HUNGARIAN PREMIER

HUNGARIAN PREMIER

a personal account of

a nation's struggle

in the second world war

NICHOLAS KÁLLAY

WITH A FOREWORD BY

C. A. MACARTNEY

GREENWOOD PRESS, PUBLISHERS
WESTPORT, CONNECTICUT

Copyright 1954 by Columbia University Press, New York

Reprinted with the permission
of Columbia University Press

First Greenwood Reprinting 1970

Library of Congress Catalogue Card Number 72-104240

SBN 8371-3965-1

Printed in the United States of America

FOREWORD

❲THESE MEMOIRS of M. Kállay obviously constitute a contribution of first-class importance to the historical literature of the Second World War. Here a man who for two crucial years directed the affairs of his country gives his own account of his stewardship, and in giving it he answers many questions which otherwise would have remained obscure forever. This is a work uniquely authoritative in its own field and, incidentally, unique also in another respect: hardly any other single man holding, during the period in question, a position of importance comparable to M. Kállay's in any of the small countries lying within the Axis orbit, and filling it in a way which would bear recording today, has survived to tell his tale. But M. Kállay's book has also another interest, a strange and melancholy one. In its pages we hear, speaking as from beyond the grave, the voice of a world which was crashing into ruin even as he sat in a German prison, himself hourly expecting that violent death from which he was fortunately spared.

In the eyes of most Hungarians that was, indeed, a world that already for a generation had been more than half a ruin. For in June, 1920, the Treaty of Trianon, imposed on Hungary at the close of the First World War, had in effect wiped out the historic Hungarian state—that large and populous, although ethnically not homogeneous, state which for 1,000 years had occupied the whole Middle Danube Basin. The north of this area was now assigned to the state of Czechoslovakia, the south to the Serb-Croat-Slovene Kingdom, the east to Rumania, a strip along the western frontier to the Republic of Austria. Even Poland and Italy received fragments of former Hungarian territory. To Hungary itself was left only the central torso, containing less than 30 per cent of the area of the historic state and just over 35 per cent of its population.[1] This was easily the most drastic of all the peace treaties of the period, for Germany's and Bulgaria's losses were by comparison far smaller and the separation from Austria and Turkey of their alien populations was not comparable. Moreover, while the dismemberment of Hungary had been carried through in the name of the national principle, yet so many concessions had been made to the strategic and economic interests of the successor states that no less than 3,200,000 persons listed in the Hungarian census of 1910 as Hungarian by mother tongue—one in three of all the persons figuring in that rubric—had been assigned to them.

Whether the application of the national principle to the Danube Basin was just or expedient; whether, assuming the rightness of the principle, the details of the settlement also were defensible, are questions which need not be discussed here. For the understanding of Hungarian policy, up to and including M. Kállay's time of office, the relevant point is Hungary's own attitude towards the treaty. This was quite unambiguous. The Hungarian government had signed the treaty in 1920 only under duress, and making no pretense that it would not seek revision or even reversal of it at the earliest possible moment; and no government there-

[1] These figures include Croatia-Slavonia; excluding them, the figures are (roughly) 33 per cent and 41.5 per cent, respectively.

after had taken up any other attitude. And in demanding revision, the governments had voiced the wish of the nation. All tendentious statements to the contrary notwithstanding, it may safely be asserted that 99 per cent of the country was united in its conviction that the treaty was unacceptable, although there was, naturally, not complete unanimity on the degree of revision for which the country should work. Some of the younger generation who grew to manhood in the 1930's would have been contented with an equitable application of the ethnic principle: if they could have recovered for Hungary the Magyar districts which the treaty had incorporated in the successor states, they would have been willing to renounce the non-Magyar areas and to co-operate on this basis with their neighbors. This school might have become more influential if the successor states, for their part, had been ready to pay so much price for Hungary's friendship; but this was not the case. Instead, the three big gainers banded themselves together for the mutual defense of all their acquisitions, and when any of them was forced to accept partial revision, as Czechoslovakia had to do in 1938 and Rumania in 1940, it was thereafter just as intransigent in demanding complete revision of the award as Hungary had been of the treaty. Failing even so much encouragement (which is not to say that much more encouragement would have converted them), the majority of the Hungarian politicians (and, as certain passages in his book show, M. Kállay was among their number) continued, while where necessary paying lip service to moderation, yet to cherish in their hearts the ideal of "integral revision," that is, the restoration of Hungary's historic frontiers— within which they were, indeed, prepared to make certain concessions to modernity in the form of autonomy for the non-Magyar areas. At the most, they became ready, as a matter of tactics, to postpone to a date which might perhaps be that of the Greek Calends the realization of revision against those of their neighbors towards whom their losses had been relatively small in return for these neighbors' support against the more important beneficiaries. Thus the small grievance against Austria—felt very bitterly in the early 1920's—was in practice buried by the early 1930's; and from about 1935 onward a movement began to offer Yugoslavia indefinite postponement of revision at her expense if she would in return break her links with Czechoslovakia and Rumania.

Thus from 1920 onward revision of the Treaty of Trianon was the central and ultimate objective of every Hungarian government. No single move made by any of them in the international field was unrelated to or unaffected by this supreme interest. The history of Hungary's foreign policy up to and including M. Kállay's term of office is, in effect, the history of her pursuit of revision. Naturally, however, the course taken by her in that pursuit was affected by a variety of factors, among which not the least important were connected with internal social and political developments, which stood, during the period, in such an intimate relationship of mutual action and reaction with the foreign political problem that no move in either field was quite independent of considerations relating to the other. Consequently, even though the purpose of these pages is simply to make clear the situation in which M. Kállay found himself in March, 1942, and the problems which confronted him, and although both situation and problems present themselves primarily in terms of foreign politics, yet they cannot be made fully clear without some reference to those internal factors which had helped to shape the one and continued to influence the other.

The non-Magyar "nationalities" had not been the only aggrieved fraction of the population of historic Hungary. Up to 1918 large masses of the population were still politically disfranchised and unrepresented, and the social condition both of industrial labor and of the much larger agrarian proletariat and near-proletariat was in many respects profoundly unsatisfactory. Not all of these evils were due to the fault of the ruling classes, but certain reforms, including in particular that of land tenure (where a disproportionate amount of the land was in the hands of a few great landowners), were long overdue.

1918 brought not only the secession of the nationalities, but also internal upheavals in the Magyar parts of Hungary; these being partly themselves national (a revolt against Habsburg rule and the Austrian connection), partly due to social discontent. The reckless radicalism of the first phase soon slipped out of the incompetent hands of its leader, Count Michael Károlyi, and gave place to a grotesque and evil Bolshevism directed by Béla Kun. In August, 1919, Kun was expelled and a counterrevolutionary regime came in. The embers of the revolution were stamped out by methods which left behind them bitter memories. After a period of transition, Count Stephen Bethlen, premier from 1921 to 1931, carried through a complex combined operation. The peasants' leaders were induced to abandon co-operation with the industrial workers and to accept the reintroduction of the open franchise in the rural areas in return for a rather more than modest land reform and promises (never more than half fulfilled) of further reforms when conditions had become more stable. The industrial workers renounced co-operation with the agrarian proletariat and promised to support the government's foreign policy in return for the secret franchise in the larger towns, an amnesty and the restitution to the trade unions of their funds and their liberty of action in the purely industrial field. Bethlen then carried through new elections which returned a parliament composed of Conservative elements subservient to himself.

In the meantime a provisional solution had been found for the question of the crown by recognizing the monarchy as still in being (although the links which had bound Hungary to the Habsburgs' other dominions were dissolved) and electing Admiral Horthy as Regent for the absent king.

Bethlen was a master of political tactics. He possessed to perfection the art of recognizing where a retreat was inevitable from an untenable position, but of limiting that retreat to the irreducible minimum. The concessions made to the dispossessed classes, urban and rural, were less than generous and in many respects the social condition of Hungary after the restoration left very much to be desired. In particular, the continued uneven distribution of the land and the deplorable conditions of the agrarian proletariat not only themselves reflected discredit on the regime but provided material for antirevisionist propaganda from the side of the successor states, where the landlords had been expropriated far more drastically. Nevertheless, it may be said at once that the accompanying political operation was so successful that up to the very last the stability of the counterrevolutionary regime was never seriously threatened from below. M. Kállay's pages show how little reason he had to fear disturbance from that quarter. The revolution carried through in 1945, although certain features of it, notably the land reform in its first stages, met the wishes of much of the population, was yet inspired, directed, and imposed from outside. Inside Hungary, neither the industrial nor the agricultural workers—nor, for that matter, the few national minorities left inside the country—constituted active political factors after 1921; least of all in foreign policy. Any sympathies entertained by any of them for the USSR played no part in influencing Hungary's foreign policy. On the other hand, the memories of Kun's regime bit deep into the minds of the re-established ruling class, and their hatred and fear of Bolshevism equaled in intensity their desire for revision. This factor in the psychological situation must be remembered in considering the later story, not least that which M. Kállay has to tell.

On this point the whole re-established Hungarian ruling class was united. All governments after 1920 described themselves as basically "counterrevolutionary" and acted in that spirit towards any manifestation of international Bolshevism. In this respect, therefore, the counterrevolution presented a solid front to the outer world—as it did also in its claim, in principle, for revision, and, for that matter, in its proclaimed determination to defend the national independence against any assault. But within itself it was deeply divided, falling into two distinct camps, the differences between which, primarily social and economic in origin, led to a strong ideological differentiation which resulted in widely differing approaches to the foreign political problem.

This division followed to some extent the old line of cleavage which had existed in the historic state between the "magnates"—the high dignitaries, lay and ecclesiastical, and great landowners, with whom in the latest period the big capitalists had associated themselves—and the "common nobles," who, despite the misleading name "noble," were essentially a middle class; but with modifications due to the altered political circumstances and economic developments. These modifications were, indeed, considerable, especially in the first years of the interwar period. For many of the active figures in the counterrevolution had been very strongly antilegitimist, and the regime had opposed the two attempts made by King Charles in 1921 to return to his throne. Consequently many of the high prelates and great landowners, who had traditionally constituted the chief support of the Habsburg connection, for some years formed what the West calls a right-wing opposition to the regime (in Central Europe the words "left" and "right" are used in a different connotation). The regime itself at this time rested largely on comparatively left-wing (in the West European sense) elements. This phase, however, passed when the legitimist question ceased to be acute after the death of King Charles. All except the most extreme and fanatical legitimists ended if not by entering, at least by ranging themselves behind the more conservative of the two surviving groups.

This was the group of which Count Bethlen had emerged as leader in 1920 and which he consolidated during his long period of office as premier, a post which he held from 1921 to 1931. Broadly speaking, it represented those forces of property, stability, and tradition in the new Hungary which were willing at least to accept the compromise of the regency. It included most of the large and medium landowners, the businessmen, a high proportion of the professional classes, and a large number of that very important and influential social class, the established civil servants. This group described their own political tenets by the word—an odd one to Western ears—"Conservative-Liberal." Their political opponents had for it other, less complimentary, phrases corre-

sponding to the English "backwoodsmen" and "last-ditchers." In
fact the adjective "liberal" in the phrase had a very special connotation derived from nineteenth-century politics: the foreign observer would have described the creed of the group, quite simply,
as conservatism in a rather extreme sense. Many, including the
present writer, have criticized very severely their class and caste
spirit, the narrow-minded tenacity with which they tried to keep
the political control in their own hands, their blindness towards
certain social problems and—perhaps most irritating of all to the
foreigner—the complacency—all the more maddening because
wholly sincere—with which they habitually denied that their
regime was in any way narrow or antisocial: denied, not only that
the dispossessed classes (or, in another field, the non-Magyar nationalities) had any cause for complaint, but even that they felt
any discontent.

Nevertheless, both the system and its supporters had qualities
which it would be unjust and foolish to deny. It is a fact that the
system had its roots in the national past and had grown up in
conformity with national conditions. Its spokesmen identified
their own interests too easily with those of the whole nation; but
they yet saw themselves as representing the national cause, and
they did so with a genuine devotion, with great courage, and with
remarkable intelligence. It was not only that they invariably resisted anything which smacked to them, however faintly, of foreign control: they did so in a way which, as it happened, made
their defense, to a certain extent, really a national one. The spiritual descendants of that Hungarian nobility which for centuries
had fought the encroachments of foreign monarchs chiefly in their
national and local diets, they had come to regard parliamentary
and constitutional methods as something sacrosanct, and they
included in the things to be defended by these methods not only
their own position, but also such rights as their constitution extended to other groups or classes. Thus, having once admitted the
principle of interconfessional equality, they opposed the abolition
of that principle to the detriment of the Jews, and having allowed

a Social Democratic party and trade unions the right to exist, while ingeniously contriving that neither force should be in a position to challenge their own supremacy, they yet refused to withdraw from them the right to continue in being. Thus, obstructive as they might, and indeed regularly did, show themselves to orderly progress in periods when such progress was not only desirable but urgently necessary, they were, at least, equally slow to follow the tide when it was setting in the opposite direction.

It must also be said that the better representatives of this school possessed a European culture and a breadth of vision which would have done honor to the statesmen of any country, and also many of the virtues of an old tradition of service, including personal integrity and dignity.

The Bethlen camp represented those who naturally desired, and could afford to defend the system, because they were the beneficiaries of it. And if their rejection of the strict legitimist thesis cost them the active support of extreme adherents of that thesis, it gave them a wider appeal to the middle classes, almost all of whom could have accepted Bethlen's leadership and ideals in the happy days before 1914, in which almost all the Magyar-speaking middle class of Hungary had enjoyed so much sufficiency to make them conservative in their social outlook. But in the 1914–18 war and the chaotic years which followed it, the savings of a large part of the fixed-income and rentier classes had melted away in the inflation; on top of which, a very special catastrophe hit the civil servants and officers who composed so large a proportion of the Magyar and Magyarized middle class. The army was drastically cut down, and the successor states expelled the officials resident in the areas assigned to them, forcing them to seek refuge in Trianon Hungary, often in a state of complete destitution. These middle and lower middle class elements, who, without belonging either by birth or by social outlook to the proletariat, now found themselves in the most precarious economic situation, under the stress of which they took a different path from Bethlen's. They were fanatically nationalist on all points, including the revisionist question—the legend so sedulously propagated in Western countries that revision was wanted only by the "feudal landowners" is completely false—and also, as a rule, on the Habsburg issue. But they were quite unable to share the complacency of the Conservative-Liberals in regard to a system which had collapsed so direfully over their heads, or their belief that the remedy for Hungary's evils lay in restoring as much of that system as possible. They wanted revolutionary changes, in the internal as well as the international field: changes which should include, in the eyes of most of them, drastic land reform and an even more drastic restriction of the rights of capital.

They were thus the enemies of conservatism; but to oppose conservatism they would not use the program of the "left." For Michael Károlyi had made a revolution of the left, which had been followed by the dismemberment of Hungary and had led to Béla Kun's Bolshevism, the supreme evil. Even democracy was suspect to them, as the pet ideology of those European forces which they regarded as especially bent on the destruction of Hungary. They took refuge in what they called "Right Radicalism," meaning thereby one form or another of Fascism.

One particular question played a large, and in time an overwhelmingly dominant part in determining what particular direction this right radicalism should take. This was the Jewish question. The proportion of Jews to the total population of historic Hungary had already reached something like 5 per cent in the last years of that state's existence, and they already then occupied a commanding position in the life of the country, controlling nearly all its finance and a high proportion of its industry and trade and being strongly represented in most of the free professions. Nevertheless, although there were occasional outbreaks in the northeast of Hungary, where the Jewish population was densest, anti-Semitism was a rare thing, and officially discouraged by the "Liberal" governments, in whose program the word "liberal" really meant "nonanti-Semitic." After August, 1919, there came a ferocious outbreak of anti-Semitism, largely due to the fact that

nearly all the leading figures of Béla Kun's Bolshevik regime, including Kun himself, were Jews. The violence of this outbreak
soon spent itself, and the regime which, under Bethlen's direction,
carried through the consolidation and reconstruction of Hungary,
reverted in this respect to the official "liberal" policy. More than
this: in the interests of the financial reconstruction Bethlen enlisted the co-operation of Jewish capital on such a scale that the
big Jewish interests became one of the most powerful pillars of
his whole system.

The Right Radicals, relegated to the opposition and excluded
from the direct benefits of the system, kept alive their hostility
towards the "Jewish Bolsheviks"; and this hostility was deepened
by the difficulties which the members of the dispossessed middle
classes, for whom, in the diminished country, place could no
longer be found in their traditional occupation, the state service,
encountered when they tried to make their way in trade, industry,
or the professions. Among some of these anti-Semitism now became a burning obsession which often banished every other
thought from their minds. Hitler's anti-Semitism therefore exer-
cized in this school an attraction which was extremely strong, although matched, of course, by the repulsion which it evoked in
the other camp.

The Right Radicals were not united among themselves. The
extreme elements (generically known as the Arrow Cross [2])
tended to form separate little political parties under various
"leaders," the most important of whom, in the late 1930's and
early 1940's, was that Major Szálasi to whom M. Kállay makes
some derogatory references in his work. But these were eccentrics,
who rejected almost every feature of the traditional Hungarian
public life and in return were treated by the rest as outcasts, almost outlaws. The true counterpart to Bethlen's Conservative-
Liberals was the great group which, until his death in 1936,

[2] Some of these groups had begun by adopting as symbol the German "Haken-
kreuz." When the government forbade the use of foreign political symbols, the
device was changed to one of two crossed arrows, each barbed at both ends (the
arrow having been the favorite weapon of the primitive).

acknowledged as their leader Captain (or, after he had taken advantage of his appointment to the ministry of defense to promote himself to that rank, General) Julius Gömbös; a remarkable figure, descendant of Swabian peasants, schoolmaster's son, Fascist-minded politician, chauvinist Hungarian, fanatical anti-Habsburgist; a man who, possessed of no more than the most primitive education and even of primitive mentality, yet contrived to have his finger in every pie and, above all, to render, in the early days, particular services to the Regent which were repaid by Horthy's special and long-enduring favor.

The two groups headed respectively by Bethlen and Gömbös waged an embittered and dingdong struggle for power, the alternations of which were obscured to the ordinary foreign observer by the peculiar workings of the Hungarian parliamentary system, as it had been re-established by Bethlen. For the system of open franchise and administrative pressure on the electorate was not so thorough that it could always prevent an Oppositional candidate from being returned to parliament, especially if he was a man possessed of local influence which could counteract that of the authorities (while in the towns it was taken for granted that a few left-wing deputies would be elected). But it did insure that the Government party would always hold an over-all majority. Thus only the hopeless extremists, who never reckoned on obtaining office, and a few individuals who found the advertisement to be gained by figuring as lone defenders of an unpopular cause more repaying than the conventional path of party discipline (and often, having created for themselves the requisite nuisance value in the Opposition, went over into the government with a secretaryship of state)—only such special cases normally stood on an Opposition ticket. The conventional way to secure acceptance of one's ideas was to enter the Government party, work from inside for control of it, and that control acquired, to alter its policy: an operation the last stage of which, if the first could be achieved, presented no difficulties whatever, since the Government party (as it was invariably, and rightly, known in popular parlance) possessed no principles whatever, beyond that it was counter-revolutionary. By the time that M. Kállay opens his narrative, even the preliminary conquest of the party from within had ceased to be strictly necessary, for under the constitution, the premier was appointed and dismissed by the Regent, who did not necessarily consult parliament when taking either step: It was the Regent's confidence, not that of parliament, that a premier had to enjoy. In normal periods, it is true, Horthy, who was conscientiously constitutional in the exercise of his functions, would not have appointed a man directly objectionable to the majority of the Government party, which would also have found a way to frustrate any such attempt, had he made it. But by 1942, as M. Kállay writes, the Regent's authority had become so overwhelming that few could have tried to resist it except under extreme provocation, and, as his narrative shows, it was the Regent who not only appointed him but kept him in office for two years in the face of the undoubted ill-will of most of the Government party.

It needs only to be explained further that the change of guard in parliament and the higher political offices was never quite complete, nor did it occur simultaneously with the change in the premiership. When he appointed Gömbös in 1932, Horthy made it a condition that he should not dissolve parliament. Gömbös therefore governed for three years with a parliament "made" by Bethlen, and many of his ministers, including M. Kállay, were Bethlen men. In 1935 Gömbös "made" his own elections, at last bringing his own men into power. As it happened, he died a year later, and none of the successors to him appointed by Horthy were pure Gömbös men (Imrédy, who swung back to that line after appointment, had taken office on different assumptions). On the other hand, none of them succeeded in evicting the "Gömbös boys" from parliament, the administration, or, above all, the army. The Government party leaders and members of whom M. Kállay complains with such acerbity were for the most part creatures of the 1935 elections.

While the question which class, or group, of those concerned, should rule Hungary was, of course, primarily a domestic one, yet it became in time, as we have said, inextricably entangled with the foreign political problem. Each side naturally sympathized with those countries whose ideological apparatus was similar to its own, bade for its support, and in return offered it its own support. This was always subject to the overriding condition of compatibility with the national interest—only a very few Communist agents on the one side and an equally small number of German agents represented by one splinter party (not Szálasi's) of the Arrow Cross on the other ever omitted this condition; but each side was naturally inclined to believe sincerely that its own friends would help Hungary towards revision, and when it became clear that concessions would have to be made in any case, each preferred that these should be to its own friends. Conversely, the resistance put up by either party to foreign influence from the quarter favored by its opponents, was partly due to fear that such influence would strengthen their opponents at home. By the time of which M. Kállay writes the foreign-political aspect of the question had become so overwhelmingly the more important that immediate domestic questions had been practically shelved. Ever since the outbreak of the European war a so-called "Treuga Dei" had been in force, which was accepted by all the political parties except the Arrow Cross. The government undertook to abstain from controversial legislation in the internal field, while the parties discussed objectively such measures as were put forward. It was obvious to all that the political future of Hungary would be determined by the issue of the war, and the parties contented themselves, in the main, with urging the government to act in a way pleasing to, or conducive to the success of, the side favored by them.

The connection between foreign and domestic politics already became perceptible, to some extent, when Bethlen was carrying through the financial and economic reconstruction of Hungary in the early and middle 1920's. The circles to which he necessarily applied for assistance were hostile to right radicalism, and it is probable that he would not easily have received that assistance if he had not been willing to liquidate the surviving remnants of the "White Terror." During his regime, in fact, radicalism of the right was repressed only a little less severely than radicalism of the left; and intimate links were forged between elements in the Bethlen camp and the West. But the ideological element did not then bulk large in Hungarian policy. Just as it would be unjust to attribute Bethlen's discouragement of anti-Semitism only to the need to conciliate foreign capital—for both he and the Conservative-Liberal elements in general disapproved of anti-Semitism, as they did also of the Fascism which Gömbös was advocating, as uncivilized and contrary to the true Hungarian tradition—so it would be a mistake to regard him as having bound Hungary irretrievably to the West. He did, indeed, secure Hungary's admission to the League of Nations, but the only important bilateral treaty which he concluded was with Italy: this being a purely foreign-political step taken in recognition of the common interest which the two countries had in resisting the overdominance of the Slavs, and particularly of Yugoslavia. In general, Bethlen regarded the time as not ripe for an active revisionist policy, which he put aside until Hungary should have recovered her strength, and the world situation should have altered. He was therefore careful to keep all doors open, and to abstain from committing his country irrevocably in any direction (it is true that, in connection with the reconstruction, he solemnly declared Hungary's acceptance of the Treaty of Trianon, but nobody, inside or outside Hungary, took the declaration literally).

Little need therefore be said of Bethlen's decade of office beyond that it brought, in fact, considerable economic and financial revival: the re-establishment, and the consolidation of his own Conservative-Liberal group. Abroad it left Hungary maintaining, despite the declaration mentioned above, all her claims, but not seriously committed to realizing them by force, since the Italian alliance was obviously a lightweight affair; on the other hand, unfortunately for him, not a step nearer realizing them by consent, since the beneficiaries of the *status quo* had utilized the breathing space simply to organize the more rigid defense of their gains.

The ideological note was first struck strongly by Gömbös when he came into office in October, 1932, a year after Bethlen's resignation (the interval having been filled by another Conservative ministry, under Count Julius Károlyi). It was an internal crisis that brought Gömbös into power; but hardly had he taken the oath of office before he was dashing down to Italy, demonstratively revitalizing the somewhat languid plant of Italo-Hungarian friendship, and eliciting from Mussolini new pronouncements in favor of revision. He was certainly largely actuated by the desire to strengthen his domestic position, and at home he did succeed (as we have mentioned) in bringing a large Right Radical element both into parliament and into the key positions in the administration and the army; one effect of this was a noticeable drawing together of all anti-Fascist elements in the country. When he had consolidated his position, Gömbös meant to introduce Fascism in Hungary and, after reconciling Italy and Germany and thus forming the so-called "Axis" (he was the inventor of that term), to bring about a foreign political combination in which Hungary, Italy, and Germany were to help one another to realize their respective national objectives.

Gömbös' regime, however, proved to be only a curtain raiser. At home, the influence exercised behind the scenes by Bethlen and his followers, and the exigencies of the renewed financial crisis, prevented him from realizing any important point of his program, or even from completing the change of guard; while the Italian alliance had the curious effect of bringing Hungary, for a while, into sharp opposition to Germany, who was now threatening Austria's independence, which both Italy and Hungary defended.

If only the Franco-Italian negotiations of 1935 had been conducted in a larger spirit, the whole European situation would have been transformed. The Hungarians were blamed at the time for not abating their claims; it is equally true that the Little Entente refused the smallest concession. Then came Mussolini's Abyssinian adventure, the rupture between Italy and the West, the Franco-Soviet and Czechoslovak-Soviet treaties, the formation of the Axis and with the Axis, the end of effective support from Italy against Germany. All other offers of help made to her were more or less openly made conditional on her renouncing her own national objectives.

Meanwhile Hitler had become chancellor of the Reich, and now, after fifteen years, a power was at last in the field which seemed both willing and able to smash the chains of the peace settlement. Many people expected Hungary at once to throw herself into Germany's arms. Instead, her policy became one of hesitations and intricate maneuverings, years of which brought her to the position described by M. Kállay, one of the chief objects of whose policy was precisely resistance to Germany.

Among the various reasons for this, one was not especially flattering to Hungary. This was that, far from being ready, as Gömbös had dreamed, to help Hungary to integral revision, Hitler courted the friendship of Rumania and Yugoslavia, and not only told the Hungarians that he would not support their claims against those two states, but even treated them with marked coolness, lest he should make his designated friends suspicious. But he did tell them that they could have Slovakia and Ruthenia whenever he destroyed Czechoslovakia, and that was a tempting offer enough, and one of which the military party was eager to take advantage. But against this there were very powerful considerations.

Firstly, perhaps, as affecting almost the entire nation, should be put the genuine fears for Hungary's independence awakened by the re-emergence of a great, united German power, more solid than ever before in history, and, after the absorption of Austria, standing, for the first time in modern history, on Hungary's very frontier. This fear was intensified by indiscreet German interference in Hungary's affairs, particularly in her treatment of the German minority, and provoked a very genuine will to resist, which reawakened and was in turn stiffened by all the old, traditional dislike of "the German," born of the centuries when Hungary had had to fight for her existence against Viennese centralization.

Secondly, there was a question of simple calculation. It was obvious that a conflict must soon break out between Germany and the West. The army officers, almost to a man, were convinced of the invincibility of the German arms, for which reason even those of them who did not sympathize with Nazism advised co-operation with Germany so that Hungary should be on the winning side when the war ended. Many of the more influential politicians, on the other hand, believed that the West would win, and, interestingly enough, the Regent, who in other respects was often inclined to back the military against the civilians, shared this view, as perhaps the one man in Hungary who understood the importance of sea power. In any case, one consideration which had always to be kept in mind was that Hungary was still practically disarmed and in no case to risk a conflict with her much more heavily armed neighbors.

And finally, sharply dividing the nation, was the ideological question, particularly in its aspect of the Jewish problem. The fact that Hitler's state represented not only the German power but also the Nazi doctrine made the question of relations with it as much one of internal as of foreign politics. The Right Radicals advocated the closest co-operation with Hitler because they hoped that this would bring them into power and enable them to carry out their program; the Bethlen group, supported on this point not only by the legitimists, but also by the genuine left, and, of course, having behind them the entire influence of the Jewish interests (all of which heterogeneous groups now lined up in a sort of shadow front) were profoundly influenced in the opposite direction by the same thought.

It should be placed on record that so far as the home front was concerned, the forces of resistance were always the stronger. Gömbös' elections were the biggest success which the right achieved, and after them, the center of gravity (some wobblings notwithstanding) moved perceptibly away from the right. Gömbös' successor, Darányi, disclaimed all thought of introducing a dictatorship and received more real support from the nominal Opposition than from the right wing of his own party. It is true that he introduced a measure of anti-Jewish legislation and also took steps to remedy Hungary's unarmed condition; also that when he and his foreign minister, Kánya, met Hitler, the question of the dismemberment of Czechoslovakia was discussed (and further discussions strongly urged by the military). But he resisted German interference in Hungary's domestic affairs valiantly enough. Hungary at this time refused to leave the League of Nations (although requested by Italy to do so) and, while not pretending to renounce revision against either Czechoslovakia or Rumania, made almost passionate appeals to the West to bring about an equitable settlement of the Danubian problem by peaceful means.

What followed may be described as a succession of short downward slides, in each case due to very strong propulsion from outside, and in each case followed by prolonged efforts, if not to regain the lost ground, at least to avoid further loss. In the spring of 1938 Darányi after all succumbed to the temptation of negotiating secretly with the Arrow Cross. The Regent dismissed him in favor of Imrédy, who was avowedly appointed because of his Western connections, and with the specific mission, on the one hand, to strengthen those links, and on the other, to take drastic action against the Arrow Cross. Imrédy began well enough. During his term of office came the Munich crisis, the story of which would fill a volume; but it stands on record that, while Hungary vehemently pressed her claim to ethnic revision at the expense of Czechoslovakia, she also made every effort, even at the risk of grievously affronting Hitler, to get her demands satisfied peacefully, with the assent and approval of the West, and to that end, while putting in a claim for Ruthenia, made a practical renunciation of the Slovak areas. Unfortunately for her Western-minded politicians, Britain and France showed little understanding for her case, and although they eventually sanctioned in principle the settlement of Hungary's claims, they washed their hands of the details, leaving Germany and Italy to arbitrate when difficulties arose. This convinced Imrédy that it was futile to appeal to the West against Germany, and when Hitler seemed inclined to take the Czechs' side, he rushed to bid for his favor by promising him international co-operation and a right-wing program in Hungary; following which he dropped Kánya, in favor of the Fascist-minded young Csáky, who promised Hungary's adherence to the Anti-Comintern pact and her resignation from the League, and in an interview with Hitler, gave him the most far-reaching assurances. At home, Imrédy introduced a new and more drastic anti-Jewish law, and began to hint at the blessings of dictatorial methods.

So Hungary had slipped a stage rightward. The slide was quickly checked when the anti-Radical forces succeeded in bringing about Imrédy's fall and his replacement by Count Paul Teleki, who was an anti-Nazi and a convinced "Westerner" in international politics. But although Teleki held new elections (on a secret suffrage recently introduced) he could not rid the Government party of its right-wing elements, and he even saw returned to parliament a large Arrow Cross opposition. Nor could he go back on the undertakings which Imrédy and Csáky had given to Hitler during those fateful weeks. He even renewed the promise to "take the Axis side" if a European conflict broke out, only stipulating that this should not involve action against Poland, with whom Hungary had collaborated in recovering Ruthenia in March, 1939. Thus the outbreak of the Second World War found Hungary deeply hostile to Germany, both on account of her invasion of Poland and of her alliance with the USSR, yet nominally her friend and no more than "nonbelligerent" on the Axis side. And although the first year of the war proved easier for Hungary than might have been expected—Hitler swallowed a refusal by Hungary to allow facilities to the German troops in the Polish campaign, and did not press her to act against the West—even

Teleki, with all his good will, could do no more than fight a delaying action against increased pressure from the right, who, after
the fall of France, when almost the whole Continent believed that
the war was about to end, within a few weeks, in a German victory,
were denouncing him as a traitor for jeopardizing Hungary's
chances of recovering Transylvania by clinging to a Western connection which had broken short in his hand. It was now (in
August, 1940) that Hungary recovered part of Transylvania; contrary to report at the time, she forced this through in the teeth of
strong German opposition, and Teleki still insisted that under no
circumstances must Hungary be involved in war with the West.
But he signed the Tripartite pact, and allowed German troops to
cross Hungary en route for Rumania, and this concession led to
complete catastrophe. In December, 1940, Hungary signed a
"Pact of Eternal Friendship" with Yugoslavia, and although this
was sincerely meant as a reinsurance against Germany, to give
Hungary a "window to the west," it was also concluded on the
assumption that Yugoslavia would follow a policy similar to Hungary's own, passively resisting Axis pressure from inside, but not
actively opposing it. The Yugoslav coup d'état of March, 1941,
confronted Hungary with a frightful dilemma. Her conduct in
the crisis was much better than the picture drawn of it at the time
(the story is too long to be told here in detail), but it ended with
her allowing the German troops passage to attack Yugoslavia, and
herself, after Croatia had proclaimed its independence, occupying
the other former Hungarian areas assigned to Yugoslavia in 1920,
and Great Britain's breaking off diplomatic relations. Teleki killed
himself in despair. To succeed him, Horthy appointed that Ladislas Bárdossy with whose dismissal Kállay's narrative begins.

As Kállay's instructions were, in brief, to reverse Bárdossy's
policy, it must be made clear what that policy was. Bárdossy was
no Right Radical; he had, indeed, no very strong views on internal
politics, in which, as a career diplomat, he had never taken part.
If anything, he was more conservative than Teleki. He was no
devotee either of Germany or of Nazism and no anti-Westerner.

He was, indeed, very attached to England, where he had served *en poste* and had possessed many friends. But precisely his English experience had convinced him that Britain was bound ultimately to support the re-establishment of that treaty system of 1919–20 which she had helped to construct and to the revisions whereof she had consented only reluctantly. In his view, Hungary could never hope to outbid the Little Entente states in the competition for the favor of the West, which could not in any case influence immediate developments in Central Europe. Hungary's only course was therefore to co-operate with Germany. The purpose of that co-operation should indeed be to strengthen Hungary, but it was a tenet of his that it was bad policy to act grudgingly or reluctantly. Germany would be content with relatively small sacrifices if offered freely, whereas if she had to bargain and cajole, she would always exact the maximum.

This reasoning determined Bárdossy's attitude in the great decision which he had to take in June, 1941, when Germany attacked the USSR. The military party, who knew that the attack was impending, had strongly urged that Hungary should associate herself with it, in order to gain Germany's favor and also to get arms from her. The Germans had not in fact provided for Hungarian participation, and Bárdossy, invoking this argument, had steadily resisted the pleadings of the war party; but at the last moment Hitler after all sent a request for Hungarian troops, this arriving almost simultaneously with the mysterious incident of the bombing of a north Hungarian town by still unidentified aircraft. Convinced that the step would have to be taken sooner or later, and acting on his principle that giving quickly meant giving cheaply, Bárdossy declared that a state of war existed between Hungary and the USSR.

It must be stated frankly that this action was not unpopular in Hungary when it was taken. The Hungarians were not, indeed, especially enthusiastic to go crusading themselves against the USSR—they would have been quite content to let the Germans do the job for them. But they were all for seeing Bolshevism wiped out; they believed that the operation would be over in a few weeks, and they accepted the view that a small-scale participation by Hungarian troops was a reasonable premium to pay for Germany's good will (for, of course, it had to be pretended, and was now universally believed, that Germany had really wanted Hungary's participation). And most of them thought that the step involved no danger of entangling Hungary in hostilities with the West. Even if Britain declared her solidarity with the USSR, this would lapse when the USSR collapsed.

Only things turned out differently. The Soviet armies, after their early defeats, began to hold their own. It became clear that the war would be long and costly. Great Britain after all declared war on Hungary. Japan attacked the United States, and Germany (and Italy) demanded that the "satellites" declare war on America. Bárdossy complied. Further, he appears (although other evidence does not entirely bear out all Horthy's indictment, recorded by M. Kállay in his opening pages) to have believed it necessary, in the interest of retaining Germany's good will, to move further to the right at home, thus again raising the internal issue.

All this filled the Conservative-Liberal politicians with consternation—a feeling which Bárdossy himself undoubtedly shared. But the fundamental difference between him and his opponents was that he still believed it necessary to go through with his undertaking to the end. They, on the other hand, were not only rigid on the point of domestic policy, but were now convinced that with America in the war the Allies were bound to win. It was therefore essential for Hungary to dissociate herself from Germany; and— and this is the most important point of all—they believed it possible. They believed that the Western Allies regarded their alliance with Russia as a wartime expedient and a necessary evil; that they would not take Hungary's military operations against Russia amiss, provided that she did not extend them to the West, and at home Hungary carried out a decent, human, and civilized policy. It would then be possible for her to regain the good will of the West and secure from that quarter and from the neutrals not only protection against Russia but also confirmation of such revision as she had already achieved, and perhaps even more. This was the program which the Regent—who fully shared the views described —decided to put into operation.

That he entrusted precisely M. Kállay with the execution of it caused some surprise when the appointment was made known, since M. Kállay had never been more than a half-hearted party politician, and for several years had taken hardly any part in national affairs on the highest level. Yet this was, under the circumstances, a necessary condition, since the Germans would never have tolerated a Hungarian premier possessed of an open and notorious anti-Axis record. Actually, M. Kállay's one full ministerial appointment—when he had held the portfolio of agriculture— had been under Gömbös; the fact that he had owed that appointment to the recommendation of Bethlen (whose secretary of state for commerce he had been) was notorious, but not on public record, and when, early in 1935, he had resigned his portfolio, he had invoked a technicality as excuse. Thus it was possible, given sufficient hardihood, to represent him to the world as a Gömbös man; whereas he was in reality, as all his friends and indeed all Hungary knew, a most typical and convinced Conservative-Liberal. A certain lack of experience in international politics might have been alleged against him; on the other hand, he possessed beyond any possibility of cavil the one quality for which, it seems, Horthy's instincts clamored in this crisis: that of being 100 per cent Hungarian. M. Kállay's was, indeed, much the same stock, background, and world as the Regent's own: the world of the solid, old-established country "gentry" of the Tisza region of Hungary: a stock whose mental and spiritual tendrils did not perhaps reach very far afield, but every fiber of its roots reached down into Hungarian soil. Here was a man whom the Regent, and those who thought with him, could understand and trust.

It is not the purpose of these lines to comment or criticize M. Kállay's narrative. Only one point may be made. As M. Kállay himself does not hesitate to confess, he operated throughout his two years with a large degree of dissimulation, using words much rather as substitutes or cloaks for action, than as interpreters thereof. Many observers at the time chose to take his words at their face value, particularly as in the first months he in fact took, or allowed to be taken, many measures which did not belie them. When, then, later, his acts became plainly anti-Axis, many supposed that his policy had changed: he had begun by genuinely cooperating with the Axis and changed his mind when the tide of war turned plainly. His present narrative gives welcome confirmation to those who always saw his doings differently: that this was not the case; that his policy was from the first that described above. Whether he always carried it out with perfect skill—whether he made too many concessions to expediency at the beginning or too few at the end (both criticisms had been heard)—is a question which the reader may decide for himself. In the light of later events, he will probably also ask himself another, more fundamental and more disquieting question: whether the assumptions on which Horthy offered him, and he accepted, this burdensome task, were in fact justified.

The event is, of course, common knowledge today. Bárdossy proved a true prophet when he foretold that no effort on Hungary's part to secure from the West any satisfaction for what she believed to be her just claims, or even protection against the Soviet Union, would be otherwise than fruitless; Horthy a wholly false one when he argued that "Germany's defeat could not possibly mean that Russia would be let into Europe." All M. Kállay's efforts in this respect were totally vain. Whether this truth can give any satisfaction at all outside Moscow; whether Kállay and Horthy did not see more clearly than those who took the ultimate decisions, what would be better, not only for Hungary, but also for the world—that, again, is a different question. At least no reader of these pages can feel that the attempt, even if it failed, did anything but honor to those who made it. If M. Kállay's world has perished, it perished nobly.

C. A. MACARTNEY

All Souls College, Oxford

PREFACE

❨THIS BOOK tells the story of the two years of struggle that a little nation waged against military and political aggressors, and of my part in that effort. I have tried to write objectively: to tell the factual truth about my land and its history during those years. But this book is also an admittedly subjective account. I have striven to describe events as we, and necessarily as I, saw and felt about them at the time. In recent years I have read many memoirs and books of political reflections, most of which seem to be colored and influenced by what happened after the event, by the wisdom and lessons of a later day. Such books may be more interesting to read than this book and may even appear to be more complete and up-to-date than one which reveals the history of a past age through the old and perhaps outmoded perspective of that age. Much truth, nevertheless, is to be found in the latter works, of which this book is an example. In history, as in painting, a subjective close-up often conveys the objects more vividly, more comprehensibly than is possible in a detached, over-all view. It is possible to make a complete photo map of a country from an airplane, but it is not possible to attain from that height the intimate view of a nation necessary to the appreciation of her spirit. What I offer here is, therefore, a spiritual as well as documentary picture of an age. It is a history that describes a grim tragedy played out on a small stage; that sets down, with neither extenuation nor malice, how we, at that time, saw ourselves, others, the world.

To tell the complete story, I would need my diaries and notes, access to material from the national archives, the newspapers of the day, my secretary's notes regarding my appointments—all these comprise necessary documentary material. Here, however, in my exile, I have no such primary source materials. On the night of March 19, 1944, when the Germans occupied Hungary, I ordered the contents of the archives burned, together with my private correspondence. My notes and those of my secretary I took with me when I fled to the Turkish legation. I have since heard that subsequently, after the Germans broke into the legation and took me away, the Turkish minister had those documents burned. I do not now have access to the newspapers or to the parliamentary records of those days. It is difficult to get anything from behind the Iron Curtain; furthermore, the Russians have taken away many of the pertinent records. I do have, however, a complete collection of my more important speeches, and I have decided to arrange my account around these. The extensive quotations from the speeches may in places seem excessive, but they show exactly what I was thinking at the time, what I was saying to the people of my country during my tenure as premier. I have been able also to draw upon the personal records of some of our ministers. I wish here to record my obligation for this opportunity to Messrs. Barcza,[1] Bessenyey,[2] Wodianer,[3] and Ullein-Reviczky.[4]

[1] George Barcza was chief of the political section of the foreign ministry, 1925–27; minister to the Vatican, 1927–37; minister to Great Britain, 1937–41.

[2] George B. Bessenyey, was chief of the political section of the foreign ministry,

Very few of my Hungarian contemporaries—alas!—survive; and, indeed, the greater number of the leading personalities of that period in Central Europe have perished. This is the first time that so many participants and witnesses of a historic period have been destroyed by the events of the period.

What is the subject of this book? What is its purpose? To describe and to demonstrate how a small nation struggled to free itself from the twin death-grips of National Socialism and Bolshevism, to preserve its honor and its humanity, and to save the lives of a million people whom Nazism had sentenced to destruction.

The first of those endeavors did not succeed and, as we can see today, could never have succeeded without a major realignment in the balance of power.

The second was completely successful up to the moment of the German occupation. After that, the nation's ideals were defiled by the usurpers of power and their hirelings. The people of my nation had, however, little in common with those despoilers.

The attempt to save the persecuted was extremely successful as long as I was at my post. Afterwards, unfortunately, about one quarter of those men perished. That the rest survived was largely owing to my two-year effort in which every true Hungarian was my collaborator.

Certain explanations of the Hungarian point of view given in this book will probably cause surprise, since foreign propaganda— some of it honorable, some of it inspired by the need of winning the war, and some of it malicious—created an entirely false idea of our people and their endeavors, and disseminated misstatements of historic facts.

I shall have achieved my purpose, probably the last service

1934–38; minister to Yugoslavia, 1938–41; minister to France, 1941–43; minister to Switzerland, 1943–44.

[3] Andor Wodianer was minister to Portugal, 1939–44.

[4] Anthony Ullein-Reviczky was chief of the press section of the foreign ministry, 1942–43; minister to Sweden, 1943–44.

which I can render my poor nation, if I have helped to restore the true colors to the picture which foreigners have of it.

I wrote these reminiscences in 1946 and 1947, when I was still most vividly under the impression of the experiences I had lived through. Although today I see many things in a different light, I made no substantial changes in my account before publication.

I realize that by now very little remains of our Hungarian way of life. The changes that have taken place are not the most important consideration, however. What is important, I feel, is that the Hungarian people should survive.

I am sorry that I have had to say unpleasant things about the Germany of those times. Today I believe that the German people, having found themselves again, will be a great asset in the development and consolidation of a new Europe.

At the present time I feel differently about Hungary's neighbors, too. I was hurt then by our differences, but now I am looking for and want to find that which brings people together. I cannot imagine anything else in the Danube Basin than harmony and peaceful co-operation.

As for the Russians, that situation, too, has changed. What I only felt and feared would happen actually did happen, and the nightmare became reality. One thing is certain, the situation cannot remain as it is, and there must be a way to solve the problem peacefully, without the use of arms. How can this be done? There must be a unity of purpose and a common will among all nations, free or behind the Iron Curtain, all governments, all individuals, so that through a combined and incessant effort the supreme goal, liberty in the whole world, will be achieved.

Rome   NICHOLAS KÁLLAY
1953

CONTENTS

CONTENTS

MAPS

HUNGARIAN PREMIER

ONE

THE REGENT APPOINTS ME PREMIER

⟨[THE YEAR 1941 was a critical year for Hungary,[1] a year of errors, when the nation was dragged into a maelstrom of political and military events. It was the year when we became belligerents in the Second World War.[2] The process was started by our partici-

---

[1] Hungary was, as is well known, a monarchy ruled by a Regent, who was Admiral Nicholas Horthy, 1868–. Horthy commanded the Austro-Hungarian fleet in the First World War. After Béla Kun's Communist *coup d'état*, Horthy was put in command of the counterrevolutionary forces. He entered Budapest with his troops in November, 1919. On March 1, 1920, parliament elected him Regent and head of the state. His premiers were: Alexander Simonyi-Semadam, 1920; Count Paul Teleki, 1920–21; Count Stephen Bethlen, 1921–31; Count Julius Károlyi, 1931–32; Julius Gömbös, 1932–36; Koloman Darányi, 1936–38; Béla Imrédy, 1938–39; Count Paul Teleki, 1939–41; Ladislas Bárdossy, 1941–42; Nicholas Kállay, 1942–44; Döme Sztójay, 1944; Géza Lakatos, 1944.

[2] See Chapter Three, "The Geopolitical Situation of Hungary," for the details about foreign policy alluded to in this chapter.

pation in the attack on Yugoslavia.[3] Paul Teleki's [4] noble gesture of suicide, a self-sacrifice intended to warn the nation and its leaders, an act whereby a gentleman sought in death to escape a dilemma that was facing the nation, saved nothing. In fact, it made our position vis-à-vis the Germans more difficult. His suicide had not, as he had probably hoped, prevented England from breaking off diplomatic relations with us and later declaring war. On top of this, Premier Ladislas Bárdossy [5] took us into the war against the Soviet Union and the United States, although there was never a state of active hostilities with the United States. The nation and the Regent felt that we were on a slippery incline. Men with eyes to see began to feel deeply uneasy.

After my appointment in 1936 as director of the national irrigation authority, I had devoted myself entirely to the duties of that office. Such free time as I had I spent at home on my estate. I was more and more often invited, however, to various political discussions of the so-called Conservative and Liberal circles, all of whose members were, of course, anti-Nazi. I had a vague feeling that I figured in the plans of these various people, but, as I had never been a professional politician, I did not take the indications very seriously.

During those years I spoke only once in the upper house,[6] when I supported an admirable piece of social legislation brought for-

[3] It is commonly believed that Hungary entered the war on Hitler's side to recover the Magyar areas of Slovakia and Transylvania. This is an error: we had recovered these territories before Teleki's death and had undertaken no military obligations in connection with the recovery of these lands. See Chapter Three, pages 56, 59.

[4] Count Paul Teleki, 1879–1941, was a geographer and political writer as well as a statesman. He served as a member of the Hungarian parliament from 1905 through the First World War. At the Paris Peace Conference (1919–20) he was the official geographic expert of the Hungarian delegation. In July, 1920, he was appointed premier by Admiral Horthy, and Teleki secured ratification of the Treaty of Trianon by parliament. He retired from politics in April, 1921, and did not return until February, 1939, when he was again appointed premier by Horthy. He committed suicide in the early morning of April 4, 1941.

[5] Ladislas Bárdossy, who had served as foreign minister under Teleki, was premier from April, 1941, to March, 1942. He was executed after the war.

[6] See page 31 note 7.

ward by the minister of the interior to provide the agricultural laborers with dwellings, hygienically constructed and provided with gardens, of which they would become the owners in free-hold after paying twenty to twenty-five installments equal to what, under the existing system, they were paying as rent.

In the autumn of 1941 Francis Keresztes-Fischer, the minister of the interior, visited me at my country home. After I had shown him my farm and told him that my deepest wish was to devote all my labors to developing it, he answered: "I can't say more than this: you had better get ready to leave this work; a larger task is waiting for you." He did not enlarge on that. About the same time Leopold Baranyai, the highly respected president of the national bank, also visited me and said that I ought to become premier. He declared that the government must not be allowed to go on leading the nation into catastrophe. Francis Chorin, of the upper house, the most important figure in Hungary's bank-ing and industrial world, and many other members of the upper house sought me out, told me their fears, and made similar ap-proaches to me. Béla Lukács, too, the president of the Govern-ment party, several times spoke to me in the same tone and asked me to come into the Government party, so I could get to know its members and make them my friends; so did the two liberal-minded vice presidents of the party, Zoltán Bencs and Paul Kos-suth, who told me that this was the wish of the sober, democratic, and liberal majority of the party. I mention all this because many people have believed that my appointment as premier was purely the result of the Regent's personal decision, whereas, as these few examples show, there was a widespread feeling in favor of my being appointed to the position.

Meanwhile I had studied the foreign situation, and I spoke in the foreign affairs committee when Premier Bárdossy an-nounced our declaration of war on the United States. I said then that, if the official rupture could not be avoided, it was our duty to keep the contact unofficially and that this policy should be applied, not only to the United States, but to all the belligerents.

The foreign affairs committee of the upper house, whose members were usually cold and reserved, received my remarks with demonstrative applause. Bárdossy did not reply to my talk. After the session Kalman Kánya, who was chairman of the committee, and Francis Chorin, a member, came to me and said that they hoped that was a program.

Before then I had had one clash with Bárdossy, when he asked me to support his bill introducing racial discrimination against the Jews. I refused and later voted against the bill.

In the winter of 1942, immediately before my appointment, Anthony Ullein-Reviczky, who was then chief of the press section in the foreign ministry, and who in that position had succeeded in acquiring a great influence, called on me and told me that he had been with the Regent on the previous day. Horthy had expressed very great discontent with Bárdossy's policy, saying that he had lost confidence in the premier and was determined to replace him. Bárdossy's successor would be a personal friend of Horthy, and a man in whom the Regent had complete confidence. Only with such a man could he collaborate in these critical times. The nation, too, Horthy felt, would follow only a premier in whom they had confidence, a man who was blood of their blood, who would follow a purely Hungarian policy free from domestic political intrigues, and who would shoulder the burden in a spirit of selfless service. The Regent had not mentioned my name, but Ullein-Reviczky gathered that he was thinking of me.

I replied that the Regent had always honored me with conspicuous marks of good will and had more than once asked for my opinion. I told Ullein-Reviczky that Horthy had even dropped certain hints of his intention to appoint me, when we had met in January, at a shooting party given for Ribbentrop.[7] I went on to

[7] In January, 1942, Joachim von Ribbentrop expressed the wish to come to Hungary to discuss our participation in the Russian war. We, to avoid attention, invited him to a shooting party at Mezöhegyes. The only persons present besides the Regent and officers of the government were Count Maurice Eszterházy, who

say, however, that I nevertheless did not believe that Horthy was thinking of appointing me just then, certainly not so suddenly and without informing me first. The rest of my answer is given by Ullein-Reviczky in his excellent *Guerre allemande, paix russe* (1947), in the following words:

Kállay said that he thought his time had not yet come, that the only policy which it would be possible to follow was that of Paul Teleki. But if Teleki had found no way except suicide of remaining true to his own principles, and suicide at a time when we were not yet at war with anyone, how could one follow this policy now, with Bárdossy's four wars on one's back? For a Hungarian premier to be able to follow again a "purely Hungarian policy," Germany must first be greatly weakened. Today, however, Germany was extremely strong. It was therefore difficult to do anything at that moment.

One day early in March, 1942, the Regent's confidential aide-de-camp, Julius Tost, called me and said that the Regent wanted to see me that same evening. I was to go to his office. I was to tell no one where I was going.

When I went to the palace, I was not expecting to be offered the post of premier, although I thought it was possible that the Regent might want me to enter the cabinet, either as minister of agriculture or as minister without portfolio. I thought the former because Horthy had once asked Bárdossy, with whose agrarian policy the Regent was dissatisfied, to invite me to a ministerial

---

had been premier under King Charles, and myself. The Regent arranged for me to enter the conversation between himself and Ribbentrop. During the talk I said that it was a great mistake to draw small nations into an offensive war. A small nation's radius of activity could never extend beyond its own historic frontiers, these being in our case the Eastern Carpathians and the Danube; in that of the Rumanians, Bessarabia; and of the Bulgarians, Macedonia. Germany could drag us and Rumania into war by dangling that apple of discord Transylvania in front of us, but this would help Germany but little, and would end by ruining both the smaller peoples. It was better not even to try to move the Bulgars; they would not fight against Russia. Afterwards, the Regent said to me that that was the way to talk to the Germans; great changes were imminent, and I should prepare myself for them.

council, where I gave my ideas on agrarian and general economic questions.

The Regent began by saying at once that he could no longer keep Bárdossy. He had been completely disappointed in him. Horthy said that he had appointed Bárdossy after Teleki's suicide —the critical time when the principal question was whether a German occupation could or could not be avoided—because Bárdossy was a career diplomat who had neither friends nor enemies in inner political circles. Bárdossy's given task was to steer the country out of the crisis as smoothly and as inexpensively as possible. The Regent had never thought of Bárdossy as the definitive head of the government. Contrary to Horthy's intentions, however, Bárdossy had plunged wholeheartedly into internal politics and even into international ideological politics. He had sought popularity at any price and had tried to build up his position with the support of the Germans and the Hungarian right. He had confronted Horthy with one *fait accompli* after another, as, for example, when Bárdossy declared war against the Soviet Union and the United States. Now the rectification of the precarious situation could no longer be deferred, for Bárdossy was trying to squeeze out of the cabinet its three loyal members, Francis Keresztes-Fischer, Daniel Bánffy, and Joseph Varga, who possessed Horthy's own confidence; furthermore, Bárdossy had even proposed to the Regent the names of three extreme pro-Germans as their successors. Then, too, Bárdossy had recently raised the question of another Jewish law, and even of deporting the Jews. A wretched state had been reached where Horthy could see no solution other than to dismiss Bárdossy and to appoint me premier.

Then the Regent told me that I enjoyed his complete confidence. I would be able to do what I liked, for he knew my ideas and approved of them. He felt that it was important that we should be of one mind on all major points, and he was sure that we would be. He said that he would not interfere in the formation of my ministry except that he would retain the power to appoint the minister of defense and he would continue his over-all control of military affairs, since, it was his belief, only he could keep the military in hand and prevent them from making politics. Horthy offered me a completely free hand in domestic and foreign political and economic matters. I was to regard the appointment he was offering me as a long-term step, for Horthy believed that Hungary could not allow herself further major political changes in wartime. He wanted to work with me, he declared, so long as he lived or remained the Regent, and he was confident that the country would stand behind me, too. If I had trouble with the Government party, then parliament must be dissolved. The new elections, he was confident, would bring me a safe majority.

In reply, I thanked the Regent for his confidence in me, but I declined his offer. In the first place, I felt unprepared and so found many rationalizations concerning myself and the nation's problems to support this feeling. I had never, for instance, thought of how I should form a cabinet. A hasty review with Horthy of that crucial responsibility persuaded me that I would have difficulty forming one from among the members of the Government party. I did not even know many members of the party because I had rarely attended their meetings—the few times to hear my friend Paul Teleki speak. And as for the leaders of the party, some of whom were members of Bárdossy's cabinet, their views differed fundamentally from mine. This conflict of principle appeared to me at the time a major obstacle, especially since my political friends and associates belonged to the "dissidents," who had been pushed out of parliament by Béla Imrédy [8] and had not been returned at the following elections.[9] Then, too, I believed that the holding of a general election while the nation was at war would

[8] Béla Imrédy, 1891–1946, leader of the Rejuvenation party, served as premier, May, 1938, to February, 1939. He was executed after the war.

[9] In November, 1938, a group of the antitotalitarian members of the Government party revolted against Imrédy, who was then premier, and with some votes from the Opposition defeated him in a motion of confidence. The Regent reappointed Imrédy, but dismissed him in February, 1939, in favor of Teleki. However, most of the "dissidents" were kept out of parliament in the new elections of May, 1939.

create problems that would aggravate the existing differences, at a time when the biggest need was for the resolution of internal differences.

These differences within the nation were bound up with the two major factors that were the deterring considerations in my mind: German political, economic, and military aggression and the reactionary influences in Hungary allied to the German policies. The Regent must know, I told him, that I would inevitably come into conflict with the Germans because I was wholeheartedly opposed to the values as well as the imperialism of National Socialism. He must realize, therefore, that he would have to reckon with Germany's hostility if I accepted the appointment. Although he offered to make me premier despite this threat, the difficulties we should meet made me pause. Could I undertake this task, I asked Horthy and myself, when I saw little possibility of repairing past errors with respect to our relations with Hitler's Germany? Could I survive, let alone be successful, if I were inextricably bound to the deadly policies of the past? For there was, too, as an adjunct to our relations with Germany, the problem of Hungarian reaction. The whole foreground of our internal politics, for example, was permeated with anti-Semitism. I believed, indeed, that only a minority of Hungarians were anti-Semitic, but it had become an attitude and force difficult to oppose because the Germans were behind it. And we were by then in Germany's grip, since we were entirely surrounded by Germany and her satellites and economically bound to that complex of nations. Our army was perishing a thousand miles beyond our frontiers, and was destined to perish because of its small size even if the Germans were victorious, when, of course, we should have need of it more than ever. Our relations with the national minorities were unpromising; we had not succeeded in gaining the affection of those in the recovered areas, and we had granted the Germans rights entirely irreconcilable with Hungarian sovereignty. These being my premises and my views, how, I asked the Regent to tell me, was I to lead the country? Was I to swim with the tide or against it? Either would lead to catastrophe.

Horthy was much cast down by my words. He thought my pessimism exaggerated. He had not lost faith or confidence. The moment Germany suffered her first defeat—and I agreed with him that that moment must come—the *Wehrmacht* would turn against Nazism, and then the possibility of a compromise peace would be there. Our own situation was not so hopeless as I thought: precisely the fact that we lay geographically between the two great antagonists, Germany and Russia, was a guarantee of our survival and our independence, since the Western powers could not allow us to come under the domination of either of them. Germany's defeat could not possibly mean that Russia would be let into Europe. Britain wanted to maintain the European balance of power and, after fighting the Germans to preserve it, would not allow Russia to overthrow it. Moreover, the Russians themselves did not need the Magyars or the Rumanians, who were not Slavs. The line of expansion of the Russians for centuries past had been towards the Balkans and the Bosporus; the Russians would rather seek an alliance with us, which they could have if they gave up their attempts to Bolshevize us. As for the past errors, that was one of the main reasons why he was calling on me. We two together, I and he, would save the country. I was not to consider present difficulties, but the way out of them, which I could find if I accepted the post. I was the only man for the task; I could not refuse it.

I did refuse it, however, definitely; and so we parted.

After that meeting, though, the Regent called me almost daily and tried to persuade me that it was my duty to accept the task. I tried to gain time and asked him at least to postpone my appointment for two months, during which time I was willing to serve in the cabinet as a minister without portfolio. I would be able then to get my bearings in the cabinet and in public life and possibly to stop some harmful policies. He rejected my proposals, and at last I gave way. When I told him I accepted, he embraced me with an intense emotion—he was almost in tears—that showed how deep his inner disquietude must have been. After I left him, his son Stephen, the deputy regent, was waiting for me on the stairs. When I told him that I had accepted, he cried out: "Now everything is all right; everything will be all right!"

Then I worked out my program.[10] It can be summed up in these words: To defend and to preserve the independence that Hungary still possessed in domestic and foreign affairs, and to work for the restoration of the independence that had been lost. I was determined to lead this effort from a position above the parties and other partisan groups—as a leader of all the people—and to emphasize this national nature of my endeavors very strongly abroad: to make it the guiding thread of both my foreign policy and propaganda. I outlined my program to Horthy thus:

In our relations with the Germans, I intended to follow a cautious but uncompromisingly Hungarian policy; to develop the highest measure of spiritual and moral resistance; to allow only the unavoidable minimum of concessions, even in the economic field. In pursuing this program, however, I was going to avoid, if possible, provoking a German occupation; for we should surely be defeated if this were attempted, and then all we had gained and preserved in our long history—our constitution, our civil rights, our independence, and all our other spiritual and our material resources—would be plundered and lost.

In my planning I reasoned that, even granting the possibility of a German victory, an independent Hungary, one still imbued with the spirit of freedom, would be much harder to grind underfoot than a country and people whose sovereignty had been impaired, whose army had been annihilated, and whose spiritual and material resources had been exhausted.

If, on the other hand, the Allies won, as I thought was certain, then a country and government which had followed a fairly in-

[10] Premier Bárdossy resigned on March 7, 1942, and I formed my cabinet on March 10.

dependent foreign policy, at least in relations with neutral countries, and which had not committed the offenses against the moral
order and against humanity that were committed (admittedly
under German pressure) by every East European country with
the sole exception of Finland—such a nation must emerge from
the war in possession of the sympathy, the respect, even the gratitude of the world. If at that moment we possessed an intact army,
we could enforce respect for our frontiers when the general collapse came, and perhaps our help would be enlisted to keep order
in all Central Europe. This would mean that the neighboring
peoples would gravitate towards Hungary, and we should be in a
position of vantage if the idea of an East European Federation
again came to the fore.

If, finally, the upshot should be a compromise peace, the fulfillment of the aims of my program would yield rich returns. It
would be clear that the Hungarian nation was the only small nation that had been able to preserve its independence, although
geopolitically its situation had been extremely forbidding. Hungary would have to be ranked after the war, along with Finland,
Poland, and Serbia, among the countries that had struggled
against a powerful aggressor to preserve independence and liberty.
To me the history of Poland and Serbia revealed that the way
to achieve this was not by armed resistance, which led to swift
defeat and complete subjection, but rather by tough, obstinate,
intransigent opposition in every field. The correctness of such a
policy of passive but implacable resistance would be proved, I
hoped, by our emergence from the war as the only country in
Central Europe and the Balkans which had been able to preserve
intact the marks of European culture, civilization, and humanity.

The principal threat to this ideal of the preservation of Hungary's integrity was, I believed, Nazism. This menace pressed on
us from without and from within: from Nazi Germany, from
Nazi satellites around our frontiers, and from Nazi sympathizers
inside our borders. This was the assault which had to be repelled.
If I had seen any possibility of victory by heroic resistance, I would

have been prepared to take the chance. But there was no point in courting certain destruction, at the hands of an overwhelmingly superior enemy. That would be merely spectacular but short-sighted and fruitless heroism. It would give total victory to our totalitarian foes.

My very appointment as premier was already an act of provocation to the Germans and the Hungarian Nazis and anti-Semites. It was necessary for me, therefore, to proceed gradually and cautiously, to cherish the end while playing for the time in the hope that the military, foreign, and domestic situation would finally allow open resistance. Meanwhile, I had to swing opinion in the nation behind a true Hungarian policy and make it alive to the reality of Germany's defeat.

I therefore told the Regent that for the moment I wished to retain Bárdossy's entire cabinet but that perhaps I would add a few new members to it. I should keep the portfolio of foreign affairs for myself, so as to resist myself the pressure from the Germans and my own right wing. I also told Horthy that in my inaugural speech I was going to announce that I intended to follow my predecessor's policy, but I was not going to make hostile references of any sort towards the Western powers. In fact, I proposed to prepare and make the first tentative approaches towards rapprochement with the West. I was going to try to establish contact with the English. In order to conceal this overture, I was going to emphasize my anti-Russian policy.

High on my list of national necessities was our withdrawal from the war. The promise already given of an army for Russia unfortunately could not be recalled, but after its fulfillment I was determined to give not a single soldier more. I wanted Hungary to raise a new army at home and to keep it intact to serve our own future purposes.

We would also have to preserve the nation's traditional standards of honor and humanity, which required, of course, that we stop anti-Semitic measures and follow an entirely new policy towards minorities. I cited the Ujvidek case [11] as an example of destructive intolerance, and I declared that in recent years anti-Semitism had almost become a touchstone of Hungarian foreign and domestic policy. The Germans classified nations according to their reliability in the handling of the Jewish question, and, unfortunately, certain elements of our own people, including officials of the Government party, were of the same mind. I had decided to choose the way which went to the heart of the problem and also offered a solution to inequities. I was determined that Jews were not to be discriminated against for racial reasons—this was inhumanity—but that they were to be judged and acted towards strictly in relation to their role in economic and social conditions in Hungary. In such, of course, were the roots of the whole question.

Everything else, I told the Regent, would have to be subordinated to these points in my program for Hungary's salvation. We were unfortunately plunging so precipitously down a reactionary road that sudden changes would cause extreme dislocations. I would, nevertheless, pursue my program with firmness as well as moderation, never deviating fundamentally from my avowed ends.

All that I thought it was necessary to tell the Regent. He, knowing my plans, gave me a completely free hand. I gave him no details at the time, and not often afterwards.

The Regent interrupted me several times, especially to emphasize his confidence in the farsightedness and purposefulness of Great Britain's policy.[12] Britain did not want to dictate to the world, but her whole position depended on her saving the free world and opposing any attempt by another nation to dominate the world. She had always fought against every dictator, not in order to seat herself on his throne, but, on the contrary, to safe-

[11] See pages 107–11 for details.

[12] At that time American policy had not penetrated to Eastern Europe, so that when talking of Western policy we referred to British policy.

guard her own liberty and freedom of action. This she could achieve only in a society of free peoples, and therefore she would always be the ally of the small nations. Horthy's second postulate was that England was bound sooner or later to square accounts with Bolshevism. She would not, therefore, bear us ill will for having taken part in the war against Russia: the anti-Bolshevik people would always be her natural allies.

The Regent agreed that we must defend Hungary's independence, but he did not think that Germany would threaten it; he had settled the question with Hitler, and it could not even arise again. The position of Hungary was different from that of the other successor states or the Balkan states. We were a nation and a people which had been formed by history; we belonged to the Western world; we were anti-Bolshevik and not Slavs. We could not, therefore, cross Germany's interests, and she had no interest in destroying such a bulwark; indeed, she had every interest in preserving it.

He accepted my domestic political program, adding only that we must make a clean sweep of our own Nazis, whom I must regard as national enemies and outside the law. It was characteristic that during the whole conversation no single mention was made of dealing with the Communists; so unimportant—indeed, nonexistent—were they in Hungary.

From the Regent I went to his deputy, to whom I repeated my whole program, with all of which he, of course, agreed. Stephen Horthy was a splendid young man and so anti-Nazi that the only difference which, had he remained alive, might ever have arisen between us would have come from his thinking me not radical enough in this respect.

I next went to Keresztes-Fischer, the minister of the interior, who greeted my news with great joy and promised me his full support. I discussed with him what I should do about my cabinet, and he agreed entirely with my idea of keeping for the time the old cabinet and not complicating my starting difficulties with the extra burden of getting a new team together and at work; the more so as it was important that nothing should interrupt the continuity and smooth flow of the departmental ministers' work under war conditions. He warned me that some of the ministers (the right-wing ones, of course) had decided not to stay on under me, but he thought they could be persuaded to change their minds. Keresztes-Fischer was willing to appeal to them, for it would look like a demonstration against the Germans if the right-wingers were left out of my cabinet.

I must explain briefly what the position of a Hungarian premier was, constitutionally and in practice, at that time. The political system of Hungary since the First World War,[13] the forms and the essence of its constitutional life, were what Bethlen [14] had made of them during his ten-year term as premier. Bethlen created the Government party and built up the position of the new form of government and, above all, of the premiership. He enjoyed unlimited authority and also, up to his last year of office, great popularity. None of his successors enjoyed as much authority or popularity.

Horthy subsequently became Hungary's authoritative and popular figure, and there was no other European head of state who exercised more authority or who was more popular. I am not comparing Horthy with the three dictators, whose alleged authority and popularity were the fruits of other methods and of a different political philosophy. Horthy was most warmly beloved by the widest circles of the Hungarian people, the middle classes, the peasants, and even the left-wing workers. There was no dictatorship in Hungary. Horthy did not seize power; his authority was

[13] See Chapter Two, "The Political Parties and Balance of Power in Hungary," for the details about the material alluded to in this and the following paragraphs.

[14] Count Stephen Bethlen, 1874–1950?, became a member of the Hungarian parliament in 1901, and he served as a delegate to the Paris Peace Conference. He succeeded Teleki as premier in April, 1921, and held office until August, 1931, when he resigned. There have been unofficial reports that he died in a Russian prison.

so great that the people accepted and approved any decision made
by him. He had grown up in the school of Francis Joseph, and so
he believed in delegating power. His working principle was that
he appointed the premier, who was to be supported in all his
actions with the Regent's authority so long as the premier enjoyed
Horthy's confidence. The Regent did not intervene in the details
of the premier's actions. The Regent fulfilled the functions of a
constitutional monarch, especially during Bethlen's time. Subsequently, however, when a premier was weak, or not altogether
to Horthy's taste, the Regent intervened more directly in questions of substance, controlling, so to speak, the premier's activities.
He did so especially in the cases of Gömbös,[15] Darányi,[16] Imrédy,
and Bárdossy, none of whom Horthy ever entirely trusted, and
none of whom, he told me, he would ever have appointed of his
free will: he had been forced by circumstances to do so. Bethlen,
Teleki, and I were the three men whom he trusted completely and
under whom he reverted, as it were, to his strictly constitutional
position. Horthy was thus the first factor in Hungary's constitutional life: not because he used any methods of compulsion, but
because his authority and, still more, his popularity were such
that the nation would not even have accepted as premier anyone
but the man designated by Horthy. The Government party also
deferred to Horthy. In Bethlen's day the party was Bethlen's. The
reason why Gömbös made new elections was that he could not
carry out his va banque policy with a party taken over from Bethlen. It is undeniable that a large fraction of the new Government
party brought together by Gömbös consisted of his personal adherents, but the shadow of the Regent's authority and popularity
still fell over it. There was no question of the party's not accepting
the Regent's nominee; even in my own case the worst I could
expect would be some hostility from the Gömbösites, that is, the
extreme right-wing, anti-Semitic elements. The same applied to

[15] Julius Gömbös, 1886–1936, served as minister of defense in the cabinets of
Bethlen (1921–31) and Julius Károlyi (1931–32). He was appointed premier in
September, 1932; he died in office, October, 1936.
[16] Koloman Darányi served as premier from October, 1936, to May, 1938.

the departmental ministers, who were appointed by the Regent on the recommendation of the premier and only afterwards introduced to the party. This outstanding position occupied by Horthy was fully acknowledged by the Opposition: there was no single party which could have imagined any sort of solution without Horthy.

I paid the customary courtesy visits to the archbishop primate, Justinian Cardinal Serédy, the Archduke Joseph, the former premiers, and the speakers of the two houses in parliament. I was everywhere most kindly received, except, of course, by Bárdossy. His unexpected fall had evoked from Bárdossy a most violent reaction, which found vent in personal hatred of myself. His sudden emergence from the colorless life of a professional diplomat into active politics had thrown him off balance, and great political ambitions had developed in him. When he resigned, a communique had been issued which, to conceal the real reasons for his going, said that he was retiring on account of ill health; and to give this story plausibility, he had gone into a sanatorium. I called on him there and, as custom required from a new premier to his predecessor, informed him of my appointment and outlined my program to him briefly. He hardly waited till I had finished before breaking out furiously:

You will lead the country into a catastrophe. Everyone knows that you are anti-German and pro-Allied, and no anti-Semite. You will run after the English and never catch them, as Bethlen could not, nor anyone else. They are committed to our enemies, the Russians and the Little Entente. They will never throw them over. You will lose Germany's friendship, and Hungary will be left alone. There is no changing the fact that if Germany is defeated we too shall finish on the list of defeated enemies. That was decided in the First World War and at Trianon.

I made no special effort to convince him that his logic was faulty, simply remarking that if, according to that argument, we were bound up with Germany, then, since Germany's defeat was inevitable, the one thing to do was to cut the bonds. We parted coldly and did not meet again.

In the cabinet I could be sure that besides the minister of the interior, the ministers of agriculture, trade and communications, and justice would support me. I had undeniable difficulties with the others; but thanks to Minister of Interior Keresztes-Fischer's efforts and the personal intervention of the Regent, I was able to get their promise to remain for the time; they loyally accepted the argument that in the existing critical situation it was necessary to set aside all other considerations and regard only the national standpoint.

The propaganda directed against us throughout the world always represented Hungarian ministries as feudal, anachronistic phenomena. I therefore give here the origins and previous occupations of the members of my cabinet:

Interior: Francis Keresztes-Fischer, country lawyer

Justice: Ladislas Radocsay, country lawyer

Trade and communications: Joseph Varga, teacher at the technical university

Finance: Louis Reményi-Schneller, bank employee

Defense: Charles Bartha, professional soldier, grandson of a Szekel peasant; succeeded by William Nagy, professional soldier, descendant of an ancient family of Transylvania; succeeded by Louis Csatay, professional soldier, son of an officer of the Austro-Hungarian army

Cults and education: Valentine Hóman, historian, university professor, and director of the national museum

Supply: Alexander Györffy-Bengyel, professional soldier, son of a peasant; succeeded by Louis Szász, university professor, sometime secretary of state for finance, son of a small village grocer

Agriculture: Baron Daniel Bánffy, representing the Transylvanian party, specialist in forestry and timber production

Propaganda: Stephen Antal, barrister and journalist, son of a village cab driver

Industry: at first, Varga; as his successor, Géza Bornemissza, engineer, director of several large enterprises, son of a level-crossing keeper

Foreign affairs: Eugene Ghyczy, career diplomat [17]

Thus as to its origins, this cabinet was truly not feudal; but it is a fact that most of these men before reaching ministerial rank had raised themselves, by their own abilities, into the leading economic and social class of the Hungarian nation.

I should like at this point to devote a few words to the accusation of "feudalism" so constantly leveled against us. It is undeniable that in many respects Hungary took over the spirit of the old Dual Monarchy.[18] Today people are beginning to see more clearly what the Monarchy was. It is not my business to analyze this problem, nor would I be so malicious as to compare the position which its peoples then enjoyed with their position today. I would confidently assert, however, that even if its political structure was not democratic—although in this, too, it was completely liberal—its economic structure was the most liberal of any European state. When we inherited that spirit, Hungary, shorn of her national minorities, had no course but to implant the nationalism which was absent from the spirit of the Monarchy into her own system.

Prewar Hungary possessed a leading social class, but it was not a closed caste and could not be because its members represented diverse elements of the population. Members of the old noble class constituted only a very small fraction of it, but they contributed greatly to its character. This group was nationalist, liberal, and social-minded in spirit; it was very honorable—corruption was unknown among its members—and unmaterialistic.

[17] After July 25, 1943, when I relinquished the office.
[18] The Austro-Hungarian Monarchy was created out of the former Austrian Empire by the *Ausgleich* or compromise of 1867. The Habsburg realm was divided into two autonomous parts: the Empire of Austria and the ancient, independent Kingdom of Hungary, which included Hungary with Transylvania, Croatia-Slavonia, and the district of Fiume.

This society was conservative in the better sense of the term.
It was strictly constitutional in spirit. It is a fact that it rejected
all such modern developments as might have endangered the nation's interests. It must also be admitted that its externals often
misled observers: it had an historical tradition, old forms, which
might be called relics of feudalism. It is, however, interesting to
note that it was not the aristocracy that put on the Hungarian
gala dress or produced the *jeunesse dorée* of the nightclubs. Those
elements were the newcomers, who were anxious to emphasize
their arrival. The concept of Hungarian feudalism was one great
bit of snobbery.

In explanation of my political outlook, I think it necessary to
state that I call myself conservative of the true Hungarian type.
My ideal, from my childhood days, has been Stephen Széchényi,[19]
the man whom Kossuth [20] called "the greatest Hungarian," and
who was, indeed, our greatest reformer in politics. I saw Széchényi's political ideals realized in those countries of Northern
Europe which had reached the highest level of democracy and
liberty without revolution: these included fidelity to well-tried
forms of life, to law and to constitution, to change and progress.

When I picture the future of my country, I can only see it
preserving its old patriotism and puritan morality, cleansed of all
the evil that has come to it in later times, but enriched by the

[19] Count Stephen Széchényi, 1771–1860, was a leader of the moderate liberal
group in the Hungarian diet in the mid-nineteenth century. Although he advocated
the modernization of Hungarian institutions, he opposed the uncompromising
nationalism of Louis Kossuth. In 1848 Széchényi became a member of the first
revolutionary government in Hungary, but he resigned in protest against those
seeking a break with Austria. Subsequently, however, he criticized the absolutist
tendencies of Austrian officials.

[20] Louis Kossuth, 1802–94, entered politics in the second quarter of the nine-
teenth century as a member of the Hungarian diet. He soon became the articulate
spokesman of an extreme nationalism that did not shrink from the prospect of
separating from Austria. He was the virtual leader of the revolutionary government
after 1848. After the fall of the Hungarian republic in 1849, Kossuth lived abroad.
So dissatisfied was he with the *Ausgleich* of 1867, that he refused an offer of amnesty
in 1890. After his death at Turin, however, Hungary claimed his body, and Kossuth
was buried in state in Budapest.

good in healthy development. It is possible to argue whether or not the destruction of the old estates was a good thing, but the land measures cannot be reversed. One may argue whether or not nationalization is preferable to private enterprise, especially in the case of large undertakings, but a private enterprise can be nationalized, while the reverse is next to impossible. The future must be built up on the good farmer, manager, technician, foreman, and—above all—on the reliable civil servant. No one must be excluded from this work, and all merit must be given full scope in Hungary's new life.

It is true that I made many speeches defending the old order. Aye, I would not throw over what was good in the old. What was good was not the title of Count or Excellency, not the big estate or financial and industrial wealth. What was decisive in those days was who was a faithful Hungarian, who would stand up against Nazism and Bolshevism. That was the point of view from which, in those days, I looked at the social classes of my nation. The expressions "left" and "right" have got hopelessly distorted since Nazism and Bolshevism invaded our phraseology. Formerly "right" used to mean a more conservative, and "left" a more progressive, spirit. Many people today regard Bolshevism as the pioneer of progress because it breaks with all that went before. So did Nazism. This has nothing to do with the persecution of the Jews; the Nazis persecuted men of their own race, too, if they were recalcitrant. The Bolsheviks, on the other hand, do not discriminate against a particular group of people, although they wipe out great masses of people in their own country. Both systems have taken all that is bad and hateful from all their forerunners, from feudalism to Marxism. What I defend in the old system is what was good, humane, and honest in it.

I must mention the reaction to my appointment abroad. Briefly: England and America were interested; Italy and the neutrals were sympathetic; the satellites were nervous. Germany betrayed no reaction whatever: the press registered the fact without comment; official circles hardly took note of it. Neither Germany nor any of the satellites sent me a single telegram of greeting.

True German opinion can, however, be read in Joseph Goebbels' diary, as follows:

April 1st, 1942. The new premier, Kállay, has long been known as an anti-German. Young Horthy is a definite pro-Jew and wants little touch with the Axis. Thank God, we have never had any illusions about Hungary, so that now we are undergoing no disillusionment.

Another extract reads:

September 23d, 1943. As for the possibilities of treachery among the other satellites, Horthy would be glad to jump out, but the Führer has taken the needful precautions [that is, by playing the Rumanians off against us]. Kállay, his premier, is a real swine. But he doesn't betray himself, he is too cautious to show his hand. For the moment, therefore, we must put a good face on a bad business.

TWO

THE POLITICAL PARTIES
AND BALANCE OF POWER IN HUNGARY

⟨[DURING normal times in Hungary the only political officials, aside from the Regent, with the power to be forceful personalities on a national level were the premier and his minister of the interior. The rest of the cabinet members were usually technical experts, naturally chosen where possible from members of the party or parties supporting the government.

I have already shown that, because of my previous independent course in politics and the entrenched power of the Government party, I had no alternative but to accept the cabinet of my predecessor. I made it my business thereafter, however, to build a Government party that would serve the program for the nation that I had outlined to the Regent.

The Government party that I inherited was no longer the same
as the Party of Unity that had been formed by Count Bethlen
out of the two large parties that had come into being during the
first legislative assembly after the First World War: the Smallholders party and the Citizens Christian party. I myself had been
a member of the Party of Unity, and as lord lieutenant through
three parliaments I had even helped to bring it into existence.
That party was the last relic of the pre-1914 Hungarian world—
partly in its physical composition but even more in its spirit, attitudes, and aims. Count Bethlen has often been criticized for
ruling undemocratically, when supposedly his historic mission
should have been to implant the spirit and institutions of the
then all-powerful Western democracies among the people of Hungary. This charge contains some truth, but it is also true that
such an aim could not have been realized because of circumstances
outside Hungary as well as those inside the country. The causes
within Hungary are to be found primarily in the country's historic
development.

Western ideas always reached Hungary, but always belatedly
and after some resistance from the nation. Hungary was the last
Eastern outpost of all Western ideas, political or religious, sci-
entific or artistic. The country became Christian a thousand years
ago, and it accepted Western Christianity and not the Eastern
Christianity of Constantinople. In fact, it accepted the purest
and most intimate version of Christianity, as purified by the
Cluniac reforms. The European Renaissance came to its last
flowering in Hungary under King Matthias Corvinus.[1] Protestantism came to Hungary after it had been already freed from strife
and had assumed a purely spiritual form. The first legislative declaration in the world in favor of the free profession of religions was

[1] Matthias Corvinus, 1443?–90, was king of Hungary during the years 1458–90
and of Bohemia, 1478–90. He, like his father, Janos Hunyadi, distinguished himself as a crusader against the Turks. He fostered learning and science in Hungary,
and during his rule the country reached her last flowering before falling to the Turks.

made in Hungary.[2] It is worth mentioning that it was the campaigns of the Transylvanian princes, Bethlen and Bocskay, that ended the persecution of Protestants throughout the Austrian empire—which then covered the whole of Central Europe.[3]

We finally adopted in their entirety the great ideas of the French Revolution: nationalism and liberalism. These were accepted in Hungary, however, only after some initial resistance, because the majority of such progressive political ideas were first brought in—or were smuggled in—by persons interested in weakening our national strength. Thus every new idea met with resistance until it and the interests of Hungary were reconciled.

To review briefly the situation after 1919, for example, we may begin by saying that it was allegedly under principles of democracy that Hungary in the Paris peace treaties [4] was reduced to one third of her former area and one third of her purely Magyar population was placed under peoples who, except for the Czechs, were Oriental pseudodemocrats. For a thousand years we Hungarians had considered ourselves the legatees of Western traditions, and we recoiled in amazement when we saw that our enemies—nations which in the course of history had never played a part in the formation of European ideas or represented such ideas—had been appointed as representatives of the West. It is not surpris-

[2] The Declaration of the Diet of Torda (1557) ran as follows: "Everyone may follow the faith he wishes, but he must not hurt those of other faiths." This referred to the antagonism between Catholics and Lutherans. The Transylvanian Diet of 1564 guaranteed the freedom of Calvinists, and that of 1568, the freedom of the Unitarians.

[3] Stephen Bocskay, 1577?–1606, was a Protestant prince of Transylvania who in 1604 allied himself with the Turks against the Habsburgs. In 1606 he signed with Archduke (later, in 1612–19, Emperor) Matthias the Peace of Vienna, which guaranteed religious freedom in Hungary.

Gabriel Bethlen, 1580–1629, prince of Transylvania (1613–29), was an adviser to Bocskay. Bethlen overran Hungary in 1620 and he was declared king. After the Battle of White Mountain in that same year, however, he renounced the royal title. He was a Protestant noble but he encouraged toleration for all religions.

[4] See Chapter Three, "The Geopolitical Situation of Hungary," for the details about foreign policy in the period between the First and Second World Wars alluded to in this chapter.

ing, therefore, that the word "democracy" was not popular in Hungary or easily accepted as a ruling idea and a national way of life. Hungary could not become a democracy because her enemies called themselves democrats and wanted Hungary democratized, not in order to strengthen her and to render her national identity more secure, but to weaken her national strength, to make her more malleable and less Hungarian. The successor states of the Austro-Hungarian Monarchy did not possess the kind of historic past or national independence and traditions as was possessed by Hungary. They could, therefore, easily adhere to the democratic ideology, under the pretext of which the Monarchy had been atomized and the successor states became "powers." But this adherence was to the externals and slogans of democracy. Under the slogan of democracy the successor states hoped to hide their oppressive attitude towards their Hungarian minorities in general and the purely Hungarian landowner class in particular, and to mask political systems that were neither democratic nor liberal but dictatorial. I must definitely state, moreover, that the respect for human rights, individual liberty, and constitutional safeguards in the Austro-Hungarian Monarchy—which had been decried as feudal and autocratic—had been far greater than was true later in the successor states, even Czechoslovakia, which, owing to its strong industry and bourgeois character, could be distinguished from Rumania and Yugoslavia. After 1919 Hungary was the only country of the old Monarchy that adapted and applied the spirit of the Monarchy. And Hungary (as always throughout her history) tried to join forces with the West, but since her enemies in 1919 had become friends of the West, this ambition became extremely difficult to fulfill. After the Paris peace treaties the situation gradually took such a turn that Hungary remained the last defeated country of the First World War. Germany became too powerful; Austria—just as today—came to enjoy a privileged position; Turkey found her own way out of her difficulties; and Bulgaria, as a Slav country, came to enjoy the friendship of the countries of the Little Entente. We Hungarians remained alone on the list of the proscribed.[5]

Thus it was not at once possible internally to adhere in our political institutions to the democratic pattern. Externally, on the other hand, we were separated from the West by an impenetrable barrier formed by the Little Entente in general and by the incomprehensible policy of revenge practiced towards us by Eduard Benes' Czechoslovakia in particular. Count Stephen Bethlen's Party of Unity was, therefore, placed between the internal and external millstones of this problem. This party was, nevertheless, the last representative of a true Hungary. Every social stratum of the nation was represented in it. Very few of its members were drawn from the old nobility. One third of its members were peasants. A leading element was drawn from the middle classes, which always tried to comprehend sensitively the values of the Hungarian people. That was the party that achieved the consolidation of Hungary after the war. Its task included the (very restrained) liquidation of the short-lived Communist dictatorship of 1919; then, the crushing of its consequence—anti-Semitism;[6] and finally, the reconstruction of the Hungarian econ-

---

[5] We know today that at the discussions and crown councils prior to the declaration of war against Serbia in 1914, it was Count Stephen Tisza, Hungary's premier, who alone opposed the Dual Monarchy's sharp ultimatum to Serbia and had it recorded in the minutes that Hungary protested against any infringement of Serbia's independence as well as against any Austro-Hungarian expansion in the Balkans. We also know now that the Czechs, the Serbs, the Rumanians, and the Poles wanted war in 1914; their point of view is quite easy to understand, since they could not achieve their national independence or territorial enlargement through other means. This, however, is not relevant when it comes to the question of war guilt. We have to add that Hungary had neither territorial nor any other aspirations and could only lose as a result of a war. What an irony of fate it is that in a war which was started with the slogan of liberty, it was Hungary—the heaviest loser of all— that adhered first to President Wilson's Fourteen Points. She could easily do this because as the oldest constitutional country of the European Continent, whose history is full of wars of independence, Hungary could hardly find any among the Fourteen Points which could not be found already a part of her constitution or of her legal system.

[6] Béla Kun and some of the other leaders of the Communist government were Jews.

omy, spiritual life, and public administration. When, however, the League of Nations could not rise to its own duty, when it did not even attempt to remedy the injustices of the Paris peace treaties and to improve the lot of the three and a half million Hungarians placed under alien rule, the Party of Unity failed. Another cause of the party's failure was the effects of the world's economic crisis, which set Hungary back very seriously on her road towards economic reconstruction.

Democracy is impossible without material prosperity and spiritual satisfaction, and the defeated countries after 1919 could not become democracies because spiritually and economically they were not healthy. Germany and Italy took the path of social dictatorships, the products of popular movements. Their nationalism became exaggerated and their political attitude antagonistic towards the democracies. Hungary, under Count Bethlen, did not follow Germany and Italy, even though her wounds were deeper and her unsatisfied claims more serious. She tried to solve all her problems in peaceful fashion, through co-operation with the Western democracies and with their support. When, for the reasons I outlined above, this had become impossible, Bethlen's policy could not avoid bankruptcy.

The reason for Julius Gömbös' succession to power was that by 1932 the people no longer believed that the interests of the country could be served through peaceful and normal means. The people were tired out by a postwar struggle that had lasted for well over ten years. An agricultural crisis, industrial unemployment, the dismissal of large numbers of government and civilian employees, and the hopeless situation in which the country's youth found itself had all created a revolutionary mental atmosphere. This situation, which was still in a latent stage, needed a safety valve, and this fact made the appointment of Gömbös as premier possible or perhaps necessary.

Gömbös' dynamic personality without doubt carried away the widest ranges of the Hungarian people; unfortunately it carried away Gömbös also, to championing extreme policies. The only

)eople who remained in opposition to him were the conservative ·nd intellectual circles: the higher clergy, the more prosperous andowners, the *haute bourgeoisie*, and the Jews. He took over 3ethlen's Party of Unity, which supported him; but Gömbös ınd the party never made friends. As a result, therefore, Gömbös ·ook his first opportunity (in 1935) to hold general elections and ·o bring into parliament [7] new representatives: his personal friends ınd younger, more active men. At these elections only Bethlen ınd I, among the former men, were returned with an Opposition program.[8]

When Bethlen left the party he had created, I was the only man who followed him. Before taking that step I had belonged, as min-ister of agriculture, to Gömbös' first cabinet, which he had formed when still enjoying Bethlen's support. The work I did for Hun-garian agriculture and for the Hungarian peasant I regard as some of the most important of my life, though I could not carry out many of my plans, including a constructive and permanent land reform. I had several other political differences of opinion with Gömbös. When at one of the cabinet meetings I, with Francis Keresztes-Fischer, the minister of the interior, protested against the asylum given by Hungarian army authorities to Croat ter-rorists, our differences became deeper.[9] (I must at once state that, as established by the League of Nations, these Croats had no part

[7] The lower house of parliament, after the Electoral Reform Bill of 1938, con-sisted of about 359 elected representatives. The members had to be at least thirty years of age. The term of office was five years.

The upper house consisted of seven groups of members: (1) 3 members of the house of Habsburg-Lorraine living on Hungarian soil; (2) about 38 male members of the high aristocracy selected by their peers; (3) about 76 members elected by the counties and cities; (4) heads of various religious communities; (5) dignitaries such as the supreme justices, the chief of staff, the presidents of the national bank and of the national institute of social insurance; (6) about 40 members elected by such organizations as the chambers of agriculture, commerce, and industry; and (7) about 50 life members appointed by the Regent. The term of office when elec-tive was ten years, and half of the elected members were elected every five years.

[8] Bethlen got in largely because my brother-in-law Tibor Kállay, a former minister of finance, gave him his own safe seat.

[9] During the debates of November, 1934, after King Alexander of Yugoslavia and M. Barthou of France were assassinated in Marseilles.

in the murder of King Alexander of Yugoslavia). I resigned soon after, when Gömbös showed his intention of subordinating Hungarian finances to Béla Imrédy, the newly appointed president of the bank of Hungary, thereby creating for him an almost dictatorial authority and sidetracking the minister of finance. This was the first occasion which clearly demonstrated the dictatorial turns of Gömbös' and Imrédy's minds. Through such an arrangement the whole of Hungary's economic life would in substance have been removed from parliamentary control, since the bank of Hungary and its president could not be made responsible to parliament.

Gömbös' new party—the Party of National Unity—broke completely with previous traditions, with Bethlen's old party and with his predecessor's economic and foreign policies. A few of Gömbös' aims were perhaps similar to Bethlen's, but his means and methods were entirely new. It cannot be said that Gömbös was not, in his own way and according to his lights, fighting for his country's cause, but he despised give-and-take, and he inflamed national passions. In fact, the whipping-up of Hungary's passions became one of his aims, and thus he drove the nation and its attentions towards the German and Italian social dictatorships. Both Gömbös and his adherents were completely misled by the apparent successes of the dictatorships and the apparent weaknesses of the democracies. There came a repetition of the mid-nineteenth century clash between the moderation of Széchényi and the impatience of Kossuth, but they had been giants of the Hungarian nation. This time little epigoni were playing with the faith and inexperience of the country. Here was the basic cause of the rift which later was characteristic of the Hungarian spiritual life. Gömbös could still ride the storm which he had set in motion, but his weak successors could not.

Paul Teleki's general election of May, 1939,[10] brought some changes in the Government party, including the withdrawal of

[10] This was after the premierships of Koloman Darányi October, 1936–May, 1938, and Béla Imrédy May, 1938–February, 1939.

the extreme right wing under the leadership of Béla Imrédy; but the party in its spirit and color was still Gömbös', especially after Imrédy forced out of it the "dissidents," comprising half the party, and its most valuable, intellectual half at that. The men who succeeded them were well-meaning, honest country gentlemen or bourgeois who had not been politicians but who had been returned to parliament as respected and popular people in their own districts. Most of them were "yes men," without definite political orientation. They saw the reactionary developments with fear in their hearts, but they had no strength to resist. The men who set the tone of the party were the noisy and dynamic supporters of Gömbös, men of a dictatorial turn of mind and above all anti-Semitic. It would not be true to say that these men were unconditional pro-Germans or the storm troopers of German policy in Hungary. Although, for example, sentiment for Italy was very strong, Fascism never took root in Hungary. Since there was far less sympathy for the Germans, National Socialism had an even more difficult time winning favor. The Trojan horse, however, inside which the ideology of National Socialism was smuggled into Hungary was anti-Semitism. The Gömbös men in the Party were anti-Semitic, but they were not Germany's hirelings. Anti-Semitism was the pivot around which their ideas turned; it was a disease with them.

I should at this point say a few words about the composition of parliament according to political parties at the time of my appointment as premier. The Government party had an absolute majority in the lower house. Admittedly, as we have seen, there were within the party important differences, but towards the Opposition it showed itself by and large to be a disciplined group.

The largest party of the Opposition was that of the extreme right, the Arrow Cross party, whose members comprised only some 5 to 6 per cent of the lower house. Its leader, Francis Szálasi (Szálosian), was a fanatic of Armenian-Austrian origin who had been a major on the general staff. He was sentenced in 1938 to three years of hard labor for extremist agitation, for propagating

ideas practically identical with those of National Socialism, and
for preaching German omnipotence. On his release from prison,
he continued his reactionary political activity, but his prison
record barred him from entering parliament. The parliamentary
leader of the Arrow Cross party was a chemist of foreign extraction who had taken the name of Eugene Szöllösi, his former name
having been Naszluhác. The program of this party was to establish
a dictatorship in Hungary, to apply the ideas and methods of National Socialism, to extirpate the Jews, to liquidate the existing
ruling classes, and to fall completely into line with Germany in
military and foreign-policy affairs.

The other right-wing party was the Rejuvenation party led by
Béla Imrédy. The members of this party upheld and sought to
implement the same ideas as those of the Arrow Cross party, but
in a more moderate and erudite manner. Imrédy was supported
by a small group of gifted people, and most of the controversy
with right-wing principles during my two years in office was between them and myself. It was a clash between two major philoso-
phies battling for survival: the Hungarian philosophy, which was
a cultural tradition that linked the country with the West and
with liberalism and other expressions of the Western spirit; and
the other philosophy, an upstart ideology which awaited a new
world and awaited it from the Germans. Imrédy, the leader of
this right-wing group, was of purely German origin, save for a certain Jewish strain; his family's original surname had been Heinrich.

The Smallholders party, the Citizens Liberty and Democratic
party, and the Christian [11] party comprised an Opposition of the
center. Of these, the first had been the most important. The
Smallholders party [12] lost much of its importance and quality,

[11] This party corresponded to the Christian Democratic parties of the Western
nations.

[12] This is the Smallholders party that was formed in 1930. Gaston Gaál, a member of parliament, became its first political leader. When he died in 1932, party
leadership fell to Tibor Eckhardt.

however, when its leader, Tibor Eckhardt, with Paul Teleki's approval went to the United States to represent Hungarian interests there. When that party was led by Eckhardt and Gaston Gaál, it had a large following among the peasantry of the country. Its large following had not, however, been reflected in parliamentary strength. A primary explanation for this political weakness was the fact that the Government party, too, was strictly speaking an agrarian party. It had more small-farmer members than the Smallholders party itself, and in elections gained the adherence of the followers of the latter party. After Eckhardt's departure the leadership of the Smallholders party was left to its two vice presidents, Zoltán Tildy, a Calvinist minister, and Béla Varga, a Catholic priest. Tildy was politically untrained and did not count for much in parliament. Varga, on the other hand, was asked by Teleki, and later by me, to supervise the Polish and French refugees in Hungary (the Poles numbering more than 100,000, the French several thousands).[13] That work, which Varga performed most efficiently, occupied most of his time, and he could take little active part in party political life.

The Citizens Liberty party had a few members in parliament. Its leader, Charles Rassay, possessed quite exceptional debating powers and remarkable judgment and consequently carried much weight. Sensing the drift of the situation and my policy, he gradually retired from public life, but he never ceased to inform me of his opinion, either personally or by other means. Although his views were often critical, I regarded his attitude as tantamount to positive support of my activity as premier.

The Christian party played no prominent part, particularly after the loss of its leader, John Zichy. The chief plank in its platform was legitimism, and that subject could not be raised effectively in those times. The party was heard from mainly on cultural questions and had several eminent members in parliament.

The Social Democratic party was a party of the left. It is worth

13 See Chapter Fifteen, "The Treatment of Refugees and Prisoners of War."

mentioning that at that time Hungary was the only country on
the Continent, besides Switzerland, Sweden, and Finland, in
which a Social Democratic party and parliamentary group existed. What made the situation in Hungary interesting was that
both the Socialists and the Democrats had Jewish members in
parliament. That was something quite extraordinary for a country under German pressure, and the Germans resented it most
bitterly. The Social Democratic party enjoyed full freedom of action, rights of assembly, and freedom of organization. It was allowed to have daily and weekly papers, and nobody disturbed
their courses of education for young people. The situation can
be best illustrated by the fact that Imrédy once came to me to
ask me to give his party as much freedom of action as was enjoyed by the Social Democrats. My minister of the interior,
Keresztes-Fischer, definitely favored the left-wing parties against
the extreme right. The Socialists' leader, Charles Peyer, was a
fair, serious, and loyal opponent. He was a man who never lost
sight of his aims, who judiciously weighed situations and possibilities, and who defended the interests of the working classes
to the last. His activity during that period was a constructive factor
in Hungarian life.

There was no Communist party in Hungary—that party had
been prohibited in 1919. There were, therefore, no Communist
members in the parliament. I can assert quite definitely that there
were neither Communism nor Communists to speak of in Hungary at that time; there just were not: the masses rejected their
program and agitators.[14]

I should like to discuss here also some of the social classes whose
attitudes and actions influenced political events in Hungary at
the time of my appointment and afterwards.

The leaders of Hungarian society—the big landowners; the

---

[14] Tito has stated that Rakosi complained to him that on his arrival in Hungary
he found only 110 Communists there.

principal financiers, among whom the Jews predominated; the higher officials; the high clergy; and the intelligentsia—all, or the vast majority of them, may be safely classed together as having been proper, constructive, and statesmanlike in their ideas.[15] I believed that I would have their wholehearted support, and I found later that I did have. There was hardly an Arrow Cross man among them; those who were were regarded as figures of fun by other members of that company. It was true, however, that Imrédy's following included a group of ambitious and dissatisfied intellectuals who were not without talent but who were wholly without roots.

The largest group of the Hungarian people included the farmers and agricultural workers—the rural population. This laboring class, in all its sections, was then and during the two years that followed the most stable group in the country. The poor peasant endured his fate with the fatalism born of centuries of serfdom—that serfdom from which he had been liberated, it is true, in Hungary first among the countries of Central Europe (such liberations occurred considerably later elsewhere). Unfortunately the liberation in Hungary had not been accompanied by necessary reforms in the economic conditions, and the rapid numerical growth of this class had aggravated their plight. Nevertheless, this class, I repeat, was quiet; it worked; it was the mainstay of Hungarian agricultural production and thus the most important factor of our existence. Politically, the rural members of the population were far removed from polar ideological trends; they were neither right- nor left-wing extremists. They had no liking for the Germans, but they were not Communists, and even the Social Democratic party could not make headway among them. They were not anti-Semitic and were completely uninfected with the spirit of class war. They were individualists and did not generalize in

[15] I may mention as a characteristic circumstance that the "Nemzeti Kaszino," a club which embraced the whole of the upper class Hungarian society with the exception of the Jews, had not a single Arrow Cross member and 99 per cent of the members were on the side of the Western democracies.

their judgments of men and things. They liked a good functionary and a good squire and respected an honest Jewish shopkeeper,
but their appreciation of all these was very critical. The clergy-
man and the schoolmaster were perhaps the only ones to escape
criticism; the independent Hungarian judiciary was the one authority unquestionably accepted as unassailable by the agricultural
population. Their positive qualities were their unbounded patriotism, their faculty for good citizenship, and their readiness to
obey the law. Their greatest strength, which makes them the im-
perishable pillars of their nation, is their immense capacity for
work and their frugality.

The political outlook of the small farmers and medium landowners differed from that of the agricultural laborers. There was
in it a latent, atavistic memory of the great political battles of
the days before the First World War. In those days it was the
culmination of patriotism and a source of pride to be an "1848-er,"
to be against the existing constitutional order and the monarchical
Habsburg state. This attitude of mind, negative in its conception, emptily chauvinistic rather than nationalistic, destructive
rather than positive in its attitude towards the state, lived on to
some extent in this social class, that very class which was most
prosperous and had least cause for complaint—a little-observed
fact which is in stark contradiction to the tenets of historical
materialism. The most prosperous were the least content with
things as they were; it was they who sought for something different, and in the last, critical stages of the war played with the
idea of reactionary upheaval. I hasten to add that all this applies
to only a fraction of the whole. The great majority of the small
farmers were loyal to the government. I do not believe that the
unquiet elements constituted as much as five per cent of our
small-farmer population. However, the proudest—I might almost
say the most arrogant—representatives of Magyardom came from
these ranks. This extremist, right-wing group was made up of
sons of the small farmers who were tired of village life and wished
to escape from the soil.

While on the subject of the malcontent right-wing elements, mention must be made of the urban and rural *petite bourgeoisie*, which included the body of minor officials and the lower intelligentsia. The vast majority of the turbulent Right Radicals, of Imrédy's and Szálasi's followers, and of the anti-Semites came from those circles. The radicalism, and especially the anti-Semitism, had economic causes. Those people, above all, were the ones whose advance was blocked by our overnumerous Jews. The frustrated members of those groups did not mind the big manufacturers and big bankers; it was the bank clerks and the retail shopkeepers who, in the opinion of the malcontents, were taking the bread out of their mouths. It never occurred to them that the explanation might be that the Jewish bank clerk was more industrious, the Jewish shopkeeper more resourceful, perhaps more cunning and more dependable, than his Hungarian counterpart. Or if those dissatisfied people did realize that this explanation might be true, it only made them more furiously and fanatically anxious that the cleverer, more successful rival should perish. I most definitely do not mean to assert that the Jewish members of the *petite bourgeoisie* were more gifted and capable than the Magyars. By no means. But it is undeniable that they were more persevering, more agile, more purposeful, and that they hung together and helped each other better. To take a simple example: in a village where there were two shops, one Jewish and one non-Jewish, the Magyar customers would be divided between the two. But it never once happened—and when I was high sheriff I asked for reports on that point from all the village notaries—for a Jew to be a regular customer of a non-Jewish shop.

It was the lower bourgeois group whose way to advancement outside of state employment, especially in business, was obstructed by the upward-striving Jews. But the way was also obstructed by the successful Hungarian upper classes, whose members filled the higher positions in business and in public life. It is interesting to note that the army was the only place where the sons of the *petite bourgeoisie* could make headway. Thus, with

difficulties barring the way to intellectual and economic advancement of those people with undoubted ambition and capabilities,
many members of that class endeavored to achieve their aims, not
by advocating, as liberals did, the removal of all hindrances to
free competition, but by preferring the use of arbitrary and violent
means. That choice was foreshadowed in their selection of soldiering as their career and partly determined by their military training in overt action. It was that class, therefore, which furnished
the greatest number of those who were untrue to the unitary national idea.

I must mention also the civil servants, the soldiers, and in general the whole category of persons whose economic existences
were secure but more or less closely linked with the state machinery. For a proper appreciation of their position it must first be
realized that even the civil servants were entirely independent of
any political or personal changes in the government. Such changes
affected only the ministers and secretaries of state, some fifteen
persons in all. The twenty-five föispans [16] may be added; those were
the party political additions to the Hungarian state apparatus.
Any other official, however high his rank, was judged exclusively
on his professional capacities, and service basis of tenure of all
officials assured their independence. That was one of the factors
which gave them their position of esteem in Hungary's public
and social life. Another was their close and intimate identification with the national idea; they were its most faithful servants.
They were drawn from every social class. The smallest contingent
was formed by the children of industrial workers. About half,
on the other hand, were of peasant stock. The old historic classes
of the untitled nobility filled only about ten per cent of the positions in the latest period. Of the non-Magyars, the Germans were
the most numerous, then the Slovaks; after them came the Serbs
and Croats, with the Rumanians at the bottom of the list. It is
interesting to note that in the Western democracies, especially
of the Latin type, the professional representatives of the three

[16] Lord lieutenants of the counties.

pillars on which the national existence rests play little part in the country's social life. It was otherwise with us: those officials formed the most respected and most influential class, and rightly so; for the Hungarian judiciary, the central and local administrative services, and, no less than they, the staffs of the state enterprises, railways, and so forth, really constituted the elite of the nation. That was primarily because the officials themselves regarded their callings as a lofty service and molded their public and private lives accordingly. Corruption was almost unknown; before the Second World War it had been practically unimaginable. Even nepotism was far less frequent than it is in some European states whose standards are high. The devotion to duty and moral standards of our armed forces were equally admirable. After saying this I need not enlarge further on the spiritual and political attitude displayed by those classes in those difficult times.

I have intentionally left for the end of this analysis of social classes the Hungarian industrial workers, not because they were not so important as the groups already discussed, but because I wished the reader to know about the other, older groups first. After the First World War an intensive program of industrialization was begun in Hungary, especially in Budapest and in some provincial towns and mining centers. Industrialization increased until industry became nearly as important as agriculture in the nation's economy, and the importance of industrial workers naturally grew as they increased in numbers and improved their organizations. They were not, however, represented in parliament in proportion to their numbers and weight; that was because representation in our parliament was based on constituencies rather than on national lists. Although the intrinsic strength of the industrial workers made them, nevertheless, a force in the nation, they naturally claimed a larger share in public life than they possessed. They were united in their will to disrupt the existing constitutional order, but there were few signs to indicate that they believed this could be done only by revolution. In fact, they did not appear to be of one mind in their ideological outlook.

It is not true that all the workers were left-wing or Marxist. A considerable number of them were for solving economic problems, not on an international, but along national socialistic lines; this national socialism must not, however, be confused with the German, Nazi variety. The principal characteristics of that Hungarian national socialism were a definite anti-Communist, anti-Marxist attitude; patriotism; and a certain not inconsiderable dose of anti-Semitism. Could the Hungarian workers have settled their own future as they themselves wished, they would never have become either Communists or Nazis. They would have developed somewhat along the lines of the British Labour party, perhaps asking for even less state intervention, and they would have taken an important part in building up a genuine liberal-democratic national life in Hungary.

I should like in the next chapter to discuss the foreign relations of Hungary after the First World War and the geopolitical situation at the time of my appointment as premier.

THREE

THE GEOPOLITICAL SITUATION OF HUNGARY

❨I COULD NOT, and did not, fail to realize that the geopolitical situation of Hungary at the time of my appointment would continue to grow worse and that the hope of finding some way out of the labyrinth caused by the country's unfortunate position would very probably diminish. Since the invasions of Czechoslovakia and Poland I had not doubted for a moment that Germany's aggressions would turn the whole world against her and that her defeat was inevitable. Even before those events I had believed that the National Socialist system could not keep itself alive in Europe. Unfortunately, however, Hungary had involuntarily and increasingly been subjected to two strong forces: expulsion from the Western group of nations and attraction into the orbit of German power. That is why Hungary, before she went to war against the Russians, could scarcely have acted in a manner different from her actions during this period. Rather than arguing here, however, whether or not Hungary committed errors—and large or small, avoidable or unavoidable errors—let us review the historic facts since the First World War with as complete objectivity as possible.

Before that war Hungary was an equal partner in the Austro-Hungarian Monarchy, in which Hungary proper together with Croatia-Slavonia, which had been connected with Hungary for 800 years, formed a magnificent geographical and economic unit between the Carpathians and the Danube. The Monarchy was an obstacle to Russia's expansion westward and towards the Balkans. The Monarchy also prevented the realization of Slav unification. The deeper causes of the outbreak of the First World War lie there. In that war Hungary, as part of the Dual Monarchy, stood on Germany's side. Germany presumably had imperialist objectives, but the Dual Monarchy entered the war in pure self-defense, which applies still more to Hungary.

After the First World War Hungary found herself on the wrong side, the side of the vanquished and even of the war guilty. The conquering Western powers did not wish to make and maintain peace with Austria and Hungary; they looked for Eastern satellites. That was an impossible, unnatural alliance, like that of the French Republic with the Russian czars or of Great Britain and the United States with Soviet Russia.

The Treaty of Trianon, June 4, 1920,[1] deprived Hungary of nearly three quarters of her territory and two thirds of her popula-

[1] Specifically, by the Treaty of Trianon: Rumania secured Transylvania, part of the adjoining plain, and part of the Banat, including Timesoara (39,903 square miles with 5,256,451 inhabitants). Slovakia and Ruthenia (23,855 square miles with 3,515,351 inhabitants) were granted to Czechoslovakia. Croatia-Slavonia and the western portion of the Banat (24,422 square miles with 4,132,851 inhabitants) were given to Yugoslavia. The Burgenland (1,554 square miles with 292,031 inhabitants) was awarded to Austria.

Needless to say, the Hungarian delegation signed the treaty under great protest, after, in fact, Count Apponyi, the leader of the delegation, had resigned. The treaty was ratified by parliament November 13, 1920.

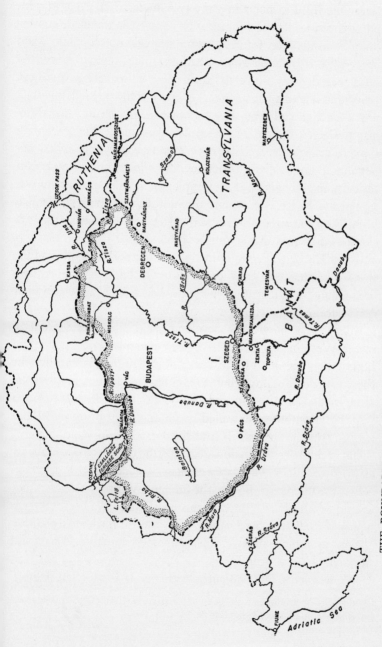

THE BOUNDARIES OF HUNGARY BEFORE AND AFTER THE FIRST WORLD WAR

From F. Deak, *Hungary at the Paris Peace Conference*, Columbia University Press, 1942

tion. One third of her ethnically and linguistically Magyar people was assigned to new states. The successor states, moreover, found consideration for their every strategic or economic wish. Hungary, on the other hand, was left as an unnatural structure, mutilated, defenseless, predestined to further partition. Nowhere (except in one small area where Austria was the other claimant) [2] was a plebiscite allowed. If we adduced those ethnic, linguistic, historical, geographical, and similar arguments, which coming from our neighbors were at once respected, we were called imperialistic, nationalistic, reactionary. *Difficile est satiram non scribere*. In the Balkans, for example, the district of Kossovo was assigned to Yugoslavia, despite the protests of its purely Albanian population, because it was a Serb place of pilgrimage. But it is not for me to give further details of this sort.

Out of the biggest country in East Europe and the Balkans they made the smallest. In the constituent states of the Austro-Hungarian Monarchy that historically had been nations with a constitutional character and with some liberty had been laid the foundations of progressive development on which a democracy of the Western type could have been constructed. Hungary had been such a nation. The best way of describing my country for those who do not know what the conditions were is to say that the same public spirit, world philosophy, discipline, freedom of and respect for authority prevailed in prewar Hungary as existed in England in the decades before the First World War. Possibly many in the Western nations regarded the conditions in Hungary as backward. It is reasonable enough to conclude that if conditions were inferior to those in the foremost Western countries they should be improved. But that this lag should have been taken as a pretext for destroying a nation, especially for the benefit of other nations even more backward, has remained something I have not been able to understand.

We were after Trianon entirely isolated in the foreign political

[2] The city of Sopron and the surrounding area were returned to Hungary after a plebiscite in December, 1921.

field, and the two attempts by King Charles to return to Hungary [3] induced our neighbors to band together in the Little Entente, [4] the purpose of which was to prevent Hungary's recovery, to isolate her economically and politically, and to thwart her attempts at treaty revision.

The Hungarian government, bound hand and foot and humiliated, could take no step to explain the injustices that had been done to the nation. The victors and their satellites born from our carcass forbade this: first, in the intoxication of victory, and then because of bad consciences. The fetters of Trianon, however, had one peculiar result in Hungary: the forming of the so-called Revisionist League. The objects of the League when it was formed were: to keep alive the idea of treaty revision in the population of Trianon Hungary, to secure remedies for the grievances of the minorities, and to help the Magyars in the successor states preserve their national character and bring up their children in Magyar spirit. Another important purpose of the League was, of course, to show the world that Hungary had not renounced the idea of treaty revision.

The League was created spontaneously out of the discontent of the Hungarian people. Members of every class were revisionist, from the peasants and workers upwards. The lower officials and the intellectuals were perhaps the most strongly revisionist of all (a million state and other employees had been expelled from the territories taken from us, and as members of the labor pool they naturally depressed the standards of the rest). The Jews, the anti-Semitic reaction of 1920–21 notwithstanding, were also conspicuous in the movement. The only classes which held somewhat aloof were the big landowners and industrialists, who had, of course,

[3] King Charles IV of Hungary (1916–18) (as Emperor of Austria, Charles I), 1887–1922, twice returned to Hungary, in March and October, 1921. In each case he was obliged to leave under pressure from the great powers and Hungary's neighbors. He died in exile on Madeira.

[4] Czechoslovakia, Yugoslavia, and Rumania came together by three dual treaties of military and economic alliance, 1920–21; by a convention in 1933; and by later agreements. They became closely bound to France by financial and treaty obligations.

interests across the frontiers. At the head of the League stood the greatest living Hungarian writer, Francis Herczeg,[5] and the presidents of the societies for promoting friendship with England and the United States, Emil Nagy and Sigismund Perényi. Otto Legrády, the proprietor of the most popular Hungarian daily paper, the *Pesti Hírlap*, placed the paper and his services at the disposal of the League. Banking and industrial circles discreetly provided financial help. Only the government held officially aloof.

The government officials regarded with mixed feelings the immense popularity with which the treaty revision movement was greeted. As Hungarians they rejoiced, but as responsible men they were unconcealedly nervous about the possible reactions. Bethlen was premier then. His attitude was very cautious, and he tried to apply a brake to the movement.

The first friendly move towards us by the great powers was in 1922, when Hungary was admitted into the League of Nations. An important result of that was the 1923 League loan, which enabled us to stabilize our economic and financial position.[6] It was entirely natural, too, after our entrance into the League that the Hungarian government worked for treaty revision on the basis of Article XIX of the League Covenant.

The work of the unofficial Revisionist League continued, however, and the movement received a powerful impetus in 1925 when Paul Teleki began a closer connection with it. As a result of Teleki's influence, the League issued a number of publications and maps with the primary object of awakening the treaty revision idea in the younger generation, giving a vivid picture of the situation of the Magyar minorities in the successor states, and making

[5] Francis Herczeg, 1863–, has written novels, plays, and short stories. Only some of his plays have been translated into English, among which are *Seven Sisters* and *The Silver Fox*.

[6] As a result of this economic assistance, the national treasury showed a budget surplus of about $15,000,000 by June, 1926, and the League at that time withdrew its commissioner, Jeremiah Smith, Jr., an American financier from Boston, who had supervised the carrying out of the provisions of the loan.

the younger people aware of the ethnical position of the Hungarian people in the Danube Basin.

At the beginning of the 1930's the League extended its work and sent representatives to various foreign states to support Hungarian propaganda there. It was thought that unofficial emissaries could do much more to make Hungarian grievances known abroad than could our diplomats, whose official positions restricted them. The first of these representatives was sent to Geneva, where many minority complaints were being brought before the League of Nations.

The treaty revision movement reached its peak when Lord Rothermere, the English press magnate, adopted the idea of "Justice for Hungary" and placed his papers at its service. The nations signatory to the Treaty of Trianon, particularly the successor states, naturally looked somewhat askance at the treaty revision activity, and Bethlen had to meet many attacks from abroad. People in Hungary, on the other hand, resented Bethlen's reserved attitude; they applauded him all the more warmly, however, when, after giving up the office of premier, he became the spiritual leader of the treaty revision movement and of that movement which sought to bring Hungary into contact with the Western powers and to win their friendship.

The treaty revision activities served Hungary's interests in various ways. During the Second World War, for example, representatives of the Revisionist League were still working in Geneva, Paris, Vichy, Berlin, Lisbon, and Stockholm, where they enjoyed the full support of our legations, used the diplomatic bag, and displayed a sort of semiofficial diplomatic activity. Before then, however, treaty revision had been realized in part. The forward thrust of the German power at Munich undoubtedly was an influence. All the emissaries of the Revisionist League were, however, strongly anti-German and worked accordingly.

These efforts by the Hungarian people themselves were made necessary by the fact that Hungary was left utterly destitute, outcast, and proscribed by the Western powers and their Eastern satellites. Teleki tried, for instance, to treat with the Czechs,[7] and the Regent afterwards sought a *rapprochement* with the Serbs,[8] but both were unsuccessful. How could Hungary have put up better resistance to the new German influence when nobody helped her to do so? Hungary's equality of rights was not admitted; she was disarmed and regarded with hostility and suspicion by both official Western politicians and the unofficial press. Hungary's desire to live was regarded and reported as being arrogance, her every protest as outrageous dissatisfaction, her approaches as intrusions. When Germany began to gather strength, neither the British nor the French desired to entangle themselves with Hungary (at this time the United States was not really interested) nor did the Western nations wish us to play an active part in European or, at any rate, East European politics. Despite these obstacles, however, and contrary to later disgraceful propaganda about Hungary, Hungary, of all the nations that ultimately were conquered by the Germans, retained her independence the longest and persisted the longest in her sympathy for and application of Western values.

The Treaty of Friendship which we concluded in 1927 with Italy,[9] then one of the victorious European powers, was our first step out of isolation and towards liberation. The world economic crisis which developed early in the 1930's tightened the economic links between the two countries and brought Austria into the combination.[10] There came into being as a result the so-called Rome Protocols [11] between Austria, Italy, and Hungary, intended primarily to defend Austria from Germany's attempt to unite with

[7] Early in 1921 Paul Teleki began negotiations with Czechoslovakia, but the formation of the Little Entente was the uppermost consideration in Eduard Benes' plans at that time.

[8] Speaking at Mohács in 1926, Horthy made a public overture towards Yugoslavia. It met with no response, however.

[9] Bethlen signed this treaty with Mussolini in Rome on April 5, 1927.

[10] A trade agreement among the three countries was signed on August 25, 1933.

[11] Signed March 17, 1934, by Gömbös, Mussolini, and Dollfuss; the detailed supplementary agreements were signed on May 14, 1934.

her. From that time Italy was a principal factor in Hungary's foreign policy. The importance of the Rome Protocols was revealed later in 1934, when the Austrian chancellor, Engelbert Dollfuss, was assassinated: [12] Benito Mussolini mobilized Italian troops in the Brenner Pass and prevented Germany from incorporating Austria.

There was, too, a historical connection with Poland (the two countries had always supported one another's struggles for freedom) which made Poland Hungary's friend during the period between the two world wars.

In April, 1935, England, France, and Italy issued a joint declaration at Stresa proclaiming a common front against all aggression.[13] Two months later, however, England, without consulting her partners, concluded a naval agreement with Germany that not only allowed Germany to reconstruct her navy, but in fact opened the first breach in the wall of the Treaty of Versailles.[14] That meant also the collapse of the Stresa Front. Then, after the outbreak of the Italo-Ethiopian War, when the League of Nations voted sanctions against Italy, Mussolini was driven into Germany's arms. Hitler could then safely disregard all the obligations of the Versailles Treaty.[15] In October, 1936, came the Rome-Berlin Axis, followed soon after by Germany's Anti-Comintern pact with Japan,[16] to which Italy adhered a year later.[17]

As a result of all those developments the Austro-Hungarian-Italian bloc lost its meaning, especially after Hitler marched into

[12] On July 25.

[13] On March 16, 1935, Hitler announced the resumption of compulsory military service in Germany and the projected increase of Germany's army to 500,000 men. On April 14, the Stresa conferees reaffirmed the Locarno obligations and consultation pacts concerning threats to Austria's independence.

[14] By this treaty, which was announced on June 18, 1935, Germany was permitted a navy 35 per cent the size of the English fleet in each category, regardless of construction by other powers.

[15] It was in March, 1936, while the League of Nations was tensely debating strengthening the sanctions against Italy by imposing an embargo on oil, that Hitler announced his intention to remilitarize the Rhineland and German troops marched into that area.

[16] Signed November 25, 1936.   [17] On November 6, 1937.

Vienna in March, 1938. Certainly Austria, abandoned by both the Western powers and Mussolini, and being German by race, had no particular reason to oppose the power-intoxicated main body of Germans. It was, of course, only by much violence and many tricks that Dollfuss and Kurt von Schuschnigg, who were in a tiny minority, had been able to hold up and postpone the Anschluss.

I know from hundreds of witnesses who were in Vienna at the time of the German entry that the Austrian people—first and foremost, of course, the youth—were madly enthusiastic. An old former civil servant of high rank told me that it was the first time he had ever seen the Viennese go wild, and he added sadly that he had lived his whole life there in vain—he did not really know them. Let nobody blame the Austrian people for that; we must realize that they had every reason for bitterness and for seeking some way out of their dead end. Nazism, like Bolshevism, holds out promises and charms for the masses, most strongly among small nations, and almost the only resistance is a nationalism above class interests. But there has never really been an Austrian nationalism. The Austrian people had maintained, administered, and exploited the Habsburgs and the great Monarchy, and they had subjugated their nationalistic feelings for a milder imperial patriotism. When their functions in the Monarchy came to an end, a great deal of purpose in life—material and ideal—was lost to the Austrians. Before the Anschluss nothing seemed final in Austria; everyone waited for something to happen, feeling that things could not remain as they were. Nothing was more natural under those conditions than for the great mass of Austrians—only a small, far-seeing, timid minority held back—to go over enthusiastically to the new ideal. The Anschluss was a solution that was forced on them but that seemed, nevertheless, to offer them some hope.

Thus Hungary, the other of the two constituents of the Dual Monarchy, was isolated. The Anschluss made us direct neighbors of Germany, then at a full tide of her expansion, and we were cut off from the West, which we could reach only by crossing Germany.

After Austria came the Sudeten question. In this connection the Regent's visit to Kiel in August, 1938, has frequently been misinterpreted. On that occasion Hitler invited Horthy to join him in attacking Czechoslovakia, offering Hungary as much of her former territories as she desired. Horthy flatly refused. While the Western press was writing of Hungary's "submission," Kálmán Kánya, our foreign minister, was venomously attacked by the Germans because the Bled agreement,[18] which recognized Hungary's equality of rights in respect of armaments, was published just when Kánya and Horthy were in Kiel.[19] The Bled agreement might have been of the greatest importance for the destiny of Hungary and indeed of all Southeast Europe, for it opened the way for co-operation between Hungary and the Little Entente and for the peaceful solution of all outstanding questions. It might have united the Danubian and Balkan countries and prevented any further German expansion after the Anschluss. Unfortunately, however, a month later the Germans were given a free hand in the East (or so they interpreted it) at Munich. Munich put an end to the French system of alliances which had stood since 1919, and the Little Entente disintegrated.

Of the new states in the Little Entente, Czechoslovakia was the strongest, the most cultured, the most civilized, and above all the best armed. She was the pampered child of Western (mainly French) politics, which was natural considering she was created by the Western nations. And Czechoslovakia gave herself to Hitler

[18] On August 23, 1938, at the Bled Conference, the Little Entente agreed to allow Hungary a military establishment in excess of that permitted by the Treaty of Trianon (an army of 35,000), on the basis of a mutual adherence to the principle of nonaggression by Hungary and the Little Entente. The implementation of the agreement, however, was to await the settlement of the minorities problem.

[19] This was the occasion of the famous incident between Kánya and Ribbentrop. Kánya explained the Bled agreement. Ribbentrop said it was so complicated that he could not understand it, and he asked Kánya to explain it again. Kánya did so and ended by saying: "The question is so simple that even Herr von Ribbentrop should be able to understand it."

without firing a shot, although we now know that the German
army staff advised Hitler not to attack Czechoslovakia because
her army was so strong. Eduard Benes did not even try to resist;
it is rumored that he himself suggested to the British and French
to advise him to yield. He himself brought Emil Hacha to power
and congratulated him on his election to the presidency after
his resignation from that office. I emphasize that it was Benes
who in this way showed Hitler that nobody opposed him, that
he could do what he wanted with small nations, that he could
embark on further aggression. Poland, Rumania, and the rest
would never have suffered had Hitler met with armed or even
passive resistance from Czechoslovakia or the Czech people. Instead Czechoslovakia lay down before him, and her magnificent
industry, her rich agriculture, and the first-rate abilities of the
Czech people and workers were at Hitler's disposal.

Today we all know the adulteration of history, geography, and
statistics which led to combining five nations to form Czechoslovakia, where the Czechs themselves were in a minority. The
"Czechoslovak" fiction was thus created; the Czech-Slovak combination had never existed nor had it ever occurred to anybody
before. (While Czechs and Slovaks had existed side by side in the
Dual Monarchy, they had granted each other little recognition;
it is an interesting detail that there had been hardly a single mar-
riage between a Czech and a Slovak on record.)

Benes' famous statement "rather Hitler than the Habsburgs"
is now well known; later he altered it, once again bowing down to
force, to "rather Stalin than the West, rather Bolshevism than
peace among the peoples of the Danube Basin."

Rumania, another partner of the Little Entente, weakened and
undermined by the Iron Guard, fell unresisting into Hitler's arms
when the Soviet Union threatened her and asked him for security and the guarantee of her frontiers against Russia and ourselves.[20]

[20] On October 7, 1940, the Rumanians announced, through their legation in
Berlin, that German troops had been sent to Rumania with her consent.

Then Yugoslavia, too, with whom we had sought friendship, putting aside our every demand, ceased to be a state.[21] She was the only Little Entente nation which resisted German pressure, and she carried on partisan warfare even after her defeat. From our point of view, however, she came completely under German domination. "Yugoslavia" was another fiction, which was blown sky-high by spontaneous combustion when Croatia turned against Serbia and went over to the Germans.

Our best friend, Poland, was partitioned between Russia and Germany, and after heroic resistance ceased to be. Poland was really the only nation on the Continent which stood up against the aggressors, which refused to buy peace from them, which fought to the end against both the German and the Russian dictatorships. Because of her legendary greatness Poland is deserving of first place among the European nations, but instead she is lost and the most wretched of all.

We had one friend inside the Axis: Italy. Italy never ceased to be our friend, but Mussolini became so committed to the German line that we could not count upon his help in anything. Paul Teleki twice sent special envoys to Mussolini, the first time in 1940 to tell him that if Italy helped he was prepared to refuse transit to German troops across Hungary on their way to Rumania; the second time in the spring of 1941 Teleki offered to do the same in the case of Germany's contemplated aggression against Yugoslavia. Mussolini, however, answered negatively both times; in fact, he advised us to fulfill the German demands.

What then could Hungary have done? Neither more nor less than she did. She went to the limit to preserve her independence, her freedom, her wealth, and her humanity, without, however, so straining the bow as to provoke brutal intervention from the Germans and the destruction of all these. This was a daring and difficult road to choose, but it was the most sensible and useful one, not for us alone but for everybody.

Until the Russian-German pact [22] there was only one danger for

[21] See pages 62–63.   [22] Signed in Moscow, August 24, 1939.

Hungary: that from the Germans. We had to resist and defer
ourselves against Germany in every possible way. If the Russia
German alliance had held, Hungary would have had to baland
between the partners, but would have probably leaned to the Ge
man side, as part of the nation instinctively turned later. The Hur
garian people feared the Soviet Union both as Russians and, eve
more, as Bolsheviks.

Then, too, a fundamental result of the mistakes of the treatic
of Versailles and Trianon was that the interests of the vanquishe
peoples coincided in certain respects.

The Hungarian government accepted with hesitation, but th
Hungarian people with enthusiasm, the two Vienna awards c
November 2, 1938,[23] and August 30, 1940,[24] which partly rectifie
the errors of the Treaty of Trianon. In each case we had Italy t
thank for what we got, since Joachim von Ribbentrop, as always
worked against us. Thus Hungary got back by peaceful means
part of her lost territories and blood brothers, unfortunately wit
the help, not of the League of Nations, but of the Axis powers, an
with Russia's full approval. In each case we first attempted direc
conversations.

The difference between what we asked of Slovakia and wha
she eventually offered us was a strip containing a population o
about 100,000. We proposed a plebiscite for this area. Tiso re
jected our proposal and asked for an Axis decision.[25]

As for the award of Transylvania—the Rumanian problem
Transylvania! This has run like a red thread through the recen
history of Hungary as an insoluble problem created by the ill-fatec
and so-called Peace Treaty of Trianon, that dictate of the mis
guided victors.

In the ocean of Slavonic peoples live two peoples who are not

[23] Arbitration of territorial dispute with Slovakia. See the next paragraph and
note 25.

[24] Arbitration of Transylvanian dispute with Rumania. See pages 58–60 and note
28.

[25] By the first Vienna award, Hungary obtained 4,566 square miles, with an
estimated population of 1,027,450.

Slavs: the Hungarians and the Rumanians. The Hungarians throughout the course of their millenary history and the Rumanians since they became an independent nation less than a century ago have sought Western culture, and the Rumanians have reached certain Western standards with extraordinary rapidity considering their short history as a nation. It is true that this applies only to their very thin upper stratum; but I also know the Rumanian peasant well, and I have rarely seen a more honest, clean-minded, and gifted people. Nothing could be more natural than for the Hungarians and Rumanians to combine. But this is impossible because of one problem: Transylvania. The Transylvanian problem is briefly this:

Transylvania was uninterruptedly a part of Hungary ever since the original conquest of the country by Magyars, continuing as an independent province even during the Turkish occupation. The first signs of Rumanian infiltration appeared in the thirteenth century. Slowly, very slowly, Rumanians settled in the uninhabited, forested, and mountainous parts of Transylvania, where Magyars never penetrated, since being horsemen and cattlemen the Magyars preferred the valleys to the pastureless pine- and beechwood regions; these areas were left free for the Wallachians, who were welcomed as settlers when they took refuge there from the Turks. During the two centuries of Turkish warfare the Magyar population dwindled, and empty areas appeared in the valleys. Thus in the course of seven centuries a stage was reached where the majority of the inhabitants in Transylvania were Rumanian. That they were oppressed is absolutely untrue: although serfdom existed, the Rumanian serfs were in exactly the same position as the Magyar serfs; there was no discrimination as regards the basic conditions of their lives. It is true that during Transylvania's independence a constitutional formula began to take shape which gave equal rights to three peoples: the Hungarians, the Szekely, and the Saxons. But this had no anti-Rumanian tendency whatsoever; it only meant that at that time the Rumanians had not yet appeared in the upper, leading stratum. Many brave Ru-

manian soldiers and other enterprising personalities subsequently
became Hungarian nobles and as such equal participants in na
tional rights. That was how matters stood until 1867. Then a
Magyarizing or, as it was later called, a re-Magyarizing process [26]
did in fact set in, with varying intensity and chiefly in the schools
This process caused resentment among the Rumanians. It did not
however, prevent them from increasing in numbers as well a.
wealth at the expense of the Magyars; considerable quantities of
Hungarian land passed into Rumanian hands, and the economic
position of the Rumanians grew stronger.

Then the Treaty of Trianon annexed to Rumania, not only
Transylvania, but also an enormous Hungarian territory which
was not even associated with Transylvania. The extent of our loss
will be appreciated when I mention that the area of historic Hun
gary given to Rumania was larger than the territory left to Hun
gary. In the ceded lands, which contained some three million
Rumanians, lived one and a half million Magyars, about half a
million Germans, and scatterings of other nationalities. More
over, except for the block of Szekely, these nationalities lived in
termingled throughout the territory.

After the collapse of the Little Entente and the concession:
made to the Germans at Munich, the position of Rumania wa:
greatly weakened by crises of domestic policy. It is a fact that it
looked in 1940 as if Hungary were going to attack Rumania and
solve the Transylvanian problem by force of arms. (Stalin's message to us to occupy Transylvania when he occupied Bessarabia did
not encourage but rather unsettled our resolution.[27]) At that

[26] To explain the idea of re-Magyarization I may say that at Nagyvarad, in the
school report, 1942, of the Rumanian boys' secondary school, almost half of the
pupils' names were Hungarian or distorted Hungarian. The leading Rumanian Greek
Catholic bishop, Hosszu, was also a Magyar, and incidentally a Hungarian noble
Maniu, the great Rumanian statesman, was also a Hungarian noble, and the docu
ment still gives his Magyar name. Similarly the Magyar origin of Vajda-Voivod·
and numbers of other Transylvanian leaders is incontestable.

[27] John Flournoy Montgomery, Hungary, the Unwilling Satellite (New York
1947), p. 138, quotes the conversation between Stalin and Joseph Kristoffy, the

juncture King Carol II, personally, and the Rumanian government asked Hitler to guarantee the frontiers of Rumania in return for concessions by the Rumanians to the Hungarians on the Transylvanian question. Hitler advised the governments of Hungary and Rumania to negotiate directly on the territorial problem.

The talks were started, but they yielded no results. The Rumanians were prepared to return only those purely Magyar areas lying directly adjacent to Hungary's frontier. After these unsuccessful negotiations the Rumanians asked Germany and Italy to arbitrate the matter, again asking for the guaranteeing of Rumania's frontiers. Teleki did not want to accept this Rumanian move, but Stephen Csáky, the foreign minister, convinced Teleki that to reject the Rumanian offer would put us into a false position, and Germany would then guarantee Rumania's existing frontiers. Teleki yielded to Csáky's argument and accepted the Vienna arbitration.

The award of August 30, 1940, in which the German and Italian arbitrators returned to Hungary rather under half of Transylvania,[28] did not bring a solution. It was true that there was a small majority of Hungarians in the ceded lands, but a million Rumanians were nevertheless brought under Hungarian rule, while several hundred thousand Hungarians remained beyond Hungary's border. (Both sides were discontented with the verdict. The Rumanian foreign minister fainted at the conference table. Teleki was so depressed on the return journey that when jubilant crowds appeared at every station he did not once appear at the window of his coach; and when the train reached Budapest, he pushed Csáky to the front to reply to the welcoming speeches, while Teleki himself remained in the background. I happened to be

Hungarian minister to Russia, on the Transylvania question. Stalin said, "Why then don't you attack Rumania? Now is the time."

[28] By the second Vienna award, Hungary obtained 19,300 square miles, with an estimated population of 2,385,987.

standing next to Teleki, and he whispered to me, "God grant that we have not now lost Transylvania for good because this arbitration, this partition, cannot be final; it will only be a source of trouble.)

The administration of the returned territory had to be taken over. Paul Teleki undertook that task with the greatest good will, and Hungary made vast sacrifices to restore the territory's economy. We built important and difficult railway lines, and we repaired the roads, which not so much as a sweeper had touched for twenty-two years. We sent in large quantities of foodstuffs. The most difficult problem was that the impatient Hungarian population and lower officials had dismissed the bulk of the Rumanian civil servants and had expelled—in a train crowded with one thousand persons—the highest Rumanian officials, who had given no cause for this; briefly put, a spirit of intolerance gained sway. The fact was that it was impossible to restrain the local Magyars; they were moved by their memories of twenty-two years of monstrous suffering, oppression, and subjection. It was impossible to make them think in political or wider terms: they sought satisfaction and were dissatisfied in the end with everything that happened.

In the disputed territory left with Rumania naturally the same thing, or even worse, was happening. I do not wish to enter here into the argument as to which nation committed the greatest number of abuses; but I can say—and this is the essence of the question—that the central authorities of the Hungarian government did all they could to curb and stop the violent outbursts in Hungarian territory, whereas in Rumania just the reverse was true. Not only were the lower officials in Rumania not rebuked for violence, but they were continually encouraged to such actions from above. This activity was easily concealed from outsiders because Rumania was under a dictatorship in which power resided in the Rumanian military officers rather than in their political officials.

When I became premier, I felt that in view of larger considerations one of my chief aims must be to reach a modus vivendi with the Rumanians. I did not, and could not, achieve this aim. Besides the objective causes, the principal reason was the infinite mistrust between us.

The crux of the whole problem was that this hostility made it impossible for us to form a common front against the Germans, who at the time of my appointment had Rumania almost entirely under their heel and were threatening Hungary: we had to compete with one another for the favor of the Germans. I never took that path, but my predecessors did and so, above all, did our army. Practically the sole reason why we entered the war and sent an army against the Russians was that the Rumanians were already taking part with full force against the Russians, whereas we were not and thus we risked losing German favor and Transylvania. The Germans emphasized this both officially and unofficially, and it was a principal weapon of German propaganda directed at the Hungarians. If there had been no Transylvanian problem—and this again is an indictment of the Treaty of Trianon—perhaps everything might have taken a wholly different course, and neither the Germans nor the Russians may have found it so easy to invade the Danube Basin.

The Germans did not like seeing Hungary's territorial aggrandizement, and they made her pay for it. After the first Vienna award, Hungary had to adhere to the Anti-Comintern pact [29] and after the second Vienna award to the Tripartite pact. [30] Thus Hungary lost much of her freedom of political action.

It is important to emphasize, however, that Hungary's occupation of Carpatho-Ruthenia was done at the urging of Poland, in the face of German disapproval, and only after Czechoslovakia had disintegrated. [31] Into the Bachka, too, Hungary marched only after Croatia had proclaimed its independence, the Serb troops

[29] On February 24, 1939.

[30] On November 20, 1940. The Tripartite pact had been signed in Berlin by Germany, Italy, and Japan on September 27, 1940.

[31] Slovakia declared her independence, March 15, 1939. Hungarian troops marched into Carpatho-Ruthenia on that day to the Polish border, and on March 16 Teleki announced the return of that area to Hungary and granted it autonomy.

had evacuated the area, and the Serb population itself asked us to come in order to forestall a German occupation.[32]

Moreover, the government and the Regent stood their ground most manfully when the war broke out. On July 24, 1939, Teleki wrote to Hitler to tell him that in no case would Hungary participate in any sort of hostile action against Poland. When Germany invaded Poland on September 1, the Hungarian government immediately declared its désinteressement and opened its frontiers, without any restriction whatever on the refugees from Poland. Csáky, our foreign minister, rejected requests from the Germans and from the Slovaks, who were joining in the attack on Poland, to allow their troops to pass across Hungarian territory and attack Poland from the south.

The first time Hungary saw German troops was during the next year, when Rumania asked permission for the transit of the "instructional" troops which she had begged from Germany. This resulted in the quartering of a small number of German supply and medical personnel at two big railway junctions in Hungary.

On December 12, 1940, Hungary concluded a Treaty of Friendship with Yugoslavia, a step intended to free us from our isolation in foreign affairs. Germany regarded our action as an unfriendly gesture. The pact, moreover, brought the Cvetkovich government in Yugoslavia into a difficult position, and it was obliged to adhere to the Tripartite pact as a counterweight.[33] This in turn provoked a military putsch in Yugoslavia, and the government was overthrown.[34] Germany regarded the military coup as a hostile act and asked permission to send her troops across Hungarian territory to attack Yugoslavia. Hungary had to choose between complying with or resisting this German request. Teleki sent a special emissary to Mussolini to ask whether we could count on his help if we refused, and Mussolini bluntly refused assistance. Finding resistance impossible, Paul Teleki sought escape from the problem in death,[35] hoping thereby to make the nation aware of the gravity of the situation, and the world aware of the tragedy in which the small peoples were becoming involved.

On April 6, 1941, the Germans began their operations. On the tenth Croatia proclaimed her independence. The Regent gave the Hungarian troops the order to march into Yugoslavia only after the Serb troops had evacuated the Voivodina, leaving it a no man's land, and it was clearly necessary to protect the large Magyar population there.[36] From a long-term point of view the extension of Hungarian rule to the Danube cut the corridor which the Germans were dreaming of creating all the way to the Ukraine. We did not encounter Serb troops, and our forces did not penetrate into territory which had been Serbian before 1914. Unfortunately, however, Great Britain broke off diplomatic relations with us,[37] although she had not taken that step towards Russia when the Soviet Union reincorporated former Russian territories on the Baltic, in Bessarabia, and in Poland, Britain's ally.

We became active participants in the war only when Bárdossy took over after Teleki's death. When Russian planes (according to one version they were not Russian but German) dropped a few bombs on Kassa, Bárdossy declared war on the Soviet Union.[38] Heinrich Werth, the chief of staff imposed his will on Bárdossy, and Bárdossy confronted the Regent and parliament with a *fait accompli*. Then on December 6 England declared war on us at Russia's wish. The far-seeing policy makers in the Kremlin knew well why they pressed Churchill so strongly to take this step: at that time they were already planning to exclude England from the Balkans. On December 12 we broke off diplomatic relations with the United States. The history of that process is that on December 11 Hitler and Mussolini announced that a state of war existed between Germany and Italy and the United States. The Hungarian government wished to avoid a severance of relations with the United States by announcing merely its "solidarity" with

[36] Hungarian Troops occupied the Bachka region on April 11.
[37] On April 7.   [38] On June 27.

the Axis. When Mr. Herbert Claiborne Pell, the American minister, asked Bárdossy whether that statement was equivalent to a declaration of war, Bárdossy replied decidedly in the negative. The next day, however, the Italian minister brought a message from Mussolini that Hungary could no longer count on Italy's support if she did not adhere to the Axis action against the United States, and at the same time the German chargé d'affaires called on Bárdossy and strongly demanded that he declare war.[39] The government of the United States and President Roosevelt realized that Hungary was acting under duress, and President Roosevelt openly expressed this awareness later in his message to Congress.[40]

Hungary's declaration of war was the gravest error committed by the government. The severance of diplomatic relations probably could not have been avoided, but the declaration of war could have been. In 1943, in a much more difficult situation, Hungary refused to declare war on Brazil and Chile.[41]

We became belligerents when we joined in the campaigns on the Russian front. In January, 1942, Ribbentrop came to Budapest to ask us to mobilize all available troops and throw them into the fighting. Bárdossy refused. Soon after, however, Field Marshal Wilhelm Keitel, the German chief of staff, appeared with a sizable military retinue and went to work on our soldiers. Bárdossy subsequently yielded, although not to all the German demands. The Germans' chief instrument of pressure against the Hungarians was their citation of the example of Rumania and the probable consequences if we did not do as well: the Germans warned that, if Rumania fought with the Germans against the Soviet Union and we did not, Hitler would find it morally and practically impossible not to revise his stand on the Transylvanian question in favor of the Rumanians.

[39] Hungary declared on December 13 that a state of war existed between her and the United States and the United Kingdom.
[40] On June 2, 1942. The United States declared war on Hungary on June 5.
[41] For an expression of German displeasure at this action, see page 182.

In March, 1942, therefore, when I took over the government, Hungary was at war—practically speaking, only nominally with the United States and England but in a real sense with the Soviet Union.[42]

[42] See the maps on pages 346 and 347 that show the situation in Europe, Africa, and in the Pacific area at the beginning of my administration.

FOUR

MY FIRST ACTIONS AS PREMIER

⟨[ON March 10, 1942, the day of my appointment, I got in touch with Béla Lukács, and he invited me to meet the leaders of the Government party. They represented the party's right wing and thus had received the news of my appointment without confidence. As I have already explained I was known to this group as an old Bethlenite and a liberal who had kept himself away from all anti-Semitism. In fact, my principles in those days were anathema to most of the right-wingers, who set the tone of the party.

I had rejoined the Government party when Darányi succeeded Gömbös as premier. I had been elected to a seat in parliament as a member of the Opposition, but I resigned it when I was appointed director of the national irrigation authority,[1] since the holding of that governmental position was incompatible with membership in the lower house. I was, however, immediately appointed by Horthy a member of the upper house, about fifty of whose members the Regent had a constitutional right to select. Very few members of the upper house belonged to the Government party and no member—so far as I can remember—to any other party. Thus I had had little opportunity to meet the members of the Government party, and that, as I had told the Regent, was a major difficulty when I was suddenly appointed premier in one of the most critical periods of Hungarian history. Lukács, the party chairman, was, however, a personal friend of mine, and he was completely devoted to Admiral Horthy's person and works. Lukács' views were different from mine, but I must say that he always supported me wholeheartedly and I could always count on his loyalty. That, then, was the relationship between the party and me. I had to win it over and to place it in the service of my aims. The alternative was to drop it and acquire adherents for my program through new general elections.

At that first meeting with the Government party members I saw Francis Bárczay, deputy chairman of the party; Stephen Kölcsey, its managing vice chairman; Count Michael Teleki, the leader of the party's agricultural faction; and many others. They informed me of the party's views on my appointment and the more immediate political issues. The picture they drew depressed and alarmed me.

Their point was that unless I accepted the party's attitude—as represented by them, the leaders—I could not govern. If, on the other hand, I asked the Regent for the dissolution of parliament, the results of the ensuing election would only strengthen the views of the majority of the party. This majority was dominated by a desperate fear of the Soviet Union and so these people

[1] The functions of this department were to supervise: the watering of the chronically dry Hungarian Plain, the furthering of hydraulic and soil-improvement operations, and the organizing of agricultural production.

wished for a German victory. They would not even hear of the possibility of Germany's losing the war, for that would automatically mean the victory of Communism. That fear was the basis of their attitude towards the Jews, too. If Germany won the war and we continued our tolerance towards the Jews, the Germans sooner or later would treat Hungary as a Jew-ridden enemy country. Moreover, no matter what we did, they argued, we could not win the sympathy of the Western powers. Since Bethlen had failed to gain their sympathy during the years of peace, it certainly could not be gained when Hungary was at war with those nations. The Western powers would hand us over to the Soviet Union, and so forth.

The party leaders said that they and the other leaders not present were willing, largely out of loyalty to the Regent, to support me as premier, but that I could not count on the rank and file of the party unless: (1) I made concessions to public opinion on the Jewish question; (2) I made pro-German declarations; and (3) I somehow relieved the anxiety of Gömbös' adherents, who had regarded me as an enemy ever since I left his government and the party.

In return I told them my fundamental thesis: that Hungary could only fight her way out of the great conflict if she tried to maintain her independence, freedom, and spiritual integrity as long as possible. I would, therefore, refuse to act in any way that would weaken these characteristics. At the most I might, in view of the circumstances, introduce a few measures in line with the party's wishes which would be acceptable on humanitarian grounds and would not be adaptations of foreign patterns. I felt that the nation's mind would be corrupted if it saw that we were forcing on it, in the interests of a foreign power, measures alien to its own tradition. In the interest of the great aims which I was pursuing, I was willing to make concessions at the expense of the Jews, but only such as did not affect the Jews in their equal rights as citizens, in their freedom or human dignity. These concessions, therefore, had to be restricted to the economic field, for such measures Hungarian Jews could bear, and, in view of the privileged position of Jews in Hungarian economic life, such measures could assume the character of economic adjustment and could be regarded by the fair-thinking section of Hungarian Jewry as their contribution to the war sacrifices of the nation. My answer obviously did not satisfy the party leaders, but after protracted argument we agreed that, in my first public speech as premier, I should declare that, even though I did not wholly accept the party's policy, I would assume an intransigent attitude on the Jewish question and would take economic measures "in order to reassure public opinion."

As one of those economic measures, my interlocutors brought up the question of the Jewish landowners. We had a law in Hungary which had limited the size of agricultural estates to a maximum of 250 hectares.[2] Jewish estates consisting of arable land could, however—with some exceptions—be expropriated in their entirety by the state on the basis of the same compensation as was granted for other lands purchased by the government. It was theoretically possible to sell such estates directly to peasants in the open market, but the law was complicated by various difficulties of procedure and rights of appeal, so that in practice the possibility hardly existed. The law was, moreover, difficult and unsatisfactory because its wording opened the door to favoritism. It said that the minister of agriculture *could* take over Jewish estates and not that he *must*. When a beginning of land reform was demanded, it seemed quite natural, under the conditions of the time, that the reform should begin on the Jewish estates. Those, with the exception of a few admirably maintained large estates, were below standard from the point of view both of productivity and of social conditions on them. In order to achieve quick results, the practice of the government had been for the ministry of agriculture to reach a compromise with the Jewish owners along the following lines: if the owner agreed to sell or let a portion of his estate and offered another portion for free distribution by the

[2] A hectare is about two and one-half acres.

state among landless peasants, he could keep a portion for himself. The results of such deals were, naturally, confusion and suspicion, and they certainly sowed the seeds of favoritism and corruption. My interlocutors suggested, then, that I should have this law altered to make the expropriation compulsory. If I agreed to this, the party would see that, even though I would not make concessions on certain points involving principle nor give up my "pro-Jewish attitude," I was approachable and might make concessions in the economic field and where it was a case of helping the small man.

During that first meeting I realized that in the future I should be unable ever to utter one single frank word. If I should merely say, even privately to any single person apart from a few intimates, that in my opinion Germany's victory was not certain, my words would spread like wildfire and would frustrate my mission. I should have to fear the unconscious indiscretion of people of my own ways of thinking as much as I feared *agents provocateurs.* I should have to keep everything to myself, never opening my mind frankly, consciously trying not to make my intentions clear to my adversaries; only by such care could I pursue my intentions safely.

After that meeting I discussed the problem of Jewish estates alone with Keresztes-Fischer, the minister of the interior. He said that in the national interest I must make any concessions which would enable the country to get through the war without losing its independence and moral integrity. The only thing that we must not do was the inexpiable. What we did in the economic field could be undone later; moreover, economic legislation would even serve the higher aim because we could perhaps save the masses of Hungarian Jewry at the price of such apparent sacrifices. As for the land, both of us knew that expropriation would be inevitable after the war. I must mention here that the land in Jewish hands was to an overwhelming extent in large holdings,[3]

---

[3] At that time 70 per cent of Hungary's arable land was in the hands of small landowners; 15 per cent in the hands of the state, municipalities, and the church; and

and there was not one single Jewish landowner in Hungary who cultivated his own lands himself.

All that would happen, we thought, was that the Jewish estates would get distributed before the other large estates. I therefore decided that in my first speech to the Government party I would announce the complete expropriation of Jewish estates. I may mention here that Jews in Hungary received this with understanding, especially as hardly one per cent of Hungarian Jews was seriously affected by this step.[4] Moreover, the expropriation included provisions for compensation, and it was my intention to give the same scale of compensation to the Jewish landowners as would have been given to other Hungarian landowners when their turn came. In any case, the compensation fixed in my proposal for the expropriation of Jewish estates was far more equitable than that actually paid after the war. Today a former landowner would regard my compensation as exceeding his most beautiful dreams.

That Government party meeting took place on March 10, 1942, and I had to deliver my introductory speech to the party on the morning of March 12.

Thus began my two years as premier, my two years of struggle on behalf of the Hungarian nation and people. I had to shoulder my burden at the moment when my country, weakened and exhausted, was facing a situation that was perhaps the most dangerous in the thousand years of her existence. During my premiership I made many speeches, for that was my only way of communicating with the country, and my great task was to win over the country spiritually to my plans at the expense of the earlier ideas.

I know I succeeded. The immediate success of my speeches was never in doubt, but their more permanent effect often depended—as was natural—on the situation at home and abroad

---

15 per cent was owned by large landholders. Ninety per cent of the Jewish estates were large holdings.

[4] The bill expropriating the lands of the Jews was passed by parliament in June, 1942, and promulgated, September 6, 1942.

and, of course, on military affairs at the time and afterwards. I
tried in my speeches to follow a consistent Hungarian policy, as if
Hungary were independent of the day-to-day events of the world.
I did this because of the two clashing worlds (I mean Germany
and the Western Allies and not Germany and Russia); I did not
wish to side with Germany, and it was impossible for me to side
openly with the Western Allies. I therefore set up a self-regarding
Hungarian policy as the ideal to be pursued. Many people failed
to understand this or regarded it as mere rhetoric. But the reader
will see that, despite all, I succeeded in making both the best men
in Hungary and the masses accept my policy as the only way out.

I have tried to reduce the quotations from my speeches to the
minimum. If certain themes and motifs recur, I have allowed this
in order to document the constancy and continuity of my policy.

My speeches contain, of course, some pro-Axis, anti-Russian,
and anti-Semitic statements, but never any anti-British, anti-
American, or anti-French sentiments. Should anyone pick out my
pro-Axis and similar statements exclusively, he could make out a
successful charge sheet against me. But such a winnowing would
be both stupid and dishonest. If a man is placed on the rack and
is forced to speak from time to time in a way sympathetic to his
tormenters, in order to postpone torture, and if he does this, not
in his own personal interests, but in order to save the cause entrusted to him, it is very obvious that he does not mean what he
occasionally must say. But if in that situation a man dares to utter
ideas contrary to the views of his tormenters, it is clear that he
really means what he says and that he wants others to know his
true feelings. I was the only one among the leaders of the countries
wriggling in Germany's clutches who occasionally dared to differ
with German views. Words like mine never came from the leaders
of Bohemia, Slovakia, Croatia, or Rumania, nor even from those
of the occupied countries of the North or from Vichy France. How
much easier my position would have been if I had not been forced
to make such declarations alone.[5]

[5] As I have said, the press and the public in other countries largely understood my

On March 12 I addressed my party. As was the custom, I first paid a tribute to my predecessor, Bárdossy, whose farewell letter had been read, before I spoke, amid loud applause, which was really meant as a demonstration against my appointment. I decided that the only thing to do was to make myself the first of Bárdossy's champions and to offer him the post of foreign minister in my cabinet. I knew that he would refuse, but I had to make the offer: first, because of the general considerations, mentioned above, which governed the formation of my cabinet; and second, because I had to reassure the members of the party and the general public who suspected that my foreign policy would mean a breaking away from Bárdossy's pro-German policy. At the same time, I declared that Hungary's foreign policy would undergo no change of direction. I said:

We should not be Hungarians, we should not be fit descendents of our ancestors who accepted European culture, but always through the course of a thousand years remained independent, if we did not take part in the struggle against Eastern barbarism, in which we must fight for Christianity and for the fulfillment of our great Hungarian ideals.

This was my first public reference to the ideology of Christianity; I really meant by it that because we were Christians we could not be National Socialists, and still less Communists, since both of those ideologies were opposed to religion as well as to the organized church and their tenets were contrary to those of Christianity. Neither could we accept racial discrimination. The reference to Christianity implied all that, but the Germans could not

---

problems and appreciated my position. But it is quite amusing to see the difference between two angles—one of which is biased and wrong and the other which is objective and correct. Marcel Hoden in his Cronique des evenements internationaux quotes exclusively such references from my speeches as lead him to the conclusion that my orientation was entirely pro-German, and that I was serving Germany's intentions. Roger Céré and Charles Rousseau, on the other hand, in their joint Chronologie du conflit mondial, quote such of my declarations—and naturally this is the intelligent and discerning way—which prove to them that I was trying to keep a distance between the Germans and myself and only waiting for the opportunity to break away from them.

find an excuse to pick a quarrel with the words because I did not call the child by its own name.

After that I expressed my faith and hope in parliamentarism; then I came to social tasks. I said:

We have to do our utmost to solve our social problems. I should like to touch today on four aspects of this. The first is the complex of material and economic questions; the second, the social implications of these questions. Thirdly, our territorial gains have now confronted us with a problem of national minorities, and fourthly, among the social problems I place the Jewish question. These are the problems I wish to discuss now. The present material and cultural situation of our people is terribly in need of improvement.

I then dealt with the first three points. Of the Jewish problem I said the following:

Fourthly, the Jewish question. I, myself, regard the Jewish question simply as a social problem, the most virulent social problem of our day. It has, of course, racial aspects, many economic aspects, and others also, but I should like to treat the whole complex, sine ira et studio, on the lines of social justice or social injustice.

The Jew is often an asocial being, individually or collectively. If we draw the balance in any country, we find that in the final implications they were harmful. Let us take the position in Hungary. Often it has been said that Jews, while their activities had often been harmful to Hungary, had also been useful. It is an indisputable fact that Jews were largely responsible for the speed with which our trade and commerce have been built up. But I am certain that we could have done that job ourselves alone. Perhaps not quite so speedily, but so much speed was not necessary, and we have had to pay a heavy price for it. On the other hand, we shall perhaps never recover from the harm Jews did to Hungary in other respects, especially during the revolution of 1918. The problem, therefore, is nothing more than this: rectification of that social injustice which has resulted in Hungary from the disproportionate part played by Jews in Hungarian economic life.

My attitude towards this problem is simply this: I regard every measure as proper which would serve the interests of the Hungarian nation as a whole. Neither more, nor less. What is genuinely valuable, what constitutes genuine progress, must be put through mercilessly and without respect of persons. The problem of Hungarian Jewry is a national one, not one of individuals. The nation, through its legislature, can bring and has already brought measures which it is our duty to execute fully. The will of the nation can always assert itself through legislation, and I undertake to execute these measures; but I declare at the same time that I shall protest and fight against individual actions—whether they overstep or whether they fail to reach the limits set by laws and government instructions—because individual action means getting round the law and is a source of abuse.

The restriction of the Jew in the economic field is a basic condition for the economic progress of the Hungarian people, at which none can take offense.

After this declaration of principle, I announced that I should soon bring in a bill providing for the final expropriation of Jewish landed property. Finally, I made a reference to actual economic and financial problems and to the supply position, and I asked the party to support me.

These quotations show that, while I did not refuse to discuss the Jewish problem, I placed it between definite limits. I treated it as an economic and social problem, as which it could and must be treated, as a problem affecting the whole nation, to the exclusion of any individual action. This attitude of mine was thus really the diametrical opposite of the German racial idea and its solution of it along the Nuremberg lines. It may be well if at this point I say a few words on Hungarian Jewry.

Before 1938 Jews made up between 6 to 7 per cent of Hungary's inhabitants; later, when Hungary regained Carpatho-Ruthenia and parts of Transylvania, this number rose to 8 to 9 per cent; but their representation in the economy bore little relation to their numbers. According to reliable statistical calculations, the Jews

owned one third of the total national wealth of Hungary, landed
property excluded, thus enjoying more than half of the total national income exclusive of that derived from real estate and from
salaries derived from state or church employment. In short, they
enjoyed a share of the national wealth and income which was entirely out of proportion to their numbers. The origin of Hungarian anti-Semitism was neither racial nor, still less, religious; it was
not even rooted in life's spiritual and ethical relationships. It
derived from this disproportion between the number of the Jews
and their wealth. To equalize this unhealthy disproportion was,
in the inflamed atmosphere of those days, more urgent than any
other social problem. It was a universal demand. Thus my introduction and commendation of the Expropriation bill was—for
all the injustice which it, like any discriminatory action or any
interference with individual liberty, perpetrated—a successful
move on my part. I had to gain time, I had to provide a safety valve
for the overstrained anti-Semitic feeling in the country and to
divert it from the racialist line and from the threatening possibility of individual action. I therefore chose a solution which—
as will be seen later—was never finally followed up and could have
been partly or wholly undone after the war or at least equalized
with similar measures applied to non-Jewish land. I shall return
to this issue more than once.

My speech did not meet with a particularly warm reception.
The older and more moderate members of the party were reasonably pleased with it; but they were shocked by my outspokenness
on a few questions. The right-wingers, the more impatient faction,
were not satisfied; in any case, whatever I had said, they would not
have believed it since they regarded me a priori with mistrust.

The first days after that address were spent in feverish activity: in the first cabinet meetings, in making hurried decisions
on the most immediate problems, in finding my bearings generally.
Since I was acting as foreign minister as well as premier, I had to
get acquainted with the whole apparatus of the foreign office. Generally, I had to find out whom I could trust, with whom I could

discuss my plans and ideas. There was only one man in whom I had implicit confidence: my minister of the interior, Francis Keresztes-Fischer.

It is very easy to ask why I did not change my men and surround myself with more reliable elements. But it was not only inside Hungary that I was regarded as a Liberal, a pro-Jew, and a Westerner; the Germans also held this view of me. My appointment came as an enormous surprise to Germany and created great consternation there. We know today from the data published since the war that the idea of settling accounts with intransigent Hungary began to be considered as early as that moment. And I had not accepted my position in order to throw my country, its people, and its material and spiritual resources into the arms of Germany, but to defend Hungary against Germany.

I had to camouflage my real intentions. It sounds paradoxical, yet it is true that in order to pursue my own policy I had to surround myself with people whose ideas were different from mine and that I had to carry out my foreign and domestic program through helpers committed to precisely the opposite program. Had I replaced these right-wing and pro-German people with pro-Allied and left-wing elements, I should have been instantly overthrown, and with my downfall would have vanished the last possibility of saving what could still be saved: the withdrawal of Hungary from the war or, if that proved impossible, the saving of her honor. These were always my two main objectives. I was not certain that I could save the country from becoming the field on which Germany and the Soviet Union fought out their struggle, but I hoped to. My hope was reasonable and realistic, too, until the moment when the Anglo-American powers abandoned Southeast Europe and delivered it up, strategically and politically, into the hands of Russia. But in any case, hope was still possible at that time, but only so long as the Germans did not occupy Hungary. Given that condition, I was confident that I could save the country's honor, that I could restrain national passions so that we should be able to hold up our heads even if we lost the war.

For although Hungary had been forced because of her geopolitical position to join the wrong side and had been driven by circumstances not entirely her fault into the war, yet, while she retained her honor and decency, she was in those respects an ally
of the West and a shareholder in Western civilization. And, in
fact, I preserved those aspects, complete and intact, up to the
moment of the German occupation.

The dreadful events which took place afterwards are Hitler's
responsibility. The blind hate, criminal lunacy, and a gutter mentality that can be found in a nation cannot justify holding the whole
nation responsible. The whole Hungarian nation cannot be held
responsible for the acts of a revolution, and the situation that
arose after March 19, 1944, was revolutionary in character. We
cannot, obviously, debit the Reformation with the atrocities committed during the Peasants' Revolts which accompanied the Protestant movements. We cannot make the great French nation responsible for the acts of the Reign of Terror. At the subsequent
peace negotiations—the Congress of Vienna is the most striking
example—the atrocities of the French Revolution were not even
mentioned and the defeated were not burdened with the discredit
for them. In those days peace treaties were made in order to insure peace.

At my first cabinet council I announced very briefly that I
wished to follow a static policy. The nation was at war. It had
undertaken certain obligations. Our task was to carry Hungary
through the crisis in such fashion that she should reach the end
of the war with as little loss as possible to her moral and spiritual
forces. I declared, however, definitely, that I would not undertake further sacrifices, liabilities, or responsibilities. We must
carry out what we had undertaken, but no more, and if we must
choose between our obligations and the national interest, then
the national interest must be the supreme law.

The cabinet council accepted this announcement, as it did all
my subsequent announcements, unanimously.

In those days I had my first meeting with the German minister, Herr Dietrich von Jagow. He was a relative nonentity, neither a politician nor a career diplomat but an enthusiastic member of the SA. He had been a naval officer, and the Germans had sent him to Hungary because they knew that Admiral Horthy had a weakness for naval officers and hoped that such a man might gain a better access to the Regent than a professional diplomat. In any case, Hitler had little confidence in diplomats. That first official meeting with Jagow was brief and formal, and our relations remained formal throughout the two years when I was premier. In the last few months I did not see him at all, always referring him to Foreign Minister Ghyczy. Later, I heard that Jagow had been instructed by Berlin not to approach me but to maintain such official contact as was necessary with foreign minister Ghyczy and his staff.

Unfortunately, when I became premier there were no British or American diplomatic representatives in Hungary. Count Robert de Dampierre, the French minister (a very correct gentleman), represented the Vichy government. Filippo Anfuso, the Italian minister, was a personal friend of Mussolini's, and he was always friendly to us, as, of course, was to be expected, given the long-standing friendship between our two countries. He was very popular in Budapest society. Of the representatives of neutral countries, I must mention Rusen Esref Unaydin, the Turkish minister, an old personal friend of mine, who afterwards worked closely with me in the interests of Turkish-Hungarian co-operation. I maintained regular contact with the other diplomats also, and can say that, with the exception of the Rumanian and Slovak ministers, all regarded my policy with understanding and sympathy.

Then, on March 19, came my debut in parliament. In my speech I announced my program, not only concerning foreign policy, but also on home affairs. Perhaps the most discussed sentence of my speech was the following:

*My program, my activity, my work can be summed up briefly
in this single sentence: we must place all the energy at our disposal
at the service of this war; I emphasize: this war of ours because
we are not driven into it by foreign interests.* And I continued:
*We are struggling in this war for our own selves, for our existence,
for our historical survival. This points clearly the way we must
take in this war.*

Our war! Thus we were not fighting for foreign, for German,
interests. That was what I wanted to express, in order that the
nation should know that for everything we did we ourselves were
responsible, we bore the consequences. We were struggling in
the war for our own existence and continuity, and not for the
interests of others, for the objectives of others. And this was what
determined our course in the war, the fact that we should bear
in mind our own interests, and look for the roads which would
lead us out of the war, for the way in which its final result would
serve the interests of the nation alone.

In the part of my speech which dealt with foreign policy I continued this trend of thought, declaring that

*The foreign policy of every nation is determined exclusively by
its own self-regarding goal, and this must, naturally, adjust itself to
the facts of geopolitics, without the consideration of which it cannot engage in realistic politics.*

And I brought this train of thought to an end in the following
words:

*This Hungarian orientation means that our nation, true to its
historical mission, is serving as the shield of Christianity against
the Asiatic danger of Bolshevism.*

And I made the following declaration for German and Italian
ears:

*The Hungarian orientation also means loyalty. Faithfulness and
perseverance at the side of our great Allies and friends, the Axis
powers, when they, and we too with them, are fighting for a juster
world order, for a new Europe. But the Hungarian orientation*

lso means peace. Peace and understanding with our neighbors of the Danube Basin, so that every nation within the encircling Carpathians should find its tranquillity, its livelihood, and its peaceful development. In the position of the Hungarian foreign policy there can thus be no change, because this is more than politics: it is a given fact, historical, psychological, and geopolitical.

I quote the following passage from what I said about the nationality problem:

We do not want to suppress the national consciousness of our non-Magyars, but we unconditionally expect them to adjust themselves fully to the idea of the Hungarian state. The nationality problem, in its primary manifestation is, first and foremost, an administrative and cultural problem. Equal treatment, consideration of the characteristics of each people, and the language problem are equally important factors. It is no less important that we should continue to work to satisfy the rightful cultural claims of the nationalities. Good administration, which deals equitably with everybody, is what reaches most quickly all strata of our people —including our brethren of non-Hungarian mother tongue. I am confident that the thousand-year-old Hungarian spirit will establish in every field, social and other, those directing and guiding points of view which make it possible and easier for our nationalities to link up with all their soul and with all their strength with the community of the Hungarian state. The problem, naturally, has social aspects too, but I need not go into these more fully, as in the social field there can be no difference between the Magyar and our nationalities.

In the following passage I defined my standpoint towards Bolshevism:

We have entered the war for ideals, because the Hungarian nation struggles with all its strength against Bolshevism. In this fight we must take part, to our utmost strength; this fight decides our fate, our future, the life or death of our entire Hungarian nation.

As in my previous speeches (and my subsequent ones also), I laid particular stress on social problems. I said that our social policy also during the war had to be transitional; we had to prepare social reforms and develop existing institutions.

I naturally had to deal again with the Jewish problem, that sea serpent of Hungarian life. This is what I said:

Among the social problems I must point out that our social structure and stratification is not healthy. That social capillarization which keeps a nation's society healthy is defective in our country. This, too, has its good reasons. When the nobles' privileges were abolished, there ought to have started a healthy blending, a seeping upwards of elements from below, while the dead debris of the upper strata vanished where it fell. But at that moment an impermeable stratum intruded, pushed itself in between the lower strata of the population and those above.

The Jews were this impermeable stratum. In this respect, the Jewish problem, too, is a social problem. The fact that so few of the Hungarian peasantry, acknowledged by us all to be gifted and even brilliant, reached the higher social strata is mainly owing to the fact that this impermeable stratum prevented healthy social capillarization.

I naturally dealt with the topical problems of finance, production, supply, and administration, and concluded my speech by pleading that the problems of the army, of minorities, and of supply should be treated outside the field of party politics. The Government party and the Opposition should regard these as three fields in which we must be united.

My speech and my debut resulted in an unexpected success. My party grew more cordial, and it can be said that for that moment at least it lined up fully behind me. The Opposition, too, heard me to the end with understanding; they did not once interrupt me, whereas there were frequent sharp exchanges between the right and left groups of the Opposition.

Public opinion in the country, too, according to the general reports, noted with great approval and understanding and for the most part accepted the way I viewed and expounded the problems and my indication of the road I wished to pursue. I can say the same of the center and even of the left-wing parties of the Opposition. The only real unrest to appear was among the right-wing parties of the Opposition, which quickly realized that my attitude and methods, aiming as they did at abating those problems the aggravation of which was their sole *raison d'être*, were dangerous to them and their aims.

I must mention also how my speech was received abroad. The Western press was divided. One part noticed those important shades in which I diverged from the policies of my predecessors: on foreign affairs, in my formulation of our war aims, on the nationality problem, and on the Jewish problem. This was the attitude of the well-disposed press. The ill-disposed press saw only, of course, that I had continued to dwell on the themes of the German alliance, anti-Bolshevism, and anti-Semitism, and quoted my statements to that effect. On the whole, however, according to the reports of our ministers abroad, my speech did not create a bad impression.

The reception in Germany, however, was frigid; the Germans were not satisfied and my person became suspect. Not only did the opinion which they had formed about my person remain unchanged, but they were also irritated because, although I had spoken of co-operation with them, of participation in the war, the Jewish problem, and so forth, I had spoken as though our objective was to serve Hungary's interests exclusively.

I must mention also an incident with Rumania that happened after my speech. The irreconcilable antagonism between Rumania and Hungary has existed, as I have already indicated,[6] since the Treaty of Trianon and will exist until the Transylvanian problem is justly solved. What happened after my speech was this. I had made statements in my address—going beyond those that I have quoted

[6] See pages 56–61.

—which indicated a wish for a friendly understanding with our neighbors, including by implication Rumania. At the very same hour, however, at a meeting in Bucharest, Deputy Premier Michael Antonescu made a sharp anti-Hungarian speech which was published after mine and thus seemed to indicate a rejection of my conciliatory policy and the announcement of a new aggression by the Rumanians.

I was exceedingly offended by the matter, but nevertheless I restrained myself sufficiently to forbid any comment on Antonescu's speech in the Hungarian press. The Rumanian press, on the other hand, published his speech with exultant comments. Long afterwards, Antonescu sent word to me that he had heard from a German source that I should be attacking Rumania sharply in my speech. He wanted to forestall this, and afterwards he greatly regretted having taken the line he did.

In spite of Michael Antonescu's sharp speech, I tried my best to reconcile our differences. I instructed the Hungarian legation in Bucharest to seek a *rapprochement* with Rumania. I endeavored to put things on a higher level, to emphasize our mutual interdependence and the danger which the mutual hostility meant to both of us.

I suggested to Antonescu that we should take as a basis the assumption that the Transylvanian problem had not been solved either by the Treaty of Trianon or by the Vienna award. It was a problem of the Hungarian and Rumanian nations, as two parties enjoying equal rights, which we could either solve between ourselves after the war or place in the hands of an international body that would be formed after the war. Until then we should consider the Vienna award as a "status quo," treat each other's minorities with greatest loyalty, stop our propaganda against one another at home and abroad, and endeavor at once to create an atmosphere which would make future agreement possible.

Antonescu replied that he could not declare the Treaty of Trianon null and void, nor could he repudiate the Vienna award in the present circumstances. (He was right from his own point of view, though it meant an illogical and essentially a total rejection of my proposals.) He was not willing to admit that Rumania ill-treated her minorities. (Why then was he not willing to offer guarantees on the point?) He claimed that he was only defending himself abroad against Hungarian propaganda: that if the Hungarian propaganda stopped, the Rumanian criticism would automatically follow suit. (Thus on this question, too, he undertook no obligation.)

He proposed, however, that we should co-operate in foreign affairs, the first step to be the mutual exchanging of information and the apprising of one another of our activities.

That would have been very fine, but the following facts must be realized: Michael Antonescu, the Rumanian deputy premier and foreign minister, was not in fact 100 per cent pro-German, but he was an absolute puppet in the hands of Marshal Ion Antonescu, the dictator, who stood entirely with fanatic honesty behind the Nazis and Hitler. One of the maxims of Rumanian politics was, as I indicated above, to weaken Hungary's position, both before the war when the West was in power and then when Hitler was. What guarantee could I have that I would not be betrayed and be handed over to the Germans at the first opportunity? I particularly feared this because I knew that Marshal Antonescu had several times protested against Hungary's preferential position, her independence, and especially against her not sending enough soldiers against Russia. He feared Hungary was keeping back her army to attack Rumania in the rear at the given moment. Then, too, the German ambassador in Bucharest practically dictated foreign affairs. How could we possibly have collaborated behind his back?

Deputy Premier Antonescu placed me in a difficult position with that proposal. Luckily, however, we decoded a telegram of his to his ambassador in Berlin in which he said that if such Rumanian-Hungarian co-operation should come into being, it

would incidentally be a guarantee to the German government
that nothing would happen which had an anti-German tendency.
(It is interesting that Antonescu later informed our minister in
Bucharest of this, saying that after his bold proposal he "had to
open a safety-valve" for himself.) I could not accept his proposal.
Rumanian politics were so wholly under German control that no
significant action could be expected or obtained from the captive
officials. I should have gained nothing and probably lost much.
In my deadly dangerous position I should have had to reckon
with one or more factors of uncertainty, and unless the whole
atmosphere between us improved nothing beneficial could have
resulted anyway.

For the time being, therefore, I replied to Antonescu that both
of us should do all we could to improve Rumanian-Hungarian
relations so that our two peoples could live together in harmony. To his proposal for practical collaboration and mutual information I replied that I should like closer and more precise details of what he meant and what he wanted: Was he thinking
of official or unofficial foreign political activity? I suggested that he
send a personal emissary to inform me of his plans and to take
back my answers.

I never received a reply to my proposal and very soon afterwards Marshal Antonescu delivered a sharp anti-Magyar speech
at the general meeting of the Liga Culturale, at which German
officers and the German ambassador were present. Marshal Antonescu said that the fighting in the East would end that year
but before returning home the Rumanian soldier would have
to turn his arms against the chief enemy—that in the north. The
meeting passed a resolution that the Rumanian frontier must extend to the Tisza.

Relations with Rumania grew steadily worse. Complaint followed complaint of atrocities committed against the Hungarians
left in southern Transylvania. They were regularly conscripted
and regularly carried off to the Russian front, always into the

ont line for use as cannon fodder. (We did not call up the
umanians for military service but employed them in so-called
labor-service," from which they frequently escaped, naturally
:porting distorted, exaggerated grievances as the reason.) The
umanians invented a splendid method of requisitioning: they
sued regulations which applied to everyone, but actually related
nly to objects which affected the Hungarians. Thus all pillows,
iderdowns, and bedding filled with feathers or horsehair had
o be handed in unless the owner held a certain official post. Since
he Rumanian people did not enjoy these amenities, the regula-
ion affected the Hungarians only. The Hungarians kept cows
nd horses; the Rumanians, goats and sheep. Consequently, al-
hough requisitioning was decreed, it was only of horses and
:attle. Everyone had to have an official permit to travel, but only
Iungarians had to show on trains their permits (if they received
hem at all). The activity of the churches was paralyzed; unknown
:ulprits burgled the houses of their leaders, the Protestants in
oarticular suffering greatly.

I do not wish to deny that many wrong, inexcusable things were
lone on the Hungarian side also, but I again repeat that the Hungarian government investigated every case brought before it and
duly punished offenders—whilst on the other side it was just the
reverse. And I repeat again: that was the difference between the
two governments in the matter of Hungarian-Rumanian relations in Transylvania.

The position gradually grew unbearable. Something had to be
done, but what? Whatever step I decided to take, I had to reckon
with the German reaction. I invited Jagow, the German minister,
to call on me, and I told him that the position was intolerable and
that I had to do something. I informed him also that I had ir-
refutable information that the German authorities in southern
Transylvania were ostentatiously supporting the Rumanians and
showing an anti-Magyar attitude. I consequently asked Jagow to
transmit to his government a request from me that it should in-

struct the German occupying authorities in Rumania not to sho
bias and not to abet the Rumanians in their excesses.

The German reply to my protest was an invitation to vis
Hitler at his headquarters.

FIVE

MY VISIT TO HITLER

[AFTER Hungary had adhered to the Anti-Comintern pact, her
premiers had, directly upon assuming office, been invited to visit
Hitler and Mussolini. It was striking that I had not received such
an invitation until my trouble with the Rumanians. During my
visit with Hitler I became convinced that the Rumanian problem was the moving consideration behind the invitation, since
Berlin held the view for the time that I should be kept at arm's
length until I showed proof of my loyalty to the cause.

I set out on April 15, 1942, with the smallest possible escort for
the German GHQ near Rastenburg in East Prussia. My special
train went through Vienna, where I received a small hint that I
was an unwelcome guest in the German empire: Arthur Seyss-
Inquart, the *Gauleiter*, did not come to the station to give me the

customary welcome. I had a good journey. I saw well-cultivate
land and sufficient laborers everywhere, but every hundred pace
along the line soldiers were posted. I do not know what they we
guarding; I do not think that anyone would have wished to attac
me, and I can hardly believe that they feared some act of aggre
sion on my part.

Hitler received me the next day at 11 A.M. The headquarte
was in the middle of a wood and consisted of a few scattered lo
concrete shelters, the roofs of which were covered with moss an
camouflaged with pine saplings. The whole area was surrounde
with barbed wire. The car that had brought me from the trai
stopped at the gate, and as I stepped out of it, Hitler left h
quarters and met me halfway. I was dressed in traveling clothe
and a mackintosh, while Hitler wore his usual simple uniform
We shook hands, and the cameras clicked and produced the pi
ture which afterwards caused amusement throughout Europe
for, as it happened, I had unconsciously put out my hand rathe
stiffly, and Hitler took it with a deep bow. This of course wa
entirely unintentional, but it pleased a large number of peopl
in Hungary. Hitler led me into his office, where Ribbentrop an
Keitel were waiting. On one side there was a desk, while in th
opposite corner four or five rustic-type chairs were drawn up t
a round table. The whole was very simple and severe.

I had always understood that one of Hitler's by no mean
pleasing customs was to pour out a flood of words from the star
without allowing his guest to open his mouth. Just the contrar
took place. We sat down, and he turned and asked me to inforr
him on the Hungarian situation. He had heard that Hungariar
Rumanian relations had become critical, and therefore he aske
me to dwell particularly on them.

I began by giving a brief sketch of the internal situation, sayin
that I saw no disquieting symptoms in it and that I had it com
pletely in hand. Then I turned to the military situation and de
clared that I must insist on the keeping of the German promis
that the Hungarian forces would not be put into the line but b

used only to occupy vacant areas behind the advancing German columns and to secure communications between the front-line troops and the hinterland, thus safeguarding the Germans' reinforcements. I pointed out that neither their technical equipment nor their training fitted the Hungarian soldiers for other duties. Moreover, it had been agreed that they should return home at the end of the summer offensive.

As for foreign affairs I said that, though we were completely loyal to our war commitments, Hungarian foreign policy could not give up the nation's independence, since for us the proof of our independence before the world was related to the question of national existence or nonexistence. I asked Hitler not to forget that however the war turned out the German people would still remain the largest ethnic group in Europe. If, on the other hand, we lost, we might disappear without a trace in the Slav ocean. In this war the Germans might lose only their ambitions, but we might lose everything. Thus for the Hungarian people the preservation of their independence and freedom of action was basic to the continuation of their national existence. Hungary's diplomatic activity was now confined to neutral states, but it was our duty to ourselves to maintain in them a sympathetic interest towards us. I naturally referred also to the food supplies sent from Hungary to Germany, pointing out that we had to contend with serious difficulties on account of two poor harvests and flood damage. I promised, however, that despite all the difficulties which this might entail for ourselves, we would send as much food that year as we had supplied to Germany before the war.

I defined my views on the Jewish problem, indicating the difference in the situations in Hungary and in Germany, where only one half of one per cent of the total population was Jewish, as against our 10 per cent. The elimination of the Jews from our national life without throwing it out of gear could only be a gradual process, and it could under no circumstances be achieved by force, I declared.

I then turned to the Rumanian problem. I reviewed the situation, referring to Antonescu's speech, and stated that I could only reply that Hungary must arm and concentrate all her forces, not to send them against the Russians, but to be ready for a Rumanian attack. I said that, although I was convinced that it was not true, the Rumanians were openly declaring that they had German support for their aggression and that they had been promised Transylvania as their reward for taking part in the war against Russia. I did not ask that he intervene in the quarrel between Hungary and Rumania but only that he should be a strictly neutral observer and put an end to any semblance of German support for the Rumanians. On this note I ended my review, which had lasted a quarter of an hour.

To my extreme surprise, Hitler had listened to the end without making a single comment or movement. Nor did I see any particular expression cross his face. When he began to speak— and in fact throughout his speech—his voice was quiet, conversational, and calm; frankly, it made me feel that he was not very interested in these affairs.

He made no remarks at all on the first part of my speech, nor did he refer to the Jewish problem either then or later, when I deliberately tried to draw him out on it. He began by saying that he would not, of course, intervene in Hungary's internal affairs, and thanked me for my information regarding them. I do not believe that he meant that he would refrain from interfering in our military affairs, but he did not refer to military matters or to broad matters of foreign policy.

He turned immediately to the Rumanian problem and said that he did not mind in the least if we settled our differences with Rumania in battle, but he could not have us disturb his plans while the war continued in Russia. Accordingly—and he would also definitely tell the Rumanians the same thing—we must find some solution so that the conflict would not begin before the end of the war in Russia. In any case, the Russian campaign would be over by autumn, and the Rumanian and Hungarian troops would have finished their task. But he warned me that the Ru-

anian soldiers were not what they had been. They had received
erman training and German leaders, and the Rumanian army
ad been hardened in fierce fighting. The Hungarian army, on
he other hand, had not merely refused German training (to my
nowledge this question had never been raised), but it also had
o experience in battle. Thus the Rumanians were no longer a
egligible factor. "I tell you," Hitler said, "that going to war is
ke kicking open a door. But I cannot know what is in a room
efore I go into it; thus it should only be done after full prepara-
ons for any emergency."

The Rumanians had also brought countless complaints about
Iungarian behavior. He could not be judge of these matters, but
nce it was the Rumanians, not the Hungarians, who had asked
or the Vienna award, he was prepared to tell the Rumanians to
dhere rigidly to the decisions of the award. He was also prepared
o instruct all German authorities and officials to preserve the
trictest neutrality and to stand aloof from the Hungarian-
Rumanian dispute, although he was convinced that they would
o so without such instructions.

With that our conversation came to an end, and Hitler took
ne into another hut, where a group of staff officers, headed by
Gustav Jodl and Wilhelm Keitel, were waiting. There Hitler
vent across to the map table and gave a long lecture on the war
ituation, gradually forgetting about me and speaking more to his
wn entourage. He asked Jodl several questions, the answers being
hiefly "ja" or "nein." It seemed that in that family circle only
Hitler had the right to speak, for during our previous discussion
lso neither Ribbentrop nor Keitel once opened their mouths.

Then we went in to lunch. Those present were Hitler, Ribben-
rop, Keitel, and Baron Dörnberg, the chief of protocol, and, of
ny own escort, Andor Szentmiklóssy, chief of the political section
f the foreign ministry, and John Vörös, head of the operational
ection of the army. The lunch was simple, consisting of soup, a
oast joint, vegetables, and fruit. There was no wine. We talked
bout general matters, and Hitler made an interesting observation:

During the war we cannot touch the large estates, since we li
on what they produce. The Junkers are the best farmers, and the
sons the best soldiers; I could not imagine an armored attack wit
out them. But after the war I shall have no need of them. The
are not amenable to discipline, nor are they obedient. By th
time we shall have no military or economic problems. The burde
of this war is being borne, both at the front and at home, by th
NCO's of the SS; these must be the backbone of the future Ge
man people, and they must have the land also.

The next day I spent in conferences with Ribbentrop, who ha
taken up his quarters in an old but rather neglected castle in th
middle of a delightful estate near the GHQ. He gave me a
arrogant welcome, and when we sat down in his study he poure
out a flood of words which lasted for two whole hours. Like
phonograph record he reeled off the German ideology and re
viewed the world political situation from the Pacific to the Atlan
tic, describing the British as the prime troublemakers and nam
ing Vansittart as the poisoning influence on British politics.
listened to him in silence. Doubtless he thought that this wa
owing to the effect of his speech, but I was extremely bored and
surprised at his stupidity. And I wondered in what circumstance
he lived and what the standards of the people he associated with
were if he thought that he could impress anybody with such a
torrent of words.

Finally he came to the very troublesome Rumanian problem
on which he showed himself less understanding and less sym
pathetic to the Hungarian viewpoint than Hitler. He brough
out a huge bundle of papers and set them on the table in front o
me, saying that these were all Rumanian complaints against Hun
garian behavior. He went with particular thoroughness into the
problem of the German minority in Hungary, the *Volksdeutsche*
In a sentimental voice he described how near this problem was to
the *Führer's* heart, for Hitler saw in each German person part of
the whole German body, of which he was the incarnation; Hitler
therefore felt that anybody who wronged a German wronged him.

Ribbentrop complained that the Vienna award had not been carried out; we were sabotaging it by not giving the Germans equal rights in Hungary, neither in schools nor in economic areas. He warned me that this was a key question for the maintenance of good relations between Hungary and Germany, and he recommended that I deal with it personally.

Fortunately there was time for me to make only a brief reply. I told Ribbentrop that I had been interested in hearing his comprehensive views and that I had nothing new to say on the Rumanian problem. As regards the German minority, I made bold to say that I did not consider the Berlin dossier a happy one. There was no conflict whatever between the German minority and the Hungarians. The Germans had found their place in Hungary's life and Hungary's economic system, where they were filling and had always filled a very important role—not, it was true, as Germans but as faithful and useful members of the Hungarian state. I called his attention to one point, that out of our twenty-seven highest-ranking generals, twenty-one were of German origin. If the Germans insisted on having a proportionate representation in all positions, perhaps there would not be even one in some. If we put their educational system on a purely German basis, I did not see how Germans could fill all the posts they were now able to obtain in the civil service, the judiciary, and elsewhere. But I said that I would really go into the problem more deeply and try to find a solution to the points in dispute. The whole question was an ephemeral one, since I knew that Hitler had announced—and he had promised the Regent—that after the war he would transfer all the Germans from Hungary. I asked Ribbentrop, however, not to listen to the German agitators in Hungary, who were trying to make themselves important, or to their advocates. I advised him to adopt my point of view that there was no purpose in creating a malentendu, since we were not considering a permanent solution.

At lunch, which was more lavish than Hitler's and included wine, only Ribbentrop spoke. That evening we boarded the train and returned home by the same route. Baron Dörnberg accompanied us to the German frontier; it is a mystery to me how he managed to squeeze all seven feet of him into the sleeping compartment.

That was my first and last sight of Adolf Hitler. I had heard much about his fascinating personality, his magnetic gaze, and how he charmed and impressed everybody he spoke to. I experienced nothing resembling those characterizations of Hitler. I spent one day with him, and during that time he was simple and direct. He had good middle-class manners, and I saw no dictatorial pose. He made no great announcements, no demands or threats—in fact, he made on me the impression of being quite a decent chap. It is said that he was a great actor; possibly he was playing this part for me, but if so, he played it very well. He was a little stout, and had a slight paunch; I was told that a winter in the dugouts had done his health no good. It is a pity that he was not the man that he showed to me.

I returned home with empty hands—it is true that I had not expected anything. Such progress as I had made in the Rumanian problem was little indeed: nothing changed and not even much promised. I felt certain that whatever might happen Hitler would always support the Rumanian side, since he needed them more than he did us. He trusted absolutely in Marshal Antonescu, and the Rumanians' servility made them more agreeable partners than we were. With us, the Germans had to fight for every wagonload of exports, and they were constantly finding themselves bunkered in our parliamentary system and liberties. A dictatorship can get on only with another dictatorship.

In connection with my visit to Hitler, I must explain my point of view towards the Germans.

I have written a great deal about them and always, unfortunately, in an unfriendly way. In spite of this, I am not, nor was I ever, an enemy of the German race except in the form in which

t manifested itself at that time and in which I was forced to deal
vith it. That period had nothing whatsoever to show of the virtues
attributed to the German people nor even of their reputed vices.
Their virtues are universally known; the charges leveled against
hem are nationalism, militarism, and imperialism.

The system under National Socialism had nothing in common
with that nationalism which came into being after the Napoleonic wars and was founded on the idea of freedom and liberalism. The nationalism and militarism of Bismark were different
again. The greatest enemy of Hitlerian militarism, particularly
at the very beginning and end, was the Wehrmacht, which was
mainly anti-Nazi, especially in the higher ranks. It is a proven fact
that the soldiers were opposed to Hitler's aggression and to the
wars in Austria, Czechoslovakia, Poland, France, and Russia. We
also know that Hitler hated the professional soldiers.

When National Socialism set itself against the whole world, it
deformed in their German aspect the German nation's leading
ideas and the basic dogmas of a national social and economic life.
National Socialism replaced conservative thought by dictatorship
and authority by terror. It set the "Party," a blind but powerful
mob, in the place of liberalism and democracy, thus restoring the
caste rule which had come to an end after the First World War.
National Socialism had nothing in it; it was merely a negation of
the past and was neither national nor socialist.

The masses of the party were made up of nobodies, of those
who had failed to make the grade in society, of incompetent place-
seekers and fanatics. And Hitler himself and all his leaders were
no different. The German people had been shaken to their very
foundations by the First World War, and the Treaty of Versailles
prevented them from retrieving their balance without providing
them with new means of life. The people became a fluid, pent-up
mass which a strange revolution turned into an unimpeded flood.
The German is what he was before 1914, and I believe that the
ancestors of the Hitler generation would subscribe to my anti-

German remarks. The judgment which I pass is on a minorit
which was a disgusting phenomenon indeed; but I know that
calling itself German it was usurping the name.

Naturally I do not use the term "fascism" in the generalize
sense brought in by the Communists. Fascism was the name
the state and social framework of Italy. It aimed at breaking u
the old order and democratic institutions in the same way
Nazism or Bolshevism, but with incomparably more humar
methods. It had nothing whatsoever in common with conser
atism or reaction, for which it is commonly, but most tender
tiously, used today.

On my return from the visit with Hitler I gave no special ac
count of it. I was compelled, however, to record the Rumania
problem as an open wound which we could not cure, which w
could at best only watch to see that it did not become infectious

Internally there was peace. Rumors began to spread in con
nection with my visit that Hitler was demanding more troop
from me and a greater degree of co-operation. It was also hintec
that I had been given a definite time within which to settle th
Jewish question. For those reasons I thought it necessary to make
the following declarations in my speech of April 20 to the party
committee:

But we are also responsible for seeing that the country does no
remain defenseless here at home. Let the whole nation take com
fort from the knowledge that there are enough soldiers everywhere
on our frontiers to defend our country's frontiers against anybody

In other words, we could supply no more soldiers for distant
battlefields, and we would defend the frontiers of the country
against anybody. At that time we were only in battle against the
Russians; the obvious interpretation of my "anybody" was "the
Rumanians"; the deeper, truer interpretation, perhaps, "the Germans."

On the problem of closer co-operation, I said:

The conception of complete co-operation also includes equality of rights. For co-operation which is to be useful and benefit both sides cannot be achieved without mutual appreciation, mutual respect, and complete recognition of each other's situation and rights.

On the Jewish problem, I announced that the Jews must be removed from all important offices and positions but that their places would have to be filled at once because the continuity of operations could not be allowed to suffer. Our needs would decide the tempo of the transfer. A final settlement of the Jewish problem could only come after the war, when the only solution would be to expel the 800,000 Jews. It was a fearful announcement, but it also meant that the 800,000 Jews would be there until after the war and that until then they would not be harmed. Before making that declaration I had discussed it with the official leader of the Jews.

I visited Transylvania twice during the spring. I wanted to encourage the local Hungarians, who were extremely despondent, and therefore took with me and announced a ten-year plan which we had worked out for the rebuilding and rehabilitation of Transylvania. The country was terribly neglected, the only positive signs of the twenty-two years of Rumanian occupation being a few dozen Greek Orthodox churches, some of them built where there were no members of this church whatsoever. They apparently thought that such a cultural activity would gain them a foothold and perpetuate their existence in that country. We, for our part, began with great energy to build railways, roads, hospitals, and similar worldly objects; we introduced rights for the individual and social measures, beginning with chambers of labor and social assurance—a list which we meant to expand. Today, unfortunately, it looks as though the Byzantine Church had had a greater cultural mission and achieved a more positive conquest of the country than did our ideals.

I made declarations everywhere on the Rumanian problem, asking for patience and understanding. I stated that public administration would be decentralized and announced:

My policy with regard to national minorities is one of equal treatment. We have never resorted to force in the past, nor shall we in the future. Naturally we shall give the Hungarians their rights after all their suffering and privations, but always without offending the others.

It was customary for the premier to deliver on the radio a speech of greeting to the Regent on his birthday, June 18. I was delighted to do so, and I used the opportunity to say something of our own views and wishes, in the hope that I should be heard outside Hungary also. For this reason I said:

Of the Continental belligerents, Hungary, with Nicholas Horthy at her head, is almost the only one to have preserved her ancient constitution, her constitutional life, and the essence of her institutions intact since the great world eruption of 1914.

This country, this permanence, this unchanged development of rights is today, as she has always been, the guardian of human laws of liberty. Once again Hungary is fulfilling her historic mission as a border fortress guarding all that has created modern European culture. She is an outpost of Roman Christianity and culture and Germanic civilization. We were the easternmost bastions of all that founded this world. The enlightenment of the Latin Renaissance, the German humanist movement, the purifying flame of the Reformation and Counter-Reformation, the flood of ideas of the French Revolution, and every movement of the succeeding century, all its peaceful yet swift progress—in all these things we took part. We lived in Europe; we stood for and still stand for Europe. It was not we, but history, culture, and civilization, that drew a boundary between us and the East. And history ordained that we should never bow to the conqueror but always fight on; and because we fought, we stand here today. The ordinance of history gave us this mission: to stand on Europe's Eastern rampart and there—always alone and unsupported—we have defended Europe against every attack; and every attack has broken down on this land—only we have lost and lost heavily.

Once more today we are fulfilling our historic mission. Let the friends with whom we are fighting, let the whole world know this: again we are fighting for Christianity, culture, civilization, and humanity; we are fighting for the purity of the home, for a child's smile, for everything which makes it worthwhile to be a man—to live; but above all we are fighting for that Fatherland which has become an aspiration and an ideal, for the nation created by history—for the ancient Hungary.

SIX

DOMESTIC POLICIES

❨ST. STEPHEN'S DAY, August 20, is a great national festival in Hungary. The historic relic—the right hand of the first king of Hungary—is carried in solemn procession from the royal palace to the Coronation church. The procession is headed by the Regent, the speakers of the two houses of parliament, members of the cabinet, and the archbishop primate of Hungary, and large crowds follow.

On August 20, 1942, as we left the chapel of the royal palace, the Regent immediately ahead of me, Béla Miklos, the head of the Regent's military chancery, came up to me and whispered "Stephen Horthy has had a flying accident. He has been killed!"

The news made me reel, but I collected myself and walked on. I could not take my eyes off the Regent, who was walking two steps ahead of me. Horthy walked very erect despite his seventy-nine years, all the time smilingly acknowledging the tumultuous, heartfelt cheering with which the crowd expressed its affection for him. The procession finally reached the Coronation church. The long, solemn Mass went on. There sat Admiral Horthy, who had lost his son and did not know it. I looked at him, and I thought how well it was that he did not know about his son and that he did not know that he would lose his country, too, unless a miracle happened. The Regent would collapse where he sat if he knew what I knew. Could he conduct his country's destinies without his extraordinary faith to sustain him and prevent him from losing heart? It was a torment for me to sit through the long Mass; to possess unshared knowledge; to be unable to share the sorrow, the loss, with any sympathizer.

After the Mass, the old Regent felt unable to lead the procession further. He asked me to take his place. But I asked that another should have that honor and accompanied the Regent back to the royal palace, with Francis Szombathelyi, the chief of the general staff, to whom the report had come from the Russian front, and Béla Miklos. The news about his son had a shocking effect on Horthy. He fainted twice, and I took him in my arms. He suffered frightfully, but all at once he seemed to master himself. He said: "I must be strong because I shall have to tell his mother." He left us to return to his private apartments.

Stephen Horthy had been elected deputy regent by the Hungarian parliament six months before his death. The Regent asked for the appointment of a deputy but did not use his prerogative of nominating a candidate. Parliament chose his son, who was in fact the Regent's candidate. The Regent was in full possession of his strength and had no need of a deputy, but he feared that he might die soon, become an invalid, or perhaps be put away by the Germans or their hirelings. When and if any of his forebodings came true, the country would be subjected to enormous pressure from Germany to elect a regent agreeable to Germany and prepared to serve her interests. That was why his son had to be elected deputy regent: such a tragic possibility had to be forestalled. For the post very few people could be considered, and Stephen Horthy seemed the most suitable. The Regent had considered Count Julius Károlyi and Count Stephen Bethlen, but both of them were men of almost the Regent's own age. Had the candidate not been the Regent's son, the pressure from the reactionaries would have set in even during the choosing of the person to be deputy; and it was quite possible that German agitation, utilizing right-wing forces in Hungary, and taking advantage of the dissension which always crops up when personal antagonisms get involved, might have prevented the election of a suitable person. As it was, only the Arrow Cross group and Imrédy's party voted against Stephen Horthy, and the Democrats and Socialists, as well as the other parties, were in his favor.

Stephen Horthy was a splendid young man: serious, intelligent, a thorough gentleman, and of extremely good appearance. He was trained as an engineer, and he spent two years in the United States as an ordinary workman at the Ford Motor Company. Later he filled very well his positions in the state engineering works and the state railways. He spoke several languages, and his accomplishments as a horseman and a pilot were well known. Above all, it was widely known that he disliked the Germans.

During his six months as deputy regent Stephen Horthy had no important duties to carry out in Hungarian politics or government. It was the wish of both father and son that, since we had to send an army to the Russian front, the Regent's son should be among them. Stephen was, therefore, sent to the East with the Hungarian flying corps.

I disliked the idea. I repeatedly suggested to the Regent that he should recall his son, but the Regent always refused. Then I took the initiative: I had a resolution passed through a ministerial council instructing Charles Bartha, the minister of defense, to order Stephen Horthy to return to Hungary. The order was sent out. The commander of the Hungarian army at the front sent for Stephen and handed him the order. Young Horthy returned with the order to his unit, and then for the first time he disobeyed an order. It was late at night when he received the order and, wanting to make one more flight, he did not hand the order to his superior officer in the morning. That day Stephen made his twenty-fifth flight over enemy territory. After taking off, he received an order from the pilot in the plane above him to fly low for observation purposes. Stephen turned too abruptly, lost speed, and crashed. He was burned to death inside his machine.

There was, naturally, an official inquiry after the tragedy. No irregularity was found, but since Stephen was a first-rate, experienced pilot, the tragedy seemed so difficult to understand that the obvious suspicion that the Germans had been concerned in it was widely entertained.

The nation, which had not quite understood the ideas behind the selection of a deputy regent, had not been especially enthusiastic about Stephen Horthy, whose modest, laconic, and retiring nature was not such as to make him quickly popular. But the country was deeply shocked by the news of his death. The whole nation mourned for him, for every Hungarian soldier fighting at the front, and above all for Stephen's parents. The Hungarian people had always loved Admiral Horthy, but on that day they took him completely to their hearts.

On the day of the funeral, which was attended by enormous crowds both in Budapest and at the Regent's country home at Kenderes, I bade farewell to my poor young friend. Joachim von Ribbentrop and Galeazzo Ciano, representing the Führer and the Duce, attended the funeral. Both of them came to see me, of course, and both tactfully said that on such a sad occasion they did not want to raise any political questions but that if I wished to discuss anything they were at my disposal. I had no wish to discuss anything with either of them, so the conversations were confined to generalities. Ciano and I talked like normal human beings, but Ribbentrop inflicted on me a half hour's talk like a phonograph record. Their visit, incidentally, raised a difficult problem of etiquette: which should precede the other, which take the right-hand place, and so forth.

Now, of course, the problem of the future of the regency came up again. The Regent was not interested in another deputy. If we had a new selection, the old anxieties would arise again in aggravated form. The only man whom the Regent trusted completely was Count Julius Károlyi, who was not very suitable for the post. Károlyi was a puritan who detested all ceremonial duties, and the job of deputy regent would have meant appearing in the Regent's place on various public occasions. Károlyi would not even have accepted the post. Then there arose a suggestion, typical of Hungarian impulsiveness and sentimentality, that Stephen Horthy's two-year old son should be made Stephen's successor, and not only a successor to the regency but heir to the throne also. The most serious people discussed this idea most earnestly. One day a deputation consisting of some of the most prominent people in the country waited on me and tried to win me over to the idea. I sent them away curtly enough.

I then wrote a memorandum to the Regent in which I described the situation and pointed out the absurdity of electing little Stephen as king or anything of the sort. It might, I said, happen that Hungary would want to become a republic or a situation might develop in which the restoration of the monarchy and the acceptance of Archduke Otto [1] would become in the national interest, but a situation could never arise which would justify plans such as were being offered in connection with the Regent's grandson. The only alternatives at the time were either to elect a new deputy regent or not to elect one at all. In my own view the only suitable successor to the regency was Count Julius Károlyi, but I listed the reasons—given above—why I did not think selection of him as deputy wise. Accordingly, I thought, the best thing would be not to fill the post of deputy regent and to leave the question open. I mentioned another possibility: the premier of the day could be authorized to deputize for the Regent

[1] Archduke Otto, 1912–, is the eldest son of Emperor Charles I of Austria (King Charles IV of Hungary) and Empress Zita.

if the latter were incapacitated or wished to be replaced. But I also immediately pointed out the constitutional objections to such a decision.

The Regent read my memorandum with an understanding which was very surprising to me. Later I heard from Madame Horthy that the Regent said that he had never in the twenty years of his office seen so frank a memorandum. He said that my candid analysis of the question won his complete trust in me. Horthy asked to see me, and we discussed the question and decided not to fill the post of deputy regent. At first he liked my idea that the premier might act as deputy regent in certain cases, and Horthy asked me to work out the details of my suggestion. But when I called on him again, he told me that he had changed his mind. The idea would not work after all, he said, for this reason: although he proposed never to let me go as premier he might be forced by circumstances to appoint another premier. Could he then find another man whom he could trust? And what would happen if the Germans forced on him a premier, and that person were then in the position to act as deputy regent? That would be a very simple and unobtrusive way of getting rid of the Regent himself. I agreed entirely with his reasoning, and so the proposal was dropped.

I must here mention the unpleasant and very painful story of the so-called Ujvidek case. Towards the end of January, 1942, news began to spread that grave events were taking place in Ujvidek.[2] Refugees and eyewitnesses arrived in Budapest, and soon questions were asked on the subject in the foreign affairs committees of both houses. I was then still sitting in the upper house and could see that the replies which Premier Bárdossy gave to the questions put there showed him to be completely uninformed. He promised an inquiry into the matter. Bartha, the

[2] In Yugoslavia, since 1919, Novi Sad. It was the largest town of the area that was occupied by Hungarian troops in April, 1941.

minister of defense, made no declaration. Later I heard that an inquiry had been ordered but the investigators hushed everything up and tried to suppress the evidence. When Bárdossy was questioned again, first in the foreign affairs committees and later in the lower house, he said that Serb partisans had attacked the Bachka and that the operation of driving them out had assumed the proportions of a state of war. The existence of a widespread conspiracy had been established and dealt with by methods appropriate to a state of war. Nothing had happened that needed any further action. Apparently that was the information given to the Regent, for I met Horthy soon after in private society and saw that he had been completely misled. Towards the end of February, therefore, I phoned Bárdossy's secretary for an appointment with the premier. I meant to tell him that the story must not be hushed up, especially it would not do to keep it from the Regent, who was making comments which suggested that he felt that his ministers were not keeping him properly informed in all matters. The interview did not take place, however, because Bárdossy resigned a few days later.

Soon after becoming premier I gave orders for a full inquiry. Francis Szombathelyi, our chief of staff, undertook it, and the provost-colonel whom he sent to Ujvidek came back with a full report of eight hundred pages. The story was the most dreadful that had ever taken place in the course of Hungarian warfare: a tale of horrors perpetrated by lunatics, criminals, and cowards. More than two thousand innocent people, including women and children, were murdered and thrown into the Danube. The motives behind the criminal action are still a complete mystery to me to this day. It was a fact that a large detachment of Serb partisans had broken into and attacked two villages near Ujvidek in search of arms, food, and booty. It was right that the attack should be repelled and comprehensible that it should be followed by retaliation and inquiries to find out whether the raiders had accomplices in Hungary. Instead of that, however, a wild massacre occurred which left precisely the partisans unharmed. A report, intercepted later, from a Ujvidek partisan recounted with delight that no member of the writer's organization was killed; the victims were the well-to-do *bourgeoisie* of Ujvidek. The victims included not only Serbs and Jews but also Hungarians and Germans, many of whom were persons temporarily stationed in Ujvidek on military or administrative duty.

When Chief of Staff Szombathelyi and I informed the Regent of the real situation, he naturally agreed that court-martial procedure should at once be instituted against the offenders. I laid the report of the inquiry on the table of the lower house and told them the whole story. Parliament and public opinion heard it with great consternation which, however, was mixed with a certain relief at seeing that even though such dreadful things could happen, the government was not hushing them up but was acting to punish the offenders. I do not think that there was another case in the course of the war where a government openly disclosed and discussed in parliament atrocities committed by the country's armed forces and in addition initiated punitive measures. I am not referring to the ghastly acts committed by the German or the Russian army but to abuses that may have occurred in other armies, too.

The inquiry and the court-martial were carried out according to Hungarian military law, and the sentences were communicated in writing to the Regent and me before promulgation. Five persons were sentenced to death and about twenty to terms of imprisonment ranging from eight to fifteen years. The Regent and I did not interfere, of course, in the court-martial procedure, and we acknowledged its decisions. By that time, however, the Germans, through some treachery, had found out about the sentences and arranged for the five men sentenced to death to escape. All five—Zeidner, Grassi, Zöldi, Déak, and Korompai—were of German origin; the last three had changed their original names.

The sentences were certainly just; the chief culprits were the five who received death sentences. They had planned the act quite systematically. They completely sealed off the area which they had decided "to clean up," cutting all communications with the capital and the neighborhood. They even cut the lord lieutenant's telephone; he made his way out and walked till he reached a telephone to report to the ministry of the interior. (His own aged mother-in-law, incidentally, was among those murdered.)

At the court-martial the defendants pleaded that they wished to provide a warning example, once and for all, to the partisans and their accomplices in the country. The Balkan peoples—at that time the Croats and Serbs were murdering each other by the hundreds of thousands—would consider a policy of restraint only as a sign of cowardice and fear.

I am sure that the incident was the work of German *agents provocateurs*, who had instigated the leaders. The relations between the Serbian and Hungarian peoples were beginning to be more friendly and a common anti-German feeling was beginning to develop. The Germans, therefore, tried to provoke an act which would definitely embitter the relations between Serbs and Hungarians and would make the *rapprochement* between them impossible. If practicable, they wanted to draw the Hungarian army into an action against Serbia. Later, I had to reject specific requests to this effect.

We found out after investigation that the five men had escaped in German military cars, escorted by SS soldiers in mufti. The German authorities were waiting for them on the frontier. Readers unfamiliar with Hungarian military law may ask how it was that the five men were not under detention. Hungarian army officers of high rank were not detained when undergoing trial by court-martial. No one ever thought of the possibility of a senior officer running away. There had been cases of officers committing suicide before the verdict, but none had ever run away. Naturally, too, we could not have expected that the Germans would help them, as rescue efforts would clearly prove Germany's complicity. After their escape I could not ask for them to be extradited, since Germany and Hungary had not signed an extradition treaty. Even if our two countries had, I could not have invoked it, for that would have endangered the safety of the two hundred thousand Polish, British, French, Jewish, and other refugees in Hungary.

The Nazis went still further in their brazen insolence in this matter. They immediately took the five murderers into the SS in high positions, and they came back to Hungary with the German army of occupation after March, 1944. Zeidner, whom I had described in the press as a coward and a scoundrel, actually challenged me to a duel—when I was sheltering in the Turkish legation.

September 27 was the anniversary of the Tripartite pact, and I had to speak on that occasion. I managed to evolve a speech in which I did not once mention either Germany or Italy but dealt instead solely with Hungarian problems. I described our relations with the signatories of the pact in the following words:

Since our adherence [to the pact] our history has entered a new phase in which we are taking part in the fight, arms in hand, thus sealing that comradeship in arms which has been maintained between the Hungarian soldier and those of other European nations in the course of our thousand years' history. Now, too, we are fighting a defensive war. We are defending our country, our faith, and our culture. We have no selfish aims. Now, as throughout our history, we are fighting in the defense of Europe.

Ribbentrop had personally telephoned to Jagow, his minister to Hungary, to ask me to emphasize in my speech our common aims and Hungary's determination to fight on Germany's side until final victory. The paragraph quoted above—the part of my speech most friendly towards Germany—was my answer. Here perhaps I may state once more the nature of the relationship between Ribbentrop and myself. Not once did Ribbentrop or any other German minister personally call me or any of my ministers on the telephone. All relations between ourselves were maintained through the stiffest official channels. I may mention, too, that when I was appointed premier, we requested that Jagow and his staff should never communicate directly in speech or writing with

Hungarian domestic officials but that they should instead submit all requests, desires, and questions exclusively through our foreign ministry.

During that autumn I made many speeches. I toured the country, emphasizing everywhere that we must follow our own line and must never become the satellite of any other power or ideology. Our aim was to maintain our independence and keep our hands free for the end of the war. I also preached everywhere the idea of peace between the Danubian nations and tried to parry the new and old accusations which were being leveled against us.

On October 18, 1942, at Ungvar, I made one of the most important of my speeches in reply to criticism from other countries. The Slovak press had criticized very strongly something on the "St. Stephen idea" as expressed by one of my ministers; the official government newspaper, too, had commented on his words very savagely. I decided not to take up the gauntlet but tried to treat the question on a higher plane, while adapting it to the contemporary situation. I said:

The idea of St. Stephen does not mean exclusively a constitutional doctrine or a peculiar state organization, as those who do not understand it, or wish to misinterpret it, try to pretend. First and foremost, it means the eternal indissoluble interdependence of those people whom destiny has borne here, has brought to this corner of the earth. The inner content, at any time, of this interdependence in the spirit of St. Stephen is always decided by the times in which these people live together. But God himself has decreed that they are interdependent; that it is their duty to support each other on this earth, to live here together, to defend as brothers the Carpathian crests. And history has laid on us the task, which for a thousand years we have assumed, of guiding this life and this community.

After this I turned to address these cordial words to our national minorities:

Among its many faults, the Hungarian race has one great weakness, which, however, is their finest characteristic: they love their fellow men. We Hungarians, alone in the whole world, are capable of loving other races. We always loved those people whom we found here and those who settled here later. When I state this, when I offer this friendship—chiefly to the people of this Ruthenia —I think I have said all I can and offered all that a friendly hand can offer. For what does this love mean? Complete equality in national life, whether in the political or in the cultural and economic sphere. This equality, however, involves not only rights but also duties, the duty of full national loyalty, of full emotional fusion with us.

Towards the middle of October, Döme Sztójay, our minister in Berlin, asked for permission to return to present an important report. He brought a message from Ribbentrop. The time had come, it appeared, when the Germans had decided to wait no longer before raising the Jewish problem. Apparently, they had given me time to show them what I could do, and the results did not satisfy them. Now they decided to take steps. Sztójay began by saying that acceptance of the German suggestions was the touchstone which would decide whether I and Hungarian policy could gain Germany's confidence, whether a German-Hungarian collaboration was possible. If I did not accept, the consequences might be fatal. He added that he personally was fully convinced of the inescapability of fulfilling Germany's demands and of the seriousness of the German threats. The demand consisted of three points:

1. The Jews to wear a yellow star
2. A ghetto in every town, segregation of the Jews in ghettos
3. 300,000 able-bodied Jewish men and women to be placed at Germany's disposal, in connection with the rehabilitation of the industry and agriculture of the Ukraine

Sztójay added that Hungary, in the whole of Europe, was a Jewish island; neither the neutral states nor even the Western Allies allowed Jewish refugees to enter; Hungary alone kept her gates open for them. There was no doubt that the Jews were the greatest enemies of the Germans and of National Socialism. The

Germans could no longer allow Hungary to remain an oasis of refuge, and they hoped that I too would see the absolute logic of this.

I sent Sztójay back and prepared an answering note. In it I gave various ingenious reasons for refusing to send the Jews into ghettos and forbidding the introduction of the yellow star and the handing over of the Jews to work for the Germans. My reasons for the last refusal were: (1) the number of able-bodied Jewish men was just the same as the number of soldiers we had sent to the Russian front, and we therefore needed the Jews at home to carry out the work of the soldiers in the field; (2) I could not abandon my principle of not compelling Hungarian nationals to undertake work abroad, even in the case of the Jews. (All the governments under German influence, beginning with France and Italy, gave hundreds of thousands of workers to the Germans, either of their own accord or under compulsion. Hungary was an exception. Before my regime we had allowed 24,000 workers to go, but these were volunteers who earned good wages abroad. We called them back successively, and during my time not one went out. There were about 7,000 who did not wish to return.)

The following account of Germany's démarches on the Jewish question is based on Eugene Lévai's Grey Book, a work which appeared in 1946, at the beginning of the present regime, and seems to have drawn upon foreign ministry files.

Hitler's Reichstag speech of April 6, 1942, marked the turning point so far as German pressure and interference in Hungary's Jewish problem was concerned. In it, Hitler emphasized the urgency of a swift and complete solution of the Jewish problem in Europe, and he spoke most energetically against the Jews. (He apostrophized them twenty-eight times very strongly indeed in his speech.) Referring to this speech, Sztójay sent the following report on August 15:

The so-called European settlement of the Jewish problem has altered in practice. Hitherto Chancellor Hitler and consequently the party and the official government had taken the view that the

Jewish question outside Germany would be one to settle after the war, on a European basis (and this view made it easy for Hungary to choose a gradual settlement rather than a swift one); now this has changed, and on the express instructions of the chancellor the problem ranks as an immediate one.

The Hungarian legation, according to the minister's dispatch, had also been informed of the following points:

The Germans wish to purge Europe of Jewish elements as soon as possible and to deport the Jews from Europe, or at least from those areas where it is possible to do so, without regard to their nationality, to the occupied Russian territories in the East. There they will be collected in ghettos or labor camps and set to work. Instructions have been issued that this transfer is to be carried out during the war. I learn from a reliable source that Reichsleiter Himmler also emphasized in a recent speech to the leaders of the SS that they wanted to complete the deportation of European Jews within one year.

Sztójay added:

Luther, the deputy secretary of state, hinted at the deportation of Hungarian Jews when speaking of the deportation of Jews in general. As I already mentioned in my previous dispatch, when, as instructed by the foreign ministry, I raised the question with Luther of the wearing of the star by Hungarian Jews in Paris,[3] he repeatedly expressed his "sincere regret" that precisely friendly Hungary did not understand Germany's intentions on the Jewish problem and protested even against the wearing of the star. And when speaking of the general settlement of the Jewish problem and of the deportation of the Jews to the East, he remarked that there would be plenty of room there for all the Jews of Europe, including the million from Hungary.

On October 8, 1942, the Hungarian minister in Berlin sent another dispatch on the Jewish problem and its relation to Hungary. Sztójay said that the Germans had ordered that all foreign Jews,

[3] The Hungarian government had protested against any discrimination in the treatment as between Hungarian Jews and any other Hungarian nationals.

including, therefore, Hungarian Jews, had to leave German territory or German-occupied Western states by December 31, 1942. So far as Hungary was concerned, the Jewish problem could be settled, according to the German government, if "Hungary were to frame and bring into force as soon as possible suitable Jewish laws eliminating the Jews completely from cultural, political, and economic life." Moreover, attention had to be given and plans made for the eviction of the Hungarian Jews. Those Jews would be taken over by German organizations and deported to the Eastern territories.

To Sztójay's objections, Luther replied that "in Germany, too, the difficulties seemed greater at the outset than they actually proved to be. He added that deportation agreements had already been made with Slovakia, Rumania, and Croatia; Bulgaria had recently introduced some very stern measures on the Jewish problem and would doubtless join in this action. Discussions were proceeding with Italy, and they already had the understanding of the Duce, or rather his promise, on the subject of deportation. Conversations were also proceeding with the French government on the deportation of Jews from unoccupied France, and these were progressing favorably." Sztójay also reported that Jagow, the German minister in Budapest, would shortly present a note on the Jewish problem to the Hungarian government.

On October 17, 1942, Jagow did in fact deliver a note to Ghyczy, the permanent deputy foreign minister. The note dealt with the questions already reported by Sztójay—the first two sections with the question of the Hungarian Jews resident in the Western occupied countries and in Germany, and the third with the Jewish problem in Hungary. On the question of the Jews in the Reich, Berlin proposed that Budapest should accept as a basis of settlement the territorial principle—that is, that each state should be completely free to dispose of the property of Jews living on its territory but nationals of the other state.

As to the Jewish problems in Hungary, the German govern-nent made the following declaration in the note presented by agow:

With a view to the speedy and complete solution of the Jewish question in Europe, the Hungarian government, for its part, is requested to initiate suitable measures in Hungary as speedily as possible. Germany has noted with pleasure the preliminary steps aken to date in this direction. They are, indeed, far from keeping pace with the development in Germany and other European states. Every consideration points to the advisability of bringing this question to a definite conclusion before the end of the war. This is an interest, not of Germany's, but of all Europe. . . .

In Germany's view, the following steps might with advantage be taken in Hungary:

1. The Jews to be completely eliminated from cultural and economic life by progressive legislation.

2. The government's measures to be facilitated and the people enabled to dissociate itself clearly [from the Jews] by the immediate introduction of distinctive marks to be worn by all Jews.

3. Preparations to be made for expatriation and transportation to the East.

On December 5, 1942, the Hungarian government sent Sztójay, its minister in Berlin, instructions to answer the German note. In its answer the Kállay government flatly rejected the German government's request to force Jews in Hungary to wear a distinguishing mark (yellow star). Similarly, its attitude towards the deportation to the East of the Hungarian Jews, or towards preparations for such deportation, was completely negative.

The Hungarian minister in Berlin handed his government's note to the German foreign office on December 14.

Luther took note with "sincere sorrow" of the Hungarian government's attitude towards deportation of the Hungarian Jews. Then he affirmed "most decidedly" that the German government would be willing to fulfill all desires expressed by the Hungarian government in connection with the deportation; in other words, the Germans would assign suitable land for the settlement of those Jews and give a complete guarantee that their livelihood there would be assured. At this point Luther emphasized that the alarmist rumors of the ill-treatment of the Jews spread by the British and American radio did not correspond with the facts.

Luther then reviewed "the present state of Jewish deportations" in the various states:

In Slovakia only about ten thousand Jews were left of the original ninety to ninety-five thousand, and they were being removed

In Rumania there had been a very large number of deportations but he had no precise figures in hand.

Bulgaria had introduced severe regulations and had made the wearing of the star compulsory. A fortnight earlier she had entered into negotiations with the German government on the question of deportation.

In Serbia there were virtually no Jews left.

In Croatia only transport difficulties had so far prevented complete execution of the deportations.

In unoccupied France the Laval government had asked the German government to help them in deporting the Jews there and the Jews were already being taken over the demarcation line.

In January, 1943, the German government once again stressed the necessity of settling the Jewish problem. On the fifteenth Luther informed Sztójay that "the *Reichskanzler* was increasingly insistent that the Jewish problem in Europe must be settled during the war."

Referring to the coolness of Hungarian-German relations and the lack of co-operation and confidence between the German and Hungarian governments and the leading political parties, "the deputy secretary of state told me, in a perfectly intimate and friendly way, but frankly and openly, that the key to these problems lay in the Jewish question."

On April 17, 1943, when the Regent of Hungary was visiting Hitler's headquarters, Hitler drew Horthy's attention most emphatically to the unsolved Jewish problem, and launched a very bitter attack on the Hungarian government. The Germans affirmed that Kállay, the premier, had sent a message to the American ambassador in Turkey, stating that

He, the premier, would not place a single soldier or a single rifle more at the disposal of the Reich; that he was, indeed, constantly making anti-Jewish speeches, but was not really doing anything against them and was sheltering 70,000 Jewish refugees in Hungary; and that the only reason why he could not at present carry on any other policy was that, if he did, Germany would occupy Hungary and exterminate all the Jews.

Ribbentrop seconded Hitler in raising the Jewish problem in Hungary with Sztójay and others. In the course of a long conversation with Sztójay, lasting till after midnight, the German foreign minister explained

all the reasons which have decided the German government to solve the Jewish problem now, during the war, and to solve it rapidly. . . . He pointed out that almost every European state, with the exception of Switzerland and Sweden, had adhered to the German action. . . . Hungary alone refused to undertake a radical solution of the problem. He remarked that according to his information, not only was the Hungarian government not carrying out the existing Jewish laws radically and completely—in fact, for some time past a certain stagnation had set in in this respect; on the contrary, it was allowing free course to certain Jewish influences, to the Jewish destructive spirit, etc., etc., and offering a safe and quiet refuge to the Hungarian and refugee Jews.

The German foreign minister emphasized in connection with the above that the chancellor was disappointed, and that the Führer had expressed this feeling to His Highness the Regent. He asked me particularly to inform the Hungarian government personally of his communication.

Sztójay, the Hungarian minister, in his dispatch expressed grave fears regarding the steps which the Germans might take:

Having said this, I now have the honor to inform Your Excellency that, in my view, the German standpoint on the Jewish question has reached a most grave position. Knowing the mentality of the German leaders and their resolution, in thought and action, in the present life-and-death struggle, I would propose, in full knowledge of my responsibility, that this problem be settled in such a way that the possibility of a third intervention be avoided at all costs.

When Lévai's book was written, the attack on prewar Hungary had already begun, and he must be given great credit for daring to remain unbiased in his three comprehensive works on the Jewish problem.[4]

Thus six months after Hitler had seemed to regard the Jewish problem as an internal Hungarian affair and had raised hopes that he would not interfere, he showed his true colors. The Germans apparently believed that I would myself take those steps so as to fulfill the requests and proposals they had already made

[4] In his second work, the Black Book (1948), Lévai wrote as follows under the title "The Destruction of the Jews in Neighboring States":

"To be able to appreciate properly the difficult situation into which the Kállay government was driven by its open opposition to German pressure on the Jewish problem, we should consider the measures taken up to that date against Jewish citizens of neighboring states. The fate of the Jews in Germany and Austria had already been fulfilled years before; only those remained in exile but alive who were able to flee to Hungary, where they were given sanctuary with the consent of the Kállay government. In Slovakia the persecution of the Jews began immediately after the formation of the independent Slovak state in 1939, completely independently of the Germans. The Nazis took no part whatsoever in the liquidation of the Jews there. At that time Hungary received some of the Jews destined for deportation and saved them with the assistance of Keresztes-Fischer, the minister of the interior."

Lévai goes on to describe the complete destruction of the Jews in Yugoslavia; part of them were deported to Germany, but the majority were killed. He also gives a lengthy account of events under the Rumanian rule; there were no deportations, but some 500,000 Jews were robbed, tortured, and then murdered in ways I cannot even quote. Lévai concludes these sections of his Black Book with the following observation:

"This was the situation of the Jews in the three states around Hungary. Thus while the Germans had more or less completely destroyed all the Jews in Central Europe, the million odd Hungarian Jews were known to Hitlerism as a virtually untouched Central European island of Jews under the protection of Regent Horthy and the Kállay government."

under my predecessor (one reason why the Regent asked Bárdossy to resign was that Horthy feared that Bárdossy would not be able to withstand the German demands). During those six months I received numerous hints to go further in the Jewish problem, but I naturally paid no attention to them. When the Germans saw that nothing had yet been done, they came forward with an ultimatum: either I solved the Jewish problem in accordance with their wishes or the fate of Hungary was sealed. They tried to bring the affair to a breaking point, apparently confident that Hungary, too, would bow to their command.

Sztójay visited me once more at Christmas, 1942, and made a dramatic appeal. He besought me to give in on the Jewish problem, to see that the Germans could not retreat in this field, not merely because of their primary interest in the question in merito, but because Hungary's refusal would entail for them a loss of prestige in the occupied states which they could not endure. He thought that another attempt to make me change my course would be made in January. If I still resisted, the Germans would try to force my resignation by every means at their disposal. If this did not succeed, they would stop treating Hungary as a partner, and a worse fate would befall us than had happened to Czechoslovakia or Poland. I merely asked Sztójay not to lose his nerve, for I was in control of mine.

Now, however, I was faced with the problem of finding the right ways and means of refusing the tactics whereby I could either avert or postpone brutal interference by Germany.

From the moment of German insistence in the matter the problem of how to save the Jews became interlocked with the problem of Hungarian independence. The question might have been asked: Could I risk involving all Hungary in catastrophe for the sake of the Jews? People often felt this, if they did not dare to say it. That question was, however, based on false hypotheses.

To have sacrificed the Jews to the Germans would have meant an irreparable liability to Hungary after the war—as we then expected the postwar world to be. It was impossible to take such a step, not only from the Christian and humanitarian point of view, but because it would not have saved Hungary's independence. To have complied with such a demand would have so disintegrated the country and so strengthened the hands of the anti-Semitic Nazi element as to turn all honest persons against us. My acceptance would really have meant the end of our independence. A huge breach would have been opened through which the Nazi spirit and German power would have rushed into Hungary, and the country's independence would have sunk still lower than Slovakia's, Rumania's, or Croatia's. The demands against the Jews would have been followed by demands against Socialists, left-wingers, pro-Jewish Gentiles, "Anglophiles," and against the whole Hungarian elite. I am describing how I saw the problem then: that the Jewish question was no purely Jewish one, but one decisive for the entire nation. I still see it so today. That period was a grave moment because I knew that it was the time when the possibility of lasting co-operation with Germany by me, and by those who felt as I, was at an end.

A gulf not to be bridged had opened between us and Germany. I had to go over to the defensive, to drag things out until Germany was defeated and until the Anglo-Saxon powers arrived on our frontiers. My task was to do my utmost to safeguard the country's independence, historic values and spirit, and its army until that day. If, I felt strongly, we were occupied before the Allies arrived, then all the horrors that had come to other occupied countries would descend on Hungary, and we should at once lose our value and interest for the Western Allies.

I discussed my decision with Keresztes-Fischer, the minister of the interior, but said nothing to the other members of my cabinet I naturally informed the Regent, who agreed with me. In order to lessen the tension and gain time, I used my old tactics and again referred to the Jewish question in my speech at the Government party meeting on October 22, 1942. It was not a very elevating thing for me to speak differently from how I thought, but

I had to lower myself in order to avoid lowering the nation. Nevertheless, I tried to win over to my side the better elements of the Hungarian nation and tried to offer some comfort to the Jews. This is what I said on the Jewish question:

I wish to establish one point here: on the Jewish question, I am prepared to take all steps which will support, satisfy, and promote the political, economic, and ethical aims of the nation. But I am not willing to promote the base, private interests of certain individuals; nor to allow the question, in these its last phases, to poison and corrupt the atmosphere more than it did in its heyday. I must contradict those people who can see no other problem in this country except the Jewish problem. Our country has many problems beside which the Jewish problem pales into insignificance. Those who can see Hungary only through such spectacles are degraded men who must be eliminated from our community. I shall do my utmost, I shall go to the utmost limits everywhere in the country's interest, but I cannot and will not allow anyone to soil the national honor and reputation of Hungary, nor to obstruct the great aim of concentrating the nation's forces, by political extremism and base propaganda.

I do not wish to appear immodest, but I wonder where else among the suffering nations a premier answered a German ultimatum by such a declaration, made under the most public circumstances, at that moment when the German troops were on the Caucasus.

As I have said, I refused to send 300,000 Jews to German labor camps on the grounds that we needed them in Hungary. After discussing the question with William Nagy, the minister of defense,[5] to whom I confided something of the background of the affair, I came to the conclusion (and he fully agreed) that we must alter the existing situation, which was really absurd. Jews at that time could not serve in the Hungarian armed forces: the Germans would not have accepted it. This, in a way, gave the Jews a privileged position. We therefore decided to call up Jews of military age and

[5] See note 4, page 140.

direct them—this was my most important argument in my reply to Germany—into labor camps or industries in Hungary. This decision I announced in the following words:

Speaking of the army, I must mention the participation of the Jews in the war. I have given instructions that all Jews of military age, whether suitable for military service or not, are to be directed into labor camps. There are, of course, technical obstacles to the immediate execution of this arrangement; we must first create the necessary framework for it.

This problem was later solved by Defense Minister Nagy in excellent fashion and at a satisfactory pace. It is possible and probable that certain of the camp commanders or foremen abused their powers, but whenever Nagy could intervene he always did so in a humane manner. The fact which really made the situation distressing for the Jews called up was that they were largely employed in occupations needing heavy physical effort, such as agriculture and roadbuilding, and very few Hungarian Jews had been industrial workers and none whatever had previously been engaged in agriculture or in heavy manual work. Before issuing the order I discussed its details with the official leaders of Hungarian Jewry, and they accepted the solution with satisfaction. Then, as on other occasions, they warned me and begged me not to provoke Germany; from their point of view, anything was preferable to being handed over to the Germans.

Towards the end of November, the lower house began its debate on the budget—the first conducted by myself. That debate was always a big event in the Hungarian parliament. On November 20 the questions relating to the premier's own department were on the agenda. Those included the press and the national minorities. In my answer to the discussion on the latter point, I again emphasized my policy of far-reaching tolerance and friendship towards our national minorities.

In the debate on the press, the right-wing Opposition, the Arrow Cross party, and Imrédy's group launched strong attacks against the censorship and the suppression of the right-wing newspapers. There were no complaints from the left-wing parties. My reply was as follows:

We treat our press more liberally than does any other belligerent country or, indeed, than do many neutral countries. There are only two ways of treating the press. We either tolerate free opinions as long as they do not violate the community's overriding interests or we take the line of the single-party government press system. When you choose to criticize the fact that certain newspapers (Socialist, etc.) still appear in this country, you seem to forget that if I chose the other way and suppressed those newspapers, then it would be my duty to leave only one single type of newspaper in this country: my own mouthpiece.

Referring to the totalitarian outlook which lay behind the criticism, I said:

I have no wish to be a dictator. In fact, I do everything to prevent a dictatorship in this country, but I warn everybody that if a dictatorship comes, it will be mine and only mine.

A few Arrow Cross party members had been excluded from parliament for suggesting a plan for the alteration of the Hungarian constitution, which would have meant the end of the country's independence and turning Hungary into a German satellite. The idea was to establish a sort of confederation of the Danubian nations under German leadership, something analogous to what the Soviet is actually establishing today. Those deputies had been proceeded against for high treason. They fled from Hungary, and the Germans received them and were using them to make the Hungarian minorities in Austria and Croatia hostile to Hungary. I found it necessary to hold those men, and their Arrow Cross supporters, up to public execration. My words, by implication, were addressed also to Germany.

The following day I had to address the lower house as foreign minister. In view of the strained relations between Germany and ourselves, my declarations were very cautious. That was the first time that I read the more important passages of my speech instead of speaking from notes. I tried to keep to the line that I had

followed in the past and that it was my definite intention to follow in the future. I therefore simply repeated, in different words,
what I had said before. I made not a single suggestion that we
were fighting for Germany's interests; I emphasized only the Hungarian and European aspects of our participation in the war, and
our unswerving loyalty to the European idea. For that reason I
quote here only the introductory lines of my speech, in which I
recapitulated the Regent's rescript to parliament. That was important because I wanted the country to see that the Regent identified himself entirely with my policy.

*His Highness, the Regent, in his recent rescript to parliament,
outlined our duties in this decisive passage of Hungarian history
with classic brevity and deep wisdom. "In this struggle," he said,
"honor, Hungarian loyalty, and the logic of life must guide our
attitude to the salvation of our race and land." And he went on:
"It is our highest duty to decide and act in every question and
under all circumstances as the interests of our country demand."*

My speech had a very unfavorable reception in Germany. It was
regarded as a sidetracking of the real issue, but they did not yet
wish to pick a quarrel over it. The second sentence from the
Regent's rescript quoted by me caused as much indignation in
Germany's official circles as it made a good impression in Hungary. It was interpreted as a plain announcement of the possibility that we might sever ourselves from the German cause.

On December 3, 1942, I spoke again, in the course of the
appropriations debate. On that occasion I re-emphasized and supplemented what I had said in my opening speech, adapting its
lines to the arguments that had been raised in the debate. Imrédy,
who was the chief speaker for the Opposition, had objected that
the government had no program or definite aim. The nation, he
declared, had to decide which road it would follow. The road
could be no other than that of National Socialism, and Hungary
must take it at once, procrastinating no longer.

In my reply, among other things, I said the following:

We must—indeed, it is our duty to make plans, establish pro-

rams, and think of everything. But it is impossible and it would e illegitimate to commit the nation to these. Impossible because e have to take into account the world around us in general and ur allies in particular, and at the same time we must do our best o safeguard our national aims and our sovereignty. The conception of postwar Europe cannot at present be said to have crystalized either in the resolutions of our allies and friends, in those of he neutrals, and still less in those of our enemies. But in that new ostwar Europe our place is assigned and our destiny outlined. In hat new world we must build up an independent, special, self-egarding Hungary, as strong and as Hungarian as we can make it. We cannot yet formulate our aims in a set of clear-cut dogmas; ut we can and must preserve, develop, and create whatever will nake us stronger, better prepared, more individual, and will make ur position more significant and more important for Europe.

Jagow, the German minister, asked Ghyczy, my deputy in the oreign ministry, for an explanation of that section of my speech ind of a further sentence. The other sentence was this:

A party is a group which is always willing to work together with others in the interests of common aims, of national aims. The party which is not willing to do this, which insists on unconditional ubjection and on the uncritical acceptance of tenets, is no longer a party, but a religion which no longer includes the possibility of adjustment and transcends the framework of a nation.

The sentence first quoted, according to the Germans, was calculated to shake faith in Germany's victory and expressed doubt in the finality of National Socialism as a doctrine. The second was construed as a direct attack against the Nazi party. Ghyczy gave Jagow a lukewarm reply.

In the second half of my speech I dealt with Hungary's previous social policy and emphasized that we meant to carry on and develop that policy with all vigor. I said:

The future can only be found in social progress and in social readjustment. The world will proceed in that direction, and even if this were not so, it is certain that we Hungarians must advance

*along that road. We have particular reasons for doing so, for only
by taking a constructive course can we maintain and strengthen
our leading position among the nations of Central Europe.*

I then reviewed Hungarian social policy before and during the
war and enlarged especially on the charge that Hungary was the
home of giant estates. I showed the statistical proportion of arable
and privately owned land in Hungary which was held by small
landowners and proved that on the basis of those figures we were
ahead of England, Germany, Italy, Sweden, Norway, or Spain.
And when our Law of 1938 had been fully implemented, I concluded, Hungary would be the leading nation in Europe from the
point of view of land distribution.

On December 16 I made my budget speech in the upper house.
I began by saying that my reply to the charge of feudalism was
that my speech followed that of a member of the upper house
whose occupation was that of agricultural laborer. After re-empha-
sizing the already familiar lines of my foreign policy, I spoke again
principally of our social problems, insisting that the nation and
the Hungarian leading class itself must solve the question, for
we could not have the solution forced on us.

That talk concluded the budget debates. I had undoubtedly
scored successes as a parliamentary debater and strengthened my
position; but I felt, nevertheless, that my position was not understood. Success as an orator was one thing; the substance of my
message was another. Very much hard work was still needed before the broad masses of the nation could feel and know what was
at stake, what I was aiming at and fighting for, what my policy
meant.

SEVEN

THE HUNGARIAN ARMY
AND THE MILITARY ACTION, 1942–43

❬[MEANWHILE our army was rolling towards the endless Russian steppes and the terrible unknown. While our soldiers were setting out to battle, I was turning all my thoughts to considering the ways by which we could withdraw from the war. The agreements made by my predecessor had to be honored, however. I pitied the unfortunate Hungarian lads. There was no enthusiasm for the war, not even from those who definitely favored the Germans and had clamored for us to form the crusade against Bolshevism. There is a big difference between making politics and manning trenches.

The lack of enthusiasm among the men had been reinforced by the negative feelings in the government about the war. The first troops started out almost stealthily and secretly; they entrained at night, so that the general public should see as little as possible of the operation. I thought that this was wrong. I ordered that the leave-takings should be with ceremonial honors, so that the soldiers should take with them at least one happy memory and should realize that the nation honored them for their sacrifice. They should not feel that they were being sent to distant foreign lands, on that journey they ought never to have taken, with flowers and farewells from their relatives but without a word from the authorities. I myself bade them farewell in Kecskemet and also Kassa, from where my youngest son, Andrew, set out as a Hussar lieutenant. I tried in my speeches to make the soldiers feel that the highest action a true son of the nation can do is to fulfill his duty, wheresoever it led him.

The Hungarian general staff and the German delegation Keitel brought to Budapest had formerly agreed that we should send to Russia the so-called Second Army, one of our three armies which we were then in process of forming. That army consisted of three corps, each composed of three two-regiment divisions and one armored division. Owing to the difficulties of partial mobilization, slow progress was made in forming the army, so that it did not arrive in time for the German summer offensive.

The Germans suffered defeat after defeat on the Russian front. A defense line was organized on the Don, and the Hungarian forces had to hold a 200-kilometer sector of it to the south of Voronezh, between the German Second Army and the Italian expeditionary force (Armir). The Hungarian divisions, each two regiments strong, had to defend some 30 kilometers each, a task which would have been impossible even with the best arms and the utmost enthusiasm. The Hungarian command immediately asked the Germans to shorten the sector, pointing out that it could not be held under such conditions. They also demanded reinforcements and fresh troops from home. Both requests, however, were refused. It must be noted that the Hungarian and Italian expeditionary forces were independent commands, while the Rumanians were mixed with German forces, both in comnands and in position. Fifty-four battalions of the Hungarian rmy, with no reserves and without the support of a single tank r plane, faced the reinforced enemy soldiers in the Russian vinter, an assignment for which they were neither armed nor uitably clothed. They had no heavy artillery whatsoever; the Germans promised it but of course did not keep their promise. The mechanism and lubricants of the machine guns of the Hun- garian force became unserviceable in the cold, and it had scarcely ny light automatic weapons. The clothing of the men was defi- ient, and their boots were light, summer wear. The situation was earful. This was not what the agreement had provided.

When Bárdossy and our military leaders agreed to supply one rmy to the Germans, it was explicitly stated in the agreement hat the Hungarian force was not to consist of front-line troops, ior to be used as such; it was to operate behind the advancing German forces as a security force. The Germans promised to nake up the deficiencies in its equipment in the field because .t was technically easier to hand the material over to the troops in the field than first to transport it to Hungary. Since the troops would not be put into the line, there would be time for them to get acquainted with their arms. The clothing was good enough because they definitely were not going to take part in winter bat- tles. The attack on Russia would be finished by autumn, it was thought, and our forces would return to Hungary then or at the most would be assigned nonmilitary duties such as keeping order behind the lines.

Everything turned out differently; not one of those promises was kept. The Hungarian forces were on the most advanced front and in its most dangerous sector. Next to them were the Italians, who likewise displayed little enthusiasm at their position. It was almost certain that they would yield under even the slightest Russian pressure, and that would seal our fate also. *Démarches,* messages, and telegrams went in long succession to the German chiefs of staff, pointing out that this was not what had been agreed to and asking them at least to make good the deficiencies of equipment. We received promises and promises, but nothing else

Our solders froze in the trenches, where the thermometer stood at 40° below zero; even their rations were meager, for the Germans controlled the supply trains. Everybody knows the effect on a soldier's morale if he is hungry and cold and he sees that his equipment is inferior to that of the enemy. The sector of the front assigned to us was so long that we could not man it satisfactorily. The number of machine guns in working order had so diminished that there were at the most two to every thousand meters. So Christmas, 1942, passed, and the new year arrived.

Not long afterwards came the news of that terrible disaster, the Russian break-through on the Don.[1] Naturally the enemy chose the weakest point; first they broke through the Italian defenses, and then they crushed the Hungarian troops. Our soldiers were benumbed by the 40° below zero temperature, and their arms refused to work; moreover, the German artillery in our rear did not help us. The Hungarians, their hands stiff with cold, could not press the triggers of their guns, and they were unable to resist the enemy in hand-to-hand fighting—the strongest point of Hungarian soldiers. The Hungarian force did not surrender, but half of our wretched, unfortunate lads met their end there. Mistaken policies—yes, but let us admit, too, in all seriousness that it was Hungary's tragic destiny also that led them thither, where they had nothing to gain, where no glory could await them but only certain destruction.

The enemy attack on us began on January 12. It was supported by artillery and tanks. Four Russian divisions attacked our 7th Division, and broke through on the second day. Another attack on the fourteenth scattered the Hungarian 12th Division. The Hungarian command asked for the German Kramer corps in their

[1] In early December, 1942, the Russians broke through the German lines west of Rzhev on the lower Volga, thus dooming the German forces at Stalingrad. By the first week in January the Germans began withdrawing from the entire Stalingrad area. Then came the Russian offensive on the upper Don, the full fury of which was clearly evident by the middle of January.

rear, which were completely inactive, to be thrown into battle, but their pleas were in vain. Our command proposed a retreat, but the German command refused, with the result that instead of a retreat there came a complete collapse. It was an outstanding achievement of the Hungarian 3d Corps that they were the last troops to leave the Don on January 26, when they covered the rear guard of the retreating German armies.

Having lost some 90 per cent of its heavy armament and 50 per cent of its manpower, the Hungarian army retreated to the Kiev area. Part of it was brought home, but the Germans stopped that withdrawal; then all we could achieve was an agreement that our survivors should be used exclusively behind the line for occupation purposes. Subsequently there were no Hungarian forces in the front line. All statements to the contrary in both the German and the Russian official communiques are unfounded. In a radio battle with the Russians—a most unusual method of combat—the Hungarian radio made this point several times. It may have happened that the almost immobile Hungarian occupation force occasionally came into contact with swiftly advancing Russian detachments, but where this happened it was usually because the Germans had not informed the Hungarian forces of the situation in time, preferring to leave them to perish.

We made every effort to save what could be saved and give help where we still could. But the German army streamed back in utter defeat and in complete confusion. The famous German order and discipline broke down completely, giving place to orgies of ruthlessness and brutality. What a difference there was between these German troops and those of the First World War, with whom ours also fought! This was, however, still not the spirit of the *Wehrmacht* but of the SS troops. Our officers said later that they still found traces of comradeship where they came across *Wehrmacht* troops in their retreat. The Hungarians tried to avoid the SS troops, however, for among them the Hungarians knew that they would find only barbarism.

Public opinion in Hungary was deeply shocked at the news of the catastrophe. We revealed the situation in official communiques, but I made no declaration. I felt that, control myself as I might, I could not have kept from voicing my real opinion, and I should have felt it dishonest to give other than the real facts or to gloss over the situation. I therefore refrained from speaking and felt more strongly convinced of my previous decisions and aims.

We made every effort to assemble our forces in the rear and restore discipline and order, to treat our wounded or bring them home, and to give new life to those who had been crippled in body or mind. Later I shall write more fully of the fate of our soldiers who remained behind; [2] here I shall say only that from that time onward we gave no more soldiers.

In making any attempt to establish the measure of Hungary's participation in the Second World War, we must first consider whether Hungary took any part in preparing for and starting the war. Anyone with the slightest knowledge of the facts will categorically deny that Hungary was culpable in those respects. We had no claims against the Allied powers, no political or any other kind of differences with them—indeed, the great majority of the Hungarian people were at heart on the side of the Western powers. We refused Hitler's proposal to take part in action against the Czechs; when he attacked Poland we most demonstratively took the Polish side; we were then on the same front as the Allies and also gave effective aid to the Poles. In the Nuremberg trials, no Hungarian leader was accused of preparing war. The new regimes in Hungary made such charges and passed death sentences, but everyone knows today that those trials had nothing to do with justice.

It is true that we had made demands on the Little Entente, but in our disarmed state we could not have realized them except by peaceful means even if we had wanted to: the Hungarian army

[2] See Chapter Fourteen, "The Military Withdrawal, 1943–44."

was only one tenth of that of the Little Entente in numbers, and not nearly so strong as that in terms of modern equipment. We had received no arms from the Western powers. (It was with equipment from the West that the Slovaks, Croats, and Rumanians afterwards fought on the German side.) The accompanying table shows the comparative military manpower strength of the states of Southeast Europe.

The participation of Hungarian forces in the Second World War was not united, continuous, or systematic. It would never have happened at all had the Germans not used pressure. Our participation was a sort of *putsch*, done without consent of parliament, and laid before the Regent as a *fait accompli*.

It is needless to remark that Hungary's part in the war was not

Nation	ARMY		AIR FORCE [a]		Total
	Active	Trained Reserves	Active	Trained Reserves	Army and Air Force
I. As of November 1, 1938					
Czechoslovakia [b]	205,000	1,685,000	6,600	..	1,890,000
Rumania	212,000	1,616,000	12,000	..	1,828,000
Yugoslavia	166,237	1,649,000	8,112	16,795	1,815,237
Bulgaria	51,610	650,000	1,610	..	701,610
Hungary	50,000	650,000	2,160	..	700,000
II. As of November 1, 1939					
Rumania	800,000	1,000,000	15,472	..	1,800,000
Yugoslavia	500,000	1,340,000	6,500	500	1,840,000
Bulgaria	160,000	510,000	3,200	..	670,000
Hungary	400,000 [c]	300,000	4,500	..	700,000

[a] The air forces of all countries listed below were part of the army, and the figures listed in these two columns are included in the figures under army.

[b] The figures for Czechoslovakia are as of September, 1936. After Munich accurate figures were not available.

[c] This estimated figure of 400,000 seems much too high to me, especially since the number of men on active duty when I became premier in March, 1942—two years and four months after this date—was about 130,000 on the Eastern front and 200,000 in Hungary.

Source: Figures released by the United States government.

a decisive factor in helping Germany's war effort; it was, in fact, no help at all. The Germans needed the Hungarian troops only as a political demonstration. Hungary's policy and the presence of her troops on the Russian front meant to the German commanders a coefficient of uncertainty with a negative value. A definite misadventure occurred when Germany in order to occupy Hungary had to withdraw large numbers of troops from the Galician front just when the Russians were advancing upon it.[3] I will not write here of the armistice of October 15, 1944, which came after my time, but this in any case added considerably to the Germans' difficulties. I will merely mention that up to March 19, 1944, no English, American, or even Russian planes were fired on by Hungary.

I naturally kept the Regent continuously informed of all our domestic and foreign problems. He assisted me in all my work and efforts with complete understanding. I was, however, careful not to tell him of those tentative steps or concrete connections I had succeeded in making with certain influential persons in countries fighting against us. In these negotiations there was always the possibility of an indiscretion. The Regent had to be kept out of them; for if news of them leaked out and the Germans heard of them, Horthy might have been compromised. The consequences of that might have been incalculable. I faithfully reported general affairs and general directions to the Regent, and I am convinced that he knew and appreciated what I was doing. The events on the Russian front came as a very great shock to him, and thereafter he made every effort to bring back the army and to form a new one at home that would serve only our own requirements.

The relationship between the Regent and the army needs some explanation. Under our constitution, which here followed in spirit that of the Dual Monarchy and Francis Joseph's system, the army

[3] In March, 1944.

was under the direct command of the head of the state, who was its leader and commander-in-chief. The chief of staff was the real head of the army, however; he settled all military problems. The minister of defense answered to parliament on questions connected with the army; his presence in the cabinet gave the army its place in the constitutional and parliamentary system.

The Regent exercised his constitutional control over the army to its fullest extent—one might even say jealously. He did not like it when a premier intervened in military discussions. Horthy's basic idea was that the army should keep aloof from politics and obey the orders given it without question. He felt the army could remain intact only so long as he himself exercised the supreme supervision and direction. Although Horthy's ideas were basically sound and admirable, they did not, unfortunately, work out in practice.

Horthy was an officer of the old Monarchy, ending as admiral of the whole Austro-Hungarian fleet. His past experiences gave him an unusual attitude towards the military. He regarded soldiers in a romantic light, seeing in them Bayards with the same conceptions of honor, loyalty, and service as those which had prevailed in the army of the old Monarchy. Moreover, as a sailor, he viewed matters from the superior moral angle natural to all sailors in every country.

The Hungarian army, sad to say, was not what he thought it to be. After the First—and lost—World War, the army fell to pieces and was also split up artificially. When the time came, therefore, to set up a national army under Horthy's leadership, most of the old officers and NCO's were already in other situations and so did not join the new army. There was, too, most unfortunately, a general feeling that those who had money or other means of livelihood should make way for those who had no resort other than to rejoin the army. Those were the primary reasons why excellent and one-hundred per cent Hungarian officers of the old Austro-Hungarian army did not join the new one.

In the old army, a peculiar situation had prevailed: among the highest officers the largest element after the Austrians was composed of Czechs. There were also many Croats and Transylvanian Saxons. A Hungarian to reach high rank in this army had to give unconditional loyalty to the ruler, and it was generally true that the Hungarians in the Austro-Hungarian army were excluded from promotion to the higher ranks, as being rebellious and untrustworthy.

When the Dual Monarchy broke up, some of the officers who had passed the test joined the new army gladly enough and obtained positions suitable to their qualifications. But the overwhelming majority even at this time consisted of Swabians and Saxons, Hungarian by nationality but Germans by blood, who were simply professional soldiers. Soldiering was the trade of those men; they regarded the army as an end in itself and were little concerned with Hungarian problems. Thus their race, their education, and their spirit soon brought some of them under German influence. On the other hand, it must be stated that the majority of them were correct and faithful Hungarian officers.

The army split into two groups when King Charles IV made his unfortunate attempt to regain the throne, an act which Horthy had to repel under pressure and ultimata from the Little and the Great Ententes. Those who were always legitimists inevitably took the side of King Charles. Thus they came into conflict with the Regent and the government, and those Hungarian officers naturally had to leave the army after the failure of the attempt. The professional military clique of German origin already mentioned were, therefore, left sole masters of the staff and of the army.

Then Gömbös took charge of the army and filled it to overflowing with social climbers, individually not without quality, but too ambitious. Under Gömbös the army became more important as a factor in Hungarian life than it ought to be in any small nation. The Hungarian army became a separate body in the country, but not as the Regent imagined it or as it was during the days of the Dual Monarchy. Far from keeping aloof from all public affairs the army wanted to direct the nation and interfere in everything. Staff officers who lacked or had one-sided training would read a couple of volumes on history or economics and straightway produce plans for reforming the constitutional law or the national economy. Army officers wanted to organize everything, and they deeply despised parliamentarism and liberal and democratic ideas. It was among them that the signs of German influence began to appear.

One of the most flagrant lies of all those leveled against Hungary was that our army was in the hands of feudal lords. Sir Stafford Cripps, in a book published during the war, wrote that the Hungarian army was Nazi because its whole corps of officers was composed of the feudal aristocracy; hence it naturally sympathized with the Germans. (When I read his remarks I took the unusual course of instructing Andor Wodianer, our minister in Lisbon, to try to inform Sir Stafford Cripps of his mistake, for at that moment there was not a single member of the aristocracy in the Hungarian army holding a rank higher than captain. Thus if it was in fact impregnated with Nazi sympathies, one main reason for this was precisely that it was *not* the Hungarian ruling classes who led the army and made up its main body.) Blinkered, slow-witted public opinion abroad had somehow conceived the idea that not only in Hungary but everywhere the upper classes, the aristocracy, and the historic classes were the enemies of parliamentary government, liberalism, democracy, and socialism. That was a completely mistaken notion of the actual situation. In Hungary at that time, just as in 1848, it was the leading classes who represented the ideas of freedom, constitutionalism, and their concomitants. A dozen times in our history it has happened that the Habsburgs clashed with the upper classes just because they represented Western ideas, and the rulers of the Dual Monarchy turned to the lower classes, the urban *bourgeoisie* or the national minorities, as a counterweight to the Hungarians. Hun-

dreds of honveds who had taken part in the 1848 struggle fought
and obtained leading roles in the American Civil War. Almost
all of them were of noble birth.

Thus the army did not represent that Hungarian nation which
Horthy professed as his own and which was ideal. Horthy, however, did not realize this; he could not see it. He believed every
report that reached him and was convinced of every man's loyalty. He saw a gentleman in every general. With great difficulty
I won his consent to a certain purge of the highest-ranking officers.
I succeeded in having some of them retired and others put in less
important positions.[4]

I myself find it hard today to account for the spiritual decay
of our whole army. In the First World War, when the professional
officers were virtually wiped out in the first year, reserve officers
and NCO's recruited from national-school teachers commanded
young recruits and old militiamen, and they endured the mud of
the trenches for four and a half years with marvelous heroism
and legendary bravery. They did not even fight in that war for a
purely Hungarian cause. Their training and words of command
were not Hungarian. They were not inspired by patriotic slogans
or least of all by ideological jargon. They fought so well simply
because they were Hungarians, and therefore loyal, brave, and
true soldiers. During the Second World War the army was more
democratic, and it did not fight for the imperialistic aims of a
great power. Its commands were not given in a foreign language.
It fought under its own officers, who had been filled from their
cadet-corps days onwards with patriotic slogans. It was a body of
comrades, led by commanders and NCO's of peasant and petit
bourgeois origin. Nevertheless, this new army's conduct could not
compare with that of the old. It was true that this was another
generation, but where did its fault lie?

It is impossible not to recognize that this was not merely a Hun-

[4] The effort to reorganize the army came to a head in September, 1942, when
General Charles Bartha was succeeded as minister of defense by General William
Nagy.

garian symptom. The spirit of the 1914 generation was clearly absent from the French army and still more from the Italian; even the Germans were affected. It would be worthwhile considering and analyzing this point. The Hungarian soldier in the First World War was famous for never leaving his officer in the lurch—that never happened. In the last war such desertions often occurred. The younger generation of commanders, with certain honorable exceptions, did not treat the soldiers as they might and should have done. Discipline was indeed not what it had been in the old Austro-Hungarian army, but it was a mistake to restore it by brutal means. Later I marveled at how the British and American forces fulfilled their duties with a friendly spirit of co-operation instead of a harsh discipline.

It had become too late for remedies, and things were made worse by everyone's feeling subconsciously that there was no point in going to Russia to fight or to sacrifice one's life for aims which one either did not accept or did not recognize. There was, however, no excuse for the higher professional officers, who had wanted us to join the war on the German side, possibly because they misjudged the relative forces and partly from political motives. It was they who confronted the Regent, Bárdossy, and—most of all —parliament with a *fait accompli* on the question of declaring war. Francis Szombathelyi, the chief of staff, once put it thus:

If we don't march of our own accord, the Germans will occupy the country. We shall still be in the war, but without a Hungarian army and without our freedom of action. If a German victory comes while we are an occupied country, we shall never retrieve our independence. But if the Germans are beaten, the Bolsheviks will not worry about the details of our behavior but will swallow us up anyhow, and more easily if they find Germans here than if we have an intact country with military forces at our disposal. In the latter case they might come to terms.

The Regent's belief and trust in the Hungarian soldier's heroism and the honor of the military leaders was so blind that it was virtually impossible to discuss these problems with him. On the

other hand, he saw quite clearly that Germany had lost the war.
At that time he made a very apt comment to a German admiral,
a friend of his who had come to see him:

*The change is quite natural. You won as long as the German
army was commanded by generals and the Soviet army by people's commissars. Now things are reversed: there are generals at
the head of the Soviet army, while the German army has become
a political one, led by the SS and the Gestapo.*

On the home front the situation was not pleasant. Under the
effect of the German defeats, the right, far from recovering its
senses, grew wilder than ever. They believed that the nearer the
Russian peril approached, the more completely we must toe the
German line. It was a simple view, not thought out to its conclusion: If the Germans were defeated, how would our resistance
have helped us? And how could our insignificant forces aid a
German victory? They should have realized that it was a mistake
to support a lost cause in any way at all, and an even greater mistake to throw all one's forces into it when defeat was certain. I
wanted us to preserve what we had left of men and material intact for our own aims and objectives; if ever they had to be thrown
into battle, it should be in our own interests and in the defense
of our own frontiers. William Nagy, my minister of defense, was
much attacked also. A liberal-minded man and no friend of the
Germans, he also tried to oppose all encroachments. In particular
he saw to it that the Jews who performed labor duties for the
home defense troops were humanely treated.

At the end of January, the Government party, which had begun
to show signs of internal dissension, decided to hold a course of
lectures on foreign affairs. The leaders thought that most of the
back-benchers were ill-informed on these matters, and would be
able to form a more mature and considered opinion if they attended such a course. I myself went to one of the lectures, and
joined in the discussion on the views of the lecturer, a university

professor. The three main points of the lecture dealt with Weltan-schauung, the foreign policy of large and small nations, and the problem of resistance or capitulation. I gave my views on each point and give here a sentence from each of them:

We are not the enemies of the so-called Weltanschauung, but we do not cringe before it or lie down in front of it.

.   .   .   .

Large nations may be liberal-minded in their foreign policy; a large nation, and it may sound paradoxical, need not always be self-regarding. But a small nation must always remember its small forces and values and must always be exclusively self-regarding.

.   .   .   .

In the course of history two dangers have threatened our nation, invasion from the East and occupation from the West. We have always defended ourselves against the East with arms, and have tried to evince spiritual opposition to the West. This decides the eternal road of Hungarian policy, even towards our friends—I repeat, even towards our friends.

EIGHT

MY JOURNEY TO ROME

[IMMEDIATELY AFTER my appointment I instructed Zoltán Máriássy, our minister in Rome, to make the necessary arrangements
for me to meet Mussolini as soon as possible. A meeting between
a new Hungarian premier and Benito Mussolini was customary,
as our connections with the Italians had been for a long time very
close. Before the war the Regent was received most cordially in
Rome and Naples,[1] as were King Victor Emmanuel III and other
members of the Italian royal family in Budapest when they repaid
the visit. It was only after the *Anschluss* that we paid systematic
visits to Hitler; those also were, strictly speaking, the result of our
Italian policy.

To my surprise, I received an answer from Máriássy that the

[1] The Regent made an official visit to Italy in May, 1937.

Italians would receive me *after* I had paid my visit to Hitler. That was undoubtedly owing to German influence. Hitler distrusted me from the very first, and he did not wish me to enter into personal contact with Mussolini. He feared, furthermore, that I would take advantage of the opportunity to meet Pope Pius XII and his entourage, and perhaps the English and American missions accredited there. Rome, however, made no approach even after I had seen Hitler. Naturally I could not press the affair, but Anfuso, the Italian minister in Budapest, continued to do so. Some months later the invitation actually arrived, but a few days before my departure it was canceled owing to Mussolini's illness. Mussolini was actually ill, and during the *Duce's* incapacitation Anfuso reported several times that I would be notified when Mussolini was well enough to see me. I received another invitation in January, 1943, but again I was prevented from going, that time by the fearful defeat on the Don, which brought disaster to both the Italian and the Hungarian troops. Moreover, the situation of the Italians in Libya had become catastrophic, and they were retreating in disorder into Tunisia. I was asked to postpone my visit on the grounds that Mussolini could not do justice to it in such circumstances.[2]

Meanwhile I learned that Hitler had asked Mussolini not to receive me. I do not think that it was lack of trust in Mussolini that caused Hitler to do that, but loss of faith in Ciano and misgivings about the Italian general staff. The fact that Anfuso explicitly asked me not to take any military personnel with me strengthened my belief.

Shortly after Ciano left the Mussolini cabinet,[3] another invitation was sent to me. I left Hungary for Italy with high hopes.[4] I believed that Mussolini was that clear-headed, strong-willed poli-

[2] On January 14–24, 1943, the Casablanca Conference was held, and the Allied policy of unconditional surrender was announced on January 27.

[3] On February 5, 1943, Mussolini forced the resignation of twelve members of his cabinet, including Ciano, who on February 7 was named Italian ambassador to the Vatican. Eight more cabinet officers were dropped February 12–13 as the crisis in the government developed.

[4] On April 4, 1943.

tician that had been depicted to me. I also believed that he was master of the situation and of his decisions.

I traveled by train through Austria. In Vienna the customary greetings from the Germans were dispensed with or were confined to the appearance of a protocol official. The *Gauleiter*, or chief official of the province, did not come out to welcome me. That did not affect me in the least, but I remembered my reception on the route when a few weeks later Michael Antonescu, the deputy premier of Rumania, made the same journey and he was greeted along the way by the civil and military authorities with the *Gauleiter* out in front. That strengthened my opinion that the Rumanians were the favorites of the Germans. Of my journey I may mention that near the Italian frontier the security locomotive which preceded our train was derailed by partisans, and we had half a day's delay before continuing our journey.

In Rome, Mussolini was waiting at the station with his cabinet, the general staff, high-ranking party and political representatives, and a large escort. Mussolini looked very ill. His head was bald, his skin yellowish-white, and he was talking quickly and with nervous gestures to one hearer or another as the train drew in. He had changed completely in the seven or eight years since I had last seen him at various international congresses I had attended in Rome; I had last spoken with him in 1938, when I visited him during my study of the magnificent irrigation system that had been established in Italy. Now, he accompanied me by car to the Villa Madama, where I was to stay with my escort. On the way our conversation was very general. We talked in French, which he spoke well but with an Italian accent.

The next morning Mussolini received me in the Palazzo Venezia, where the Austro-Hungarian embassy had been located. Giuseppe Bastianini, Ciano's successor as foreign secretary, was present during our conversation. Mussolini welcomed me briefly and mentioned that he was preparing to go see Hitler in a few days' time. Mussolini then turned the conversation over to me and requested that it should be in German.

I then expounded my ideas in a speech which lasted for some three quarters of an hour. I was very cautious. I wanted to explain everything, but in such a way that neither I nor, more particularly, Mussolini should be placed in an awkward position. I had nothing to hide so far as my own standpoint was concerned—that was very well known in Rome at this time. I could not, however, rush matters; for this was not a private conversation, and I had to have some regard for him. If I were to come out into the open and ask questions, Mussolini could do nothing but break off our conversation or divert it from dangerous ground, even if he agreed with me. On the other hand, it was my task to explain everything, to call his attention to everything, and to gather his point of view —from the way in which he received my communications if he should avoid direct answers.

I began by saying that I did not wish to speak about the military situation and its strategic relationships. As a starting point I confined myself to the discussion of one fact—that the Axis was withdrawing on every front. He interrupted me to say that Hitler had assured him that in the summer he would settle with the Russians once and for all.

I repeat, I replied, that I can only discuss our situation on the basis of the present position, not on suppositions. If, however, there is talk of a German summer offensive, then we must also consider the fact that last summer's offensive did not achieve a decisive success, and that failure occurred when the Russo-German balance of power was undoubtedly more favorable to the Germans than it is at present. And I must draw your attention to this: this year there is every possibility of the Anglo-American forces going into action on the Continent. In that case there would be the possibility of a war on two fronts, which all German military science regards as catastrophic.

I also pointed out that Hungary could not give a single soldier for this offensive, whereupon he claimed the same for Italy. I continued:

It follows from this, that we have reached the end of that time

when all Axis calculations were built on one supposition, that
of a swift and complete German military victory. Thus we cannot
neglect any device which may give our countries the possibility of
breaking free. There are political devices and methods, equally
effective in home and foreign policy, none of which we may neglect.

I may state quite openly that in the realm of foreign policy I
see first and foremost the need for greater activity and independence, and it is the chief purpose of my visit to offer collaboration
in this realm. Today, as I see it, the situation is very strange; of
the states which adhere to the Axis powers, only Hungary has
her foreign policy, her own particular ideas and actions officially
represented abroad. We are the only state that does not follow
slavishly in the footsteps of the Germans but that tries instead
to show that those who adhere to an alliance or friendly regime
need not be servile towards it too. It grieves me to have to say
that not even the Italian representatives are showing independence. It looks as if Italy were entrusting the direction of her foreign policy entirely to the Germans, the only distinction between
the two nations being that the Italians are liked and the Germans
are not. The Italians seem to have become the subrepresentatives
of German policy; it is true that they are more graceful at it in the
salon, but they have no ambition to pursue any other course.

Then followed a short exchange of opinions.

Mussolini said: I don't understand how you can make such an
independent approach, and how in your geopolitical situation
you dare come forward almost provocatively like this. Don't you
think that it will lead to trouble?

I replied: If I were in your geopolitical position, and if I had
forty-five million Hungarians, you can imagine what an independent policy I would pursue.

I beg you to consider, I continued, whether or not there would
be security, possibility, and hope of our breaking free in the event
of either a German or an Allied victory, if Italy and Hungary—
and, if possible, Finland—were to formulate within the Axis a

separate common policy, which would not be at variance with our
duty of loyalty to our alliance. Within the Axis this would mean
that we were not completely at the mercy of German predomi-
nance or of German policy, which unfortunately commits mistake
after mistake. Our importance would grow within the Axis, and
outside it we should not be associated entirely with the Germans.

I added that reasonable German policymakers would be only
too glad to receive such a suggestion; for our friendly relations
with other nations could grow into a significant factor in their
own policy also should the necessity for compromise arise, whereas
in the present situation our policy could not aid them in the least.
Such a bloc, counting on the sympathies first of all of Finland,
Poland, and Turkey—countries threatened by Bolshevism—then
of the subjugated Balkan states and Sweden, and of the neutrals
such as Spain, Portugal, and so on, who were afraid of Communism, might give some hope of free development. In any case,
the mainstay of the combination working for political freedom
would be the Vatican.

I carefully avoided mentioning the question of a separate peace,
but I could see that Mussolini was disturbed at the thought that
I might raise it. He tried to answer, but I asked him to listen to me
until I had finished.

The Balkans, I went on, were another field where we ought to
pursue a common policy. Italy and Hungary would always remain
neighbors of the Balkan peninsula, above all of Serbia and Croatia.
The policies of Italy and Hungary should, therefore, be guided by
considerations different from those motivating the German policy.
The prospect of irrevocably losing the friendship of these peoples should be considered because of its possible postwar effects,
quite irrespective of the outcome of the war. Policy in the Balkans
was at that moment dictated by Germany; Italy participated in it,
but Hungary had hitherto succeeded in avoiding becoming involved. At this point I mentioned that during the winter the Germans had requested us to provide three divisions for the occupation of Serbia so that German troops could be diverted to the

Russian front. I told Mussolini that I had rejected the German request categorically.

I reminded Mussolini that Italo-Hungarian *rapprochement* had begun precisely with the object of forming a common policy in the Balkans, and that it was Italy which had sought our co-operation, and that of Austria, in that field. That policy had no aggressive intentions and aimed only at the economic and cultural consolidation of the area on a friendly basis, under Italian influence. For twenty years, Italy had done her utmost to win the sympathy of Yugoslavia in order to exclude German influence from that country. Yet Italy had come to be hated in the Balkans more perhaps than Germany was. The Balkan peoples, accustomed to invasions and foreign oppression, appeared to suffer the Germans more easily because they were convinced that German rule would end when the war ended. The anger and hatred of the Balkan nations were reserved for the Italians, who, those countries feared, wanted to remain after the war also. The situation would have been different had Germany and Italy divided the occupation of the Balkans between themselves—things having proceeded that far—and had Italy been able to attempt, in the zone of occupation allocated to her, to create, by means of wise administration or by the grant of self-government, conditions which would not destroy the chances of agreement and pacification at the end of the war. Then in the event of an Axis defeat, neither the mixed Italo-Yugoslav coastal area, which had been inherited from the Austro-Hungarian Monarchy, nor the northern Adriatic would necessarily be lost. Under such conditions it would also be possible to come to terms with General Draja Mikhailovitch, whose forces although at present showing signs of weariness nevertheless comprised the true patriots of Serbia. Now, on the contrary, the position was that the occupying powers, particularly the Italians, were seeking co-operation with the Communist partisans (the later Titoists) rather than with royal Serbia—that is, with Mikhailovitch, who not only represented legality but also was more desirable politically. I warned Mussolini that the destruction of an independent and legal Serbia, or for that matter of any other Balkan state, instead of serving Italian interests might well rather open the gates to Pan-Slav imperialism.

The third point that I wanted to raise with Mussolini was the Jewish question and its implications regarding Hungarian Jews in Italy. I asked him not to take it amiss if I expressed my point of view in a matter which might appear to be no concern of mine —at any rate not in its Italian aspect. I explained to him that I could not help being interested in the attitude of Italy in this matter because of its inevitable effect on my position in Hungary. Anti-Jewish measures were now beginning in Italy too. I could not understand why this was necessary. The number of Jews was so small—hardly 60,000—that not even the political or economic reasons which were used, for instance, by Hungarian anti-Semites could be invoked. In those days every action of the Axis powers was interpreted so as to make our bill of indictment even longer. This was true particularly in respect of Italy, because no opportunity was lost to identify Fascism with National Socialism. It was quite incomprehensible to me that, while little Hungary did not tolerate outside interference in this matter, while we refused to be swept away by the tide, and while I was able to resist deplorably strong internal pressure and categorically to refuse German demands, he, Mussolini, in the total absence of popular anti-Semitism in Italy, should have given in to Nazi Germany. I repeatedly said that I had taken it for granted that he would stand by me in this question—and now I found myself alone among all the leaders of the Axis powers. The official spokesmen and the press of Rumania, Slovakia, Bulgaria, and Croatia were openly inciting the Germans against Hungary as "the last haven of the Jews"; even in Poland and Bohemia not a finger was raised in the defense of the Jews. Finally, I asked Mussolini most emphatically that there should be no discrimination against Hungarian Jews in Italy and that they should be given the same treatment as other Hungarian subjects. If a state had the right—however questionable it was—to discriminate between its own subjects, in no circumstances could it claim the same right against aliens living on its territory, Jews or not. The Italian government had, therefore, no right to discriminate between Hungarian subjects living in Italy.

These were the three problems which I wanted to discuss with him. I had turned to him with confidence, not only because I knew that he was our friend, but also because when, after the collapse of 1918 we had set out together with Italy to fight against the injustices of the Treaty of Trianon and had aligned ourselves with Italy politically, Mussolini had accepted his share of responsibility for Hungary's future.

It was not only owing to the errors and weaknesses of my predecessors, and Csáky's and Bárdossy's mistaken foreign policy, but very largely also to our Italian orientation, and to the Duce's intervention or personal advice, that Hungary now found herself in a painful predicament. Hungary's relations with Germany had formerly been cool and reserved. This was natural, for the Italo-Austro-Hungarian triangle had been definitely formed and shaped to oppose the Anschluss, and Germany's ambitions in the Balkans. Bethlen had initiated this policy; but Mussolini had recognized its significance and had put it into practice. No doubt he knew of the negotiations I had conducted with Dollfuss with a view to establishing closer relations between Austria and Hungary.[5] After the Anschluss our own tripartite pact ceased, of course, to exist, but the friendly relations between Italy and Hungary remained unchanged. Italy became a neighbor of Germany, while we found ourselves cut off by the Reich from Italy and the rest of Europe. Hungary was cut off from the West, and we and, with us, the other peoples of the Danube Basin and the Balkans were surrendered to the Germans. In the political, military, economic, and indeed in every other sense, the new state of affairs

---

[5] In 1933–34, when I was minister of agriculture, I often traveled to Vienna to negotiate commercial agreements. I became a close friend of Dollfuss and conferred with him on Austro-Hungarian relations.

simply drove us into Germany's arms. Hungary was left no alternative but to join the Axis; otherwise even her friendship with Italy could not have been maintained. Hungary would have remained completely isolated because her neighbors refused to come to terms, which had made it impossible for Hungary to approach the friends of her neighbors. Hungary might have counted on Poland, but Poland herself signed a ten-year nonaggression pact with Germany; [6] thus even Poland directed our path towards Germany. The development of closer relations between Germany and Hungary followed the pattern of Italo-German relations. Gömbös' pro-Axis policy notwithstanding, Hungary was not bound in his time to Germany by any pact or direct agreement; we had got into our present position only later, and only as the ally of Italy.

I observed, moreover, that after Germany had come to terms with the Russians, the Germans had compelled us to re-establish diplomatic relations with Moscow.[7] We had to do this precisely at the moment when Soviet imperialism was trampling under-foot our best friends, the Poles, and starting out in other directions also. If we had not been compelled to re-enter into diplomatic relations with the Soviet Union, there would have been no need to sever relations again at a later date, and we would have been spared the humiliation of reversing our policy towards the Soviet Union under orders from Berlin.

It might have been possible for us to avoid joining the Anti-Comintern pact had Italy abstained from it, although Hungary was being threatened by Bolshevism and Soviet expansion from much closer quarters than Italy, which, geographically and militarily, lay much farther from the Soviet Union than Hungary.

But above all, I was convinced that we should never have

[6] Signed January 26, 1934.

[7] Hungary established diplomatic relations with the Soviet Union in February, 1934. Diplomatic relations were severed in February, 1939, after Hungary had adhered to the Anti-Comintern pact. Diplomatic relations between the two countries were resumed in September, 1939, and severed by Hungary on June 24, 1941.

entered the war had not Italy done so. In all probability, we should have been able to maintain neutrality, which was impossible without support.

I told the Duce quite frankly that I wanted gradually to extricate my country from the war and to lead it back into a state of nonbelligerency. I asked him to help me. Only in such a position could Hungary—the only Axis country which was still independent and unoccupied by German troops—be of use to Italy both during the war and at the coming peace negotiations.

The basis of my whole policy, I informed Mussolini, was to safeguard Hungary's independence and create conditions necessary for her freedom of action. I was working to achieve these ends, and I was convinced that my efforts could succeed. If they did, and if at the end of the war Hungary found herself where I wanted to place her, she would be saved, whoever won the war. Only one thing could upset my calculations: a German occupation of Hungary. I did not expect this to happen, though, because it would be a major blunder, even from the German point of view. When the fortunes of war were on the decline for a nation, however, one could not always rely on reasonable decisions from her leaders. I was asking—and expecting—Mussolini to stand up for Hungary if ever the dreadful eventuality of a German occupation arose. With the occupation of Hungary by the Germans, Italy would lose her last partner. The Italian people would also be painfully affected, I told him, not only because their sympathies were with us, but also because it would raise in their minds the frightening possibility of the occupation of Italy herself.

I concluded with a few warm words of personal tribute to him.

Mussolini remained silent for some time. Then he began to speak. He assured me of the Italian people's and of his own personal friendship—which, he said, remained unchanged. He thanked me for having spoken so frankly; he regarded this as a sign of confidence and friendship. In all his actions he was guided by a sense of responsibility; this had always been the case when he had influenced the shaping of Hungary's destiny or given us advice. But he had never pressed his opinion on us—Hungary had made her decisions as an independent state.

As for his political line, which had led to Italy's participation in the war, he wanted only to observe that ever since the Entente had let Italy down at the Paris Peace Conference, all legitimate Italian aspirations had been thwarted. Had Italy remained neutral, war having broken out, none of her aspirations would ever have been fulfilled. The Allies had made some attempts to keep Italy neutral, to eliminate her as a factor in the war, but they had not offered her an alliance. In that situation Italy would have once again lost the opportunity of achieving her aims, whichever side won. She would not have been accepted as a partner on equal terms but would have been forced to provide naval or air bases for the Allies. She would have become a theater of operations without deriving any benefit from it. These were the petty arguments to justify Italy's entry into the war in the eyes of petty people.

The great and true reason, however, worthy of the heritage of the Roman Empire and the historical necessity, was that the war was for Italy the moment of destiny. It was the occasion which if missed would not recur for making Italy a real great power, with that place among the great nations rightly due her people on the strength of her numbers, her culture, her geographical position, and her historical heritage. If she missed this opportunity or if she failed, Italy would remain a beggar among the great powers of the world. She would never again reach the position rightly hers—a great nation and respected as such by the other powers. For twenty years he had worked to prepare the Italian people for that, to make them understand it. Hungary's position was similar. Only in the war could she make good the injustices of Trianon.

I interrupted to observe that at Munich the process of revision had begun by peaceful means. He answered that immediately after Munich it became clear that the mutual mistrust was so great as to make a lasting settlement impossible.

After those preliminaries, Mussolini went on to say that he would come to the root of the matter. He understood and appreciated my policy, and I could count on his support. He assured me that as long as his word had any weight with Hitler he would always be at my disposal if I turned to him. But he wanted to warn me not to commit any gross blunder; the Germans were not to be joked with. He laughed heartily when I interjected that the Germans appeared to have reserved for themselves the monopoly of committing clumsy errors. The Germans, he went on, were becoming very touchy and suspicious; he himself had had many unpleasant experiences in this respect. Had I any concrete reasons for referring to the possibility of a German occupation?

I said that I had and had not. I was not afraid of the intelligent Germans, and I was giving them no cause to regard an occupation as inevitable. But not all Germans were intelligent. It was peculiar to the German group mentality that when things went badly the least intelligent Germans always came to the fore. Actually, there were three reasons that might induce Germany to occupy Hungary. First was the military: the soldiers disliked seeing a country within the radius of their operations which was not an unconditionally obedient satellite. Second were the actions and example of the Rumanians: they, with an eye to Transylvania, were trying to persuade the Germans that the Rumanians were Germany's reliable friends and the Hungarians were unreliable; that the Rumanians were satisfying all Germany's military, political, and economic demands, and so it was unfair that half of Transylvania should have been given back to the Hungarians, who sabotaged the German effort; that, while the Rumanians were sending more and more troops to the front, the Hungarians had stopped participating and we were obviously preparing to withdraw from the war because I was talking about nonbelligerency Third, the Jewish question, too, could become dangerous; the Germans were irritated because—as they said—Hungary had become a citadel of Jewry and I refused to take any radical measures

These were suppositions and possibilities. As for definite symptoms, the official and unofficial Nazis in Budapest were in ever-
closer touch with the pro-German Hungarian political parties and
their most extremist representatives. And among the German
minority, whose loyalty had so far been beyond reproach, a certain
restlessness was becoming noticeable. So long as they only worked
inside Hungary, I was not particularly worried. But when they discovered, as they were bound to do, that they could not get the
regime changed by such methods, it was not impossible that these
Germans might resort to those methods of force which they always preferred. As the front moved closer to the Carpathians, the
Hungarian question would undoubtedly become more urgent
for them.

Mussolini agreed that there undeniably was a certain restlessness in the air—he had sensed its presence in Italy, too—but
this was quite comprehensible. The Germans must be reassured,
however. That was the only way of avoiding worse trouble. He
declared emphatically, however, that he had no information or
knowledge of any facts which would justify my worries. He was
meeting Hitler in the near future, and the question of Hungary as
well as my policy would certainly come up. He promised me that
he would watch with particular attention for any signs of coming
trouble. He assured me repeatedly that he would oppose any such
plan and would stand by Hungary with Roman loyalty.

What I had said about Italo-Hungarian co-operation within the
Axis was wise and timely, Mussolini told me. I was right in saying
that, with the Blitzkrieg period over, there were other things to be
thought about. But Italy's position was difficult. Whatever he did
would be regarded, not as the natural gesture of an independent
nation, but as an effort or intention to withdraw from the war and
conclude a separate peace.

Then he looked hard at me and said the following words, very
seriously:

We cannot even think of a separate peace. Firstly, because honor would not allow it. Secondly, because Italy would achieve nothing by it. Her position would not improve; her prospects would not become more favorable. She would become a battle-field. The Germans, too, would become her enemies, and the country would suffer terrible destruction. In any event, the Allies' insistence on "unconditional surrender" excludes the possibility of such a step. Thirdly, nobody has been able to show me that getting out of the war is a practicable possibility.

He was not, however, rejecting my suggestion and was even sympathetic to it. Should his coming visit to Hitler fail to convince him that by autumn the war would be over or a separate peace concluded with the Russians (as he was going to suggest), he would decide that the time had come for us to serve our own interests by independent action.

He then complained that Hitler was not giving him sufficient support in Africa, that the German leader underrated that theater of operations and was seeking a decision only in the East. That was Hitler's great error, Mussolini declared, because, if the Allies won in Africa, they would open the second front in the south from bases in Turkey. Such an invasion would be very dangerous because the enemy would have to be fought over a widely scattered area, and the German and Italian forces would be faced with an almost impossible task. On the other hand, if the Anglo-Saxons were unable to attack from the south, they would have to attempt it from the west, and that would mean certain defeat for them. Hitler could hardly wait for that moment which, he had promised himself, would entail the destruction of the American and British fleets and open the road to England for him.

Perhaps Mussolini sensed my depression from my silence. He rose, walked up to me, placed his hand on my shoulder, and said:

Trust me. I am judging events correctly. If the promises which I have been given fail to materialize, and if things turn out as you expect, I shall know what to do, and your nation can always count on the Italian people.

I can only repeat, Mussolini went on, *that everything depends on whether we finish the war or, rather, on whether Germany finishes the Russians by autumn. Before these decisive questions are settled, one way or the other, nothing must be done which would weaken, if only morally, the strength and driving power of the Axis. If autumn fails to bring victory, then—but only then— your line of thought can be considered. But I am prepared to state now that I accept your point as worth keeping in mind. I shall remember it, and I myself will return to it at the proper time. I must ask you, however, to do nothing that could weaken our position before that time, or to shake faith in our unity. The faith in victory in the German and Italian soul is unshaken, and even stronger is the faith in our armies.*

Finally, with regard to the Jewish question, he said that it was true that there was no anti-Semitism in Italy; the number and the position of the Jews in Italy were insignificant. He had had to take certain measures because the Germans, who were incredibly intolerant and inflexible in this matter, had insisted. He could afford concession precisely because the problem was so unimportant in Italy. He appreciated and approved of my policy on this question, and he recommended that I persevere in it and congratulated me on having withstood all Germany's pressure and threats. He accepted my views on nondiscrimination towards Jews of Hungarian citizenship in Italy. He did not know the exact position in this respect, but, so far as Hungarian Jews were concerned, he would act in accordance with my wishes.

Later I found that Mussolini had kept his promise and that no harm had been done to Hungarian Jews in Italy. Unfortunately, that situation did not last long, for after the fall of Mussolini atrocities occurred in the German-occupied areas and the Neo-Fascist Republic.

Our discussion went on after that for a considerable time, lasting in all almost three hours. It included other problems of lesser general interest. Italy's internal political situation was mentioned, and I remember the words with which Mussolini outlined the

160

MY JOURNEY TO ROME

differences between the Italian and German governments.

In Italy, he said, there are no factions, cliques, or powerful personalities who have their own organizations, followers, and means of independent action. I stand alone, and I can change people, as I have done recently, whenever I think it necessary. I do this from time to time to prevent the emergence of governments within the government and the rise of individual ambitions.

In Germany, he said, things are different. The SS, the Gestapo, the Reichswehr are so many separate powers; and there are even powerful individuals whom Hitler is compelled to consider—Goering, Himmler, and Goebbels are so many kinglets. That is why one can never be sure whose influence will ultimately prevail with Hitler.

During the whole conversation Mussolini was fresh and alert and showed no signs of fatigue. Cabinet secretary Bastianini was also present; but, as he spoke little German, he never once intervened, although he took notes. As soon as I returned to the Villa Madama, I dictated an account of our conversation.

The next day I, Máriássy, our minister in Rome, and Szentmiklóssy, chief of the political section of the foreign ministry, who accompanied me, were guests for luncheon at the Palazzo Venezia. The only Italians present, besides Mussolini, were the secretary of his cabinet and Anfuso. Lunch was simple but excellent: soup, fish and vegetables, sweets and fruit. I remember that at other dinners and social occasions—and the party given by the King was no exception—the quality of the food was remarkably poor, and the meat was invariably uneatable.

The conversation at Mussolini's table covered many subjects. I raised the subject of the Balkans, observing again that it was a matter that concerned Italy and Hungary more than the Germans, who were dictating policy there. We were the immediate neighbors of Yugoslavia; we were to bear the consequences of any events to come; and yet everything was taking place according to the orders and interests of the Germans.

Mussolini answered that wherever the Germans trod only one policy was possible: the one they would impose. Agreements with them would be useless; they would not keep them. He added, not without irritation, that while I was refusing to send troops to the Balkans in order to avoid becoming involved—an argument he approved of—I was effecting the very thing I was trying to avoid by supporting Mikhailovitch. The Italians were supporting Marshal Tito because they felt that he was the weaker of the two; Mikhailovitch would be a greater danger to them. Supporting Tito was the way to disrupt the unity of the Yugoslav resistance. There was no danger of Yugoslavia's going Communist: the Serbs were the most nationalist people in the world. In any event, the question of Communism was not being decided in the Balkans but on the battlefields of Russia.

Afterwards, thinking over the discussions I had with Mussolini during the two days, I felt that, although no concrete agreements had been reached between us, I had achieved my aim. I could not hope to push him towards any major decision at our first discussion. On the other hand, I had had a good opportunity to tell him everything I thought he should know; and from my words he should have been able to feel and gauge the extent of my concern over the course of events, while I, in my turn, had been able to sound his intentions. Unfortunately, I was compelled to conclude that he had no firm plans or decisions ripening in him but was letting himself be carried with the tide. The illusion of German strength and Hitler's forceful convictions were dominating Mussolini's personality and were limiting his independence of decision. At the same time it was not hard to see that he was worried and undecided. From him I did not hear any of those optimistic platitudes to which I would have been treated in abundance by the Germans. He was worried about his own position and about Italian domestic politics. The fact that he himself had turned the conversation to this subject and the way in which he had boasted of his "total power" could only prove to me that the ground was becoming shaky under his feet. What he had said about separate peace gave the impression of a well-studied slogan rather than an earnest and spontaneous expression of his thoughts.

It was obvious to me that the idea of a separate peace was constantly in his mind.

Mussolini was not an unbending and determined despot like Hitler. Mussolini's whole past was full of irresolution and contradiction. He had been a Socialist as well as a freethinker and had changed his tenets often enough before coming to power. He was swept up to the surface by the situation which arose in Italy after the First World War.

Italy had been a monarchy based on royal authority. The people carried on their day-to-day struggle for existence and gained some additional satisfaction from their great spiritual and artistic gifts and traditions. Italy had been among the victors of the war, but she was greatly weakened by her efforts and proved unable to take up the threads again where she had dropped them in 1915. New ideas, too, then made themselves felt in Italian life. Foremost among them was strong nationalism, which should be distinguished from the prewar *Irredenta*, a spasmodic and limited rather than a universal and nationalistic movement. The nationalism which appeared after the First World War was real, even though a little forced and perhaps not very deep. It was a feeling new to the Italian people, and it shook them out of their inertia. Apart from the movement led by Cavour and Garibaldi which resulted in a united Italy, the Italian people, perhaps alone among the nations of Europe, had not known real nationalism. There had, to be sure, been local patriotisms, but those currents lost their importance with the union in 1870. The irredentist feeling for the territory held by Austria received full satisfaction in the Paris peace treaties. The Italian nationalism that arose after the First World War was vague in its aims and aspirations, but in spite of that, or perhaps for that very reason, Italian nationalism became one of the waves that carried Mussolini to power.

The other new ideological, political, and cultural current was democracy, which domestic and foreign propaganda alike pressed on the Italian people. In this respect also the Italian people had been more backward than any other of the cultured peoples of Europe. Though possessing a constitutional government, the

Italian people had been little interested in the wider issues of government. Their life had been almost completely patriarchal. There had been no oppression; in fact, there had been possibilities of social fluidity, and contact between the various strata of Italian society had been very direct and friendly. Democracy as a conscious guiding principle of politics had, however, been absent. Then the process of democratization began in Italy. But the basis of democracy in every country must be high standards of life, material and cultural, and a middle class which has a trained understanding of statecraft, which is ready to make sacrifices, and which is willing to lead the state. If such a group is not present, or if its members are not fitted with a sense of duty that is recognized as such by the people at large, then the basic conditions for democracy are lacking. So it was in Italy.

A democratic movement always begins with the emancipation of the class with the lowest cultural and economic standards, and such a proletariat is correspondingly merciless, radical, and crude in its methods. It accepts the tenets of Marxism, which lead not to democracy but to totalitarian class war. The totalitarian idea is realized in true and conscious form, easily defeating the hesitant bourgeois ideology, which is cowardly precisely because it fears to lose its economic standards. Such a totalitarian ideology can only have two really effective opponents: another dictatorship or real democracy. It is, however, not enough for this democracy to exist merely in the hearts of the bourgeoisie; it must be something established, strong and able to defend itself against the totalitarianism of the right as well as of the left.

Italy's tragedy began when she proved unable to develop into a democratic country. The democracy which she tried to create, the democratic principles that had become the official Weltanschauung of the world after the war, were threatened with extinction by mutually warring masses revolutionized by the liberties created by democracy and by the slogans of nationalism, socialism, and Communism. Things were made still worse by the great impoverishment and unemployment resulting from the First World War and by the embitterment felt by the Italian people when the

Paris peace treaties of 1919 did not give the country all the rewards the Italians had been expecting. The Italians could not see why in the councils of Versailles only accomplishments on the military field were held decisive or why Britain and France regarded themselves as sole victors of the struggle, disregarding Italy's military achievements and refusing to accept her as an equal partner.

Those were the sentiments that unsettled the Italian people and weakened the authority of the government, and in the clash of political slogans democracy proved the weakest. It failed to establish itself in Italy, as democracy failed also in the defeated countries where the Allies tried to establish it but where there occurred instead Communist revolutions—in Russia, Germany, Austria, and Hungary alike. The upshot in Italy was that, while the monarchy retained a certain authority, the main field was disputed between nationalism and left-wing socialism. Fascism then appeared, and it appropriated the slogans of both nationalism and socialism and exploited their doctrines and spiritual forces.

Mussolini and his friends used all the catchwords: they proclaimed national self-assertion, and they adopted the socialist and Communist tenets, including the dictatorship of the people, the nationalization of the means of production, workers' control over production, the omnipotent "working man." The Italian people rallied to the Fascists because they promised order and work. The lower middle classes were Mussolini's first supporters because they hoped he would protect them on the one hand against the old aristocratic rule, a "democracy" which to the lower middle class meant the rule of the upper middle class, and on the other hand— a still more potent motive—against the Communism that threatened the most important purpose of the lower middle classes— their peace of mind. The masses of workers were won over by the totalitarian and radical-socialist doctrines of Fascism, whose great strongholds remained till its last days those industrial cities of northern Italy, which today are the bulwarks of the Communist movement in the country.

Fascism would never have come to Italy if democracy had been strong enough to take over and hold the power or if the Italian monarchy had been strong enough and determined enough to broaden its basis of power by allying itself with democracy. By the time Fascism appeared on the scene, democracy had already been beaten, so only two choices were left: a dictatorship of the left or one of the right. King Victor Emmanuel and the overwhelming majority of the Italian people chose the latter.

The Fascist dictatorship, like all dictatorships, began with great initial successes: wonderful technical achievements, social reforms for the masses, and a strengthening of the Italian character. Nevertheless, these were followed by a growing inertia, self-interest, a clique system, and corruption—all heralding internal disintegration. Finally, internal enthusiasm slackened, external pressure increased, and so the system was unable to meet the exigencies of the times. Italian Fascism never employed that entirely ruthless terror which is a dictatorship's sole method of self-preservation in the wholesale way in which German National Socialism tried to use it and Russian Communism still uses it. Fascism just ran on and gradually ran down, until it stopped during the Second World War. Not only men are the victims of wars but also ideas which lack real permanency.

In 1943 Fascism was already in decay. It no longer had any spiritual force. I do not know whether Mussolini himself perceived that, but he had no power of decision or action left. His regime was already reaching its twilight.

That was the state of Italy and Mussolini at the time of my visit, and the weaknesses in both were, I feel, why I failed in my aim, which was to get Hungary and Italy to join in extricating themselves from the Axis, in following a separate path from Hitler's Germany, so that when National Socialism collapsed, as it was bound to do, it would not inevitably drag us down with it. In Mussolini's eyes, Fascism and his own person were identical with Italy. But Fascism and his own person were doomed: sentence had been passed on them, not only by the enemy, but by the Italian people as well, and later, as we were soon to see, would be passed on them by King Victor Emmanuel also.

My audience with the King was for a quarter past twelve, to be followed by an official luncheon at one. Entering the Quirinal, I passed the ranks of the royal guards—fine strapping men, not one under six feet tall. The King received me in his simply furnished study.

I had met him before: the last time in Budapest in 1937, when he was returning the Regent's visit. Those were marvelous days, perhaps historic Hungary's last festival. There was a magnificent cavalcade of Hungary's past, the nobles and their ladies in ceremonial dress, while the streets were thronged with villagers in their colorful national costumes: every outward sign of a great country, strengthened and inspired by tradition and by national vitality.

I found that King Victor Emmanuel had changed little since 1937—for that matter, he had early become the little, elderly man which he was by the time of my visit.

During our conversation we discussed no serious or immediate problems. The King, perhaps intentionally, gave me the impression of being unconcerned with or even uninterested in the war, the military situation, foreign politics, the domestic situation in Italy—in fact, in any important problem. That, of course, was not the case, but the outward impression left was that Mussolini was the sole master of the situation and responsible for it. I mentioned the situation at the front, but the King's remarks were restricted to generalities. I mentioned Mussolini's impending visit to Hitler, but got no reply at all. The King then turned the conversation to Hungarian history, of which he showed an amazing knowledge, extending to the smallest details. I thought I knew the history of my own country tolerably well, but I had to be on my mettle. He knew dates far better than I. And when I mentioned that one of my ancestors in the fifteenth century married Aloysia de Aragon, of the royal house of Naples, the King delivered a most enthralling lecture on lesser known details of Italo-Hungarian relations in that period. Unfortunately, that was hardly the purpose of my visit to Rome. When luncheon was announced, the King looked quite cross. "What an interesting talk we had," he said. "And now we must sit through a wearisome official lunch! Don't you find them boring too?"

At lunch I was seated on the King's right, my other neighbor being Vittorio Ambrosini, the chief of staff, who had been appointed a few weeks before. I talked mostly with him. After a few introductory sentences, the general said that Italy had already lost the war and that Germany would lose it too. Hardly knowing who my interlocutor was, I was naturally surprised to hear such candid opinions voiced at the lunch table by the head of the Italian army. As I did not know who the other guests were, who might be listening, and whether or not German spies were among them, I answered the general only shortly, but invited him to come to Budapest and discuss plans and possibilities there.

After lunch we went into one of the state rooms, where I saw Gobelins of the same pattern as those in the Hungarian premier's official residence. Though this was the first time that his attention had been called to it, the King at once knew how the Gobelins got to Hungary.

The next day I was received in audience by Pope Pius XII. This was the most moving, as well as the most important and interesting, event of my visit to Rome.

I had met the Holy Father in Budapest at the Eucharistic Congress of 1938, when he was papal secretary of state. That was the second beautiful event of Hungary's last years that I remembered in Italy. On that occasion, too, there was pomp and pageantry, but the spirit brooding over it all was that of the Catholic Church, whose bastions St. Stephen had established on the easternmost fringe of Europe; what inspired the vast crowds was the Hungarian faith. I shall never in my life see anything so beautiful as the tens of thousands of country folk in their rich, colorful local costumes. We saw groups representing at least twenty-five various regions of Hungary, in their beautiful dresses that are worn every Sunday at home. I doubt whether any country

in Europe could have matched that spectacle. At the Midnight
Mass at the Heroes' Square, more than a hundred thousand men
took the Sacrament, while Cardinal Pacelli sat on the throne,
most worthily representing the head of the Roman Catholic
Church.

At that time the dreadful tragedy of the Second World
War was already casting its shadow ahead. Austria had already
been occupied, and Germany was feverishly preparing for war.
No one was allowed to attend the Congress from either Austria
or Germany; only a few prelates reached Hungary by an indirect
route.

In January, 1943, when I received my second invitation to go to
Rome, I drew up a long memorandum to the Pope, setting forth
my views. When I had to postpone my journey, I sent it to him
by courier. I composed the memorandum myself, with great care,
as I did all my speeches and writings. Where I quoted the Pope's
declarations, however, and those of his predecessors on Communism and the dangers of dictatorships, I had got our primate,
Justinian Cardinal Serédy, to help me.

The memorandum was a cry for help, a supplication from the
eastern borders of Catholicism to the head of the Roman Catholic
Church and through him to the Catholics and Christians of the
whole world. I explained that I was writing, not on behalf of
Hungary in particular, but on behalf of all those small nations
who were a forward defense line of European culture against
another world which was Asiatic and Communist. I was writing on
behalf of all the states primarily threatened by this dreadful danger: Finland, the Baltic states, Poland, and the Balkan countries,
as well as Hungary. I argued that the real frontiers of Europe were
the frontiers of Catholicism and Protestantism, beyond which
came another world. Our Hungarian ancestors had pushed this
line forward, from the eastern valleys of the Alps to the Carpathians, and now the danger threatened that Russia's victory might
push it back to where it had stood a thousand years ago. This
prospect was a dreadful threat to the whole world, but first and

foremost to the Catholic world and to its culture. I pointed out that, while even the Church's visible struggle was being waged against the Nazi regime and its atheism and while that struggle would end by the victory of the West for Christianity, the greater threat against Christianity was from the East. The victory of the Allies would mean a Communist victory as well, and then woe to Protestants and Catholics alike because Russia had never been either of these.

When I took my seat facing the Pope, I saw my memorandum lying on the desk in front of him. He began to discuss it at once. He condemned the system and methods of the Germans, which independently of the war were inhuman and brutal, especially towards the Jews but also towards their own race. He emphasized the dreadful sufferings of the Polish people, who had been subjected to the terror of both the Germans and the Russians. The Roman Church could never co-operate with governments which followed methods like Germany's or Russia's and built up their systems on those methods. Russian Bolshevism had already shown its true colors when it exterminated millions of its own citizens, but that the Germans could be capable of the same horrors was a great and painful personal surprise to him, who had been papal nuncio in Germany for several years. He had not during that period seen any trace of anti-Semitism among the German people.

He thanked me for having succeeded in keeping Hungary from such inhumanity and said that he felt confident that, with its culture and Christian faith, the Hungarian people would never follow such paths.

Then we discussed the war. I told the Pope openly that then as before I considered that the Axis had lost the war. If I had one partner, even Italy, I should hold it possible to halt Germany, which was heading straight towards a catastrophe. But I had no partner, not even Mussolini. The small nations around Hungary dared not move; they were completely subservient to Hitler. There was no point even in a heroic gesture from me, because if I turned single-handed against Germany, the only possible result would be that I would hand Hungary over to Hitler, and the same beastliness that was taking place elsewhere would come in Hungary, too.

Expanding the ideas in my memorandum, I told the Pope that unless something were done the resultant tragedy would be far greater than that economic collapse of Europe which must follow Germany's defeat, apparently the only aspect of the disaster of which most people thought. My own view of the situation was that the world was already splitting into two camps. On one side were nations whose majorities were neither Roman Catholic nor Latin in culture. On the other—the losing—side were the Roman Catholic and Latin nations, headed by France and Italy, and the nations of the Latin culture, Hungary, Poland, and Croatia. Spain and Portugal did not really count and, in any case, would not share in the victory. This was the first great war in the history of the world in which the Latins and the Catholics were all on the losing side; in fact, they were in a way out of the war as it was being fought by non-Catholic powers. And the coming peace would be the first large-scale peace settlement in world history in which the Latins and Catholics would have no say. By this I did not imply that the victorious Anglo-Saxon races did not represent the highest degree of contemporary culture and civilization, but through their alliance with Russia they were tied to barbarism. Thus, they would not be alone when dictating the peace. In fact, in the dictated peace to come the power of the dictators would weigh heavier than the powers of democracy, humanity, and Christianity.

The head of the Roman Catholic Church had now a task: to step forward boldly and to lead not only the Catholics but the Christians of the world in a campaign to save our European culture and our universal faith from destruction from the East. I feared that if the small East European bulwarks of Christianity, of which Hungary was the first, were sacrificed, the forces of destruction would not stop at their frontiers.

The Pope showed the utmost interest in my point of view. He

said that my interpretation gave historical depth and significance to the events of our day. Then he made me the following declaration: The Holy See so far had made no attempt to mediate a peace, and he could not take any such initiative. No single belligerent had approached, or even sounded, the Holy See with respect to peace overtures. His impression was that both sides were fighting for total victory and that they aimed at dictating total peace terms. The doctrine of totality was foreign to the Roman Catholic Church, and in such an atmosphere the Church's conception, which desired a real, just, and permanent peace, was not an actuality. The situation then was so embittered that it was certain that if the Vatican made peace proposals, and if one of the belligerents accepted those proposals, the other side would reject them. The Church would then, willy-nilly, become a partner and ally of one of the belligerents, and the other side would *ipso facto* turn against the Church. So the purpose would be defeated because the impartiality of the Church—its broad superiority over worldly events —could be attacked by evil tongues. But he was well aware that the Italian people desired peace and, being Italian born, he would be glad to lead the Italian people out of the catastrophe. For the given reasons, the Pope could take no initiative, but he could and would do all in his power if his own Italian country or its government asked him to do so. In that case, the Church would not be taking the initiative and would not be responsible for a refusal, and its attitude could not give rise to misunderstandings.

I thought the Pope's declaration extraordinarily important and asked whether I could communicate it to Mussolini. He agreed and said that he regarded it as his duty to listen with understanding to anyone who turned to him for help and to try to help if he could. He asked me, however, to formulate precisely what I wanted to tell Mussolini.

I therefore drew up the following extracts from our conversation as suitable for communication to Mussolini:

1. The Holy See had so far not offered its mediation to either of the belligerents and had received no request to do so. So long as

the inhuman methods and systems of certain of the belligerents did not change, the outlook for peace was almost nonexistent and to represent the cause of such groups was incompatible with the Church's moral position.

2. Should Italy turn to him for help, the Pope, being the head of the Church of Peace would consider the proposal and would be happy if he could help his people.

3. The Pope acknowledged that the attitude of the present Italian government towards the Church had been correct and its behavior in the war humane. Both these things derived from the religious and humanitarian character of the Italian people.

His Holiness gave me a free hand to inform Mussolini of that part of our conversation of which the above three points constituted a summary.

After that the Pope and I continued our conversation for some time. I sadly remarked that the position of small countries was tragic: the Pope and I were talking of mediations for peace, and I could not even ask him to undertake such negotiations for Hungary. Hungary not only could not conclude peace, she could not even surrender; we were powerless to sue for peace because we were only a tiny cog in the machine, and we were unable to surrender because none of our enemies was near enough to be approached. We had no wish to harm anybody, yet we were at war and inescapably doomed.

The Pope showed genuine sympathy and infinite kindness during our whole conversation. He spoke with much affection of my country and people, and he dwelt on his memories of Budapest. Then he reverted to my memorandum and expressed his complete sympathy with it. In contrast to my pessimism, however, he expressed his strong trust and faith that humanity and Christianity would, in the end, conquer the world of pagan doctrines and barbaric methods.

After our conversation, which had lasted an hour and a half, the Pope gave me his blessing, in the Hungarian language. The members of my entourage, including Baron Gabriel Apor, our envoy to the Holy See, were then called in, and the Pope exchanged some words with them. Then we left.

I left the Vatican in an entirely different state of mind from that in which I had left Mussolini. The Pope's real spiritual greatness, that lofty power built on the past and future which I felt in him, made an overwhelming impression on me. Compared with what he radiated, the triumph or despair of us men of a day seemed small, ephemeral, and unimportant.

The audience had lasted half an hour longer than had been planned, so I was late in calling on Cardinal Maglioni, Pacelli's successor as papal secretary of state. We had a few special problems to discuss, chiefly relating to the still unsettled position of the Greek Catholic Church in Transylvania. I told Cardinal Maglioni of the difficult situation in which the Hungarian Roman Catholic bishopric in Transylvania found itself under the Rumanian rule, and we discussed a few personal questions of the Hungarian Catholic church. I then repeated to Cardinal Maglioni what the Pope had told me about his attitude towards mediating for peace. Cardinal Maglioni replied:

The Anglo-Saxon powers would at once answer any peace feelers by saying that they could in no circumstances negotiate with Mussolini and Hitler, with Fascism and National Socialism. There must, therefore, be a change of regime in Germany and Italy before any initiative could have the smallest chance of success. But we could not say this to Hitler or Mussolini, unless they themselves took the initiative and approached us. Overtures on our part would simply be a useless affront, which would react disagreeably on the position of the Roman Catholic Church in present-day Italy and Germany.

We walked out again between the lines of chamberlains, knights, and guardsmen and went to St. Peter's Church, where I ended my day in the Vatican with the usual ritual. Then I arranged an appointment with Mussolini for six that afternoon. When we met, I told him what the Pope had, not charged me, but authorized me to repeat of our conversation, which I could repeat verbatim, having in the interval dictated the material to my secretary as a record for our archives.

Mussolini was greatly surprised and impressed by what I told him. I sat in the chair that I sat in during my first visit, but he sat, not in the chair at the other side of the desk, but on the desk itself, quite near me. When I finished my account, he began to sway backwards and forwards on the desk. "Interessant, tres interessant," he said; he then interjected a few words in Italian and, a few seconds later, sat up and answered:

It seems that it is a waste for me to keep an ambassador to the Pope, for the Pope trusts you more than he does him. I have the greatest respect for the Pope, and it is unfortunate that I cannot speak to him personally. I believe, and I know, that he means well, and would do everything for the Italian people; but it is impossible, impossible. . . . Do you remember what I told you about a separate peace—for the Pope can only have been thinking of that? Impossible, impossible. . . . Everything depends on my coming journey to Hitler.[8] That's all I can tell you now. . . . But thank you for passing on what the Holy Father said. Perhaps one day I can thank him myself.

Then I took my leave of Mussolini. I do not know whether my step led to anything.

I am convinced that the Pope believed that both dictators, Hitler and Mussolini, would have to disappear from the scene before there could be any possibility of peace. But naturally, and primarily, the German regime and its methods would have to go as the precondition of any peace. Whatever other political considerations might apply, the Pope, as the supreme representative of Christianity and humanity, was morally precluded from having any commerce with the dictators.

Of Mussolini's subsequent visit to Germany, I managed to establish two facts. His idea was to propose to Hitler the conclusion of a separate peace, at any price, with the Soviets, and the

---

[8] Mussolini and Hitler met in Germany, April 7–10, 1943. They met again in Verona July 19, 1943, when it was evident that Mussolini was losing power in Italy.

return to the basis of the German-Russian nonaggression pact. With the Soviets out of the war peace could be concluded with Britain and America on a compromise between the Munich agreement and the principles of the Atlantic Charter.

Naturally, there was little hope of achieving those two conditions by that time. The Russians would no longer have been satisfied with what they had got by their agreement with the Germans in 1939. It was already evident that their imperialism and their ideology were now directed towards further aims. It was also highly unlikely that the Anglo-Saxon powers would backtrack and accept those victories of German imperialism and ideology they had been forced to swallow at Munich.

Hitler and his circle weakened Mussolini's resolution by showing him the new "secret weapons" and by talking of a "total warfare" which was to make the maximum use of Germany's strength and which looked very attractive on paper. They persuaded him that Russia would be decisively defeated by autumn, after which the Anglo-Saxon powers would be forced to accept peace without any concessions from the Axis.

I also found out that Mussolini had made representations on behalf of Hungary and of myself and had declared that he would, in no circumstances, allow any violation of Hungary's independence.

During my stay in Rome I attended a few more receptions, at which I met practically all the men then important in Italy. I saw many of the members of the old regime at the Caccia Club, and at dinner at the same club I talked to many of the supporters in a narrower sense of the Italian monarchy. I also attended an afternoon reception given by the governor of Rome, where I had a sight—unfortunately only a hurried glimpse—of the Roman Forum.

I met the diplomatic corps at a reception given for me by the Order of the Knights of Malta. At that social function a curious little incident occurred. I happened to be standing in a corner, giving some instructions to my secretary, when a lady passed us, the wife of a prominent German diplomat, whom I had known quite well when her husband was stationed in Budapest. I had already exchanged some cordial words with her at this party. As she passed me, she suddenly whispered to me: "*Geben Sie acht, Sie sind gehasst bei uns.*" I knew already from the old days, that she was no enthusiast for the German regime.

The German ambassador, Hans Georg von Mackensen, called on me, but we spoke only of generalities.

Baron Apor, our envoy to the Vatican, who was the senior member of our diplomatic staff, gave a small lunch for me, which was attended by a few notables from the Vatican and by Count Ciano, formerly Italy's foreign minister and then ambassador to the Vatican. After the others had left, Ciano and I had a little private conversation.

Ciano said quite openly that, not only Italy, but also Germany had lost the war, that the fall of Mussolini and of Fascism was inevitable, and that there were only three possible successors to Mussolini—himself, Marshal Pietro Badoglio, or Marshal Rodolfo Graziani. He thought a reasonable separate peace for Italy quite a possibility, since the only real aim of the Allies was to crush Germany. Italy was not in the way either of the Anglo-Saxons or of the Soviets. Mussolini said that he had to try to realize Italy's national aims by victory in the field. That might have been worth trying in the past but not then—in 1943. All that could be done by the Italians was to save what could still be saved.

Ciano impressed me then—as he always had—as an extremely intelligent person, who was, however, not serious-minded enough for the times in which he lived. We Hungarians must, however, acknowledge that he had always taken Hungary's side, especially during the two Vienna awards, when he supported our point of view against Ribbentrop.

That was the end of my visit to Rome. I had also a few last economic discussions, and I received some decorations from the

talian government and some charming presents from the Pope.
God alone knows where those things are today. They were looted,
presumably by the Russians, from the Turkish legation in Budapest.

I drove back by car to Florence through Orvieto and Siena,
wanting to see how the Italian country, which I had known from
previous visits to Italy, was looking now. Every acre of country
seemed to be cultivated, and in the towns the people looked tolerably well fed and clothed. The picture I saw was not one of war;
I saw hardly any soldiers and no Germans at all. It is true that my
road lay far from any place of military importance.

In Budapest I was received at the station with ovations. People
entertained great expectations about my mission to Italy, but I
brought back nothing except a clear recognition that Italy, too,
was a broken reed. In the near future we would be standing
alone, and we could, therefore, follow only our own way.

NINE

INTENSIFICATION OF THE GERMAN PRESSURE

❰[AFTER my visit to Mussolini, the Regent was unexpectedly invited to visit Hitler. The date of the invitation was fixed for April 16–17, 1943, and the reason for it, as given by Jagow, the German minister in Budapest, was that Hitler wished to discuss the general military situation and that of the Hungarian troops. There was no hint that the invitation might also have political discussions for its object. Consequently, the Regent went without any political advisers, whose presence the Germans always tried to avoid on those occasions.

I went through the various questions with the Regent, and we agreed that he should reject all requests for more troops and make no promises of further concessions by us in the matter of exchanges of goods. I begged him—but he needed no asking—to be

irm on the Jewish question and to adhere to our well-known atti-
ude that this was a Hungarian domestic problem, whose economic
ind social aspects were on the best way towards solution. I showed
Horthy a report which had fallen into my hands accidentally from
i high German functionary who had taken part in the Hungaro-
German economic negotiations. This report, which was endorsed
by German military officers, was to the effect that a removal of
he leading Jewish persons in economic life would be injurious to
he continuity of production, and that was so, not only because
hey were indispensable, but also because the Magyar economic
experts capable of replacing them were unwilling to do so—a fact
o which the writer of the report drew the attention of the Ger-
nan circles concerned as "a typical symptom of sabotage." The
only solution offered was either to leave the Jews in their present
leading positions or—and this would be in effect the final and
necessary solution—to fill these leading positions with German
experts, as had happened in Rumania, where such men were acting as advisers.

Should any political questions come to be discussed, I asked
Horthy to lay all responsibility on my shoulders. If possible, however, the Regent was to avoid all argument, for he would never be
able to convince Hitler or get him to understand.

The first day of the Regent's visit was marked by stormy scenes.
Hitler declared that I was a political adventurer, enemy number
one of the German people, and he demanded my removal. To all
this the Regent, as he subsequently told me, replied that he had
been invited to discuss military and not political questions, or he
would have brought me with him. He was not competent to discuss these questions without his responsible premier, and he could
not go into the proferred accusations. Horthy declared, however,
once and for all, that just as he had never dreamed of trying to
influence Hitler or the German government in their choice of
ministers so he would accept no prompting, nor even the expression of a wish or an observation, that his premier, who enjoyed

his full confidence, should be replaced. To yield in the matter would be a violation of his oath, and the Hungarian premier was responsible to no one but the Regent and parliament. The first day's discussions ended on that note.

On the following day Hitler changed his tactics; he made no mention of the questions of the previous day. He came out instead with a demand that we should give him a new army against the Russians. He argued that the Rumanians had returned in full force to the fight, had called up all their age groups, and were thus fulfilling their obligations as allies.

Ribbentrop, for his part, brought out a *dossier* and tried to show Horthy various documents, primarily intercepted telegrams from British and American legations in neutral countries, which showed that members of the Hungarian legations had indirectly, and even directly, informed them that Hungary was not going to give a new army for the 1943 summer campaign.

The Regent refused to look at these documents, but accepted, and agreed to hand on to me, a note from Ribbentrop. It ran as follows:

April 16, 1943

For some months past the German government has received increasingly numerous reports that the present Hungarian cabinet, under the premiership of Herr von Kállay, has been observing a conduct which in the last resort is manifestly inspired by a defeatist point of view. Apparently Herr von Kállay has lost faith in the victory of the Axis powers, and as a result of this attitude of mind he permits political steps and machinations of which he cannot be ignorant and which aim at reducing to a minimum Hungary's participation in the war waged by the powers of the Tripartite pact, if they are not, in fact, designed to achieve contacts with the enemy with a view to preparing Hungary's withdrawal from the solid block of the powers of the Tripartite pact.

This attitude of the Kállay cabinet is reflected, for one thing, in the fact that, according to a whole series of perfectly reliable reports, an increasing number of Hungarian persons are traveling to neutral countries in order to establish contact with English and American personalities, on which occasions it is always asserted that the Hungarian people are in reality hostile to Germany and in addition convinced that the Axis powers are going to lose the war. The most notable moves in this direction are the journeys to Turkey of Andrew Frey, the editor of the Magyar Nemzet, and of Professors Julius Mészáros and Albert Szent-Györgyi.[1] The German government has learned from unimpeachable sources that these trips are designed to convey to English hands the information that the Hungarian government is resolved on no account to fight against British and American troops. Professor Szent-Györgyi went so far as to hand to an American middleman in Constantinople an exposé which actually offered the enemy military cooperation with England and America as soon as Germany was faced with a serious invasion. At that moment Hungary would open her frontiers to Allied troops.

Instead of categorically stopping such treasonable machinations by the most drastic measures, the Hungarian government has taken them passively and has even aided and abetted these journeys.

A further instance of Hungary's endeavors to establish contact with the enemy is furnished by the recent journey to Rome of the former Hungarian minister in London, von Barcza. According to reliable reports received by the German government, special efforts have been made to win over the Vatican for Hungary's peace aspirations, as a means of getting into touch with the enemy camp.

In other ways, too, the Kállay cabinet has evinced an endeavor

---

[1] Unlike the other persons named, Professor Szent-Györgyi had received no commission from me. Before his departure I discussed my policy with him, and I consented to his seeking contact with the Allies in order to enlighten them on our standpoint; but I entrusted him with no mission to enter into negotiations with them. I have the greatest respect for master scientists, but they are specialists only in their own field, and then, too, politics is not an exact science. I was not surprised when upon his return Szent-Györgyi talked of his far-reaching negotiations, for I had already received confidential reports from Constantinople which told me that his negotiations had been conducted with members of the German secret service. That was how Ribbentrop learned of them.

See Chapter Sixteen, "My Foreign Policy," for the details about our negotiations with the Western nations alluded to in the note and in this chapter.

to draw away from the Axis powers and to take as little part as possible in the actual fighting. As the German government has been reliably informed, Premier Kállay, on February 19 declared unambiguously in the foreign affairs committee of the Hungarian house of representatives that Hungary's participation in the war on Germany's side was confined to the quarrel with Soviet Russia; the quarrel between the Axis powers on the one hand and England and America on the other was no concern of hers.

That the reports received by the German government give a true picture of the Hungarian premier's sentiments has for the rest been confirmed by the Hungarian government's attitude towards the German legation in Budapest concerning various questions which have recently arisen. Thus the deputy head of the Hungarian ministry of foreign affairs,[2] when informed by the German legation of our wish that Hungary, in conformity with Germany and Italy, should break off her relations with Chile, took the standpoint that Hungary's adherence to the Tripartite pact placed no such obligation on her. Further, at the beginning of April, General Vörös, the head of the operational section of the Hungarian general staff, told the German air attaché in Budapest that the Hungarian air squadrons at present in France for training were on no account to be employed operationally, as they were designed only to be put in against Russia. This was a plain indication of the Hungarian government's desire not to be involved in any warlike action against England and America.

Furthermore, it is evident that the Kállay cabinet is at pains to reduce Hungary's share even in the war against Bolshevism, and to withdraw from participation in the war even in this field.

Finally, the whole attitude of the Kállay cabinet is characterized by the communications which the German government has received, not, as might be thought, from the Hungarian Opposition benches but from government circles, which tend to prove that the present composition of the Hungarian government precludes both a heightened war effort on Hungary's part and in-

[2] Eugene Ghyczy.

creased agricultural production. The cabinet shifts to and fro and pays court to our enemies.

The Regent definitely refused the request for a new army, as well as a further request that the one Hungarian division that was then guarding the railway lines should be ordered up into the front line. He argued that Hungary was in no position to send a fresh army beyond her frontiers. The Hungarian equipment was wholly inadequate: we had neither the uniforms, the arms, nor the motor vehicles for an expeditionary force. The annihilation of our Second Army on the Don, moreover, showed that, contrary to all promises, our men had been employed with insufficient equipment to perform tasks far beyond their strength. He would never again consent to see a hundred thousand Hungarian soldiers wantonly destroyed, without benefit to their own country or even to their German allies.

The case of the Rumanians was wholly different, the Regent said, because they nourished the secret hope of one day using the army which they were setting up with German assistance and German arms to attack Hungary. That was a consideration of which we could not lose sight.

Thus all Hitler's requests were rebutted. The German leader begged, however, that, in order to neutralize the effect of my extremely ambiguous speeches, he and Horthy should issue a joint declaration which would show the world that Hungary had no intention of cutting adrift from the Axis powers but that she was rather standing squarely by their side.

The Regent agreed to that, approved the text of the communique, as shown to him, and traveled back to Hungary. During Horthy's return journey, the German telegraphic agency asked our agency to publish in Hungary a communique on the results of the meeting, which had already been issued to the German press. The text as submitted to us ran as follows:

The Führer and the Regent gave expression to their determined resolve to continue the war against Bolshevism and its British and American Allies till the final victory. . . . The Hungarian nation will mobilize its forces to the last man for the liberation of Europe and the security of the Magyar people. . . .

Ullein-Reviczky, chief of the press department in the foreign ministry, rushed to me in despair with this text. I forbade its publication until the return of the Regent, and I got in touch with Horthy as soon as he arrived. He told me that the communique had been shown him but that he had not signed it because the understanding was that we should issue one in similar terms on our own account that would not contain any mention of the English and the Americans.

I naturally acted accordingly, with the result that the communique appeared in Hungary one day later and without any reference to the English and Americans. It may readily be imagined that this not only caused some stir at home—and what indignation in Germany!—but also roused a certain amount of interest abroad. Once again the Germans had mismanaged their affairs. Had they refrained from smuggling the reference to the English and Americans into the text of the communique, they would have got a more or less reassuring declaration. Furthermore, it would not have been made manifest that in point of fact the Hungarians did not consider themselves to be at war with the Anglo-Saxons, did not look on them as enemies, and categorically refused to subscribe to any declaration placing them on that footing.

The reaction in Germany was immense. Telegrams, telephone messages, special couriers, and planes flew back and forth between Berlin and Budapest. Finally, Jagow, the German minister in Budapest, made a démarche to Ghyczy, my deputy in the ministry of foreign affairs, demanding an explanation. We answered that we could not undertake to publish a declaration which had not been approved by the Regent—apart from which, it was by no means to Hungary's interest unnecessarily and senselessly to affront the Anglo-American powers, with whom we had so far not been involved in any warlike action.

The matter had, however, its political consequences at home.

A busy traffic started and grew between the German legation and numerous members of the right-wing Opposition. I was able to ascertain that Béla Imrédy, Andrew Jaross, and Francis Rajniss of the Rejuvenation party and Gabriel Vajna, Ladislas Baky, and several others of the Arrow Cross group, called at the German legation or met in other places. They tried to voice their views in their own press, but I stopped them mercilessly through the censorship. All the more violent were the attacks leveled at me in the foreign affairs committee of the lower house, where those gentlemen were becoming very daring and aggressive.

The foreign affairs committee, unlike the other committees and plenary sessions of the lower house, met in secret, and its members were bound by oath not to divulge its proceedings. But I was dismayed to find that the members of the German legation, and even the German press reporters, had full knowledge of all that went on. I even obtained palpable proof of this in a very amusing way. A journalist member of the Croatian legation managed to steal from the pocket of the German press attaché the written report of a member of the foreign affairs committee, and it was passed on to us by a member of the Croatian legation. The writer of the report was Ladislas Baky. I read the stolen document aloud in the foreign affairs committee, without mentioning the author's name, for I had no legal proof. But I declared that I would not tolerate having my parliamentary work obstructed by traitors, and if in future the foreign affairs committee was not informed as fully as it should be of what was going on, the responsibility would not be mine. The whole case made a most painful impression on me. It was a blow to my idealism, for what had happened was treachery and that was an unusual, even an unknown, thing with us.

A session with the foreign affairs committee of the lower house was always followed by one with the corresponding committee of the upper house. The committee in the upper house was very different both in composition and quality. Its chairman was the excellent old diplomat Kalman Kánya, and its members were se-

lected from among the highest secular and ecclesiastical dignitaries. Stephen Bethlen was its intellectual leader. It was a joy
to participate in the debates of that committee; the high standard
of the speeches, the freedom from party politics, and in particular
the understanding which my policy met with there were refreshing
after the sessions of the lower house committee. In the upper
house I could be much franker about my policy and my intentions.
I could be absolutely sure of secrecy. It was certain that in this
company there was no informer carrying tales to the Germans.
The entire membership of the committee was anti-German or,
as they called it at the time, Anglo-Saxon in its sympathies. The
committee was sharply opposed to any trespassing into politics by
the army, and its members showed no trace of anti-Semitism. It
is a curious phenomenon that this body, composed partly of indirectly elected and partly of nominated members, should have
been more representative of the country's mentality and incomparably more aware of its true interests than the deputies in parliament elected by ballot on the basis of a wide suffrage. The foreign affairs committee in the upper house represented the continuity of the national idea, whereas the mind and policy of the
representatives in the lower house were dominated by the currents,
catchwords, and party prejudices of the day.

Stephen Bethlen, George Prónay, Ladislas Ravasz, Anthony
Sigray, Chrisostom Kelemen, the archabbot of Pannonhalma, and
many of the younger men of the foreign affairs committee of the
upper house openly expressed the view that the country did not
want war, had no wish to fight on the side of the Germans, and was
not in a position to accept material and economic exploitation by
Germany. And they were opposed to all anti-Semitic measures
Several Jews, or baptized Jews, belonged to the foreign affairs
committee of the upper house and took an active part in its de
bates.

Mention may be made of the violent reaction evoked among
the Germans and their partisans in Hungary when, after Fran
cis Chorin's mandate as chairman of the National Federation o

Manufacturers had expired, the Regent seized upon the first vacancy to appoint Chorin as one of the fifty members of the upper house that the Regent was entitled to nominate.

After the Regent had refused to furnish more soldiers or to let Hungary participate in a fresh offensive against Russia, at least so far as front-line action went, there was a period of calm. But it did not last long. A few weeks later the Germans announced that, since we had refused to take part in the 1943 summer offensive they were mounting against the Russians, they were forced to withdraw three divisions from the Balkans. If we said that the Hungarian army was not fit for front-line service, or for other reasons was disinclined for it, they would concede the point. There could, however, be no obstacle to our replacing the divisions which had been withdrawn from the Balkans: That would involve no act of aggression towards any side; in fact, there was every reason to assume that the Serbs themselves would be well content if the German troops were replaced by Hungarians; and so forth went the German reasoning. We were to take over the control, with three divisions, of the territory stretching from the Danube to the regions occupied by the Bulgarians. The Germans were prepared to equip fully, not only these three divisions, but also a further two, in order that we should be in no anxiety concerning the battle fitness of our home army. Our army command, with the exception of William Nagy, the minister of defense, would have accepted that offer with joy; all that mattered to them was that the deficiencies in the equipment of the army should be remedied.

I rejected the proposal, however, without a moment's hesitation. Such a step would have meant a complete reversal of my whole policy: our army would have moved outside the country's frontiers; our relations with the Serb nation would inevitably have been aggravated; and we would have come into armed conflict with the Serb partisans. All that would have occurred, moreover, at a time when I had already established contact with the Serb partisans and had even aided them with gifts of war material (not arms). My refusal evoked no visible reaction from the Germans.

The minister of defense, William Nagy, an army general who had been recalled from retirement to take over his post, had before his appointment been chairman of a small industrial concern that had been formed with Jewish capital. He naturally resigned from the business on accepting office. He made the mistake, however, of allowing his brother to be put in his place, thereby making it appear as though Nagy's ties with the concern still continued. Such a lapse had never happened before in Hungarian public life; we were meticulously careful about that sort of thing. Nagy, apparently, had a soldier's disregard for appearances. But a right-wing member of the Opposition gave notice that he was going to ask a question on the matter.

A supplementary question in the inquiry, I learned, would ask the government to range itself openly by Germany's side in the military field as in its internal and external policy and to place every assistance and support at her service. I was to be asked to offer Germany a million Hungarian soldiers. A third question would demand that the Premier should openly condemn those endeavors and factions which, under the collective title of "Peace Party," were trying to disrupt Germany's and our own common struggle and to destroy the national morale. Furthermore, information would have been asked on the rumors current that certain of our diplomats had established contact with the Anglo-American powers. Yet another aim of the projected inquiry was to question the policy of Ullein-Reviczky, the chief of the press section of the foreign ministry, and his connections with the enemy press.

I invited Imrédy as the intellectual leader of the right-wing Opposition to see me—I did not think it worth my while to deal with the Arrow Cross crowd, knowing it to be intractable. After frankly explaining to Imrédy both the military and the political situation, I appealed to his honor and his conscience as a patriot to stop these questions from being put. I told him that I foresaw the utmost danger for the country if they came to be debated. I said that the whole thing had only one purpose, to discredit my policy in the eyes of the Germans and to put the Regent in a difficult position. He replied that it was in fact the intention of his supporters to bring matters to an issue. The only policy open to Hungary was, he said, to range herself by Germany's side: to conquer or to fall with her.

Imrédy thought a complete defeat for Germany to be an impossibility. The Germans would have a voice when peace was concluded, and if we could not count on them when that time came, we should be left without a single friend. But he still had faith in a German victory, and our conversation had helped to convince him that, in view of my pessimistic outlook, I could not be allowed to remain in office; I must yield my place to someone who possessed the confidence of the Germans. If I resigned, the Regent could not refuse to appoint as premier someone acceptable to the right section of Hungarian public opinion and to the Germans. Imrédy was sorry to have to take his attitude; he would be pleased to see me at the head of the government if I were willing to co-operate with the right. They themselves had no personal ambitions of any kind, but it was necessary to form a unified right party, eliminating the left elements in my own party. Afterwards a new general election should secure the power by an immense, sweeping right-wing drive.

Thus all my hopes of solving the parliamentary situation in a peaceful manner were frustrated. Imrédy's remarks about my person did not interest me; for, as I told him, I could in no circumstances leave my post, and his group had not the slightest chance of evicting me. They would never succeed in inciting public opinion against me. The majority of my party stood loyally behind me. And as for the Regent's dropping me, not even the much-vaunted German pressure, let alone the influence of the Hungarian right, could achieve this object. Thus the alternatives open to me were: either I could accept the challenge or I could withdraw and prevent a conflict from arising. The outcome or issue of a parliamentary battle, should one arise, was not in doubt, but it would have been extremely dangerous and unpleasant. It would have incited the Germans against the country, and would have suggested that it was my policy which stood in the way of our friendship with Germany or rather of our unconditional subservience to her interests. A parliamentary battle at that juncture would, moreover, have endangered my foreign political activities, which at that moment seemed to be nearing fruition.

I decided to prevent the conflict from being aired in parliament. Once again I confided my resolve to no one but Keresztes-Fischer, my minister of the interior. Then I proposed to the Regent that he should prorogue parliament. By this means I would prevent the putting of the questions, and I would be able to examine the case of the minister of defense, on which I myself was not quite clear, and, incidentally, to make it impossible for such charges to be leveled against a minister of defense in wartime. I should also ward off the airing of the other questions and gain a breathing spell, with the hope that a few weeks would see me safely through the crisis.

The prorogation of parliament is a fundamental right of the head of the state, secured to him by law, qualified only by another provision under which fifty members of parliament may demand the convocation of the legislative body. The Regent accepted my proposal, although he would have recommended a more drastic measure. His soldier's mind envisaged having these men arraigned for antinational activities, and he was certain that they would have been convicted in a court of law.

Wednesday afternoon was the customary day for questions. Immediately before the ordinary morning session on that day, I called an extraordinary ministerial council in my official rooms in the lower house. I described the situation to those assembled and announced the Regent's decision. Then, when the speaker opened the session, I handed him the Regent's rescript.

The perturbation in the right-wing benches was intense. My own party also was taken aback, for even its chairman had only been informed at the last moment, when he could no longer communicate with his fellow members. His shout of "Long live the

Regent!" taken up on our side drowned the hesitant voices of he Opposition, and meanwhile the speaker closed the session.[3]

Thus I arrived where I never thought to arrive: I was forced to govern without a parliament. All my endeavors were centered on restoring the possibility of parliamentary life. Until I was able o reconvene parliament, I had every important measure debated by the so-called Committee of Forty-two,[4] and I naturally kept in all things within the prescribed limits of the Enabling act.

There was, in any case, no urgent legislative work to be done, although I should have been glad to get a few bills of a social nature debated, primarily one on the insurance of agricultural laborers, similar to that already existing for industrial workers. Then, too, the bill for industrial workers needed amendment and extension. In other respects, however, it was perhaps just as well that parliamentary activity should have been suspended for a while. In the prevailing—comprehensible and excusable—war-time tension, and our peculiarly delicate situation, almost every speech, whether emanating from the Opposition or from my own party, contained something which would have been better left unsaid.

The left-wing Opposition, and its acknowledged leader, Charles Rassay, received my decision with understanding, and Rassay called on me to assure me of the fact.

There was no comment or reaction from Germany. All that the German deputy foreign minister said to Sztójay, our minister in Berlin, was: "Mr. Kállay seems to be a clever tactician."

It was in those days that my tentative approaches towards the Allies began to show concrete results. Our ministers in neutral capitals, and more especially my confidential agents in Constantinople, succeeded in making some valuable contacts. There was

---

[3] This prorogation of parliament occurred on May 6, 1943.
[4] Parliament delegated a committee of forty-two members, drawn from all parties, to exercise control over the government's actions during the suspension of sessions of parliament and to issue ordinances of a nonconstitutional nature. So far as I know, we were the only country in which an endeavor was made to secure parliamentary government even during the suspension of parliamentary sessions.

every prospect that I should be able to consolidate these links and start negotiations between Hungary and the agents of the Allies. The gist of these conversations, as described in the report which reached me, was that, while Hungary's fair dealings with the Allies in word and deed were acknowledged, and it was considered particularly significant that we had never once fired on Allied aircraft and that we had helped the Poles to escape to the army in Syria, it was, nevertheless, thought desirable that we should make a public and decisive declaration that we would put no more troops into the conflict on Germany's side and that we did not wish to make ourselves part of the German sphere of interest.

Parliament having been prorogued, some time had elapsed since I had made any public pronouncement. Thus I had given no account of the military situation following on the reverses on the Don and had offered no personal explanation to the country of why I had to prorogue parliament. I therefore convened a big Government party rally in Budapest on May 29, 1943. To such a meeting, with an audience several thousand strong and including, of course, members of parliament and the leaders of the various parties, I could render account almost as officially as if in parliament.

I spoke first about the military situation. I then went on to explain that the prorogation of parliament had been necessary in order to save parliamentarism, to prevent persons who in any case were ideologically disbelievers in the parliamentary principle from disturbing the peaceful working of parliament. When I came to my statement on our foreign policy, I picked my words very cautiously. Nevertheless, I made decisive declarations on every point on which the Allies had asked for a declaration: that we would give no more soldiers; that we would not get swept away by ideological torrents; that our destinies were identical with those of Europe; and that we refused to be drawn into any sphere of interest. My actual words were as follows:

A country's foreign policy, like every other policy, rests in the last resort on its people's spirit of self-sacrifice, for in elemental crises it is impossible to live without sacrifices. But there is a limit beyond which sacrifice cannot go, for it is not an end in itself: the end is the interests of the nation. I have never lost sight of this fundamental standpoint, and consequently will undertake only such sacrifices as are proportionate to the nation's strength.

Another characteristic of Hungary's foreign policy is its solidarity with Europe. We are a European people, a faithful member nation of this Continent, a nation which in the course of its grand and tragic history has been a cradle of Christian culture and an outpost of human progress. It was this European consciousness, this European sense of obligation which set us, in 1941, to fight the Bolshevist aggression and menace, this which armed us to defend all that was valuable in our eyes. We are fighting a defensive war. We have no other interest than to live in peace within our frontiers as one of those independent nations which wish to work for the great aims of human progress within the framework of their own traditions, their own institutions and forms of life.

In recent times we have heard a good deal about the unfitness for life of small nations—it would seem that they have no right to live at all except in the shadow of some big nation, drawn into spheres of interest, always deferring to the wishes of the stronger and more powerful. Hungary will have none of this.

In the further course of my speech I went through the whole gamut of our current problems. On the Jewish question I once again made it clear that Hungary would never permit herself, any more than in the past, experiments irreconcilable with her Christian culture and morality, nor deviate from those humane principles which she has practiced throughout her history in racial and denominational questions.

I was surprised myself at the effect of this speech. The whole of Hungarian public opinion—except, of course, the extreme right —received it with extraordinary approval, and regarded it thereafter as a compendium and charter of Hungarian internal and external policy and of Hungarian aims.

Still more interesting was the effect of the speech abroad, although, as I have said, and as may be seen from the quotations, I had picked my words with extreme caution. The press, not only of the neutral countries, but also of the Western belligerents and America dealt with it in detail, commenting on it as a declaration of nonbelligerency and concluding that Hungary's policy had turned clean about. A member of the American legation in Berne personally translated the speech for the benefit of President Roosevelt; and it was not long before my entire speech appeared in English, French, and Italian.

The leading figures of Hungarian politics, among them Stephen Bethlen, Kalman Kánya, Charles Rassay, and Andrew Bajcsy-Zsilinszky, came to see me one by one to express their appreciation and satisfaction. In the German press, on the other hand, there appeared not a word, not even the fact that I had spoken.

I thought that the period of parliament's suspension was the right time to make a comprehensive survey of the entire body of our social legislation up to that time and to elaborate and prepare for parliamentary debate such bills as the future would necessitate. Most of these had already been drafted in the respective ministries, and I wished to lay them before the lower house before the end of the war, if possible that same year.

The prorogation of parliament prevented my laying new bills before it, but it did not prevent my gathering the existing legislation into one voluminous codex and having those still in preparation completed. This was done. Later, when writing of that autumn's legislative work, I shall refer to these at greater length; here I shall only mention that I outlined my ideas in regard to my new agrarian policy in a speech at Szeged on June 27, 1943.

In 1939 Hungary had adopted an agrarian law fixing the maximum arable land to be possessed by one private person at 250 hectares, which would have meant the transference of more than half of the arable big estates still in private ownership into the hands of small landowners in allotments of five to ten hectares.

Because of the war and because our army, and with it the greater part of our younger agricultural population, was at the front, this law had not been carried out. At first I myself was of the opinion that it would be better to defer its execution till after the war. I did not wish it to cause unrest among the soldiers at the front who might fear that they would be overlooked at the distribution, and I feared it might impair production at home.

I became increasingly convinced, however, that the matter could not be put off any longer. My former fears were lessened, partly because by now we had comparatively few men at the front, and I was not anxious about the fighting spirit of our soldiers because they were only serving behind the lines. The problem of production also influenced me less than it had done; for if the law were carried out gradually, the incidental drawbacks could be eliminated. Then, too, our surplus had in any case to be given up to the Germans.

I prepared a new act, amending the existing one and extending its scope to cover ecclesiastical and municipal as well as state property, although I did not propose the complete abolition of these. The result would have been to turn exactly 90 per cent of the country's arable land into small farms of less than 50 hectares. The owners would have been indemnified by receiving bonds to the full value of the expropriated land, issued by a bank set up for the purpose. The bonds would yield no interest, but the recipients of land would amortize the bonds at the rate of 4 per cent per annum. It would have been a sort of purchase on the installment system, on the same lines as the still more radical bill which I had prepared in 1934, when I was minister of agriculture. I did not mean to ruin the old landlords, nor to throw to the new owners a piece of land unprovided with equipment or capital. What I wanted was to create genuinely viable small subsistences. The indemnification of the old landlords appeared to me necessary; even though rudely deprived of their accustomed living standards, they must still be able to enjoy a certain income, sufficient to maintain their families and educate their children for new professions. The bank would have advanced them the value of the bonds, but only if they were prepared to invest the money in the land left to them.

Forest properties I did not intend to touch, for these were best managed in private hands, and partitioning them into allotments would have meant destroying them. In any case, state control in this respect was so strict that not a tree could be felled without a government permit.[5]

I quote here some passages from my Szeged speech, in which I described my plans for agricultural reforms:

The primary task and the destiny of the Hungarian soil is to give bread and subsistence to everyone in this country, to produce as much, and of as good a quality, as possible. The second requirement is that it should be in the possession of those best qualified and most capable of producing good results. Law XV of 1942[6] has brought us nearer to this. In the future, as in the past, I shall aim at the total national good, not that of individuals, and I shall pursue an agricultural policy which insures that the country is fed and that the worker on the land can subsist.

I consider that the time has come for a calm, wise, and sane transfer of the land, under the proper conditions, into the most suitable hands. Not all can have land, because there is not enough to go round, and because to tie anyone down to an allotment so small that it cannot yield him a livelihood would be the most antisocial and reckless of policies, only good to serve the purposes of demagogy. The function of the land is not solely to draw sweat from the laborer; it must also give better and more abundant food to the entire community. The cultivation of the soil is a vocation which entails obligation, but not only obligations; it also confers

[5] The Forestry act, also drawn up during my term of office as minister of agriculture, was subsequently acknowledged by the International Forestry Congress held in Berlin to be the most up-to-date of its kind in the world, and it was commended as an example to every state.

[6] The act expropriating Jewish landed property (see p. 71). Laws reaching the statute book in Hungary are thereafter officially described by a serial number and the year of enactment.

the right to an adequate livelihood. This must be the basis of all our measures and decisions in future.

The reference to Law XV of 1942 roused some animadversion among the big landowners, who, in other respects, were well-disposed towards me. It seemed to them to foreshadow the total expropriation of all landed property and to justify the anxiety which they had expressed when it was passed that it would prove impossible to stop at the Jewish estates and that all landed property would meet with the same fate.

Once again the nation was preparing to celebrate St. Stephen's day. The Regent, whose son had been killed on that day twelve months before, took no part in the celebrations. I represented him and led the procession.

On the preceding day I broadcast a message to the country. I shall quote parts of it because it was mentioned in a very friendly and approving spirit, not only in the neutral, but also in the Anglo-Saxon press. On the other hand, it was interesting to observe the fury with which some English and American papers—without exception such as were influenced by Benes—attacked this speech, although it was purely concerned with our festival and had nothing in it of either a political or polemical nature.

On St. Stephen's Day we celebrate Hungarian unity. The nation stands as one man behind the country's Regent—today he is the symbol of Hungarian concord, strength, faith, and loyalty.

Look around you in our country in this fourth year of the terrible world conflagration. Here everyone has the same desire: to insure the existence, destiny, and future of the nation and of every loyal son of the nation.

This nation is working as it never worked before. Every acre of land is cultivated. The country cottages are kept in good repair; never have so many new cottages been built. The factories are working full blast. And it is for ourselves that we work, for the arduous today and for the Hungarian tomorrow.

It is said, nevertheless, that there are parties, both in parliament and outside it. Of course there are, and all the better! I have no wish to put Hungarians into uniforms—it is their souls that I want to unify. They must never become slaves, but they must be ready to sacrifice all in the service of the country and the nation. It is the unity of souls that I preach, not that of externals. This is what I trust and believe in, and I know that this is how it should be.

Because of this faith I can shoulder the task which destiny has assigned me. Because of it and with it. For without it all is vain. If there is to be order in the land there must be order in the souls.

With this faith our people and our nation stand or fall. It was never from outside that enemies, destruction, or assistance came to us. We are answerable for ourselves.

Around us all is still aflame. Never before has the world seen such flaming pyres. It is not we who lit them, and it is not in our power to put them out. But if we guard our own homes, if we keep watch and do not give way to panic, the fires will burn themselves out without setting light to our little cottage; and we may be able to help in putting out the embers of the burning world.

A mission awaits us—the mission to work for justice, peace, regeneration, and the maintenance of order. To this end we must have at home tranquillity, discipline, and a strong army; and abroad, the understanding of friends unswayed by prejudice and passion. Both these things depend on us. Internal order and the strength of our army will gain us friends—there is no other way to gain them. This will be the triumph of Hungarian justice.

My grave and resolute words were received with much approbation at home as well as abroad. All the more surprising and painful—painful as only a blow can be which comes from a quarter on which every hope, every aim and ideal is fixed—was the response which came over the radio from America. Who inspired it I cannot tell. But I am certain that the message transmitted next day as THE VOICE OF AMERICA emanated neither from the American people nor from the American Government. I shall quote first a message received a month before my speech—and about a week after the Allied landing in Sicily—and then the message that followed my speech.

London, July 16, 1943. From the Hungarian transmission of 12:15 A.M. [Once again the British are threatening bombing raids. In his introduction, the speaker pointed out that as a result of the Allied advance in Sicily, the Allied bombers have come much nearer to Central Europe and thus also to Hungary.]

The Hungarian authorities are well aware that the Allies can easily reach Hungary from the Sicilian air fields. It means that sooner or later a devastating rain of bombs may descend on Hungary's military and industrial centers and buildings.

The Hungarian people must act, and act quickly, for if they do not, if they continue to tolerate their masters' subservience to Germany, then their towns and factories, built with the sweat of their brow and untold sacrifices, will shortly lie in ruins.

There is only one way for the Hungarian people to escape further fruitless sacrifices: they must without delay dismiss the ruling government. They must realize that the present regime, for all its false promises and surreptitious attempts, is driving Hungary into catastrophe.

The regime is endeavoring by various underhanded methods to mislead public opinion in Hungary and abroad. It tried to do this in the past, and now thinks to hoodwink the Hungarian workers by appropriating the program and aims of the so-called Popular Front.

But it is not so easy to mislead the Hungarian workers, peasants, and intellectuals.

Let the Hungarian people expect no salvation from outside. The Hungarian people can only save themselves by their own efforts, by liquidating all those political factors which are driving it to perdition. They must without delay get rid of all those Hungarian factors who have made Hungarian economic life and industry completely subservient to Germany.

In this fateful hour we can say with conviction that it is no idle talk if we declare that the end of this regime is drawing near.

London, August 24, 1943, Hungarian transmission, 7:45 P.M.
Hungarians, your leaders, who revel in Nazi catchwords, have

joined in the Hitlerian pastime of throwing dust in the eyes of the people. They make it appear as though they were doing all in their power to save what can still be saved [passage unintelligible]. Recently your Quisling Kállay declared that it was not you who lit the fires. Kállay, who is responsible for all your sufferings, is not ashamed to lie to you that his policy will defend you against the mortal wounds caused by the war. But how will Kállay or Stephen Antal protect you from the bombs? [Unintelligible.]

Hungarians, listen to the words of wisdom! All that your leaders, who have cheated you innumerable times, will achieve by their policy is to hurl you into the bottomless abyss of horrible catastrophe.

Attention! This was the Voice of America calling to you, Hungarians. Listen to our messages, and spread them among your friends, always and everywhere!

TEN

THE FALL OF MUSSOLINI

˹THE MOST critical period for our foreign policy was during the
˻veeks when Mussolini fell out of power and then later, after his
˼escue by the Germans, when he announced the establishment
˻f the North Italian Fascist Peoples Republic. At home and abroad
˼ny decision was awaited with cries of "hic Rhodos hic salta."
˼ur American and British friends, but also our enemies, were
˼emarkably unanimous in their concern about our future course.

My whole policy within the Axis, like that of Paul Teleki be-
˼ore me, had rested on Mussolini and Italy. In the past this policy
˼ad been—as I have explained in detail elsewhere [1]—largely re-
˻ponsible for our being dragged into the German sphere of in-
˼luence. After the fall of Austria, Teleki had gone so far as to

[1] See pages 55, 62, 152–54.

think that every means must be employed to draw our relations with Italy closer. There was ample basis for this attempt in the great mutual sympathy that prevailed between the two peoples. This attraction derived from the historic past, when it had a cultural and psychological basis, and then it had been reinforced by strong economic reasons. The principal reasons behind Teleki's endeavors, however, after the expansion of Germany's power, were political. Teleki did not stop at theory but tried actually to link Italy with our interests. We know from Ciano's diary that Teleki inquired whether it would be possible for an Italian prince to occupy the Hungarian throne: Teleki hoped that this would assure the nation's independence and defend it against Germany. Our Treaty of Friendship with Yugoslavia in March, 1941, was concluded with Mussolini's knowledge and behind Hitler's back. Twice Teleki left vital decisions to Mussolini: once in 1940 when he sent Baranyai to Italy to go with Frederic Villani, our minister to the Quirinal, to say that if Mussolini would back him up, Teleki would reject Rumania's request (which Germany, of course, was supporting) for instructional troops to be allowed passage across Hungary; and again, in even more emphatic form, Mussolini was consulted when the war against Yugoslavia was breaking out in April, 1941. Unfortunately, in each case Mussolini returned refusals, saying flatly that we could not count on him and advising us to do what Germany asked.

Committed as Mussolini was to the German line, I yet hoped that a position might arise when he himself would look for a way out. Even after my conversation with him I did not regard Mussolini's withdrawal from the war as impossible, although the propaganda campaign of the Allies against his person and system was (justifiably enough) growing more vigorous. It would not have been morally impossible for the Allies to come to terms with him; if they were able to co-operate with Stalin, they certainly could have with Mussolini. In any event, Mussolini was until then our only possible support against Hitler in all our problems, and I was sure that Italy would find a way out of the war, with Mussolini or without him, and that we would be able to accompany her in that withdrawal.

That was the situation on July 25, 1943, when the news of Mussolini's fall and arrest reached us. Ever since my return from Rome I had somehow expected something of the sort, although I thought a military *putsch* more likely than a revolt among his own creatures and adherents.

The Badoglio solution was a half measure. The Marshal could not win the full confidence of the Allies, and he put nothing into the place of the vanished Fascist system. We naturally at once communicated with the new regime, and agreement was quickly reached between its excellent foreign minister, Raffaele Guariglia, and Apor, our minister to the Vatican, that the relationship between the two countries remained unchanged and that we would give each other mutual support in seeking a way out. The King's and Badoglio's declaration of loyalty to the Germans was a surprise to me. I knew that for them it was only a step to gain time, but for us it meant a loss of time and opportunity. The Germans were able to make their preparations against the Italians and against us also. If Badoglio had turned against the Germans at once, large Allied forces would have been there on Italian territory. The Italian army itself greatly outnumbered the *Wehrmacht* contingent in the country, and in such a situation we might have had a chance to make the *volte face*. The *Wehrmacht* tied down in Italy and quite unprepared in the Danube Basin, the Rumanian troops far from the Hungarian frontier, and, most important of all, the Russians not yet recovered from their earlier losses and not yet threatening us—in such a situation we should have had every chance.

It is the world's pity that this did not happen. As things were, we had no possibility of acting. The great moment for our country again slipped from our hands by a nuance, never to return.

I had been ready for it. I had talked over the whole situation with Foreign Minister Ghyczy and Keresztes-Fischer, minister of the interior. When I saw that their views of the situation, and

of our proper policy, were the same as my own, I brought Louis
Csatay, who had replaced William Nagy as minister of defense,
and, a little later, Francis Szombathelyi, the chief of staff, into
the conversations. The dominant feeling in the two soldiers' minds
was at first that of loyalty towards our ally, and I could not take
this ill of them. I managed to convince them, however, that
the supreme *lex*, the national interest, called for bold decisions.
They were anxious for the fate of the sixty to seventy thousand
men we had left on the German lines of communication, on
whom the Germans might revenge themselves. Subsequently
sealed orders against such an event were taken out to the troops by
a trustworthy courier. Finally they assured me officially that if the
Regent gave the order, the army would obey it. They cautioned
me, however, against overhasty action and against overestimating
the strength of Italy's resistance and warned me that the Allies
did not at the moment appear strong enough in the south to
invade Italy successfully. I remember Szombathelyi's words: "The
Italian people and their leaders have the courage to surrender, to
look the consequences, however serious, in the face; but they have
not the military devotion to fight." And so it was. Eisenhower's
appeal to them to turn against the Germans, and his offer of help,
which he issued four days later, went unheeded. The Italians did
not stir, nor did any other move occur which would have enabled
us to take action.

We got, however, information that under the cover of reports
to the contrary, which were put out to lull the Germans' sus-
picions, the Italians were discussing unconditional surrender. I
inquired of Guariglia, the Italian foreign minister, who replied
in the negative. To our minister's question whether it would be
possible for Hungary to be included in such case, the Italian foreign minister replied that he could answer only if the case arose.

I naturally kept the Regent constantly informed. His own point
of view, as always, was correct: it was that our relationship with
the Italian dynasty and people had not been changed by the

events. One might regret or one might be pleased at the fall of Mussolini, but the event did not affect the big questions. When I said that we might have to prepare for great decisions, Horthy said that he would do what the country's interests enjoined. There was, in fact, only one thing that he would not do: he would not stab the Germans treacherously in the back. Before taking any step he would inform Hitler. He would give notice that our co-operation was at an end, and he would, if need be, declare war. But, he repeated, he would not stab the Germans in the back.

This declaration from the Regent was quite enough for me. It left me a free hand to prepare the ground for a decision, and I began, most cautiously, to take my diplomatic steps towards the Allies [2] and to prepare public opinion at home. Szombathelyi's and Csatay's declarations proved that the army was not irrevocably hostile.

Our ministers abroad sent in mutually contradictory reports and suggestions. Some of them tried at all costs to get me to forget my hesitations; others advised me to be cautious, but to move gradually away from the Germans. The demand for radical action was not unanimous, and still there was no word of what would happen afterwards if we did move.

Nothing much came at that moment from the Germans or from Sztójay. The Italian legation was, at least outwardly, the quietest of all, but we heard that inside the legation a Latin civil war was raging. Anfuso officially passed on Badoglio's declaration of capitulation,[3] but we did not know what Anfuso's personal attitude was. When Szentmiklóssy congratulated him on Italy's decision, Anfuso did not react. His whole attitude was reserved, but the gen-

---

[2] See Chapter Sixteen, "My Foreign Policy," for the details about our negotiations with Allies alluded to in this chapter.

[3] On September 3, 1943, Badoglio signed a secret armistice with the Allies calling for unconditional surrender, but the formal announcement was held up until September 8, when the Allies landed at Salerno. The Italian government did not declare war against Germany until October 13, after the capture of Naples and the stabilization of the front along the Volturno River.

eral impression was that neither he nor his staff were drawing the consequences; they would remain at their posts.

Immediately after Italy's surrender I convened a ministerial council and announced that all agreements which bound us to the Italo-German Axis had, by Italy's act, become automatically non-operative. Hungary had recovered her moral freedom, and her policy would now be determined exclusively by her own needs and decisions.

My declaration was received in deathly silence. Keresztes-Fischer remarked: "Of course." Bánffy asked: "And what do we do?"

I answered Bánffy: "We act at the appropriate moment as our interests demand; pending this, our policy remains static."

It was true that we had already broken from the Axis in our souls and our political sympathies, and now any formal obligation also had ceased. With Italy leaving the Axis, the structure to which we had adhered had been weakened by the removal of the pillar on which we rested. Now, therefore, no moral or legal obligation bound us to the old alliance. The legal situation was, indeed, not quite so simple as that, but by and large the thesis was undeniably plausible.

Our British and American advisers—almost without exception —urged us to break away from the Axis. They said that this was the moment when Hungary must make her vital decision—to be or not to be independent; that decision would be the touchstone by which she would or would not win the good will of the Allies. It would be enormously important from the strategic, political, and propaganda standpoints if, following Italy's secession, that member of the German bloc which had succeeded even better than Italy in keeping its military, political, and economic independence, the one state on whose territory there were no German soldiers, immediately broke away and defied the Germans in the heart of their own sphere. That would really have created the appearance that the whole system was collapsing—but alas! only the appearance. The real consequences would have been different.

Let us first consider the point of view of the Western nations. The Allies saw only the obvious facts. There was no need to go deeply into the question. A glance at the map showed that Hungary was a transit and supply area of the first order for Germany. It was not generally known how much resistance we had put up to the Germans in this area, how many difficulties and delays we had made for them.[4] Perhaps the Western nations did not believe our accounts. We were undeniably contributing with our agricultural and industrial production to the German war potential, and even giving them certain military assistance. I may say at once that if our defection would have brought the cessation or even the diminution of this assistance, it would have been my duty immediately to fulfill the wishes of the Allies, and they would have been entitled to take my refusal as a hostile act.

The real situation was not what it appeared to be, however. The Hungarian forces in the East were serving behind the lines, not at the front; only 10 per cent of them were under the command of the Wehrmacht.[5] Economically, we were not giving Germany half of what we could have given her. Our oil and our transport were used for nonmilitary purposes, and our trains were running on the prewar time tables. One may mention, too, the freedom in our foreign and domestic policies and the unexampled position enjoyed by our Opposition parties, the Jews, the press, and our refugees.

Italy, after her surrender, did not tie down any important part of the Wehrmacht. She did not join the Allies in any serious attack on the Germans. We had no agreement with the Allies, no prospect of immediate help, not even any concrete promise regarding our future. In those circumstances we could at most have taken the negative step of ceasing to be Germany's allies. The consequences would have been catastrophic, but it could have been done. The positive step of turning against them was the ultimate goal of our policy, but unfortunately it was not possi-

[4] See Chapter Thirteen, "Our Economic Policy."
[5] See Chapter Fourteen, "The Military Withdrawal, 1943–44."

ble then, nor, alas, later (not at any rate in the direction we wanted, that is, towards the British and Americans).

The Allies were on Italian soil. After the surrender of Africa Italy had lain outside the zone of the great German military operations. Italy's geographical situation was quite different from ours; Italy's size, its inaccessibility, and the presence of Allied troops there made the occupation of it by the Germans an impossibility. The Germans might try to defend Italy, which would tie down certain military units there, but they could not occupy it. Or the Germans might give up Italy, which would be a factor in their collapse, but not from the military point of view. Militarily, withdrawal from Italy would even bring the Germans a momentary advantage by shortening their line.

Hungary, however, lay at the focal point of Germany's military operations, on the roads both to Russia and to the Balkans.[6] There was no doubt that the Germans would have to assure their hold on Hungary at all costs. It was probably only the deftness of Hungary's policy and Hitler's personal respect for Horthy that had prevented the Germans from closing the grip on us altogether; for otherwise it is incomprehensible why Hitler had not resorted to that expedient, so simple and in all respects so advantageous to him. For what would the occupation of Hungary have meant?

From the military point of view: Hungary possessed almost 1,000,000 trained soldiers. About 300,000 of them were organized in three armies, not indeed perfectly equipped, but yet fit for action. Compulsion and propaganda could have placed this force at the disposal of Germany within a year. (They would also have got from Rumania the ten extra divisions which Marshal Antonescu had refused them, saying that he would give no more soldiers until the Hungarians did their part.) That might at the least have substantially delayed the progress of Russia's operations, and the *Wehrmacht* would not have needed to withdraw so many divisions from the Western front.

[6] See the map on page 346.

Transport and supply: Hungary's considerable store of locomotives and rolling stock would have been at the unreserved disposal of the Germans, who could thereby have made up their own deficiencies and speeded up the movements of their troops. Our motor cars (we had at the time more private cars on the road than England) and oil supplies would have fallen completely into their hands.

So would have our agricultural production, in which field, as the statistics show, there was much resistance and sabotage. The agricultural laborers would have gone to work in Germany.

As for industry, there could be no doubt that the Germans would at once have seized our coal mines, oil wells, and bauxite deposits (these the largest in Europe) and have exploited them mercilessly to secure the maximum of production for their own use, leaving nothing for our home consumption. The highly skilled Hungarian workmen would have been integrated into German war production, either at home or in Germany, certainly in the most critical spots—not to speak of the fact that Germans would have been put in the places of the "unreliable" directors and clerical staffs of our enterprises.

Politically, Hungary was the sorest point of the German satellite system, the only country not militarily occupied. Hungary was the one in whose internal policy Germany had least to say and whose foreign policy was the most independent.

The refugees, numbering nearly 200,000 persons, would have fallen into German hands.[7]

This is my answer to those *friends* who urged us to break away.

But our enemies, who certainly also possessed considerable influence with the Soviet government, particularly its press, urged us to break away even more vigorously. We could trace this through three channels. One of these was the Communist propaganda, at home and abroad; the second, the Benes-Károlyi line; the third, the attitude of the British secret service in Istanbul. Their points of view and plans can be summed up as follows: at

[7] See Chapter Fifteen, "The Treatment of Refugees and Prisoners of War."

all costs to bring about a German occupation, the sooner the better. This would completely disintegrate the existing Hungary The Germans would eliminate the leading patriotic pro-Allied circles, whom the nation followed, and set Arrow Cross scum in their places. Hungary's military, political, and administrative system then would crumble away. A condition of chaos would exist at the end of the war, and then, when the German army was beaten and the Russian troops entered, there would be no organized force in the country to take over the power except the Communist movement then forming underground. Thus when peace came to be concluded, the vanquished and compromised patriotic, conservative, and pro-Western forces would have nothing to say. The underground workers would emerge and represent the country, adhere to the Benes-Stalin pact,[8] and form a new Danubian Bloc under Russian protection. I could deduce this from reports rendered me by the persons observing the activities of the Communists and the extreme left in Budapest; from letters written from Stockholm by an ex-Communist Hungarian émigré named William Böhm to Michael Károlyi; from what Andrew Frey reported of the activities of a George Pálóczy-Horváth, who was working as a British agent in Constantinople; and many other sources. Unfortunately, therefore, it was not our friends but our enemies who saw the position clearly.

Seen in this light, it appeared that a "jump out" by Hungary, at any rate a withdrawal not properly prepared for, together with the German occupation which was bound to follow, would bring temporary advantage to the Germans and long-term advantage to the Communists, but none to anyone else. This is exactly what happened later. It was really only the Communists, whose object was to destroy Hungary, who thought the matter out to the end. The Allies would have had no gain from Hungary's withdrawal

[8] The provisional Czechoslovakian government in London and the Soviet Union concluded a twenty-year alliance which was signed December 12, 1943, during Benes' visit to Moscow. Czech-Russian relations during the war period began, however, in August, 1941, when the Soviet Union accepted Zdenko Firlinger as minister of the Benes government.

except a certain political success, and the possibility of one or two effective broadcasts and leaflets.

Really, if one thinks this question through, with any regard for the Hungarian point of view, one can come to no conclusion other than that which I have stated above. All the intermediaries with whom we dealt, most of whom were friendly to us or at least not actively hostile, began by saying: "Jump out as quickly as possible!" But after the matter had been explained to them, all without exception saw that this was impracticable and senseless and reported to that effect. But it is equally interesting that after a short interval they returned to the same point: "Yes, yes, we know your arguments, but all the same you must do something," and so forth. Obviously, superior political or military authorities had taken their line once and for all and were not to be moved from it.

We thought over the question and dissected it again and again. I should most certainly have preferred the solution recommended by the Allies. If it were practicable, it was to the nation's interest; and if I could get the very smallest guarantee for my people, it was my duty to take the greatest risk.

I therefore began to put out feelers along every line at my disposal. I had semiofficial contact with the English through George Barcza in Switzerland, but he was not an accredited emissary and could not negotiate officially. I accordingly asked our partners in Istanbul, via our transmitter—and this time the message went expressly in my own name—what guarantee the British and American governments would give if we carried out their proposals, under instructions, and jumped out, incurring all the consequences. We made only one condition: that we should not be occupied exclusively by Russian troops, but that British and American troops should join in the occupation (I thus on my own responsibility dropped the rigid Hungarian condition that the Russians were not to occupy the country) and that we should be given an express assurance that we should not come into the Russian sphere of influence. The person on the receiving end in

Istanbul—Pálóczy-Horváth—immediately replied: "I can assure you that you will get no reply." And he was right. I repeatedly sent this message: "All right, but if we do as you want, what comes after?" I never got an answer. Throughout the negotiations the Allies were correct. They did not lead us up the path, and they did not promise what they were not themselves certain that they could perform.

After this discussion of foreign politics, which I shall cover more fully in another chapter, let us see what the feeling and the public opinion was at home. There is no doubt that nearly everyone agreed that we must avoid being occupied. But there were dissentients, and there were nuances.

In the first place, there was a curious psychological factor born of history, education, gentlemanly feeling: the older generation, who were precisely the most strongly anti-German, interpreted Italy's action as a repetition of the "treachery" of 1915, when Italy had forsaken the Dual Monarchy and joined the other camp. This almost softened them towards the Germans, and they protested against our following Italy's example. With such people, the idea of "behaving correctly" dominated everything else, and there were many such precisely in the age groups most influential in civilian life. Practically all the ex-soldiers and, consequently, many of the peasants were of this mind. So also was Horthy, in spite of his awareness of other considerations and his strongly Anglophile feelings.

The extreme right and the extreme left were, thank God, not numerous, but in their own egocentric fashions, and with the designs which I have described, opposed most strongly the idea of surrender. Then, as so often afterwards, the Nazis and Communists advocated identical methods to reach their opposite ends. The representatives of what one may call the "idealist" policy described above gradually came to see that their feelings must be subordinated to the real interests of the country. The most important group, that which had formed round Bethlen and

Baranyai, became dominant. They were in favor of jumping out, and then tried to convert me to it. This was how they put it:

It is impossible that the English and Americans should not take our side. We must ask a guarantee of this. They will not allow a million Jews and others to fall into the hands of the Germans. Even if the occupation comes, let the government fly out; it will be recognized as a government in exile and can go on working abroad. Certain as it is that the Germans have lost this war, it is equally certain that the Allies will not allow the Russians into Europe. And if that does happen, then nothing will matter; we shall be devoured from both sides. But we shall have done everything the English and Americans wanted, and they won't leave us in the lurch. And so on went this argument.

The sober-thinking masses, however, the majority of the nation, who were not adventurers or revolutionaries of the right or of the left, thought differently. So, I could not doubt, did the small farmers and the agricultural laborers. The attitude of the Smallholders party parliamentary deputies was not quite clear-cut. They wavered between the points of view of the villagers and of Eckhardt's American friends, while Bajcsy-Zsilinszky's immediate followers definitely wanted the radical decision. The leader of the Citizens Liberty group, Rassay, was for moderation; so was Peyer, the leader of the Social Democrats and the acknowledged spokesman of the workers. They looked at the prosaic situation and the masses behind them, and the decisive factor in the eyes of these leaders was how to save the lives and safeguard the interests of the people. What dominated them was fear of a German occupation. There is no doubt that the German rule would have had terrible consequences for the masses. I have explained why above. The moderate leaders estimated that an occupation would cost 1,000,000 lives, not to mention the material and moral destruction. Their sentiments were 100 per cent pro-Allied, but they saw too little profit in a gesture which might save us at some distant date but which would immediately bring so much destruction.

The rescue of Mussolini on September 12, 1943, caused general pleasure, which was owing to sympathy for his person and admiration for the gallant feat. Hitler's apparently chivalrous gesture only gave Mussolini his life. The Germans had nothing but trouble with him, and from my point of view he caused me very great distress in the most difficult struggle that I was conducting.

The crisis reached its culminating point on September 23, when the news came of Mussolini's formation of a new government and then of the proclamation of the constitution of the new North Italian Fascist Peoples Republic. That meant fresh trouble for us. The new state was a puppet show in itself, but it freed north Italy from German devastation and "evacuation." (The Germans never plundered, ravaged, or murdered on their own initiative or for their own benefit, only on orders, which they then carried out systematically.) The new state put off the collapse of internal order almost up to the arrival of the Anglo-American troops, which was immensely fortunate for Italy and, since Italy's values are the world's, for all humanity. During the last days of the regime I was in prison with some German staff officers, including one who had been sent to prison for refusing to carry out the orders given him when Naples was abandoned. There were among us also some senior Italian partisan officers. I heard what both groups were supposed to do before the Allied troops arrived.

But to revert to the main thread: the liberation of Mussolini and the formation of the new Italian Republic upset our calculations. We heard the news on the radio (we got no official notification), and immediately Jagow, the German minister, called at our foreign ministry and left there a telegram from Ribbentrop asking us to recognize the new Italian Republic immediately and to establish diplomatic relations with it. Jagow added that the German government attached particular importance to our unconditional and immediate recognition and to our drawing all consequences therefrom: that is, accrediting a minister and breaking off all relations with the royal government, which had defected to the Allies. Hard on Jagow's heels arrived Döme Sztójay, who informed us that Baron Ernst von Weizsäcker of the German foreign office had told him that the démarche to us had been delayed for twelve hours because Hitler had first wished to discuss the entire Hungarian position. The military had, for the first time, participated in this discussion. In the middle of it Hitler had telephoned Marshal Antonescu of Rumania. Weizsäcker had said that he did not know what had passed during this conversation, and he had no right to make guesses about it, but he advised us to co-operate. Sztójay's own view was that, if we did not do as Ribbentrop asked, the Germans would regard our refusal as open defiance and act accordingly. I had never seen him so positive.

Our problem was therefore not simply that of the recognition or nonrecognition of Mussolini, but the determination of our own future, as dependent on our decision. We might return an insolent refusal to the German request (which was the first time, since I had become premier, that they had tried to intervene in our foreign policy, or had even expressed an opinion about it); but we should have then had to pay the bill immediately. Such was our impression as we studied the question and sought a solution.

There were three theoretical possibilities:

1. To recognize Mussolini's new state, send a minister to it, and break off relations with the royal government

2. To disregard the request and maintain relations with the royal government

3. To grant de facto recognition to the new state and take up official relations with it, but also to maintain relations with the royal government

We rejected a priori the first solution or, at any rate, that part of it which would have involved withdrawing recognition from the royal government and declaring that we were at war with it. (The Germans had gone so far as to try to push us into this position, and in their later declarations interpreted their demands as including the dethroning of the House of Savoy, an absurdity

such as only Ribbentrop's foreign policy could perpetrate, as con
trary to law as it was to common sense.) We naturally could no
even consider this.

Another possibility might have been to refuse to recogniz
Mussolini, not to take cognizance of his new state. The mildes
form of doing this would have been to leave Ribbentrop's tele
gram unanswered, as any answer from us would have aggravate
the situation. Silence, however, would have constituted, no
merely a rejection of the request, but an act of downright rude
ness. With a sensible partner one could, of course, have talked an
reasoned, but in our position that was impossible. The situatio
would have been very different if Rumania, Slovakia, and Croati
had instantly rejected Ribbentrop's wish, so that we could hav
acted together. But they failed us then, too; all of them had alread
recognized Mussolini.

The third alternative would have created a confused situation
Both Italian regimes would have regarded themselves as repre
senting the whole country. The position in international lav
would have been disputable, and we should have got the wors
of both worlds: we should have recognized Mussolini, and callec
down the threat of occupation from Germany for failing to breal
with royal Italy.

Days passed, and our situation grew more and more difficult
Our neighbors recognized the Fascist Republic without reserva
tion. Jagow and his faithful partner, Sztójay, got more and more
nervous, as (presumably) telegrams from Berlin flooded in. We
had to make some decision. Keresztes-Fischer then made a sug
gestion, which we adopted in the end. We should simply make a
declaration, which was to be expressed only in our answer to
Ribbentrop (not to Mussolini), taking note of the fact com
municated to us that Mussolini had formed the North Italian
state. The final text of our telegram ran as follows:

H. E. RIBBENTROP, REICH FOREIGN MINISTER: WE HAVE TAKEN
NOTE FROM YOUR TELEGRAM OF THE FACT COMMUNICATED BY
YOU THAT MUSSOLINI HAS FOUNDED THE NORTH ITALIAN FASCIST

REPUBLIC. WE TAKE THIS OCCASION TO INFORM YOU THAT WE
ALWAYS POSSESSED IN MUSSOLINI A TRUE FRIEND OF THE HUN-
GARIAN CAUSE.

This was the Hungarian declaration which we afterwards called
"recognition *de facto* and not *de jure*."

Our message was in fact nothing more than an answer to the
message conveyed to us by Ribbentrop for our information. It
was taking cognizance of, not recognizing, the new state. The
essential fact is that we sent no note to Mussolini, either then or
later. It was really not even *de facto* recognition, but simply communication to a third party that we had taken cognizance of what
he communicated to us, which was an existent fact. We could
not, in our position, have done less without incurring perfectly
useless sacrifices. We made no concession of principle. There was
nothing in our declaration which could have served as a basis for
a change of our position vis-à-vis the Italian royal government,
nothing contrary to international law. Those members of the
Italian legation accredited to Budapest who remained loyal to the
dynasty took it in that sense, with great pleasure. There was nothing in our message that restricted our freedom of action.

I must explain the second sentence of the telegram. When I
submitted the draft of the message to the Regent, he accepted it,
but suggested that we should make a gesture towards Mussolini,
some expression of feeling. We must not, he said, be ungrateful
towards one who had been our true friend, even if our ways were
now parting. The Regent's suggestion was the origin of the telegram's second sentence. It did not change its essence and even
contained a sting directed against Ribbentrop, who had not been
our friend and against whom Mussolini had several times been
obliged to take our part.

Our attitude must be judged in the light of our position. We
let three days pass after our neighbors had recognized Mussolini
before issuing our entirely noncommittal declaration. This gave
full expression to our dissociation from the event; our delay expressed this completely, in terms of diplomacy. The Germans

swallowed it, but, according to Sztójay, they never forgot it
Weizsäcker told him that this was the first open declaration of
our opposition to Germany's foreign policy.

Those people on the Allied side who were interested in our
affairs—if I may so express myself—had awaited our decision with
feverish expectancy, and our declaration filled them with great
hopes. They thought this a grand opportunity for Hungary to
come out into the open and break away from the Germans. Such a
step was, indeed, a temptation. There were great advantages in
taking a point not directed straight against the Germans as a
pretext for showing our political independence. The great draw-
back to this, however, was that the Germans would undoubtedly
have decided to square accounts with us radically. Even if settling
with Germany was our own final aim, they and not we would have
chosen the moment, and at that time I still hoped that we might
find the means to take the initiative. So our text caused a
certain disappointment among people in the West. They thought
that we had missed an opportunity and that my policy was undecided. Many people, however, understood and appreciated the
independence, courage, and dissociation from German interests
expressed in the text and regarded it as a good beginning.

Looking back, I now think that we acted correctly. This chapter,
and, indeed, the whole book, will show the reader the motives
behind our policy, and subsequent events proved amply that
we should only have lost by hanging up the hatchments in our
windows a year sooner.

No answer came to our telegram, either from Berlin or from
Mussolini. Sztójay had nothing to report, but he thought that
the marked stillness (the German papers did not publish our telegram) was not a good omen. No reaction came either from the
Italian legation in Budapest. Mussolini rang up Anfuso, however,
and asked for his adherence. Anfuso immediately consented. He
was the only Italian head of a mission to do so. That was just our
luck. Everywhere else the legations remained in the hands of
Badoglio's followers. Only in Budapest the new Fascists took
control, although the great majority of the legation staff, includ-

ing the first counselor, Baron Carlo de Ferraris, and the military attaché, Count Emilio Voli, remained loyal to the King.

For the moment we left both of them their diplomatic status. Both visited the foreign ministry; both used their diplomatic titles and insignia. Politically, we had really no official dealings with either. There were, of course, incidents, as when the head of the Italian-Hungarian bank rang up in despair to ask what he should do, since both legations were asking him to hand over to them the funds—I think it was 30,000,000 lire—deposited with him. Louis Reményi-Schneller, the minister of finance, at once blocked the whole sum, and a hurriedly convoked legal court decided that since General Voli had paid the money in, it must be paid out to him, but under the circumstances, we decided that the bank should pay Voli only a monthly allowance for expenses. I should mention that when a republican minister arrived, the question came up again. He was completely without funds and asked us at least to treat his staff on the same footing as the others and give them a subsistence allowance out of the money. We refused this, whereupon the republican minister kept back some hundreds of trucks that we had ordered in Turin and were already entrained. We maintained our attitude in principle, but allowed the republican legation a certain sum for expenses, deducting this from further payments made to Italy for orders.

But what about our legation in Rome? On orders from me, George Bessenyey, our minister in Berne, took up with Mr. Allen W. Dulles, then chief of the OSS in Switzerland, and Mr. Royall Tyler, of the American legation in Berne, the question whether the British and American authorities, when they entered Rome, would leave our legations in enjoyment of their diplomatic privileges, or tolerate them at all. The Americans found the question extremely interesting but, after making inquiries, said that they could give no guarantee on the point. I should therefore recall Máriássy, minister in Rome. I pressed that solution very hard and raised the question also with the Badoglio government, which also returned a refusal. An interesting and significant position would have arisen if my idea had been realized. The Hungarian minister,

a legation, a Hungarian point, the first to come into contact with
the Allies, would have seceded, and the first de facto possibility
would have been realized.

Soon afterwards Raffaele Casertano, minister from Mussolini's
North Italian Republic, arrived in Budapest with regular letters
of credence. I did not like having to receive Casertano, for
this meant that de jure recognition which we had so far escaped
giving. But it could not be avoided; refusal would have been a
declaration of war, not only on Mussolini, but also on Germany,
and a quite purposeless gesture, after we had already chosen the
course of balance by our de facto recognition. We continued to
follow that path. Casertano presented his credentials, but neither
then nor later did we send the Italian Republic a minister or even
a chargé d'affaires. So the republican government was represented
with us, but we were not represented with it.

We treated Casertano, who was, incidentally, no very winning
personality, with the greatest froideur. No one held a single discussion with him on political questions. His contact with the
foreign ministry was limited to the affairs of his legation. I saw
him only once: in connection with his subsistence.

The staff of the royal Italian legation continued to enjoy full
liberty and diplomatic privileges, even after the armistice, and our
social and official contact was with them alone. Once the Fascists
and Royalists came to actual blows, in a struggle for the possession of the Italian Cultural Institute on Sandor Street. Our police
decided in favor of the latter. Then we closed the house.

After Italy's surrender the Germans in other countries and at
the front rounded up the Italian soldiers and civilians and sent
them to Germany, under dreadful conditions. Some of the transports went across Hungary. We did what we could. We gave them
food at stations, let the Voli legation set up kitchens for them,
and supplied victuals. Those who were able to escape found safe
shelter with us, and none of those in our own country were
touched.

That was the situation, and so it remained until the German

ccupation on March 19, 1944. The Hungarian government only
ook note *de facto* of Mussolini's regime, and afterwards recog-
ized its minister *de jure*. Hungary did not send a minister to
aly, and we did not speak to the Italian minister, but rather
emonstratively favored the old regime. In the soul of the people
great sympathy and affection for the Italians lived on unaffected
y any of this.

Outside the Axis we had no friends. Inside it we had had one.
Now we had lost that friend.

ELEVEN

INTERNAL POLITICAL UNREST

❪THE GREAT MASSES of the people paid little heed to international events or even to the military situation. They went about their business, occupied with their own daily cares and troubles. Two complex groups ordinarily directed affairs. One was the house of representatives, or lower house, with its complements of party members, organizations, societies whose political agitation was reported faithfully in the newspapers serving these factions. The other legislative body was the upper house and the element which it represented and led without appearing to do so; the upper house was characterized by fewer blocs, a less strident press, and a far more discreet propaganda.

I had had much difficulty with the lower house but never any with the upper house. The activities emanating and irradiating

rom the lower house, whether sponsored by the right or left
ving, had made troubles for me and created awkward situations.
could not because of the Germans make an adequate stand
gainst the right wing, and I had no wish to do so against the left.
To obviate misunderstanding, I must state once again that in
hose days there was not a trace of Communism in Hungary.)

Imrédy's group and the Arrow Cross contingent were daily grow-
ng more daring. They were overtly speculating on the Germans'
efusing to tolerate me any longer, when their time would come.
\t first the right-wingers tried to gain the ear of the Regent.
mrédy, Jaross, Rajniss, Szálasi, and other extreme-rightist lead-
:rs made repeated attempts to lay their case before Horthy, but
ie would receive none of them. The lucubrations they addressed
o him were forwarded to me by the chancellery with the dry com-
nent: "Referred to the premier on his Highness' instruction." [1]
', for my part, naturally had some discussion with the right-wing
eaders.

I received Szálasi only once, however. He stayed two hours, and
iis confused talk and meaningless phrases, of which I cannot now
ecall one word, made the worst possible impression upon me.
There is no doubt that he belonged to the tribe of possessed fa-
iatics. I do not think that he knew what he wanted beyond the one
nagic thought of obtaining power because he was chosen to guide
:he destinies of the country. Some time after our conversation
[received from Szálasi a long memorandum to which I sent the
following brief reply: "I can give no substantial answer to the
lines that you have sent me, for they are un-Hungarian both in
thought and composition and therefore incomprehensible to me."

The thesis of all the extreme right-wingers was always the same:

[1] There are those who assert to this day that the Regent had Nazi sympathies.
The above fact is sufficient proof to the contrary. To have made himself inaccessi-
ble at the height of the German power to the adherents of that power, and at the
same time to receive those of the other side, was the frankest possible proclamation
of his attitude and must count as a gesture of resistance. To do this with your head
in the lion's mouth is somewhat more of an achievement than to thunder your
opinions, however loudly, in full security over the radio.

Hungary had to choose between siding with the Germans or wit
the Russians. No other possibility existed for those extremist
Hungary's choice, therefore, had to be the Germans. Furthermore
we had to make our choice clear or else we should lose the friend
ship of the Germans, gain no other supporter, and thus be th
enemy of every nation. Our lot was inextricably bound up wit
the fate of Germany. There was no escape from that destiny, an
we should bear the consequences of it. If we were to perish, w
should at least perish heroically. It goes without saying that mo1
baseness than exalted virtue lurked behind those thoughts an
phrases.

There were, it is true, some fanatics of good faith among thos
extremists, but few, very few; and they were mostly men of limite
outlook. Most of the leaders were speculators who thought c
themselves when they talked of the nation. A lost cause for then
meant the foundering of their individual fortunes and ambitions
and catastrophe was their own disappearance from the scene. Th
hope of saving their own skins was behind their call to heroisn
that was addressed to ten million Magyars. Besides the scoundrel
among the leaders, there were madmen. The retinue of those fa
natics was formed mostly of: broken-down failures; restless, half
educated elements; the loafers of the villages; and, principally and
in vast numbers, anti-Semites.

On the basis of reports obtained from mayors and lord lieu
tenants of the counties, Keresztes-Fischer, the minister of the in
terior, computed the probable strength of that extremist right
wing element in Hungary, and he came to the conclusion that i
formed no more than 5 or 6 per cent of the population. (His com
ment on the subject was interesting and characteristic of his clarity
of vision. He said that, in his estimation, the same percentage
would be found in the left wing were our relations with the Sovie
Union what they then were with Germany—which is to say tha
in Hungary the subversive, untrustworthy element always form
about 5 or 6 per cent of the population.) I must repeat, to prevent

misunderstanding about internal conditions in Hungary at that time, that the greatest part of the country's population was conservative in the old-world sense of the term—the people were intensely nationalistic, law-abiding, resentful of authoritarianism, honest in their dealings, and excellent citizens.

The right-wing element could not, therefore, be called in any way important, but it was, nevertheless, provocative and dangerous. On the one hand, it presented with its loud-voiced manifestations an incitement to German intervention, and it formed a fifth column for German aspirations. On the other hand, and that was the aspect which troubled me most, the rightist clamor created the impression abroad that there were serious Nazi sympathies and forces at work in Hungary. The Arrow Cross movement was particularly dangerous to the Hungarian nation because it had behind it base and unscrupulous people. It was backed, too, by that faction of anti-Semites whose hatred of the Jews was made rabid by self-interest.

The agitation carried on in the country by the right wingers was dealt with very energetically by Minister of the Interior Keresztes-Fischer. He tried, within the restrictions imposed by the law, to reduce the effectiveness of the rightist campaign to a minimum. Imrédy once said to me that all he asked for was that his party should be allowed the same freedom of action as was enjoyed by the Socialists. Because of the restrictions on their activities, the right-wing agitation produced little effect, and the order and tranquillity of the country were not endangered by those reactionary elements.

It was very different in parliament. What was said at provincial meetings went no further than the ears of the actual audience; nothing which might endanger the country's interests could appear in the press, for it was suppressed by the censor. What was said in parliament, on the other hand, could not be kept from the public, not even out of the newspapers. It was thus natural that the Opposition should choose parliament as the platform from which to sound its real propaganda. Right-wing deputies seized every occasion and every subject to air their own phraseology. They particularly abused their parliamentary privileges on Wednesdays, which were question days. On that day the right-wingers would produce by the dozen subjects which could cause us trouble and render our difficult position still more troublesome and difficult.

At first I tried to disarm them. I made a gesture to Imrédy, appealing to his patriotic sentiments. This produced a few weeks' calm but naturally no final solution. What happened was this: during a debate I spoke very sharply to Imrédy. After the debate he walked towards me to ask when he might call on me, and I stretched out my hand to him in open session. To explain this gesture I must quote the last passages of the debate.

Imrédy, turning to my own party, had said: "You applaud everything the premier says or does. But we, the Opposition, look through the other, outer end of the telescope which reduces the size of things, and consequently we judge them differently."

Commenting, in the closing sentences of my reply on this figure of speech, I said that "it was only when we were children playing that we used to look through the wrong end of the telescope. In these serious times I would beg the speaker and the Opposition to look through the right end. For the rest, neither 'reduce' nor 'enlarge' are the proper terms to use in this connection. Looked through in the right way, the telescope *brings things closer*."

The deputies in the lower house, who were aware of the political tension, were so electrified by this that not only members of my own party but also Imrédy's supporters rose in a body and clapped. The handshake, in this setting, assumed far greater significance than either of us had contemplated. He had walked towards me with the intention of explaining his conduct, and I had stretched out my hand to him for no special reason. It would have been a fine thing indeed had I been able by means of such a slight, melodramatic gesture to detach Imrédy and his circle from the German influence. But this was far from being the case, not so much, I believe, because of Imrédy as because of the arrivistes who formed his immediate circle and the general staff of his party.

The Arrow Cross camp I did not regard as of any consequence. I looked on them as the sort of hooligans who hover on the fringe of every movement. I could not take them seriously; I loathed and despised them. Perhaps that was a mistake; for there are times which bring such men to the top and invest them with power, as we were not long after to witness in Hungary. The same thing happened at the other end when, not much later again, the moderate left-wing parties were ousted from power by a similarly small, similarly denationalized Communist group, animated in its turn by hatred and lust for power.

I was most concerned, however, with adjusting the conflicting currents within my own Government party. Like every party which tries to adhere to a middle way between two opposite extremes, my party was in a difficult position, principally because not every member of the party was convinced that the middle way was the only right one. As in every parliament and every party in history, my own party had its right and left wing. Temperament, sympathies, and ambitions all played their part in this. As a rule, the extremists on both flanks are the most ebullient, the most greedy for action, and the most ambitious. In a moderate, middle-course party, it is precisely they who are doomed to silence and inaction, get no hearing, are given no tasks, and obtain no posts. As a result, the discontent engendered by their forced inaction is added to their original vacillation of purpose. It was so in my own party; it was bound to be so. In the interests of accuracy I must observe here that I had no trouble with the left wing. At most, I was reproached by the members of the left for not being stricter with those elements in my own party which revealed right-wing sympathies. Otherwise, however, my policy met in the left group with wholehearted approval and support.

It must be said in excuse of the oppositional faction in my own party, however, that it was unaware of the underlying motives of my policy, for I could not reveal them to anyone. All those members saw was that our relations with Germany were deteriorating, while at the same time the British and American radio attacked, threatened, slandered, and abused us with increasing virulence. Meanwhile, too, the Russians approached our borders. It was easy to understand that those not upheld by intuition, by an implicit trust in my own person, or by wholehearted dislike of the Germans should view with anxiety and apprehension the situation towards which we were drifting. I naturally endeavored to reassure those anxious party members and win them over, and I succeeded for the time being. The core of their anxiety was not removed, however, and I saw them, more and more frequently, seeking to establish contact with various members of Imrédy's camp, dining together in isolated groups—in short, displaying all the symptoms of the impending formation of new factions and alliances.

Finally, in the fall of 1943 a memorandum was produced by the dissident members of my party and handed to Béla Lukács, the party chairman. Lukács held out a long time against passing it on to me. In the end, after repeated prompting, he brought it up to me with the explicit assurance that he was acting solely as postman in the matter. The memorandum embodied everything against which I was fighting. Conception, build-up, angle of vision, all were erroneous—erroneous, that is, from the point of view of anyone better informed, more at home in world affairs, and commanding a wider perspective. But the policy formulated in the memorandum was also reprehensible because it was that policy which produced the moral debacle which was the most grievous part of the tragic times following the German occupation. Nothing that those men in my party conceived or imagined to be in the country's interest materialized afterwards; instead, the presence of the Germans and the weakening of the nation's healthy and decent instincts brought into being every sort of villainy.

I shall quote the principal passages of the memorandum because it was an important and revealing document. It will enable the reader to appreciate what the public temper of those days and the forces against which I had to contend were. More particularly, the reader will be able to see the erroneousness of the policy of Britain and America, a policy which refused to see those conditions in Hungary and which by attacking my regime strengthened and supported precisely the spirit which animated the memorandum.[2]

The memorandum began by claiming that it was the duty of the signatories and of the "majority" of the party which they represented, as patriots and legislators, to raise their voices against certain phenomena which might endanger the existence and the future of the nation. The text went on:

We see with disquiet that some of our representatives and members of organizations abroad are endeavoring to persuade the government—in opposition to the opinion of our leading military factors—to base its conduct on the assumption that the Anglo-Saxons have won the war. It seems pertinent to ask what will happen if the said representatives are mistaken? For years we have been told that we must not stake the country's existence on a single card [that is, a German victory: that was what I used to contend] because our existence and our future are treasures so sacred that they must in no circumstances be jeopardized. And yet there are people who would stake the country's future on the card that the Anglo-Saxons will win the war without the aid of the Russians, nay, if need be, against them.

The memorandum pointed out that such an attitude could only be explained by individual predilections and asserted that it was a total error to suppose that a mistaken foreign policy could be remedied by a leftward orientation at home.

The memorandum then argued the impossibility of imagining an Anglo-Saxon victory capable of warding off the Bolshevik influence. Were Germany to be defeated, the argument ran on, and

[2] See Chapter Sixteen, "My Foreign Policy," for the details about our relations with the Allies alluded to in this chapter.

were Bolshevism to gain the upper hand, the fate awaiting Europe would be unimaginably desolate. The text continued:

It is thus clear that the spreading of the Bolshevik deluge cannot be stemmed by the course described above. For even assuming that the English gave some promise to this effect, no one with a sense of responsibility and a sane appreciation of recent events could accept such a promise as valid. One need only look at the Polish question and the Italian tragedy; the daily intensification of the Bolshevization of southern Italy under the armed protection of the invaders, the persecution of the Church, the miserably dependent situation of the Badoglio cabinet, and the resolution to remove the head of the Italian state. It is an equally well-known fact that in the Balkans the Anglo-Saxons have officially recognized the Communist Tito and therewith brought Bolshevism right up to our southern frontiers.

The memorandum then pointed to the grievous consequences which would ensue if we turned away from our German allies, and stressed that fundamental thesis of political history which argued that the Hungarian people, nipped between the arms of the Slav pincer, was predestined to make common cause with Germany against Pan-Slavism. The text continued:

Certain circles labor under the delusion that, in case of a rupture with the Axis and an Anglo-Saxon orientation, we should not have to regard the Anglo-Saxon's ally, the Soviet, as a serious menace. It is in this notion that we see the motive for the left orientation of our internal policy.

The most serious consequence of a leftward trend in Hungarian domestic policy appears to us to be that the closer war approaches us, the greater becomes the danger that the German army, having lost trust in us, will enter Hungary as not an ally but the occupying force of a battle area. This might produce a tragic schism in Hungarian society, infected with Anglophile sympathies and worked upon by untimely anti-German slogans.

No nation can survive without the determined intention to defend itself. The nation is lost in which the serious nationalist resolve towards self-defense is lacking. Unfortunately, in this respect, Hungarian public opinion is completely confused and at sea. And meanwhile, an unbridled agitation, which underrates even the Bolshevik menace, is carried on.

As a result of this vacillating foreign policy of ours, our country, which under the inspiration of the Szeged Idea [3] had passed through years of advance unparalleled in our history, is being driven in spirit towards the left by forces secretly in revolt against the Regent's government. The conflict between the two forces, the right-wing Szeged Idea and the more and more prevalent left trend, is producing not only uncertainty and disorientation but also a state of impotent lethargy, the most disastrous result of which is that it breaks down, shrivels, and disintegrates the clean, vital instincts of the nation and the fighting spirit, moral energy, and courage demanded by the struggle.

In order to show what are the more and more alarming proportions assumed by the left trend and what headway it is making against the disintegrating national forces, we feel it incumbent on us, in view of the responsibility assumed by our party for the continued existence of our nation, to draw attention to a few important and burning problems.

What is the objective data which leads the government to permit the disruption of a responsible right-wing formation faithful in the guardianship of national traditions and wholly dominated by the Szeged Idea?

The leftward trend is evinced, first and foremost, by the freedom allowed to the Social Democratic party and to the so-called Popular Front to organize itself. The leaders of the Social Democratic party are allowed full liberty to agitate, to hold meetings, and to rebuild their organizations, notwithstanding the fact that by now the mass of the workers has turned, in spirit, away from international socialism. The Social Democrats' training schools

[3] The counterrevolution against Béla Kun's Communist rule in 1919 began at Szeged, and the Szeged Idea refers to the strongly rightist and nationalistic ideals of the extreme anti-Communists.

for agitators, for example, pursue their activities unhindered in Nagyvárad, Mezöbereny, Szarvas, Kondoros, Szombathely, Fel-sögalla, Salgotarjan, Kassa, and Szentes. The police are debarred from attending these schools—apparently by higher orders—and we hear that latterly some of the lecturers have been telling their hearers that these training schools for agitators are needed in order that this time the power should not slip from the hands of the Marxist working classes as it did twenty-five years ago.

The minister of the interior has tried to reduce the meetings of the various political parties to the standing committee meetings, whereas the Social Democratic party is permitted to hold meetings at which the attendance reaches hundreds or even a thousand. The circumstance that the meetings of the Social Democratic party proceed apparently unhindered leaves the masses under the impression that this party has the support of the authorities. This impression is strengthened all over the country by the official permission given for the wholesale distribution of Népszava's [4] special-size "Day of Rising" posters at a time when, owing to the well-known paper shortage, the national press and book publications are subjected to a stringent control. The Social Democratic leaders nourish the popular belief by openly advertising their close contacts with government circles; and their contention finds support in the fact that their most active centers of organization are in the state concerns or concerns closely connected with the state.

After pointing out the error of supposing that this essentially Bolshevist organizatory work was in the hands of Peyer and his circle, the memorandum went on to describe the disruptive activities of the so-called Peasant Alliance.[5]

We have been horrified to see the organization of the farmers on a class basis [6] launched, on official instigation, a process which,

---

[4] The official daily newspaper of the Social Democratic party.

[5] The Peasant Alliance was formally founded in September, 1941, with Ferenc Nagy as its first president and Béla Kovacs as its national secretary. For details, see Ferenc Nagy, *The Struggle behind the Iron Curtain* (1948), chapter 4.

[6] A task entrusted to Ferenc Nagy, with the purpose of diverting the farmers from ideological politics. See pages 256–57.

wing to the collaboration of the Social Democrats, has spread eft-wing tendencies to other layers of society also. This mistaken domestic policy has pushed aside the proven farmers' organizaions and, by letting the left-wing leaders come to the fore, has not merely set on foot a movement reminiscent of the spirit of George Dózsa [7] against the natural leadership of the middle class, but has lso directly made possible the emergence of distinctly agrarian-Bolshevik elements.

This officially fostered peasant movement had brought back resh multitudes to the debilitated relics of the Independent Smallolders party. And what are the goals towards which this party's econd team, after the departure abroad of the first,[8] is leading he farming masses, which it bewitches with its slogans, is made ufficiently clear by the reiterated public announcements of the party leaders of their collaboration with the Marxists. This is the nore dangerous since it is well-known that in 1919 the farmer lass offered a wholehearted resistance to the proletarian dictatorhip. There is no better proof of the irresponsibility displayed by he leaders of this so-called organization of the peasantry and of he ideological and political attitude which they have taken up, han their public speeches (at Miskolc, etc.) and the memoandum which the Independent Smallholders party handed to he premier and publicized in wide circles both abroad and at ome.[9] The fact that so far the authors of this memorandum have scaped retribution is causing almost irremediable damage in the public opinion of the country. . . .

A whole army of press organs is openly working to win over the ducated classes to the Popular Front, practically unhindered by censorship which in other respects is meticulously severe. For nore than a year pamphlets bearing the signature of "Peace Party" have been distributed in large quantities, and the political ection of the state police, so efficient as a rule, has found no means o stop this. Very wide circles of the public have been disquieted

---

[7] George Dózsa led a peasants' revolt in Hungary in 1514.
[8] This refers to Tibor Eckhardt's move to the United States.
[9] See pages 237–44 for discussion of and quotations from this memorandum.

by receiving these pamphlets in the mail, but we have not heard
of any single case of a perpetrator being punished. It is such phenomena which turn, in more and more numerous social associa-
tions and semiofficial organizations, the exponents of left ideas
into parlor Bolsheviks.

As the war draws nearer to our frontiers, the Jewish problem,
the methodical solution of which was retarded on the plea of wartime conditions, has once more become acute. Acute because, in
a country called upon to defend itself, possibly with direct German
assistance, the situation of eight or nine hundred thousand Jews,
whose vital interests cause them to nourish aspirations at variance
with the Hungarian war aims, inevitably requires to be regulated
by new and effective measures. Those Jewish masses, which by
their disruptive and black market activities are instrumental in
undermining the home front, should without delay be placed
under strict surveillance and be employed on public works.

The premier, in his opening speech, explicitly stated that the
only solution of the Jewish question in Hungary was deportation.
If there are at the present day obstacles to the methodical execution of this inevitable process, at least it should be possible to set
about the preparatory work. It is an impossible situation that for
a considerable time past a whole array of press organs, political
parties, and social factors should have been able to work unhindered at the rehabilitation of the Jews in Hungarian public
opinion, while the censorship makes it practically impossible to
air the Jewish problem with due regard to Hungarian interests.

A trend to the left has manifested itself, ever since the beginning of the war, also in the field of economic life, and this prevents
the government from placing its economy unreservedly in the
service of a defensive war. To this must be ascribed the fact that
the direction both of the production and distribution of the raw
materials needed for common necessities had not been concentrated in a single hand and placed under more stringent government control. It is also the reason why there is a greater shortage
of consumer goods than can be justified by the restrictions of war-

ime production, while, at the same time, goods still flow in pro-
usion through the channels of the black market. The dispropor-
ion between the prices of agricultural and factory products can
10 longer be maintained.

The last few years have shown a conspicuous deviation also in
he control of the press, although in this respect a slight improve-
nent is noticeable since the departure of the former chief of the
>ress.[10] A glaring example is furnished, in the field of foreign
>olitics, by the Budapest daily papers. Apart from the Pester
Lloyd, the Függetlenség, the Uj Magyarság, and the three Arrow
Cross papers, not a single Budapest daily can at present be called
>ro-German. The government's own organ, the Magyarország,
>ublished in its New Year number a leading article entitled "The
Principle of Unconditional Surrender" that was so unprecedent-
:dly defeatist in spirit as to cause the utmost scandal abroad and
>ainful consternation at home.[11] The news items in the daily
>apers are in no wise calculated to strengthen the morale of Hun-
;arian society in the degree required by these times of historic
:ribulation. Another only too effective factor in this moral disin-
:egration is the radio. It is very desirable that all the factors adapted
'or the purpose of propaganda: press, control of the press, radio,
films, etc., should be placed under a unified, undeviating, and truly
national control.

We must also mention, in view of their outstanding importance,
the anomalies manifested in the field of book publication. At a
time when intellectual life in Hungary has to struggle against the
greatest difficulties on account of the paper shortage, publishing
houses, mostly under Jewish control, multiply like fungi. The publications of these firms familiarize their readers with the ideology
of our opponents, and teach them—without their perceiving it—
to be "citizens of the world." It is imperative, not only from an

[10] Anthony Ullein-Reviczky, who in September, 1943, was appointed minister
to Sweden.

[11] The leader, written on my instructions, was an answer to the Allied propaganda,
and said in effect: "All right, we will lay down our arms, but to whom? To whom
shall we surrender? We have only Germans around us, for a thousand kilometers."

economic but also from a national standpoint, that this matte
should be remedied without delay.

The memorandum spoke of the "extremist fluctuations" o
our minorities policy, which, it said, had had particularly harmfu
effects on the Magyar inhabitants of the recovered territories. Th
chief reason why things had gone so fast downhill was that th
men who led and directed the Magyar movement of resistanc
and solidarity during two decades of foreign occupation were no
associated in the practical transaction of affairs. The memorandun
continued:

On the above grounds we must emphasize that the path alon,
which the country has for some time past been proceeding wil
lead to moral disintegration, moral lethargy, and most certainl
to moral demilitarization. It is possible to compute with almos
mathematical precision that in consequence of these reasons, n
worse catastrophe could happen to the nation than that the pre
dictions of certain circles should come true and the German
should lose the war.

The conclusion finally drawn ran as follows:

We must follow a hard, militant right-wing policy, based o
the Szeged Idea and permeating and embracing the whole o
society in one disciplined unity.

The document concluded:

We are too close to the events which followed the last worl
war to have forgotten that it is impossible to pull up on the edge o
an abyss, nor have we forgotten that once before the failure t
bridle subversive forces called forth the judgment of the Wester
world, democratic even then, in the words since become histori
of a French general: "Vous êtes tombés si bas?"

This must not occur again. Therefore, we must see to it that we
have a strongly nationalist state, morally armored as well as mili
tarily equipped, to confront every hazard without regard to the
possible consequences; for if we do not take this road, but con
tinue to pursue the other, we jeopardize all.

In the full consciousness of our responsibility, we beg our chair

man, in the name of the great majority of our party—while there
is yet time—to make it possible for the country's foreign and do-
mestic policy to return to the path which will lend us and the
nation the moral force to shoulder undismayed the burden of
responsibility and the great struggle which we must and shall see
through for our country and for His Serene Highness, the Regent.

These were the essential passages of the memorandum. It was
signed by thirty members of the Government party, all from the
lower house. The signatories were one and all unimportant men
who played no role in politics or in public life. There was only one
name of mark among them, that of Valentine Hóman, the distinguished historian and university professor, who for ten years
had been minister of cults and education.

I never replied, in any form whatever, to that memorandum
nor referred to it even in private conversation. The only thing I
could have done about it would have been to expel the signatories
from the party. They would have then gone over to Imrédy, and
besides strengthening his hand, the world would have been made
aware of the split in my own party.

That was one of the groups which demanded that I should come
resolutely out into the open and take the consequences, come
what may. More important and exhaustive, both in contents and
construction, was the memorandum handed to me by Andrew
Bajcsy-Zsilinszky and Zoltán Tildy in the name of the Independent Smallholders, Agricultural Laborers, and Democratic party.

This document, thirty-three pages long, started with a description of the historic background, sketching Hungary's prolonged
struggle to preserve her independence. The second part showed
how we were drawn into the Second World War and contended
that Bárdossy "declared war first on the Soviet and then on the
United States of America in the face of every rule of constitutional law." The third part developed Hungary's position
in the Tripartite pact from the international, legal, and political
points of view. This part contended that "Hungary's adherence to
the Tripartite pact did not in itself constitute an alliance in the

strict sense of international law." It was only later that the relations between Hungary and the three Axis powers turned, in
practice, into an alliance; legally this alliance was still open to
question. Hungary's entry into the war was not required by her
alliance; it occurred in consequence of the incessant German pressure which materially impaired Hungary's right of self-determination. Her entries into the war had, without a single exception,
occurred in opposition to the spirit and letter of Hungarian constitutional law. The law postulated the preliminary consent of
parliament before a declaration of war. Bárdossy announced all
of his declarations after the event, with ruthless disregard for the
fundamental principles of parliamentarism, in such a manner as
to make it impossible, under the rules of the lower house, even to
discuss them.

After this the memorandum developed the imperative necessity of our returning to our neutrality, and then it demanded: the
re-establishment of constitutional order; the rescinding of the
Jewish laws; the drastic repression, by systematic measures and
by adequate punishment of offenders, of the growing lawlessness;
reconciliation with the Serbs, Croats, and Slovaks; and the establishment of self-government in Transylvania and Carpatho-
Ruthenia. The concluding section ran as follows:

1. THE RISK

We are perfectly aware, Mr. Premier, that our withdrawal from
the war and the restitutio in integrum of our neutrality involve
considerable risks. These risks must be reduced to the minimum
possible, but they cannot be wholly eliminated. A government
which sets itself the task of guiding Hungary out of the maelstrom
in which she is now caught must be prepared to take the unavoidable risks.

The memorandum next referred to the example of other countries and urged the necessity of paralyzing the fifth column working in our midst. It continued:

And this not merely by insuring that the leading posts, both in the political and the military field, are manned by convinced, loyal, and devoted champions of the cause of Hungarian independence, but also by taking steps to bring home to the misguided public before it is too late the mortal danger which is threatening the country and its own patriotic duty. This can be achieved only by a wholly new press policy and by granting to the democratic parties much greater liberty of movement than they have hitherto enjoyed. In these grave times the patriotic Opposition parties have a right to demand, not in their own interest but in that of the country, that they should be allowed to speak more freely and frankly to the Hungarian people. It is my [sic] conviction that a few weeks' instruction would suffice to bring people of good faith back to the right national outlook—for, fortunately, the overwhelming bulk of the working masses themselves have always at heart remained faithful to the ideal of Hungarian liberty and independence. There is no fear that these masses, if allowed more freedom of self-expression, will ultimately carry the country in too radical a direction and sweep it into revolution. On the contrary, the focus of revolution, or rather of civil war, lies today not among the masses but in the middle classes. The masses, peasants, and workers alike, see things sanely and realistically; and a liberating movement in the Kossuth tradition will turn them into champions of the national cause, as devoted and resolute as were, in 1848, the peasants freshly liberated from serfdom.

Another potent instrument for lessening the risks involved is the complete restoration of the constitutional order. The third potent instrument is the Hungarian honvéd army, strengthened in its morale and its leadership and imbued with the Kossuth spirit, the spirit of the war of liberation. The fourth potent instrument is a liberal solution of the nationalities problem by a courageous application of the Nationalities Law of 1868 [12] and the an-

[12] Law XLIV of 1868 established the Magyar language as the official tongue of Hungary, but it allowed the widest possible use of other languages in the country consistent with political unity. The political and judicial rights of people speaking other languages were upheld by this law. Mr. C. A. Macartney in his book, *Hungary* 1934), page 102, said: "As a model for the treatment of national minorities within national State, this law could hardly be surpassed."

nouncement, within the shortest possible time, of the introduc
tion of those extensive territorial autonomies which have become
imperatively necessary.

A Hungary so ordered can shoulder without fear all the risks
which our withdrawal from the war might entail. A Hungary
whose foundations rest on constitutional order, on the principles
of a purified democracy and on racial and social appeasement, a
Hungary with an army a million strong, under a firm, efficient, and
pronouncedly Hungarian leadership, could in a few months raise
itself to stand like a rock above the breakers of the Central Euro
pean maelstrom.

2. OUR ROLE AS THE CREATORS AND PRESERVERS OF ORDER

Having proclaimed her neutrality, Hungary should render herself so useful and indispensable in the exalted role of creator and
preserver of order during the reorganization of Central Europe
that even our enemies should be forced to admit our merit in this
respect. It is in this task that we must seek our salvation, and not
in vain attempts to curry favor with the victors, nor in the dis
credited antics of diplomacy; still less in a foolish and odious imi-
tation of the clumsy somersaults and self-abasement displayed by
Michael Károlyi and his circle.

It goes without saying that we must harmonize our policy, and
in good time, with that of the victors, but only in regard to the
highest fundamental principles. A proud and free nation like the
Hungarian, conscious of its high destiny, can pursue no policy but
its own. Even the victors will accord it credit and respect only if
it stands up, courageously and large-heartedly, for its own cause,
which is also the cause of Europe. Free and courageous peoples
which are conscious of their destinies, are seldom comfortable
partners in international life. Switzerland, Turkey, Finland, or
Poland are none of them humble henchmen of the Allies. We
Hungarians have only to harmonize our true, original, traditional
policy with the principles already evolved by the Anglo-Saxon
world for the reconstruction of Europe.

Within the framework of these principles we can render a very great service to the peace and better order of Europe as well as to humanity at large, if we dauntlessly defend our own independence and that of the Danubian Basin, the heart and core of Europe, as we have done for a thousand years, and make it possible for a Hungary as Kossuth conceived it to join with a new Poland to form the nucleus of a federative alliance and collaboration—on a strictly defensive basis—of the smaller nations and countries, from Scandinavia to Greece and the Dardanelles, which lie between the great German and Russian ethnic seas. The ideal of uniting in their common self-defense these many small or medium peoples who together number one hundred to one hundred and forty million souls, has come to live in the public mind of the world, and it cannot be realized without Hungary.

Another reason why Hungary's declaration of neutrality is important, nay, essential for the further course of the war is that it would make evident the natural limitations which govern our nation's traditional and never-outworn role in world politics; the role, that is, that, because Hungary is situated in the heart of Europe, where all this Continent's arteries meet, she can never go beyond self-defense—just as the human heart cannot decide to join up with the body's right side against its left, nor vice versa.

We must recall our troops to the last man from the Russian frontier, thus returning before it is too late to that traditional policy which was never hostile even towards Russia. At the same time we must make it clear that we cannot, either now or at some future date, take part in any vilification of or hostile policy towards the German people and the German Reich.

3. OUR MILITARY SITUATION

It remains to consider Hungary's military situation in view of a possible Anglo-American invasion of the Balkans.

Certain military and political signs and considerations seem to indicate that in this war the Balkans will not, after all, become a battleground of decisive importance. The Anglo-Saxons have no imperative need of the Balkans for the invasion of Germany, while the German high command, for its part, will hardly undertake to hold a front of several thousand kilometers after the Italian divisions stationed there have withdrawn, as presumably they will do. But we must prepare ourselves for the least favorable possibility, the possibility of this country's becoming a theater of war, either through an Anglo-American attack from the Balkans or through an attempt, either by the Germans or the Anglo-Saxons, to possess themselves of Hungary's central position by utilizing large-scale air forces. If this happens, Hungary must settle clearly and decisively her relations both political and economic with Germany.

It is our conviction that Hungary must oppose with all her political and legal argument, as with her military strength, not only any attempted invasion by Germany, but also any passage of German troops across her territories; and that even though our army, for all its numbers, should prove, by reason of insufficient equipment, unable to prevent a temporary German occupation. It is, however, unlikely, both for political and military reasons, that Germany would try to occupy Hungary if we withdrew from the war or proclaimed neutrality; and the attempt if met with serious resistance would assuredly prove hopeless.

German aggression would open the way, not only from a military but also from a moral point of view, for a portion of the Hungarian army to march down into the Balkans, after first occupying southern Transylvania.

Whatever course the war takes in the Balkans and Central Europe, a Hungary once more in possession of her right of self-determination, freedom, and neutrality must accept a conflict with Germany rather than fight the Anglo-Saxons. This is the standpoint of our party.

A Hungarian army a million strong, even though insufficiently equipped, can yet, if led by strong and capable Hungarian commanders and imbued with the spirit of Kossuth's soldiers of liberty, become the most important military force, after the Turkish, in the entire Danube Valley and the Balkans. If necessary, the army must be used to secure the country's freedom and continued existence.

Certain hints in the British press suggest that this Hungarian army might eventually be entrusted with the task of an international police force, should chaos supervene in Central and Eastern Europe.

Mr. Premier! In this memorandum we have expressed what our national conscience and our duty as parliamentary Opposition bade us say; setting forth at the same time the attitude which, in these days of supreme national emergency, our party takes up towards the decisive questions which confront our Hungarian destiny.

Budapest, July 31, 1943

Andrew Bajcsy-Zsilinszky brought me that memorandum, when it was still in draft form, and asked my opinion on two points: (1) Did I think it advisable for him to come out into the open at all by producing a memorandum of this nature and addressing it to me? (2) What did I think of its general trend? He said, however, that he did not guarantee to defer to my opinion.

I replied that the memorandum contained nothing to which I should take exception as a private individual. It was another question how much of its contents I, as premier, might regard as practical politics. The memorandum would justify their policy and condemn mine. But self-justification was no part of my task; such considerations could not affect my conduct of the embittered day-to-day struggle which I had to carry on as best I could. The good of the nation demanded that we should each of us work within the range of the possibilities open to us and not obstruct each other.

We discussed the entire subject matter in detail; I enlightened Bajcsy-Zsilinszky on many particular points, and concluded by telling him that I was willing to accept the memorandum officially. We parted most cordially.

That memorandum was much more important than the memorandum that was issued by the right. The underlying motives of the right-wing one were hatred and a refusal to see things as they

were, and it was wrong on every point. It approved what had been
ill done in the past and proposed to repeat the same errors in
aggravated form in the future. The memorandum of the Smallholders party, on the other hand, was based on a serious estimate
of the situation. It contained more than one mistake, but I may
describe the impression it left on my mind by saying that I would
have signed it myself had I not happened to be premier. Its greatest merit was that it was free from prejudice, and it was right in
its diagnosis of past errors and in its proposed remedies. In short,
therefore, the memorandum of the Smallholders party saw the
situation in the right light and showed the right way out, while
the memorandum of the right-wingers was wrong in every particular.

The terrible and tragic part of the situation, however, was that
the right-wing course—to lean still further towards Germany—
was the one that was technically, politically, and militarily open
to me. That course presented no difficulties whatever, for it meant
leaning on that power which at the moment was actually pressing
against us, the only power with which we had to reckon, the
German. The correct course, on the other hand, could not be
pursued because it was obstructed by that same German power.
Paradoxically, those who advocated the wrong approach were
reckoning with the facts, while those who saw things in the right
light were failing to do so. What the Smallholders proposed was,
word for word, my position. I wished to realize it, however, in such
a manner as to reduce the attendant risk to a minimum and to
reach our goal without squandering in the process those national
forces which were imperatively needed for the realization of our
common program. If our national forces were destroyed, our goal
would never be reached for lack of effective spirit, tactical vantage
ground, and men to compass our ends.

It was not that I did not dare to risk a military occupation for
my own personal and political purposes. What I dared not endanger was precisely the very aims which the Smallholders memorandum advocated. *For I knew, and had often said to these very*

riends, *that what I had to fear in case of an occupation was not
he fall of my own regime but the fall of all my friends, the de-
truction of the regime of the future, without which the Hungary
hey wanted could not be preserved.* I already knew that what
Iungary had to fear was not the opposition of that day. I told
hem in so many words that I should be happy could I know that
hey would succeed me. But I was afraid that my successors would
e, not they but disorder, chaos, and dissension, from which would
merge not a bourgeois democratic Hungary but a dictatorship,
vhich, after all that would have happened, could only be a Bol-
hevik one. There was no surer preparation for this Bolshevik dic-
atorship than a German occupation, a so-called partisan move-
nent, devastation wrought by Allied bombs, and, above all, a
Russian military occupation. Occupation by Russia would be un-
voidable if Hungary passed into German hands and German
oldiers confronted Russian soldiers on Hungarian soil. Previous
o this, however, the Quisling regime which a German occupation
vould set up would have destroyed the country's moral assets and
created an atmosphere in which everyone would hate his neighbor.

The final memorandum (which was not as good as the earlier
Iraft) was brought to me by Andrew Bajcsy-Zsilinszky and Zoltán
Tildy. A few days after reading it, I summoned to me the leaders
ot only of the Smallholders party but also of the Citizens Liberty
arty and the Social Democratic party, including Charles Rassay
nd Charles Peyer. I told them, at somewhat greater length but
vithout substantial difference, what I have written immediately
bove.

Bajcsy-Zsilinszky was the first to reply. He said that the risk
nust nevertheless be taken, for even if all my predictions were
ealized, there was no other way out. He reminded me that I was
lways saying we must go our own way. Bajcsy-Zsilinszky regarded
he taking of the risks as our way. The only difference between us
vas that he was prepared to take risks for his aims, while I wished
o achieve them without risk. He did not believe that my policy
ould succeed. If it did, he would be the first to range himself at

my side. He was certain, however, that this would not happen, and we should only lose the few good marks which an open withdrawal would gain for us in the future.

Rassay followed. He said that he had long seen what I was driving at and approved of my political tactics. He did not think anything would be gained by showing our hand. This would merely expose our resources to destruction. It was much better to husband them. He would not, therefore, recommend any course which would precipitate catastrophe on us for the sake of a noble gesture. But he concurred with those sections of the Smallholders memorandum which demanded a more vigorous, extensive, and radical purge in the general staff in particular and in the corps of officers in general. I should also be firmer with my own party, and dismiss those two or three ministers who, to his certain knowledge, were my personal as well as my political enemies. I should take more effective measures against the press propaganda of the Imrédy and the Arrow Cross factions—in fact, suppress all propagandist activity from whichever party it emanated.

Peyer, who linked his arguments with Rassay's, said that for his part he could not anticipate any result of any kind from anything we did, open or covert. Our fate was not in our own hands, it was completely immaterial what we did. The only thing which mattered, therefore, was to stave off the German occupation as long as possible, insuring meanwhile—and on this he would categorically insist—that Germany should not intervene in our domestic affairs. Unlike Rassay, Peyer thought it of the utmost importance that propaganda should be permitted, and he naturally demanded this in the first place for his own Social Democratic party. The Social Democratic party must be strengthened throughout the land, for it was the only one which could withstand and oppose the German or the Bolshevik pressure.

After that, Tildy spoke, or rather tried to speak, but before he had uttered three sentences, Rassay interrupted him to say he had better shut up: the times were too serious for him to be talking.

In the end, I identified myself with Bajcsy-Zsilinszky's spirit nd his aims, applied Rassay's tactics, paid due heed to Peyer's practical methods—but followed my own line, exclusively.

Among the Oppositional politicians of that day, Rassay was by far the most outstanding personality. He had not only brains and bility, but the courage to express his convictions, not only to his dversaries but also to his own followers.

Outside my own party, but spiritually most closely akin to me nd incontestably the truest representatives of all that was most valuable in Hungary, was that group, or rather (as "group" would mply organizatory ties which did not exist between them) those persons who acknowledged as their leaders first and foremost Stephen Bethlen, and after him, such individualists as Leopold Baranyai. I have already described who these persons were and what circles they included; it might be said further that they embraced all those persons whom the Bolsheviks are liquidating, or have already liquidated, by various methods but with consistent purpose. I had amicable personal relations with them, as they belonged to my old circle of friends. They had no need, therefore, to hand me memoranda, since I was always at their disposal. Our co-operation was continuous and complete. They were Magyars first, last, and without question, and natural opponents both of Nazism and Bolshevism. The more conservative among them were Anglophiles who wished to imbue Hungary with the English pirit. The more radical section, on the other hand, was composed of intellectuals who looked rather towards France and made French Radical Democracy their ideal. It must not, however, be supposed that there was any divergence among these men as to the inevitability of radical reforms, both social and agrarian, after the war. But they accepted Bethlen's doctrine that such proposals must not be brought forward openly at that juncture; for this would start each group bidding against the rest, and once this started we should be playing into the hands of the Bolsheviks, who would be quite unscrupulous in their promises. But it would

be a mistake to think that this group, which comprised the mos
important factors and classes of the Hungary of that day, woul
have in any way opposed any progressive social policy or any rad
cal democratization of the country.

The same applies to the legitimists, whose legitimism had noth
ing to do with conservatism. It might almost be said that quite th
contrary was true, for it was the theory of the legitimists tha
small countries cannot be democratized without a fixed point,
factor of continuity. A policy built exclusively on a system of part
rule cannot, they thought, achieve stabilization. They pointe
to the monarchic regimes of the northern countries, from Eng
land to Sweden, where the democratic principle seemed to then
to have assumed truer and purer forms than in many a republic
The higher clergy, too, was by no means averse to ideas of reform
and large sections of the lower clergy favored reform in every field

The complaints of the right wing of my own party showed hov
much I helped the Opposition—as I have described it above—
to get a footing in the country and to influence public opinion
What the parties and factions of the right and the public opin
ion commanded by them objected to in my policy was perhap
not so much my stubborn opposition to all Germany's efforts to
influence us and penetrate our system as my handling of the lef
groups at home. It seemed to the right-wingers that I not onl
handled the left with kid gloves but that I actively supporte
them. The best proof of the correctness of their charge is that
sent, not only the Smallholders memorandum, but subsequentl
also that of Peyer's Social Democrats to Switzerland by foreig
office messenger. This Social Democratic memorandum is not in
my possession, but copious excerpts from it were published in th
press at the time.

TWELVE

THE RECONVENED PARLIAMENT

[IN THE AUTUMN of 1943 I felt that the time had come for the re-
convening of parliament, which had suffered a prolonged, forced
suspension. The fact that the debate on the budget for 1944 could
no longer be postponed was not my sole reason for wishing to
reconvene parliament. I should in any case have thought it im-
proper to deprive the country of its full constitutional life at a
time when the situation in respect of the war, of external relations,
and of economic questions was nearing its crisis. The time had
come, in fact, when we were confronted with the immediate problem of to be or not to be.

I had long felt, as Paul Teleki knew, that the gathering world
conflict had set this great problem for our country. Teleki and I
had often discussed the matter, and we had been much of a mind,

except that he had been somewhat more pessimistic than I in re
gard to the country's internal forces. I shall here interpolate a
episode to illustrate my forebodings at that time about Hungary
future.

In June, 1939, the International Congress of Agricultural In
dustrialists met in Budapest. I was its chairman. It had been n
easy matter to get the Congress going in the troubled politic
atmosphere following the *Anschluss*, but somehow it was don
The majority of the delegates came from France, Belgium, an
Holland, for this alliance of industrialists, whose permanent sea
was in Paris, was primarily sponsored by the economic and sc
entific world of those three countries. But delegates also cam
from England, various countries overseas, the Axis powers, an
the Balkans. Practically every major country except Russia wa
represented.

My own personal friends at that meeting were from among th
French and Belgians. After one of the afternoon sessions, I climbe
with several of them to the top of Gellért Hill to look at th
panorama of Budapest in the light of the setting sun, with th
mighty Danube dominating the scene, and to watch the lamp
leap up one by one as the dusk slowly passed into night. It was
lovely sight, and there were cries of admiration from all around
"*Quelle merveille! . . . beauté . . . . splendide!*" At that ver
moment an unspeakable sadness descended on me, and I said
as though History herself spoke through my mouth: "Yes, Me
sieurs *et Mesdames*, it is a wonderful sight. Look at it well, for
is the last time you will see it. The royal palace, the bridges, a
will be annihilated. What you see will be a heap of ruins." Ther
was general embarrassment after my remark, yet one could fee
that subconsciously everyone had been thinking along the sam
line, but nobody had dared utter what I had blurted out.

Teleki heard of my remark and asked me to come and see him
When we met, he asked why I had said what I did. I replied tha
it had been a sudden impulse but that behind my words la
a profound conviction that a great clash was inevitable and tha

Hungary, lying far from the West and wedged between the two giants, Germany and Russia, would be in the center of the fighting, the havoc, and the destruction. Exceptional political skill might perhaps save her national, ethnical, and constitutional existence, but nothing could prevent her from becoming a battleground and the center of destruction.

Teleki shared my views. He was, however, more pessimistic than I about the Magyar people's inherent strength but more optimistic in regard to Britain's policy. He saw a solution in the formation of a Central European and Balkan bloc guaranteed by Britain, France, and the United States and stretching from Finland to Turkey. And he said an interesting thing. This bloc, he said, must be anti-Bolshevik; and yet it would be to Russia's interest that it should be formed, for it was the only means of defending the small states from German aggression, and it would be Russia's best protection against German attack. The first link in the chain would be an alliance with Yugoslavia. We had already established complete understanding with the Poles, and we could very easily come to agreement with the Bulgars and the Turks. All that would be wanting then was the adhesion of Rumania and Czechoslovakia. Well, Teleki continued, Rumania, surrounded in this way by Bulgaria, Yugoslavia, Hungary, and Poland, would have everything to gain by falling into line. We on our side must endeavor to make this easy for her by the most far-reaching concessions. That would leave only the Czechoslovak problem, and he had no manner of doubt that Czechoslovakia would disintegrate into her constituent elements—Ruthenia, Slovakia, and Bohemia—if Benes did not accede to the policy of the bloc. Teleki said that, for his part, he would never trust Benes: everything that man touched became a source of catastrophe.

I knew indeed that we were approaching a climax, but at this time—the autumn of 1943—I was still filled with confidence, believing in a favorable solution and therefore in the plenitude of my strength and fighting powers. The nation, too, was beginning to feel with me that the final development was at hand. In the following paragraphs I shall endeavor to outline the major trends in the various parts of the population.

The economic situation of the largest section of our people those engaged in agriculture, was showing marked improvement Within this group, however, there were varying degrees of de velopment.

The big landowners, with their mass production, came under strict state control as regards prices and marketing. Their tax returns, too, could be checked. They could not, in the nature of things, sell in the black market, where they were forced to acquire, second-hand and at exorbitant prices, most of the farm implements, machinery, and so forth, which had disappeared from the markets. The tax on net income was steeply graduated, rising to 80 per cent for incomes over 400,000 pengö (10,000 dol lars at the rates then prevailing); and any concealment of income was both ethically and practically unthinkable for Hungarians of that group.

The small farmers, the so-called smallholders class, on the other hand, had things all their own way. They were able to sell at ex cellent prices their small produce—vegetables, fruit, wine, and, above all, the poultry and swine which they slaughtered without license. The most revealing symptom of their economic condi tion was that they were able to repay in large measure their long standing debts to the banks. Members of this class lived well, and they were able to satisfy all their wants, even if not always in the legal markets. For the first time, perhaps, in the history of their class these small farmer peasants enjoyed a state of ordered pros perity.

Less well off were the landless agricultural laborers and farm hands. Their fixed wages were hardly sufficient to keep them, par ticularly as manufactured goods—especially clothing—had be come extremely dear. An alleviating factor was that nearly all these landless laborers, and, of course, the farm hands owned their own cottages and gardens. They were thus able to eke out their slender resources with poultry, eggs, and the like.

I made every effort to ameliorate the lot of the agricultural laboring class. The problem was a difficult one. An immediate, overhasty land reform would, of course, have been no help at all and would have wrecked agricultural productivity. A rise in wages would have involved a rise in the prices of price-controlled products, in the first place of grain. There would have set in then that vicious spiral so well known in economics, with increasing inflation and with nobody benefiting. My collaborators and I explored every avenue of possible reform. The only remedy appeared to be some arrangement that enabled agricultural laborers to procure manufactured articles, at prices within their means and directly, thus cutting out both the retail and the wholesale tradesman and preventing the possibility of the goods falling into the hands of black marketeers. This would have been a big help, and we did all that we could in this direction. The trouble was, however, that there were not enough goods to go round. What there was of any value in the way of boots, clothing, underwear, and blankets had to go to our army; the remaining stocks were scanty and of poor quality. Thus we were, unfortunately, unable to help the real working peasants as I should have liked and as they deserved.

Despite their difficulties, however, there was no unrest among the agricultural laborers. Their patience was remarkable. They were the most valuable social class in the nation. I say without hesitation that had we been spared the catastrophes which in fact overtook us, the postwar consolidation could have safely been entrusted to the agricultural workers.

The masses of small farmers, who were so well off, also supported my regime. As I stated above, however, it was the discontented sons of this group, together with the malcontents of the urban and rural *petite bourgeoisie*, the minor officials, and the lower intelligentsia, who became the followers in the right-wing factions of Imrédy and Szálasi.[1]

The large landowners, together with the high clergy, the higher officials, and the leading industrialists and intellectuals, were also

[1] See pages 38–39.

behind the government. Naturally, however, even this leading class was not entirely of one mind, especially with respect to external affairs. Although they were homogeneous in that none wanted the Germans and all feared the Russians, there was a right and left shade among them. The left wing, headed, of course, by the Jews, dreaded the German occupation more than a Russian invasion. The right-wingers felt the other way around. Both sections, however, fully understood and were ready to support my "Hungarian" policy which aimed at avoiding both contingencies. These differing shades of opinion led to anomalies not infrequently met with in Hungarian politics: for example, the Jews, and also a fair proportion of other left-wing elements, were so afraid of a German occupation that they continually tried to persuade me to go to any length, yield to any demand, to avert the supreme disaster of occupation; on the other hand, the Conservative elements, the Roman Catholic high clergy and Bethlen's group, were for resisting the Germans more stubbornly. In fact, to bring home to my foreign readers the full complexity of the situation, I offer the complete alignments on this issue: Our army, the Jews, the Arrow Cross, all shades of the right and the extreme left of the industrial workers—all these were for compromise with the Germans, for procrastination and concessions. The Conservatives, the aristocracy, the distilled essence—as represented in the upper house—of every national factor, the high clergy, the genuine Magyar masses who dared to think independently, rallied around me, stood for the principle of intransigence and resistance, and advocated it as the policy to be pursued towards the Germans. The Russians, of course, were desired by neither of these groupings, and they were never mentioned.

I discussed above the rightist and anti-Semitic orientation and behavior of the *petite bourgeoisie*, the minor officials, and the poorer intellectuals who comprised the turbulent Right Radical and the groups headed by Imrédy and Szálasi.[2] For some of the grievances felt by these elements, there were extenuating circum-

[2] See pages 39–40.

stances, factors which reflected on Hungary's social policy. In each case the position was governed by the country's situation and its limitations, which, unfortunately, often made it impossible to realize desirable social objectives. It was this class of whose support I felt least confident: I feared that at a critical juncture this group would develop political unrest, as was more or less the case later on.

The economic situation of the industrial workers at this time was by no means bad. As their situation was, in fact, better than that of the agricultural laborers and the civil servants, the industrial workers were a constructive factor in the national life. Their political organ, the Social Democratic party, was free from extremist tendencies, though it had to fight against the infiltration into its ranks of communistically inclined radicals. Yet it was indubitable that even the latter were not Moscow-sponsored internationalists, but merely more radical than the official leaders.

In the foregoing I have endeavored to give a picture of the country's situation. The preponderant majority of the population did not want war, and wished neither for a German nor a Russian victory, as they expected no solution for our problem from either nation. What most Hungarians wanted was peace, tranquillity, humanity, order, and a human existence—not the triumph of this or that ideology but the coming of peace and the arts of peace. For this reason the Hungarians were constructive in their outlook, the best possible people for the work of reconstruction that peace should bring and deserving a leading role in the life of Central Europe and the creation of a new order. It was not the fault of Hungary or her people that things turned out otherwise.

Everyone felt that we had no concern with the war; that everything, whether avoidable or not, which had forced us to take part in it was a mistake; and that we had to find a way out to save ourselves. Possibly there was not another people, not excepting the actual neutrals, which desired so ardently to be neutral in the world conflagration as we did. If there was a splinter, a vociferous little group, which ranged itself by Germany's side, and another less vociferous group which advocated an immediate move against Germany, no one except a few insignificant cranks and paid agitators advocated those courses for the sake of Nazism or Communism; most holders of these extreme views saw them as a means of escape from our predicament. It might be said that, paradoxically, the greater part of the pro-Germans came from those circles which feared Germany so much that opposing her seemed to them the greatest danger of all, and the other camp saw no escape from the Soviet menace but to come to terms with it.

It was in that atmosphere that the new parliamentary session opened with the debate on the budget. The several parliamentary parties had used the interval to prepare themselves. My own Government party—the Party of National Life—had employed the time in strengthening its provincial organizations and taking up the fight against extremist tendencies whether of the right or the left.

The party's endeavors against the right met with the complete favor and support of government organs. But the party was surprised and shocked to find that the left-wing parties met with the benevolent indulgences, if not the open or tacit support of these organs. This indulgence applied in the first place to the Smallholders party and the Social Democrats. The high sheriffs received definite instructions from Keresztes-Fischer, the minister of the interior, to let those parties work and organize freely, unless they definitely set themselves against the constitutional order of the state and endangered that internal order and tranquillity which were so necessary in time of war.

Ferenc Nagy, a Smallholder deputy, had been specially encouraged by Minister of the Interior Keresztes-Fischer to form the so-called Peasant Alliance. This organization was to wean the class of small and medium farmers from right-wing influences and to organize them on expressedly anti-German lines. Nagy was to fight, not only the Arrow Cross contingent and Imrédy's followers, but also the right-wing elements in the Government party. He was to endeavor to gather round him a thoroughly patriotic, constructively-minded group which after the war and under different political auguries might form the nucleus of and develop into a new Government party. As I said, Nagy undertook the task with the encouragement of Keresztes-Fischer, who personally promoted and assisted his work in every respect. Naturally the movement had my full approval and support. I myself discussed with Nagy the best lines to follow.

Keresztes-Fischer kept in constant touch with the Social Democrats also, and I frequently received Peyer and their other leaders. In my conversations with him as well as with Rassay, the leader of the Citizens Liberty party, and Zoltán Tildy, of the Smallholders group, I invariably emphasized that their task and real historical mission would begin after the war. They would inevitably be called upon to take over the direction of the country's affairs, and they must not therefore look on themselves as leaders of insignificant Opposition parties, nor exhaust themselves in the airing of ephemeral grievances. I told them that they must not impede my work by small pin pricks and breaches of tact, made possible by the existing freedom of speech and of the press, and that they must not aggravate my already sufficiently onerous difficulties with the Germans. They must always remember the historic mission awaiting them and prepare for it by laying down its moral bases.

I helped that group in their efforts to organize themselves and to gain ground in the public opinion of the country even against my own party. For that support, I was sharply attacked by my party, as I have shown,[3] not to speak of the immense repercussions which my conduct aroused in the right-wing parties and primarily, of course, among the Germans. I supported also the contacts which the Social Democrats had abroad. Their articles, memoranda, and letters were not infrequently carried to neutral coun-

[3] See Chapter Eleven, "Internal Political Unrest."

tries by foreign office messengers; I also helped some of their emissaries to get across the frontier.

I must, however, state that not one of those parties adequately
realized the importance of its mission and future role. All were
more conscious of their actual insignificance and balked ambitions than of the great aims for which they should have been preparing themselves.

Inside my own party the balance of forces had shifted considerably in my favor. The sane, patriotic, not pro-German, and
not anti-Semitic elements had become preponderant. Events at
the front and the gradual worsening of Germany's position naturally contributed to this. Although the group of intransigent pro-
Germans and anti-Semites in the party had dwindled perceptibly,
they had become all the more restive and determined. That group
began to flirt with Imrédy, but it had no connections with Szálasi's
extremist right wing, just as Imrédy himself at this time was still
strongly opposed to the Arrow Cross group. Those right-wing
members of my party could cause trouble during the budget debate only if its speakers struck a note which created discord abroad
and imperiled my Anglo-Saxon orientation. I tried to prevent
them from doing that with the help of the party leaders, although
the attitude of the leaders was not far removed from that of the
rightist members. But three quarters of the members of the
party were good Hungarians, loyal and devoted to the national
cause. The judgment that has since been passed upon the Government party is unjust. It produced far fewer collaborators after
the German occupation and many more men of courage, fortitude,
and unyielding patriotism than the parties that came into power
under the Russian occupation and Russian influence.

I can sum up the political attitude of parliament and of the
country at large after eighteen months of my administration by
saying that my position and authority had been very greatly enhanced and strengthened and the number of my friends and followers much increased. The camp of my opponents had dwindled
and had lost much of its influence; on the other hand, it was

primed for a sharper conflict. The period of waiting to see how I should behave was over; the Germans and the parties under their influence now knew my aims. Thus I started the new parliamentary session strengthened, indeed, but faced with the prospect of open war.

But I envisaged that prospect calmly, for I believed that both in my internal and my foreign policy I had so far taken the right line and had achieved results. My country's situation was in every respect the most favorable that circumstances allowed. German influence was very much on the wane, and the Germans made little attempt to interfere in our policy. The economic situation was satisfactory; the food problem was improving, and our deliveries to Germany were diminishing. So far, too, we had not been bombed. Those things could be seen by all, and everyone must feel, I thought, that there were freedom and security in the country for everyone. But what was nurturing my hopes and sustaining my self-confidence was something the public did not know, could at most only suspect: that I had my contacts with the Western powers and that I believed that Hungary would win the peace with their help, perhaps even by fighting at their side.[4] That was the culminating point of my policy: the point when it seemed reasonable to hope that we were advancing, not towards the end of all things, but towards a new world.

The budget debate opened in the lower house on November 12, 1943, with the discussion on the premier's budget. I had asked the house to discuss the budgets in that order, a reversal of the usual procedure in which the premier's was the last order of business. And, again contrary to the customary practice, I rose to speak at the beginning of the session, saying in explanation of my action that since the house had not met for some time, I thought it necessary and only fair to inform parliament of the situation, of my views, and of the direction in which the country was being governed. I did this to forestall a multitude of questions and speeches

---

[4] See Chapter Sixteen, "My Foreign Policy," for the details about our relations with the Western Allies alluded to in this chapter.

which might have been justified if I had not given my exposition in the beginning. I wished also to prevent the controversies
which might have sprung up on many such points between the
Opposition and members of the government and which might
have gained acerbity in the course of the debate and thus created
an envenomed atmosphere before my turn came to speak.

In my speech I stated that my whole political attitude and
course had been laid down when I spoke on May 29, 1943.[5] Passing on to our foreign policy, I expressed the hope, without entering on specific details, that our aspirations would ultimately be
victorious. Then I went on as follows:

*I believe and profess that however insignificant a pawn we may
appear in this conflict between the world's giants, a mere grain
of dust compared with them, our destinies lie largely in our own
hands. That is why I struggle and wrestle, refusing to let myself
be forced into comfortable, oversimplified decisions which would
take no account of the life-or-death problem of our nation and
would jeopardize its existence. I shall move neither right nor left
from the only firm rock there is, the single-minded pursuit of
Hungarian aims, Hungarian interests, and Hungary's ultimate
good.*

*Recognition of three facts are needed if we are to maintain this
course: that as things develop we may come to be the focus in
the struggle waged in Europe by the three world powers; that the
military force of the German, the Russian, and the Anglo-Saxon
world is drawn up around our frontiers; and that the great fight
draws nearer on every side. But the moral and spiritual influence
of our enemies, too, must be reckoned with; it may come to fray
our nerves, since the war of nerves has come to be an accepted
fact and can easily affect the impressionable.*

*We cannot dream of taking up the fight against these gigantic
armed forces with our own strength, but that makes it all the more
important that enemy propaganda and alien influences should*

[5] See pages 192–93.

not disrupt our unity, cloud our vision, or bring confusion into our ranks.

The duty of Hungary's political leaders is to reckon with these indubitable facts and to prepare the nation for all eventualities.

The second conclusion we have to draw from the present situation is that we must increase our military preparedness to the utmost by utilizing all available resources. It is our duty to see to this at the cost of any sacrifice, any effort. For I hereby declare that while we harbor no thoughts of any kind of aggression, we shall—and let everyone take cognizance of this—defend our frontiers. On this point we shall never yield. It is not a point that can be made the subject of political consideration, nor even a question of military capacity; it is a national duty, imposed on us by the problem of our national survival. A provocative attitude would be mere senseless braggadocio; not to husband our strength to the utmost, recklessness. But he would be a dastardly traitor who would not defend our frontiers, our country, and our freedom, or who even stopped to consider possibilities and relative forces. Let no one imagine that anyone else will accomplish this task for us. It is our duty and can be only ours. These are the two great facts which the nation must face open-eyed, for which we must stand prepared and which will decide our fate.

The third requisite, on which depends all possibility of this decision being a favorable one, is the maintenance, preservation, and securing of order within the state.

After dealing with some questions of internal policy, I ended as follows:

Every war contains the germs of social revolution. While the war lasts, they remain latent, to break out after it. To recognize the symptoms and prepare remedies and solutions against the time when they are needed is the only correct and possible precaution we can take. War sweeps away the weak not only on the battlefield but also after the battle. A nation will only be strong if it realizes this and acts accordingly. Two things have to be done *in this direction: to assist with every resource that war conditions allow the poor, the indigent, and the weak; and if this is impossible —but only then—prepare to accomplish the task tomorrow.*

In the course of the debate, I was sharply attacked by Imrédy's party. Other attacks came from members of the so-called *Volksbund*, while the Transylvanian deputies discussed the nationalities problem, for which the premier was responsible, in great detail. Ladislas Nagy, an Imrédist deputy, fell on a collection of my public speeches published at that time and enumerated various statements of mine which he alleged were contradictory. Among other things, he mentioned that, in the speech in which I introduced myself to the house, I had said that "we must take part in this campaign." He then called on me to be consistent and to raise a new army to support the Germans in their fight against Bolshevism, which was still raging and looked more dangerous for us than ever.

I replied:

In my first speech in the house I could not say what the honorable member must be well aware of, that I was taking over a fait accompli. I must draw the consequences from the losses suffered by our 300,000 army as my Magyar conscience and Magyar sense of responsibility bid me. The situation has changed, gentlemen! I cannot agree with you that we must throw a second Hungarian army—everything we have raised since—into this fight, in which, as I said this morning, we must not dream that any one will defend us. We need all our forces in our own struggle. They must be held in reserve.

That same party urged me to introduce a capital levy on Jewish property. I replied that Reményi-Schneller, the minister of finance, had given careful consideration to the problem but had "come to the conclusion that we have neither the theoretical nor the practical means to carry such a measure through at the present time without seriously affecting the course of economic life."

Certain Transylvanian deputies suggested, in view of the Rumanian atrocities, that we should resort to reprisals against the

Rumanians in our country. I rejected this suggestion, saying that "to ill-treat my own citizens because my neighbor has ill-treated Magyars would be contrary to Hungarian ideals and to our nationalities policy."

The German deputies protested against the policy of assimilation. I answered them at length, reviewing the question from the historical angle. In my concluding remarks, I said that we were not the gainers by the process of assimilation, which had enabled the Germans to occupy so many high posts in official and economic life. We should be better off were they to choose other paths and make no claims to these high posts. (This remark caused great commotion among the German deputies, who immediately rushed to report it to the German legation and discussed it with Berlin for days on end, even threatening to leave my party. It was no easy matter to smooth things over.)

The Imrédists and the Arrow Cross party made a strong attack on the censorship. The left-wing parties raised no objection to it.

The discussion of the ministerial budgets was followed by the debate on the appropriation bill, after which on December 4 came my reply.

By custom, the first speaker in the appropriation debate was the leader of the most important Opposition party; thus the duty devolved, as it also had the previous year, on Béla Imrédy. He attacked my policy in all its aspects in a comprehensive speech lasting fully two hours. He described my program as vacillating, lacking definite aims, and contrary to the national interests whose fundamental axiom was that there was no issue for us nor salvation for Hungary except by Germany's side and with German aid. In relation to domestic affairs, he developed the thesis that the National Socialist idea was the only one on which a nation could be built up in the world to come. The crumbling edifice of our historic constitution could no longer be bolstered up; it must be pulled down to give way to a new structure consistent with the spirit of the new age and of National Socialism. Practically every deputy of any importance in the lower house, both on the Government party's side and on that of the Opposition, spoke in the course of this debate. In my reply I dealt only in a general way with the questions that were raised, and I concentrated on joining issue with Imrédy.

An essential part of Foreign Minister Ghyczy's comments had concerned the right of small nations to live. This was a favorite subject of mine but I thought it best to let the foreign minister be the one to develop the theme, for the foreign ministry's exposition always aroused especial attention abroad. At the beginning of his speech Foreign Minister Ghyczy spoke, with the customary prudent circumspection, of Germany and Italy's important role. He then went on to the subject of the small nations, viewing it in an extensive historical and political perspective before he turned in this connection to Hungary. And then it happened that, whereas at the mention of Germany and Italy the right-wing parties had broken into ostentatious applause, when he came to speak of Hungary's rights and her claim to have these rights recognized, there was silence on their benches.

Referring to this incident, I said some words which seem to me worth mentioning because they aroused immense indignation in Imrédy's party, an indignation which endured during the whole of that parliamentary session. I said:

It is the fundamental question, not only for our own future but also for that of Europe at large, whether the rights of small nations are to be recognized everywhere in the world. Victory will go to the nation which recognizes them; even if it is conquered in the field, it will be morally justified by history. During the foreign minister's speech I was shocked to see that the references to our German and Italian allies were applauded, while those to our own country were heard in silence. Gentlemen! Here, at this point, a chasm opened between us.

After that I argued that we must not listen to any voice that came to us from beyond our frontiers; propaganda, from whatever side it derived, must be silenced among us. I declared that "this country's policy will be modified neither by threats nor by promises."

In an improvised part of my speech, when I was speaking of the need for caution in party politics before impugning the good faith of our opponents, I made a declaration of faith and referred to the example of Stephen Tisza. I said:

What must have been the hidden tragedy of that man when he left the crown council in Vienna and assumed control of a war of which he was perhaps the only one—and in any case the first—to disapprove! And he died without uttering a word in his own defense, having sponsored a policy which was not his own but which he had yet been compelled to represent in the nation's interest.[6]

Then I turned openly against Imrédy in the following words:

The honorable member's speech was repulsive. He repelled everyone and also repelled men from communal thinking in order that only his thinking should prevail. This will have a disintegrating effect on the nation and is unworthy of a Béla Imrédy.

Naturally I replied also to the spokesmen of the other parties. It may not be without interest to mention my reply to Peyer, since his subsequent conduct really confirmed what he had said on this occasion. I said:

I take note that the official spokesman of the Social Democratic party has made a public profession of faith in favor of Hungary's territorial integrity, liberty, independence, and freedom from all alien influences.

I dealt at great length with the questions of reform and social progress. I showed that we had done in this direction all that the war and circumstances had allowed, and I expressed doubt that any belligerent or even any neutral country had done as much as our impoverished Hungary. I referred to the comprehensive

[6] Stephen Tisza, premier of Hungary in 1914, never revealed the fact that he opposed the sending of the ultimatum to Serbia in July, 1914; his position became known when the documents were published after the First World War. He was assassinated in October, 1914, precisely on the ground that he had "dragged Hungary into war."

survey which Minister of Justice Radocsay had published on our social welfare laws and regulations and described any attempt to deny our achievements and our difficulties as unpatriotic and subversive malice (I was thinking principally of the dastardly propaganda carried on against us abroad). And I concluded my speech in the following terms:

I know that all this is little enough, far from exhaustive, and not yet the beginning of a new world. But to promise what present circumstances preclude from realization is to prepare, not reforms, not social progress or a better future, but revolution. Possibly certain individuals or parties hope to weather the coming time by this means. Let them! I can undertake no more than to lead my nation and my people to the point where they can decide their own fate according to their own free will. The preparatory work is going on. But it would be dishonest not to admit that it is often simply turning in a vacuum until our nation has come safely through the present terrible times and the destruction of which we hear such shocking tidings from every side. But for this we need faith, industry, soldiers, and a Hungarian policy. It is for this I work, for this that I ask for the acceptance of the appropriations bill and the rejection of the amendments.

That sentence in the foregoing passage in which I said that the nation would have to determine what it wanted when it was free to come to completely independent decisions gave rise to lively comments. To very many people it was the first startling intimation that we could not hope to continue after the war as we had lived and thought before it.

On December 16, 1943, Imrédy challenged me to make a clear statement on my attitude towards Bolshevism. I said, "From the first minute the whole of my foreign and domestic policy has been governed by the need of defense against Bolshevism, its power politics, and its expansive tendencies."

For that declaration I was sharply censured by the British and American press and radio.

After the budget had been debated in the lower house, it came up for discussion in the upper house. Of the speeches delivered during the debate there, I must especially mention those made by Stephen Bethlen, Ladislas Ravasz, Leopold Baranyai, Anthony Sigray, and George Pronay. The debate was on a very high level throughout and was entirely free from party politics, which was natural, since there were no parties in our upper house, whose members were chosen partly on a vocational basis and partly because they were men eminent in public life. There was not a single Imrédist or Arrow Cross man in the upper house. There were right-wing and left-wing groups, about equal in strength, but the great majority of the members were nationalist, liberal, and conservative.[7] There was no question of antidemocratic or antisocial tendencies, although, of course, certain individuals were inclined that way. But I am convinced that the upper house contained men as progressive as many party politicians who made a greater parade of their sentiments. The intellectual standard was inevitably a very different one, since the members included, ex officio, representatives of all the higher state offices and church dignitaries; about fifty members were men prominent in public life nominated by the Regent, and the provinces were represented by delegates elected by the urban and county administrative bodies.

The characteristic feature of the upper house was its markedly anti-German, liberal, and pro-Allied sentiment. In the budget debate, for example, Count Sigray, who was Archduke Otto Habsburg's representative in Hungary, made a speech in praise of democracy; the spokesmen of the bench of bishops made a decided stand against National Socialism and anti-Semitism; and all the speeches dealing with domestic affairs without exception condemned the Arrow Cross party and National Socialist disturbances.

In conformity with the specialized capabilities of the members, there were many speeches on economic questions, led by Leopold Baranyai, the eminent president of the Hungarian national bank.

[7] See pages 36–37.

The other paramount subject of discussion was external affairs
treated, naturally, on the high level to be expected from the com
position of the upper house. In one of my replies, I observed tha
it would be a mistake on the part of the victors to imagine tha
there could be a Europe without Germany or Italy or—assuming
another contingency—without France. In whatever way the wa
ended and however great the havoc wrought in these countries
Europe could not be rebuilt without them. The foreign ministry
begged the speaker of the upper house to have this sentence
omitted from the journal,[8] for Foreign Minister Ghyczy feared
that my remark might cause bad blood in all quarters—among the
Germans because it presupposed their defeat and among the
Anglo-Saxons because it declared the two Axis powers to be in
dispensable factors in Europe.

I shall quote in full the essential and concluding part of my
speech. It was my last parliamentary utterance.

Both my speeches delivered before this debate and that made
by me in the lower house reflect the same unaltered course. Nat
urally and inevitably the foreign minister's exposition is integrally
linked with this. I wish, then, again to stress the unchanging
nature of Hungary's policy; its consideration of ultimate issues,
its devotion to the country's interests; and its conformity with
the Hungarian character, which connotes, in the first place, honorable dealing.

I am happy to be able to state that this policy of mine is meeting
with understanding in ever wider circles of the country, and I
would add—not out of boastfulness but because the nation's interest is served if this is realized—that, some extremist dissenters
apart, my conduct of our foreign policy and its objectives have the
backing of the entire nation.

If you have done me the honor of following my speeches with
attention, you will have seen that from the first moment, but—

[8] This could only be done in very exceptional cases and then only by a special
procedure; the matter also had to be laid before the editorial committee of the
upper house.

I repeat—perhaps most markedly since last spring and in the foreign minister's latest exposition, we have been increasingly occupied with the fate and problem of the small nations, a problem of primary interest for us not only on our own account but also on that of all Europe. It may possibly be in some degree owing to us that this question is assuming world-wide importance and is coming more and more to the fore among Europe's important international problems. I am glad of this, for Europe belongs to the Europeans, and it is the small and medium nations which determine its character. In their common evolution through the centuries with the great powers, the small nations went through the same process of development as the latter in respect of culture, civilization, and social institutions, and the small nations produced all those assets by which the world today judges its values, and which made the advance of other nations possible. I therefore do not hesitate to say that without the small nations there is no Europe, just as without Europe there would be no world; at least none worth living in for human beings.

This is why I, why we, talk so much about the small nations. For it is my conviction that they must have a part in the drawing up of the new world peace; if not, that peace will be no peace. Recognition of this fact will naturally have to penetrate all nations, big and little; and the latter must see to it that they are worthy of the pedestal to which their past has raised them.

The fundamental condition of this is that they should remain true to that past and to themselves, preserving and developing those special values which Providence has assigned to them. The value of the small nations resides, not in adaptability and the mutability of their political creeds, but, on the contrary, in the independence of their spiritual and political attitude, in the permanence of their institutions, and in their stubborn defense of these, possibly in the preservation of the distinction between the institutions of others and their own.

The greatest service the small nations can render is to remain true to themselves and even in times of tribulation faithfully to guard their own achievements and the fundamental values of humanity.

The wiping out and destruction of nations with a historic past may destroy more than lies within the frontiers of that nation; it may recompose the synthesis of the world. If we were to remove one color out of the rainbow, not only that one color, assuredly, would be lost to the world; the sun itself would shine differently, and its vivifying force would be one ray the poorer.

The scene of war is coming ever closer to our frontiers, and the great offensive of the war of nerves has already reached us. We are flooded with promises and threats—primarily threats—which foretell a horrible fate for us if we persist in our present policy. Simultaneously we are accused of having entered the war in the hope of easy loot, of aspiring to the acquisition by force or by stratagem of alien possessions.

Hungary has not waged war for the sake of conquest; she has sought neither easy nor hard-won loot; she has sought only her right. Naturally she has regarded as hers that which had always been hers and which only Trianon deprived her of—she never made a secret of this. But no thought of conquest or expansion led her into this war. What we wanted and still want is to live. It was not possible for us to remain outside the universal hazard of war; we could not isolate our country from the spreading conflagration. But it was not we who started the blaze, and it cannot be accounted to us as a crime that we were caught up in the flames. Indeed, Providence never designed the Danube-Tisza regions and the Carpathian Basin as an Arcadia; Hungary's destiny has never been one of carefree safety or of cunning profiteering. We took up, because we had to, the burden imposed on us by our situation. But it was not we who, at Trianon, determined what the situation should be.

And now, while war rages round us, I must emphasize that Hungary, Germany, Austria, and Bulgaria were not the sole victims of Trianon, Versailles, St. Germain, and Neuilly; all Europe, perhaps the whole world, suffered with them. The devastations of ar may perhaps be kept within limits or repaired in the ensuing eace, if that peace is a real one; but a bad peace, which is merely he continuation of war by different methods, poisons the entire orld. The human organism may survive the effects of an isolated fection, but continuous blood poisoning is inevitably fatal.

These considerations apply in an increased measure to the small ations. We know that the risks run by them are quite different om those of the great powers. Small nations are, so to speak, ontinually faced with the question to be or not to be; more espe- ially Hungary, whose geographic position has set her at that point here great peoples and great interests clash.

The policy of small nations is conditioned by the need of self- reservation. They follow existence politics, not power politics; or they want to survive and develop, not to conquer. The nation hich deviates from this path and seeks to secure its own pre- onderance by methods which have already failed once and have een proved catastrophic sins against the fundamental interests f the small nations and thus of all Europe. That state cannot be nduring which seeks its security not in itself but in external, alien upport, which tries to replace territorial and ethnic inner har- nony by international political combinations, and which sees its wn mission in services rendered by or rendered to another ower.

If small nations wish to survive, they must in the first place eek the path of mutual understanding, mutual support. Mutual nderstanding, especially between neighbors, is one of the primary tages on the path towards self-preservation. This understanding annot, of course, mean subservience, but must be based on a nutual regard for rightful interests. Good neighborly relations are condition of further co-operation, evidence of honest good-will nd of a sense of responsibility.

Small nations cannot, in the nature of things, pursue a pro- ocative policy, and they must consider not only each others' ightful interests but also those of all other nations; for the fact f being a small nation confers no laissez-passer and does not

justify irresponsibility. But this must never reach the stage where
a small nation is pressed into the sphere of interest of any great
power. In my speech of May 29 I dealt with this question, but in
view of recent events I feel it necessary solemnly to reassert our
standpoint.

We can see no promise of security in the establishment of
spheres of interest, only the seed of renewed conflicts; for since
these spheres of interest serve the needs of single states, they must
sooner or later clash with other, similar formations. There is no
other guarantee of security than a just peace, which gives every
state, big or little, the conditions of existence to which it is entitled and which may thus become a basis for the productive and
constructive co-operation of all.

There is another point on which I should like briefly to touch
on that revolutionary propaganda which is one of the chief instruments of the war of nerves. We know that all wars bring changes
in the social, economic, and political structure of countries, and
that at the end of a war it is never possible to continue where we
left off. But we also know that wars can only hasten the gradual
course of development, they cannot eliminate the intervening
stages. A war may breed peace, but anarchy can only breed disaster and confusion; anarchy can multiply the grievous consequences of war, but it cannot cure them and does more harm than
good to the cause of necessary change.

Some of the speakers have dealt with recent events, such as
certain speeches emanating from the side of the Anglo-Saxon
powers, the Atlantic Charter, and the Benes-Soviet agreement.
One of the speakers extolled the democracies as alone profitable
Unfortunately, however greatly we may admire the democracies
of Western and Northern Europe and the United States, and
their epoch-making significance, I cannot at the present moment
and in the light of cold reality see that the bare fact of democratic
government is a guarantee for the correct solution of international
problems. Finland is the very incarnation of democracy, not impaired even by the intrusion of a so-called plutocracy, and the

Baltic states have developed on the same lines, and yet their lot is by no means enviable. In order that they may be jettisoned to satisfy the selfish purposes of higher power politics, their democracy is being called in question. Yet, if there is democracy in the world, then it is to be found in Finland, for there it is presided over by an admirable word, and that word is "integrity." The terms of the Atlantic Charter are also beginning to grow blurred and are more and more markedly, and even officially—witness the Russo-Czech treaty—replaced by the conception of spheres of interest.

His Excellency Géza Szüllő has broached the question of unconditional surrender. I believe that we can all agree with his words and remind the world that the small nations are all, without exception, the products of wars of liberty; that they have developed during secular struggles for freedom; and that, since they are ready to take up the fight again, it would be folly to force it upon them.[9]

[9] I was informed by Ullein-Reviczky, our minister in Stockholm, that a member of the British legation, in the course of a confidential conversation, expressed the view that in England and America the idea of "unconditional surrender" was not universally accepted as a commendable and happy solution even after the total victory which was a foregone conclusion. In fact, our minister had received the impression that in official circles it would by no means be taken amiss if the question were made the subject of criticism. I consequently resolved to mention it in my speech. But as Ghyczy, our foreign minister, feared that the Germans might, not unjustifiably, charge me with publicly discussing the contingency of their defeat, I decided to ask a member of the upper house, M. Géza Szüllő, well-known for his anti-Nazi and pro-Western sentiments and famed for his courageous outspokenness, to take over this part of my speech. It was given to him in writing and he read it aloud. I have not got the text by me, but I remember it.

The principle of unconditional surrender was, he said, objectionable from three points of view: that of international law, that of political ethics, and that of practical expediency. After reviewing the obvious arguments provided by the two former aspects, he proceeded to show that after unconditional surrender only one factor was left in the field: the victor, who was thereupon compelled to assume full responsibility, while the vanquished party ceased to be responsible for anything that might occur. Unconditional surrender excluded the possibility of concluding peace, for this demanded two free agents; there can be no obligation unless it is shouldered voluntarily. After unconditional surrender the victor would have to take over the entire administration of the vanquished country, its food supply, its economic burdens, etc. Only a victor who meant to incorporate and spoliate the vanquished country, to destroy its constitutional life and force on it a prolonged period of slavery, could look on this as an advantage. The Anglo-Americans, he continued, had no

274 THE RECONVENED PARLIAMEN

In my speech in the lower house I declared that neither threat
nor promises could make us abandon our political objectives.

We have never joined in any political race for favor, and w
shall not do so. For the primary duty of small nations is not to ru
races but, as I said before, to be true to themselves. I therefor
assert and maintain that we adhere to our own line. Our value ii
the world is commensurate with our intrinsic worth, our impor
tance with our self-respect and integrity.

The traitor may be paid, but no gentleman will clasp his hand
And the Hungarian people want to be able to clasp hands un
ashamed with all the peoples of the new Europe and the new
world. It believes that its intrinsic values will insure its existence
and permanence, and therefore it will go its chosen way. Thus only
can it protect itself and the cultural, human, and humane inter
ests entrusted to it. Whatever shape the coming world assumes
it trusts that recognition of these will determine a nation's destiny
For unless these factors are accepted as decisive, the new worlc
will only bring new struggles for our nation: struggles for which i
is as much our duty to prepare as it is to do all in our power—a
in fact we are doing—to further the advent of that new world anc
a better understanding. Such are the convictions which guide my
domestic and my foreign policy. I beg for the acceptance of the
budget.

That speech was my political swan song, and it was also the
swan song of Hungary as a free, independent, national state. Ar
attentive perusal of the above quotations from my budget speeche

such purpose; therefore unconditional surrender would not be conducive to thei
interests; it could only serve the interests of those to whom this sort of peace ap
pealed. The Anglo-Saxons had no need of the assets of the vanquished nations
they had nothing to gain by the destruction of liberty and the creation of a new
world of slavery. Consequently, he did not understand the adoption of this slogan
He went on to remark that Anglo-American broadcasts were continually recom
mending us to accept this principle and to surrender unconditionally. He would lik
to know, he said, in what manner the spokesmen expected this to be done. To
whom should Hungary, for example, capitulate? It required two to make a capitula
tion: one to capitulate and one, who was on the spot, to replace the suspended con
stitutional order by his own system and rule.

THE RECONVENED PARLIAMENT

will reveal how the confident note with which I began changed towards the end to one of resignation. Rumors were reaching us of the Teheran Conference; [10] I sensed a change of atmosphere in my negotiations with the English and Americans; Benes' journey to Moscow [11] and other things combined to awaken in me, if not yet full awareness and despair, a feeling of uncertainty and fear.

The optimism with which only a month before I had viewed the trend of affairs had not, however, been entirely unjustified nor unfounded. I was not alone in taking a hopeful view of my country's future—neutral observers were under similar impressions. Many people were coming from the Axis states and even from neutral countries to settle in Hungary, not only because our country seemed to offer the freest, most normal, most comfortable and secure life in Europe, but also because it seemed likely to weather the war and postwar disturbances more smoothly than other countries promised to. To cite only one example: the minister of a nonbelligerent country, accredited to the most Western neutral state in Europe, with whose country we still maintained diplomatic relations although it was an ally of Great Britain, asked to be transferred to Budapest and came there with his family because he thought it not only the pleasantest but also the safest and calmest post in Europe. Official recognition of this privileged situation of ours manifested itself in two other cases.

In the first instance of official nature, the Spanish minister of foreign affairs inquired of our minister in Madrid whether Hungary would support a peace proposal emanating from neutral and nonbelligerent states and based on the ideas of the Pope's Christmas address. He said that, apart from Hungary, he had so far approached only Sweden in the matter, for only in these two states did he discern the courage to sponsor a move of this kind, notwithstanding their delicate position in regard to Germany. Obviously, therefore, he regarded us as a nonbelligerent, courageous

[10] Held November 28–December 1, 1943.
[11] In early December, 1943, after the Teheran Conference.

nation disposing freely over our own fate. I naturally received the proposal with joy and promised my wholehearted support. But the enterprise soon collapsed, other neutral countries having been dissuaded from participation by England and the United States.

The second attempt was more serious. The Turkish minister, Unaydin, called on me and, remembering a conversation which we had had a month before and which he had reported to Ankara, asked whether I should be willing to enter into an immediate agreement with Turkey to work out a detailed military plan to form a "Bloc of Order" in Central Europe and the Balkans after the war. The Turkish government—that is, General Ismet Inönü, the president, Sükrü Saracoglu, the premier, and Numan Menemencioglu, the minister of foreign affairs—were convinced that in the Balkans, where guerillas were even then fighting not only against the Germans but also against each other, where the most sanguinary religious wars were being waged between Catholics and Orthodox, and where the Macedonians were already organizing for civil war, pandemonium would break loose as soon as the German troops withdrew and Bulgaria collapsed. They believed that in those circumstances Turkey and Hungary would be alone in preserving order, calm, and intact armies. Thus it might devolve on us to maintain order in the Balkans, since it was possible that neither Russians nor Anglo-Saxons would allow the task to be undertaken by the other. Neither of our countries wanted territorial gain and were thus absolutely marked out for that not exactly agreeable duty. Even though we could not know how events would shape themselves, we must be prepared for such a contingency, which was why they were making their proposal.

I saw at once that this Turkish offer was prompted by their fear of the Balkans being occupied by Russian troops, a prospect which they (rightly) thought we also disliked. I gave my unreserved consent to the plan, the main points of which were to be discussed in Budapest. John Vörnle, our minister in Ankara, was known to be very friendly with the German ambassador, Franz von Papen, so that I could not entrust the business to him.

What would have lent the matter special importance in our eyes was that since Turkey was an ally of England's, it would, we thought, give us a chance to draw nearer, even if only indirectly, to the British Central European policy. But the project came to nothing. I must remark that the Turks' cipher was very easy to break. We always read their telegrams straight off. When our negotiations began to assume a concrete form, I called Unaydin's attention to this; and the Turkish cipher was changed; but I continued to receive the deciphered texts without a hitch. When I asked whether the Turks had changed their key, I was told that they had. That, however, did not hold things up even for a day, for our cipher department was still able to read the text straight off. When, after the Teheran Conference, Anthony Eden invited Sükrü Saracoglu, the Turkish premier, to come and see him in Cairo, the Turkish official sent reports of the discussions home; and in one of his reports I read that, when he informed Mr. Eden of the proposal he had made to us, Mr. Eden conspicuously refrained from entering into the subject. In a subsequent telegram I read that Premier Saracoglu had ordered the negotiations with Hungary to be broken off. It needed little imagination to guess, first, that Turkey had been warned off all anti-Russian moves, and, secondly, that Hungary had been put on the wrong side of the line, as being not in the British sphere of interest. The October, 1943, Conference in Moscow, which spoke of Italy and Austria but left open the question of the other small states on Russia's frontiers, had, indeed, already thrown its ominous shadow before. And Benes' journey to Moscow had rendered our abandonment almost a certainty.

As isolated instances, the two things are not particularly important, but they are incontestable proof that the far from negligible factors in the official policy of the nonbelligerent countries did not regard Hungary as beyond hope and thought her political course trustworthy. It is also proof that we caught at every straw which might extricate us from the German war without throwing us into the arms of a Russian peace. Unfortunately, the arbiters of the new world, or rather those who should have been its creators, the English and Americans, did not recognize this.

In the excerpts from my speeches that I have quoted, and particularly in the last fragment, I drew attention to mistakes, dangers, and crimes, all of which unfortunately afterwards came to pass. In the autumn of 1943 I defined all the weaknesses of unconditional surrender, its incompatibility with peace and the responsibility which it laid on the victors. When speaking of small nations, I made plain the dangers and immorality of spheres of interest, and showed that they harbored the germs of a third world war. This is a sad satisfaction, if indeed you can talk of satisfaction when defective vision has destroyed all, perhaps irretrievably, and brought us within sight of the ruin of the world.

Little by little I was brought to realize that all my efforts had been in vain. In times of great historical upheavals the voice of a small nation is not heard; it cannot change the course of events. Even the depositories of the power and the force, the men into whose hands the direction of affairs has been laid, somehow prove strangely unable to direct events, even if they see clearly. In these mighty storms it is no longer the man at the helm who guides the ship; it is delivered over to the mercy of the winds and the waves.

I am convinced that Winston Churchill saw and knew all this. But as an Englishman he perhaps took refuge in the time-honored English axiom that in a difficult situation you must go for one thing at a time. The first thing was to win the war; the rest would follow automatically. We small nations viewed the situation in the opposite way: what troubled us was the question of what would happen after the war. And that difference of perspective was the rock on which my tentative approaches towards England and America were wrecked and on which, incidentally, the destinies of Poland, Finland, the Baltic states, Czechoslovakia, Rumania, and the Balkans were thrown against to their undoing. England was fighting for her life and was only concerned with what those nations could give her, in what degree they could aid her, in her own struggle. She could not see and did not realize that they could contribute very little to her victory. Their importance lay not in war but in peace, and there it was great and indispensable. That England and the United States would win the war was a certainty, whether the small countries were for them or against them. But the peace they could not win because they sacrificed those countries, both those which had fought with them and those which had belonged to the enemy camp. I am not being wise after the event; I knew, saw, and felt all this at that time.

And since I saw it clearly, the question had to arise: *quid nunc?* In my account of negotiations with the Allies—Chapter Sixteen— I deal at some length with the alternatives which presented themselves and which, briefly stated, were these: either to issue a declaration that we were withdrawing from the war, thereby exposing ourselves to an immediate German occupation and the most rigorously hostile treatment, or in despair to side unreservedly with Germany. I shall in Chapter Sixteen show why I chose neither of these alternatives. Here I shall only deal with the effects of my decision on the home front.

All my personal feelings prompted me to resign and withdraw from politics or else to go abroad and try to do something for my country from outside. It is quite certain that in this way I could have salvaged my own personal position. But this point was so unimportant that I wasted not two thoughts over it. I only asked myself what would be more advantageous for my country. If I resigned, I thought, the Regent would have to appoint a new premier. Incidentally, this could not be done then without German interference. So far the Germans had not dared to dream even of intervening in any civil or military matter; but after the bad experiences they had had with me and in their critical situation, they would intervene if I left office. I could not imagine whom the Regent would choose: he would probably have to appoint some soldier as premier, with a cabinet of political officials to support him. A soldier would be thought suitable because he was no politician. But this would have its own drawbacks, for precisely a man without political training and routine would be easily—rather inevitably—drawn into following a bad policy.

Then there was the problem of my own Government party. It would inevitably split. The right-wing members of the Government party and the right-wing Opposition parties would form a new coalition. This would be the largest single party and, with the German influence behind it, would dominate the lower house even if it did not have an absolute majority. The serious and moderate elements in the Government party would be left isolated, and since they would not be able to unite with the left-wing, democratic Smallholders and Socialist parties of the Opposition, parliament would no longer reflect an independent nation.

Naturally such a regime would, willingly or under duress, place all the country's military and economic resources at Germany's disposal; and the Jews, the socialists, and the foreigners who had sought refuge with us would be delivered over to the mercies of their Hungarian enemies and of the Germans. In fact, the Germans would get all they wanted, and the country would in every way be the worse for a selfish decision by me. Complete disintegration would set in, and the only safeguard against it would be the presence of the Germans.

Since I could not resign, What was I to do? Change my policy? If I did, Which way should I turn? To Germany—since to Russia I would not and the Anglo-Saxons, apparently, would have none of me? And what was I to tell my people? What reason should I give if I went? And if I stayed, Was I to tell them that I had abandoned all hope, that we were lost, and that all was lost?

I made the only decision that I was capable of: to stay. I was told of various childish plots against me that had been concocted by Arrow Cross people, but I disregarded them. Some German plans against me were more serious. I was told that a plot was laid when Edmund Weesenmayer, who became German minister plenipotentiary after the occupation, visited Budapest before the Germans took over. Then they decided to put off their action until I could be got to Austria to shoot chamois. (Before the

Anschluss I had shot in Austria every year, as the guest first of Dollfuss and later of Schuschnigg. This naturally stopped after the *Anschluss*. Suddenly, I received an invitation of the same nature from Jagow, the German minister in Budapest, I should, in any case, never have accepted the invitation, but a lady connected with the German legation warned my wife, without giving reasons, that I had better refuse.)

I discussed the question of my resignation with the Regent. He would not hear of it. He said that he had several times most flatly rejected German requests that I should go. I had no right to suggest such a thing myself. In his opinion the general public, the entire country, all honest, right-thinking Magyars, were on my side. What, then, could justify my resignation? The attitude of the Opposition? Or that of an insignificant faction of my own Party? That the Germans were dissatisfied with my policy or that I did not do everything just as the English and Americans wanted? Were these reasons for me to go? Was I free to abandon my post because I was suffering all these difficulties? Even if I felt, as I had explained to him, that the expectations on which I had based my policy had not been realized as I had hoped and wished, that was not a sufficient reason for my resignation. He would understand my action were it prompted by the consciousness of mistakes committed. But he could not consent to my leaving my post merely because of my country's enemies and because those we sought to join could not comprehend the only policy which the circumstances allowed Hungary to follow.

What, then, were the problems confronting me? In the first place, the stagnation of my negotiations with the English and Americans. Secondly, the military situation, and, in particular, how to retrieve the remnants of the Hungarian Second Army from Russia and to eliminate the pro-German elements among the officers, especially in the general staff. Thirdly, how to stave off the attacks of the Imrédists and the Arrow Cross and disarm the right-wing elements in my own party.

There were, of course, such permanent problems as wartime

difficulties with public supply, centering with us on industrial articles, and connected with this the task of evading German demands, the growing nightmare of inflation and its effect on the fixed salary class, and other matters that are discussed in the next chapter. All these were in themselves very important concomitants of the war conditions, requiring constant work and care, but not political in nature. They might and did cause difficulties, but they could not sweep the country into a real crisis and into catastrophe.

That conversation with the Regent confirmed in my mind the direction in which my sense of duty impelled me, and I spoke no more to him of resigning.

THIRTEEN

OUR ECONOMIC POLICY

OF THE VARIOUS LINES along which Hungarian resistance was conducted, our economic resistance was the most successful and the most systematically carried out. There are various reasons to account for this. The nation's economy was the field in which the government found it easiest to develop and to conceal its resistance to Germany. Our domestic needs, the demands of our own army, the counterclaims of those from whom we bought abroad—all these were titles under which we could reduce the satisfaction of Germany's demands and conceal our real position. It was difficult for the Germans to prove that sort of passive resistance against us because we never let them see the genuine statistics, and that they had not been able to get hold of those illegally we could see from the fact that the figures on which they used to work were incorrect. But good intentions on the government's part would not have sufficed unaided to make the resistance effective; the main cause of our success was that all the economic groups concerned participated with enthusiasm.

The farmers were anti-Nazi almost to a man, and also they were naturally prone to hoarding, especially in periods of inflation. Hoarding was particularly easy for the small farmers whose stocks it was difficult to control. The result was that at the beginning of 1944, before the German occupation, the farmers possessed stocks, known to the ministry of supply, of 7 million quintals [1] of bread grains over and above the stocks required for the national consumption till the next harvest, which were in the ministry's depots. The Germans' chief complaint was of our failure to deliver livestock; here we hung matters up so successfully that at that date—that is, in the fifth year of the war—the country's livestock population was 6.25 per cent higher than in 1937.

As for industry and wholesale trade, the sabotage was conducted with a zeal which almost outstripped the government's own intentions—a fact easily explained by the circumstance that Hungarian industry and distributive trade, like our banking, was almost entirely in the hands of anti-Nazis, a large part of it being, indeed, owned and controlled by our Jewish fellow-citizens. The majority of the industrial workers were Social Democrats, and they naturally took their share in this salvage operation. I wish, however, to state at once that this resistance did not take the form advised by the Communists in their whispered underground propaganda or by the British and American radio broadcasts in their trumpeted exhortations that the workers should destroy means of production and stocks, refuse to work, or otherwise follow a policy of hara-kiri. All groups concerned understood that the object was not destruction or diminution of production, but letting the German war effort get as little as possible. That was much the more effective course and, indeed, the only one which achieved its purpose, suited us, or benefited the Allies. The violent

[1] A quintal is 100 kilograms or 220.46 pounds avoirdupois.

1ethods proposed by the Allies would have at once brought down
n us an equally violent German intervention, and we should have
·een the sole losers and the German supply services and war in-
.ustry the sole gainers.

A testimonial to our effort was when late in 1943 Karl Clodius,
vhom the Germans had sent down to negotiate with us, said to
1e: "Take care, Mr. Premier! The conviction is beginning to gain
round in Berlin that it is not good policy for us to tolerate Hun-
ary's independence; for we are getting incomparably much more
rom the occupied countries, especially Czechoslovakia, and also
rom Rumania, which grows and works for us as we want."

Before adducing a few data which are in my possession to sup-
ort these statements, I shall invoke the testimony of a prominent
nember of the present regime (that is, the Communist regime).
van Boldizsár, postwar secretary of state in the foreign ministry
nd one of its most important personalities, director of propa-
·anda, and an extreme Communist, wrote for the postwar govern-
nent, in 1946, a little book entitled *The Other Hungary: the His-
ory of the Hungarian Resistance Movement*. Boldizsár can hon-
·stly not be accused of prejudice in favor of the old order; indeed,
1e never missed an occasion to attack it most passionately. Never-
heless, he had to admit that the regime did everything possible
luring the war to resist Germany's pressure and demands.

The present study . . . must present to the world the funda-
nental truth that the present democratic Hungary is not a sud-
len, overnight growth produced in a forcing-house of party poli-
ics nor an artificial structure. Hungarian democracy had been a
iecessity of the logic of history, a natural phase in the evolution
>f that other and truer Hungary that fought for democracy long
* igo in the past and for democratic ideals laid herself open to grave*
isks and made unselfish sacrifices.[2]

Boldizsár went on to show how the Western powers and the
-ittle Entente by cold-shouldering Hungary (Czechoslovakia, for
·xample, imported cereals from overseas) forced her into a Ger-

[2] Ivan Boldizsár. *The Other Hungary*, page 5.

man economic orientation. To escape her isolation Hungary first
turned towards Austria and Italy. After the *Anschluss*, however,
and after Italy had linked up with Germany, Hungary had no
choice left but the German market. Even before the war the percentage of our exports going to Germany had thus risen from
11 to 50. Boldizsár then turned to details and wrote as follows:

GERMAN TRANSPORT HAMPERED BY RESTRICTING
MEANS OF TRANSPORT

[In 1939] *The ministry of transport lent five seagoing Danubian
motor barges to the British admiralty and one to the French ministry of marine. . . . Later on the government consented that the
barges should ply under the flag of Panama so that they would be
safe from German attacks. After the outbreak of war the Danubian
oil tankers belonging to the shipping interests of the Shell Oil
Company were in secret rebuilt as seagoing barges and one by one
withdrawn from the Danube. This maneuver had the full consent
of the Hungarian ministry of transport. The same ministry first
lent 120 oil-tank wagons to Switzerland in 1941 and 50 in 1943.
Of these the first number reached Switzerland, thereby causing
no inconsiderable inconvenience to German oil transports. After
the resignation of Mussolini the Hungarian government co-
operated with Badoglio's adherents at the Budapest Italian legation and agreed to take over 700 oil-tank wagons in transit from
Italy. Until the German occupation 400 of these were still being
kept back by the ministry of transport.*

*The rail transport for the German war machine was interfered
with by various means. Some lines were closed down as, for example, the one between Szeretfalva and Déda; new locomotives
were kept back in the work shops under various pretexts; oil transports were held up by the customs authorities, the alleged reason
being the need for minute customs examination.*[3]

The author then enumerated various acts of sabotage carried
out in different industrial enterprises and listed the factories which

[3] *Ibid.*, page 42.

it proved possible to close against any deliveries to Germany, at least to this extent, that they offered terms which the Germans would be unable to fulfill. Others delayed delivery, or supplied poor quality goods; some managed to evade German orders by rebuilding or moving to new premises.[4]

THE FOREIGN EXCHANGE POLICY OF THE
NATIONAL BANK OF HUNGARY

The national bank had accumulated by now the experience of many years of how the German-Hungarian trade exchanges could be effectively obstructed. In this context we mention first the foreign exchange policy of the national bank. A high rate of exchange for the reichsmark [5] would have served as an encouragement for exports. Therefore the national bank tried to keep the official rate of exchange for the reichsmark low, and as long as it could it paid a high premium to exporters who delivered hard foreign currencies. When the national bank saw that the method by "quotation" would not serve the purpose any longer, a number of other financial expedients were resorted to in order to skim off the profit which exporters to Germany would pocket while on the other hand it insured a favorable premium to those who delivered non-German, hard foreign currencies. With such and similar methods the national bank tried to divert the flow of our foreign trade from Germany. It must be known that the reichsmarks for deliveries effected were remitted to the national bank which paid out the amounts due to the exporters in Hungarian pengö.[6] The clearing department of the national bank was constantly delaying payments even of amounts for which it had already received settlement from the Germans, the intention having been that exporters should by and by lose interest in selling to Germany.[7]

[4] Ibid.

[5] The average rate of exchange in 1941 for the reichsmark was 39.968 American cents.

[6] The average rate of exchange in 1941 for the pengö was 19.77 American cents.

[7] Ivan Boldizsár, The Other Hungary, page 42.

THE RESISTANCE OF OUR EXPORT TRADE

The practice of the various official export trade organs did not remain much behind the policy of the national bank. Hungarian resistance had already made itself felt during the negotiations leading up to the commercial treaty. The negotiations were taking place in a very strained atmosphere, but it was nevertheless often possible to decrease the bulk of exports to much below the level of the surplus by painting the economic conditions of the country in much darker color than the real situation would have justified. Then again no allowances whatsoever were made from the rigors of qualitative and quantitative prescriptions for German exports so that the export quota was never fully reached. In this context we might mention the so-called "junctions" regulations according to which an export license to Germany was granted only on condition that a certain quantity of the same produce would be sold on non-German markets. This system was kept up until the Germans got to know of it and made a sharp protest. And now we have arrived at the richest chapter in the description of our economic resistance from which, however, we shall cull only a few facts. These are taken from the period 1940–44 and are a convincing array of proofs adduced to what we have said already.

The export of wheat and maize—although the surplus in the crops was rising—was kept under the quota as regulated by the commercial treaty; we saved thereby 259 million reichsmarks worth of wheat and 169 million reichsmarks worth of maize. The quota for the export of horses was gradually being diminished but even so in 1940–43 only 50.7 per cent of the quota was exported while in 1943–44 this figure fell to 7.3 per cent. Thus all in all 26,000 horses were kept in the country. The saving realized by not exporting the full quota of cattle amounted to 78,000 head, and as only the poorer quality animals were exported and the better quality kept at home, this was equivalent to 33 million kilograms saved. As regards the export of pigs only 189,000 pigs were exported as against the quota of 640,000, which meant a saving of 451,000 pigs. The quota for lard and bacon was decreased from 14 million kilograms to 3 million kilograms and even of this quota 2 per cent was delivered. The export of sheep also showed a decreasing tendency and stopped altogether in 1942. These figures show that during the war Hungary not only sabotaged the German demand for livestock, but she managed to increase the amount of her own stock.[8]

Boldizsár went on to show how we encouraged our trade with the neutral countries, often asking to be payed for our exports with machinery of which we then put off acceptance. The state steel works, among others, adopted this device. He mentioned that we, and only we, succeeded in resisting the German "Frachtverfahren" regulations for directing transport of goods. He showed that we introduced the rationing system mainly in order to paint our situation in colors blacker than the realities justified. Finally, he mentioned one very important measure which we, again, were the only state to take: it was laid down that at least two thirds of any fresh capital subscribed or invested must be proved to be of Hungarian origin. Machinery of German origin or patents were not accepted as substitutes for cash subscriptions.[9]

It would be possible to adduce data more detailed and giving an even clearer picture of what we did, but that is unnecessary. Boldizsár's pamphlet, issued under the Russian occupation by a Communist official, gave the best proof that our economic policy during the war was, not one of unwilling service to Germany, but, on the contrary, a tenacious and unremitting resistance in every field.

The importance of that economic resistance becomes clear if we cast a glance at the map (see page 346). With Austria incorporated in the Reich and the small states north and south of us completely under German power, we were held in an iron grip. We could only reach our principal market, Italy, by crossing German territory, using Germany's railways, roads, or air space.

[8] Ibid., pages 43–44.   [9] Ibid., page 45.

Germany wanted to take in her own hands and organize the entire supply system; she was to distribute the stocks. We opposed this stiffly and insisted on maintaining direct exchanges with Italy. We were also able up to the last to keep a free hand in our dealings with the three neutral countries within our range—Sweden, Switzerland, and Turkey. That direct bilateral exchange infuriated Germany because we were able thereby to get many materials which she could no longer obtain. We had a lot of trouble with the Germans because of that, and they tried to make it a condition that they were to receive a certain percentage of the goods that crossed their territory in transit; but that demand, too, we managed to ward off.

A few words on our economic negotiations with Germany: while I was premier, I used to preside over those negotiations myself. The immediate conduct of them lay in the hands of Louis Reményi-Schneller, minister of finance, whose sympathies were, indeed, strongly right-wing and pro-German; but it was not my experience that he failed to represent our case energetically and according to my instructions in those negotiations. The program used to be that early in the year a German economic delegation, headed by Clodius, minister plenipotentiary, would arrive and present a list of desiderata. Then the endless haggling would begin. We would try to whittle down each item; and all acknowledgments are due to the Hungarian delegates, headed by Alfred Nickl, for the Sisiphean labor which they performed. Finally, the important questions were brought to me for decision, and that was the end of the discussions. I should stress that the German government and foreign ministry never once intervened; or rather, I remember one case: in 1943 we refused to export any maize, and the German minister intervened to ask us to send a few wagons of maize to Hitler's personal physician, who was conducting some experiments on infant nutrition.

Clodius was a very decent man, in whom I did not detect excessive enthusiasm for the cause he served. Sometimes, when calling on me, his attitude was practically that of a suppliant. He would

explain how difficult his situation was; he would get the sack if I
sent him away empty-handed again. Once I asked him about
German conditions. His reply was: "We exist. We eat; we clothe
ourselves, more or less; children get born; but there is no pleasure
in any of it. The Reich is not losing the war; but the German
people has lost its joy and its smiles, and it will never get them
back."

The case of the Bachka was an interesting and typical one. The
Bachka, which had been assigned to Yugoslavia in 1920, had been
the richest agricultural area of historic Hungary. Its population
was a mixture of Magyars, Germans, and Serbs. After the collapse
of Yugoslavia, the Germans proposed to take it under their own
management until the end of the war, as a separate economic unit.
We refused to accept that plan, but in the end agreement was
reached that the export surplus from the Bachka should go to Germany and Italy in the proportions of 60 and 40 per cent. While
those negotiations were going on, the whole surplus filtered up our
way; when the inventory came to be taken, therefore, the cup-
board was bare. The same thing happened every year. It goes without saying that no German official was ever allowed into the area
under any pretext whatever.

In spite of everything, however, Germany's passive balance with
us (that is, her excess of imports over exports) rose in 1943 to
one billion reichsmarks. The debt itself was not such an overwhelming one, but we had to issue the equivalent of the reichsmarks in pengö to finance our own production. The substitution
of pengö for the frozen reichsmarks was one of the main causes
of our inflation. The pengö had originally been equal in value to
the Swiss franc, but by that time had fallen to under 10 centimes.
Our national bank succeeded in cushioning the effects of that on
our economic life; the domestic price level did not fully reflect
the fall in the pengö's value abroad, retail prices having risen only
200 to 300 per cent. But already this rise in prices was weighing
heavily on much of the population, first and foremost on the
fixed-income classes, but also on the workers, whose wages could

not be raised in step with the rising prices without initiating an inflationary spiral.

At the Hungaro-German conversations which opened in January, 1944, I said that I could not grant any more reichsmark credits: we must be paid in goods for any further exports. We realized that this would not of itself remedy the inflation, but at least the national wealth and production would be increased. In exchange for our exports we wanted German machine tools, machinery, raw materials, and half-finished products—all things which we had stipulated in earlier negotiations, but without receiving delivery. I asked further for the transfer to ourselves of Hungarian assets held in Germany, such as shares in Hungarian companies held by German shareholders, and the Hungarian property of the Danube Steamship Company, consisting of the winter port at Obuda and the coal mines near Pécs, which Germany had appropriated after the *Anschluss*. I knew that it might not be possible for us to keep for ourselves after the war such of these assets as Germany had acquired by conquest, but it was still better than nothing. Then, too, the claim at least constituted a counter-demand to theirs which was difficult for them to accept and thus made it harder for them to insist on their own demands.

After much initial indignation, the Germans agreed in principle. We had thus gained a point; but now came the harder part, the execution of the agreement. The transfer of the shares was relatively easy. The process was set in motion: the Hungarian banks and industries could now recover possession of such of their shares as had been in German hands, and the danger of German penetration diminished correspondingly. The transfer of real property from German hands involved more difficult negotiations which were, unfortunately, never completed. When Czechoslovakia disintegrated, Germany laid claim to Czech interests in Carpatho-Ruthenia. We did not admit Germany's title to these assets and took them into our own possession. Germany's largest set of Hungarian assets was that part of the property of the Danube Steamship Company which had been Hungarian even under the

Dual Monarchy. There were two main items: the Obuda harbor, with extensive premises, docks, etc.; and the coal-mines near Pécs, which were the most important mines, both quantitatively and qualitatively, in Trianon Hungary. We managed to reach agreement over the harbor. We agreed on a valuation, with which Germany was credited. The German military command, however, intervened in the case of the mines because it was from them that they took their coal for their Danube shipping and other purposes. We got out of them in the end a written promise that after the war they would hand over to us the mines with all equipment and legal rights. The Germans insisted, however, on keeping the mines in their own hands up to the end of the war, as they had no guarantee that under Hungarian management the claims of their armed forces would be adequately met. We got as far as agreeing that the whole enterprise should at once begin using the Hungarian official crest, etc., while the conversations on the valuation had to be concluded before the next year's economic negotiations, which were not to open unless this point was settled. I do not know whether that agreement was ever initialed, but I do not think it was.

So much for the way the negotiations were conducted. How the agreements were carried out is another story. Neither party delivered what it promised. But there was a difference between the two kinds of nondelivery. The Germans sent short measure because they had not got full measure to send, and they knew at the time of their promise that that would be the case. We promised at the negotiations only half of what we had, and in the end we delivered only a fraction of that.

It is interesting to observe how human frailties contribute to such results. Both Louis Reményi-Schneller, the minister of finance, and Louis Szasz, the minister of supply, had definite German sympathies; yet both fought our battle bravely. Reményi-Schneller, the minister of finance, resisted the Germans because he was fanatically keen on his own anti-inflationary monetary policy, and he feared the effects on it of putting into circulation the value of the reichsmark balances in pengö. His colleague, Szasz, also resisted because he was naturally anxious for his supplies—he dared not resort to requisitioning for fear of losing popularity. The third holder of an economic portfolio, Daniel Bánffy, the minister of agriculture, was a fanatical hater of the Nazis and did everything he could to sabotage deliveries. The right-wing parties kept on demanding the unification of the ministries of agriculture and supply, for which there was much to be said under wartime conditions, but I refused to do it because the disagreement between the economic ministers suited my book.

The part played by Leopold Baranyai, the president of the national bank, was an important one. He was an outstanding figure not only of our economic life but of our whole public life. His intellectual and moral distinction gave him a special position. He was most definitely anti-German, and everyone knew that he was co-leader, with Stephen Bethlen, of the group which personified Hungarian resistance. As a zealous Catholic, Baranyai possessed much influence among the higher Catholic clergy, and he was a close friend and frequent adviser of the Regent's.

Baranyai was an inveterate opponent of Reményi-Schneller, whom he thought I ought not to retain as minister. Unfortunately, the relations between the two men became so strained that when Baranyai's term of office expired, he refused to accept reappointment if Reményi-Schneller continued as minister of finance. Here, again, I was faced with one of the dilemmas which confront public men. Baranyai was my friend and a first-class man. Reményi-Schneller was my opponent. One man's ideas were identical with my own; the other's, the opposite of mine in every respect. Every member of Baranyai's circle belonged, politically and socially, to my own circle, while Reményi-Schneller had round him men with whom I had no contact in either respect. Yet I was unable to let Reményi-Schneller go, even for the sake of my dearest and most admired friend. Of all the decisions which I had to make as premier, that one was perhaps the most painful. If I dropped Reményi-Schneller (who also took the opportunity to offer his resignation, for he would have liked to be free of the restrictions under which I made him work), the logical next step would have been to appoint Baranyai to succeed him. But the position in connection with our economic negotiations with the Germans would then have been catastrophic. Baranyai's every action, any objection raised by him to Germany's demands, would have been put down to his Germanophobia. The economic negotiations would have ceased to be economic at all; they would have become a purely political tussle. So Baranyai went, and I was more alone than ever. It was, incidentally, a gain for himself and for our cause, for as a private person he was able to devote himself more freely to various other activities at home and abroad in which we continued to co-operate.

This whole subject of economic resistance deserves a special treatise. I have not the space to enter here into much detail, but I shall give a few statistical data in support of what I have said in these pages. The material is fragmentary, for I have been unable to undertake systematic research. It is impossible to get books, especially books about the past, from behind the Iron Curtain; moreover, the data in the contemporary records are not reliable—not that the struggles and results of my administration are represented too favorably, but the reverse.

I give figures from various sources even where they conflict.[10]

All the following tables are from the *Hungarian Statistical Review*, a nonpolitical source whose figures I consider reliable. The statistics that follow the tables are from the notes and the *Aide Memoire* submitted by the Hungarian government to the Western powers in 1946. Although the postwar administration was hostile to the old regime, its figures were compiled for the peace negotiations and may or may not be entirely impartial.

[10] Further details may be found in the following works: L. Jocsik, former secretary of state for industry, *German Economic Influences in the Danube Valley* (1946); L. Jocsik, *Hungarian Economic Resistance against German Penetration*; Government of Hungary, *Note to Principal Powers*, February 1, 1946; Government of Hungary, *Aide Memoire*, September 3, 1946.

AREAS UNDER CULTIVATION IN HUNGARY, IN MILLIONS OF HOLDS,[a]
BY CROPS, 1937 AND 1943 [b]

Crop	1937	1943
Wheat	2,625	2,731
Rye	1,969	965
Barley	827	767
Oats	412	422
Total	5,833	4,885
Maize	2,093	1,850
Potatoes	515	463
Sugar beets	82	96
Total	2,690	2,409

[a] A hold is approximately 1.405 acres.
[b] The total arable land under cultivation, in millions of holds, was: 1938, 9,556; 1941, 8,836; 1943, 9,269.

AGRICULTURAL PRODUCTION, IN MILLIONS OF QUINTALS [a]

Crop	1938	1941	1942	1943
Wheat	26,883	18,855	17,032	22,785
Rye	8,046	5,601	5,132	6,692
Barley	7,240	6,027	5,114	7,053
Oats	3,104	3,394	2,792	3,516
Total	45,273	33,877	30,070	40,046
Maize	26,620	18,062	14,493	12,462
Potatoes	21,406	21,196	18,038	18,212
Sugar beets	9,694	9,060	7,382	7,259
Roots	35,210	29,572	24,677	19,951
Total	92,930	77,890	64,590	57,884

[a] A quintal is 220.46 pounds.

HEADS OF LIVESTOCK IN HUNGARY

Animal	1938 [a]	1942	1943 [a]
Cattle	1,882,000	2,376,000	2,124,000
Horses	814,000	900,000	774,000
Swine	5,224,000	4,468,000	3,716,000
Sheep	1,629,000	1,708,000	1,197,000

[a] The statistics for 1938 show 85,000 quintals of meat in cold storage, and those for 1943, 180,000 quintals. The figure for 1943 is, however, far below what it actually was.

MINING [a] AND SMELTING OPERATIONS, IN TONS [b]

Product	1938	1943
Coal and lignite	9,369,000,000	12,161,000,000
Steel	648,000,000	776,000,000
Bauxite	467,000,000	998,000,000
Crude iron	336,000,000	418,000,000
Iron ore	298,000,000	342,000,000
Manganese ore	46,000,000	102,000,000
Petroleum [c]	43,000,000	839,000,000
Aluminum	2,000	8,000

[a] The total numbers of persons employed in mining were: 1938, 45,000; 1943, 64,000. The total payrolls were: 1938, 66 million pengö; 1943, 112 million pengö (at 1938 rates of pay).

[b] The figures have been rounded to millions.

[c] The production figures in state-owned oil fields were: 1937, 2,000 tons; 1940, 253,000 tons; 1943, 842,000 tons.

STATISTICS ABOUT FACTORY PRODUCTION

Factor	1938	1939
Units of horsepower	1,082,000	1,293,000
Number of production workers	289,000	392,000
Total number of employees	344,000	484,000
Value of production in millions of pengö	3,044	8,643
Value of production in millions of 1938 pengö	3,044	3,710
Price index	87	203
Average annual wages of skilled workers in pengö	1,752	4,537
Average annual wages of skilled workers in 1938 pengö	1,752	2,623
Cost of living index	88	152

VALUE OF INDUSTRIAL PRODUCTION, IN FORINTS [a]

Year	Value [b]
1938	13,883,000,000
1943	19,385,000,000
1947	10,840,000,000

[a] The forint in 1947—the rate used in this table—was worth 8.58 American cents.

[b] Figures rounded to millions of forints.

NATIONAL INCOME, IN PENGÖ,[a] 1938–44

Fiscal Year	Income [b]
1938–39	5,192,000,000
1939–40	5,506,000,000
1940–41	4,312,000,000
1941–42	5,171,000,000
1942–43	5,467,000,000 [c]
1943–44	5,241,000,000

[a] The pengö at the 1938 rate—an average 19.727 American cents—is used throughout the table.

[b] Figures rounded to millions of pengö.

[c] From agriculture, 1,345,000,000 pengö; from manufacturing, 1,741,000,000 pengö.

NATIONAL COST-OF-LIVING AND WAGE INDEXES

Index	1939	1943	1944
Cost-of-living	100	226	339
Wage	100	191	332

PRICES OF WHEAT PER QUINTAL

Year	Price in Pengö
1938	21.42
1939	20.36
1943	35.09 [a]

[a] Official price.

VEHICLES AND RADIOS IN HUNGARY

Item	1938	1943
Trucks	19,000	18,000
Motorcycles	11,000	22,000
Radios	419,000	716,000

HUNGARY'S FOREIGN TRADE, IN MILLIONS OF PENGÖ [a]

Year	Imports	Exports
1938	472	600
1940	603	515
1941	602	648
1942	631	767
1943 [b]	597	672

[a] The League of Nations price index in 1929 pengö—average of 17.44 American cents—is used throughout the table.

[b] The figures for 1943 are slightly too low, as the index did not allow for the rise in prices during the year.

HUNGARY'S TRADE WITH GERMANY,[a] IN MILLIONS OF PENGÖ, 1939-43 [b]

Year	Imports	Percentage of Our Total Imports	Exports	Percentage of Our Total Exports
1939	204	50	265	51
1940	360	60	281	55
1941	474	64	531	66
1942	544	58	718	62
1943	699	61	867	67

[a] The figures in this table include trade with Austria, the Protectorate, and occupied Poland.

[b] In 1938, before the *Anschluss*, our trade with Germany amounted to only 28 per cent of our total foreign trade.

Hungary's Trade with Neutral States, in Pengö [a]

Country	1938	1941	1943
Switzerland			
Imports	10,400,000	21,600,000	55,700,000
Exports	16,700,000	66,400,000	78,000,000
Sweden			
Imports	3,700,000	14,800,000	25,700,000
Exports	10,000,000	17,600,000	32,400,000
Turkey			
Imports	2,600,000	21,100,000	64,200,000
Exports	4,300,000	17,200,000	32,300,000
Finland			
Imports	1,200,000	3,200,000	15,100,000
Exports	1,100,000	3,900,000	13,400,000

[a] The decline in the value of the pengö must be taken into account in considering these figures.

Germany's Reichsmark Balances [a] at the End of 1944

Country	Amount [b]
Belgium	$3,327,000,000
Holland	2,309,000,000
Denmark	560,000,000
Hungary	199,000,000

[a] The prices of goods and values of services owed by Germany.
[b] The amounts have been rounded to millions of dollars.

According to these documents, the Futura (that is, the state silos) had in storage at the time of the "liberation" 18 million quintals of bread grains which had not been delivered to Germany. According to the same sources, the number of swine rose by 32 per cent between 1938 and 1944 and the number of cattle by 16 per cent.

Between 1940 and 1943 Hungary delivered only one quarter of her quotas. Her exports of foodstuffs to Germany were: 1939,

40 million dollars worth; 1941, 21 million dollars; 1943, 12 million dollars. Hungarian economic policy aimed at reducing its exports of agricultural products. These products formed the following percentage of our exports to Germany: 1940, 81 per cent; 1941, 76 per cent; 1942, 68 per cent; 1943, 69 per cent.

In 1943–44 Hungary delivered only 57 per cent of the agreed quantity of agricultural products. She kept back promised deliveries of cattle, swine, poultry, etc. Hungary fulfilled only 69 per cent of her promised quota of cattle. Between 1940 and 1944 she delivered to the Germans only 189,000 swine instead of the 640,000 which she had agreed to send. In 1943–44 none of the agreed quotas of fats and bacons were met. The exportation of horses during the period 1940–44 was lower than before the war. "That," says the government source, "was why the Germans had to occupy Hungary."

Hungary tried to fill up the unmet quotas on agricultural products and livestock with light industrial articles. The Hungarian government resisted Germany's price policy more successfully than did any other government. Between 1939 and 1944 export prices from Rumania to Germany rose by 128 per cent and import prices by 614 per cent. The corresponding figures for Hungary were 117 per cent and 180 per cent, respectively.

In 1941 there were working in Germany 35,000 Hungarian and 80,000 Slovak workers; in 1943, 14,000 Hungarian and 120,000 Slovaks.

The sources point out that whereas in Rumania the Germans acquired possession of the Resita, Malaxa, Continental Oil, and other concerns, in Hungary their holdings on the whole diminished.

I should like to add the characteristic detail that at the end of the war Hungary was preparing to manufacture her own synthetic rubber and to build a plant for the production of synthetic aviation fuel. The Germans had refused to give us the formula for either product, a refusal which cost us years of experimentation. At that period Hungary had on the roads the largest number of private cars and trucks (absolute, not relative figures) in all Europe, including England. That was done on purpose to leave as little gasoline as possible for Germany.

I repeat that the above figures and quotations were taken from publications of the postwar Hungarian government, which was naturally anxious to conceal anything creditable to the prewar governments or nation. Paul Sebestyén, secretary of state in the foreign ministry, almost conceded this in a letter that he sent to George Bessenyey in Paris. When the peace negotiations opened in Paris, I sent my son Christopher with some data to Stephen Kertesz, who was preparing the material for the peace conference as the foreign minister's permanent deputy in Paris. Kertesz replied by thanking my son but saying that he had unfortunately received strict instructions not to use any material, even if it was valuable to the Hungarian cause, which might reflect credit on the old regime or any member of it.[11] What sort of peace negotiations are those in which the true interests of the nation are misrepresented? Can such negotiations have any validity?

I repeat once again that there was not a nation, a people, or a government within the German power sphere which put up a resistance in the economic field so stanch as Hungary's. But I will go further. What of the nations outside that sphere—Turkey, Sweden, or Switzerland? They had to give way before Germany's threats no less than we, although their general and geopolitical situations were incomparably better than ours.

The object of our resistance was, of course, not only to keep Germany short, but also to have our economic potential intact at the end of the war. This was the government's plan and purpose. As the figures quoted show, we were entirely successful up to the moment of the occupation. The capital assets of our agriculture increased, as did our industrial capital and productive capacity. Besides all this, we had considerable potential reserves because no branch of our economy was producing to full capacity.

[11] Kertesz, incidentally, afterwards went to Rome as minister, seceded, and is now doing excellent work in the emigration.

Our correct attitude towards our foreign creditors is perhaps best indicated by the fact that even after England's declaration of war on us we continued to pay the interest on our debt into the Anglo-Hungarian clearing account.

I shall also mention that we, and we alone, sent aid and supplies to distressed peoples and states. The only figures I possess are some issued by the Red Cross, which show that in 1943 Hungary sent goods to the value of 19 million Swiss francs to the starving French, Serbian, and Greek peoples, to children, and to others. This figure does not include the very considerable deliveries made by us direct to the children of Belgium and Holland, nor what we sent regularly every year to the Vatican, whose entire supply of flour came from us.

I received many requests—official, semiofficial, and above all by radio—to sabotage our productive facilities: not to reduce our deliveries to the Germans but to destroy our own production and its sources. We did not accede to those requests, which were inconsistent with democratic thought as they were neither humane nor practical. A scorched-earth policy may bring a momentary advantage in a military campaign, and it is true that military success is the indispensable precondition for victory in war. But it is always necessary to consider whether some action of the moment which cannot influence the final result is worth what it costs. The war had to be won, of course, but what came after the war was important, too—of permanent importance to the defeated but still more to the victors. That is why the policy followed by us in the economic field was—looked at from a longer perspective—right for Hungary, the victors, and for humanity.

FOURTEEN

THE MILITARY WITHDRAWAL, 1943–44

❨HALF of the Hungarian Second Army, which was sent against Russia in 1942, was lost in the Don offensive of the Russians in January, 1943. We managed to bring home half of the remainder as disabled or sick or on other grounds; the remaining quarter was kept in Russia by the Germans despite all the efforts of government and army officers to secure their release. In the months following the military collapse at the Don, we made continued requests and demands for the withdrawal of all our troops from the Russian theater of war, and a crown council resolution was even passed on the subject. (It was a constitutional custom that in matters of supreme importance the Regent called a crown council of the leaders of the country—namely, the members of the government, the speakers of the upper and lower houses, the president of the supreme court of justice and the court of appeal, the chief of staff, and such prominent individuals as, for example, former premiers and foreign ministers.) It was easier, however, to pass such a resolution than to carry it out. After the meeting of the crown council the Regent gave the order for the troops to return home independently. The Germans replied with a counterorder that no vehicles were to be allowed the Hungarian soldiers and that any troops which attempted to return on foot were to be stopped by armed force.

Even without this intervention by the Germans, it was imagining things to believe that the decree could have been carried out. Our forces were several hundred kilometers from the Hungarian frontier, and they were scattered in various areas in the severe wintry weather which had settled on the land. The Hungarian soldiers were prisoners and hostages in German hands. One thing they could have done: lay down their arms if they received the order. Then they would have become German prisoners of war, but it is more likely that they would have suffered the worse fate of being divided into the smallest possible units and dispersed among the German forces, to perish altogether in the combat actions.

And what should have been gained by that? Doubtless we should have made some show in the eyes of the Allies, but should we by provoking the other side have gained as much as we lost? Of course, the Germans would have regarded further resistance as open defiance, and we would have drawn the harsh consequences. The events of March 19, 1944, would have taken place in Hungary a year earlier, and the Germans would have had an extra year to carry out what happened after their occupation of Hungary. We realized how anxious the British and Americans were for us to resist openly, but my first concern had to be for the interests of my country, and I could not follow advice which, in our view, would not even have helped the Allies.

Thus some sixty to seventy thousand of our men remained in the East. Their equipment was poor. They were armed with what remained of the light artillery weapons and small arms, but they had no tanks, motorized equipment, or planes. In accordance with an agreement made shortly before, the Germans gave the Hungarian soldiers the primary task of securing the lines of communication.

In the beginning of the withdrawal our men did not come into conflict with regular Russian troops. In fact, such engagements occurred sporadically only towards the very end of the Eastern campaign, when some slight contacts were made owing to the rapid advance of the Russians, or when the Germans infringed the agreement and did actually throw certain Hungarian regiments into battle. There was, however, fighting with the partisans, but I do not mean by "partisans" those irregular troops who were really fighting for Soviet Russia, of whom there were very few. The partisans I am referring to were not supported by the Russians nor did they operate in co-operation with the Russian high command. Most of the irregular soldiers were Ukrainian exiles and refugees, who fought the Germans bitterly but were not expressly Communists. There were White Russian formations of the same type and a considerable number of Polish partisans who were Polish nationalists. These groups without exception fought against the Germans, but they regarded in a different light the Hungarian troops who were fighting on the German side but were not of German nationality. Soon there came into existence between the Hungarian soldiers and these insurgent forces a kind of sous-entendu agreement, and the two groups tried as far as possible not to harm each other. The Hungarians defended the roads, railways, and military objects entrusted to them. If they were attacked by the partisans and there were skirmishes, the fighting soon died down and prisoners were exchanged. If at all feasible, the Hungarians and the partisans avoided clashes between themselves.

This whole strange state of affairs began in the ranks, and at first the high army officers tried to ignore the development. Finally, however, the relationship proceeded to the point where we brought a Russian, a Polish, and a Ukrainian partisan commander by plane to Budapest, and our staff officers worked out a certain *modus vivendi* with them. They were to restrict their activities as far as possible to the German forces and leave Hungarian-occupied areas alone, while we would naturally not attack them unless we were compelled to. In case we were forced to attack them, we were to give them warning and even help them by furnishing medical supplies and bandages. This scheme functioned well until the continued Russian advance forced backward the partisans also, and they came into increasing contact with our troops. This made it difficult to continue the game. Then we received a proposal from the partisans that a party of about 100,-000, including many women and children, should try to break through the German lines. If they succeeded, they proposed that Hungary should receive them as refugees and shelter them as she had previously given shelter to the Poles.

I should have much liked to accede to this request, but unfortunately it was not practicable to give a favorable reply immediately. The success of their plan was very doubtful, and it seemed very likely that if they began to put it into action, our part in it would become evident. Then, too, if they did reach Hungary, the Germans would want to lay hands on them there, and this would have led to a very serious conflict. If we resisted, the Germans would have a ready excuse for intervening. If, on the other hand, we gave in, we could justly have been charged with leaving the partisans in the lurch. Whether the attempt succeeded or not, the Germans would have said that we were conspiring with the enemy.

This does not mean that we denied refuge to the partisans but that we deferred our decision and the danger and responsibility arising from it until a time when the situation was such that we could not delay it further. Our military leaders stated that the request of the partisans for shelter could only be taken seriously if the partisans approached the Hungarian frontier, when it would be a political problem, not a military one. In any case, the military could only bring it before the government as a *fait accompli*. The partisans took note of our reply, but, as we knew, could take no action. Subsequently the rapidly advancing Russian forces wiped them out.

Thus, with reference to the whole problem of the military, I was unable after the reverses on the Don to do more than before. We refused any more men or equipment, and we waited for things to change. We made our plans for the time when we would be able to do something really practical towards a radical solution of the problem.

Such a possibility arose at the end of August, 1943, when Louis Csatay, the new minister of defense, returned from the German headquarters bringing with him a proposal from Keitel that the place of the German troops being withdrawn from the Balkans should be taken by Hungarian forces, who would serve as occupation troops or as guards for the supply lines. Csatay was for this proposal since it opened up the only way for us to bring home our occupation forces from the Russian theater of operations and use them for the direct defense of the frontiers of Hungary. Csatay's proposal was as follows:

The Hungarian government, with the agreement or at the request of the Croatian government, should undertake the duty of maintaining order in the present state of Croatia, and for this reason should bring home the Hungarian Second Army; after the necessary refits and reinforcements, this Army should be sent to Croatia as an occupying force.

Chief of Staff Szombathelyi, expressed his views on that proposal at a meeting of the supreme defense council over which I, as premier, presided. I quote the following extracts from Szombathelyi's long speech (it lasted at least an hour) because it throws light on the mentality and ideas of our soldiers and it also gives a clear picture of the much-discussed problem of the inner motives which caused our army to be charged with one-sided, Germanophile feeling. Moreover, the speech shows the nature of the difference between the ideas and outlook of the military commanders and those of the political leaders at that time.

The Allied powers have in part taken the initiative and have met with some successes. In Africa the British have forced back the Germans and the Italians, while as a result of the Russian offensive begun in the winter of 1943 the Axis powers have suffered severe blows to their military strength. Not only have they been compelled to give considerable ground, but their losses have also been great.

In the opinion of the chief of staff, in mid-April, when he accompanied the Regent on his visit to Hitler,[1] the situation of the Axis powers gave no cause for anxiety. The initiative was, indeed, gradually passing into the hands of the enemy, which meant that the prospects of the Axis powers were growing steadily more remote. It appeared quite certain, however, that they were determined to do everything possible, and if they were not victorious, they could avoid the worst fate—their own defeat—or at least they could not be vanquished quickly.

Taking everything into consideration, the year 1943 did not at first promise decisive results. It seemed perfectly possible to make all preparations and plans for the Axis powers to renew the attack on all fronts in 1943, although the full effort was more likely to develop in 1944 than in 1943. Hungary also seemed likely to fulfill her military program because she had not yet had to reckon with an Allied invasion in the Balkans. It proved possible to carry out the withdrawal of the Second Army which had played such an unfortunate role in the winter offensive of 1943; losses could be made good, the forces trained anew, and finally we might hope to secure the withdrawal of our occupation troops also.

The Germans promised that they would not compel the Hungarian army to take part in their war effort either on the Eastern

[1] This was the meeting discussed in Chapter Nine, "Intensification of the German Pressure," pages 179–83.

front or in the Balkans, after their request on the latter point had
been rejected in February, 1943.

The year 1943, however, turned out quite different from what
seemed likely in April of that year. The first great surprise took
place in May, 1943, when the German submarines suffered such
great losses that they were forced to withdraw from the high seas,
and since that time they have not ventured far. As a result, the
number of enemy ships sunk fell, surprisingly, almost to nil. The
sea communications of the British and Americans grew more secure.

But the greatest surprise was the collapse of Fascism and the
fall of Mussolini. The strategy of the Anglo-Americans, or rather
of the British, the essence of which is to break the enemy's will
to fight, and thus compel the enemy forces to lay down their arms,
wringing the victory from them by this means, has, even if it has
not led to complete success, nevertheless once more brought material advantages in the offensive against Italy. Increasing bombard-
ments so reduced the resistance of the Italian people (which in
any case was weak) that they threw over Fascism. In the 1914–18
war, just as in the Boer War, the British resorted to the blockad-
ing of food supplies, and this was a considerable aid to their victory. In the present war they have gained a more powerful and
effective weapon in the airplane, which is more suited to achieving swift results than was the blockade. This has made it possible for British warfare to develop surprisingly fast all along the
line. The commercial spirit which has brought such riches to
this otherwise hard people has also reached complete expression
in warfare. The commercial principle of acquiring the maximum
profit on the minimum investment has been fully applied on the
field of battle too. This type of strategy is the complete opposite of the annihilating, "heroic," strategic principle of the Axis
powers, and more particularly of Germany, who has sought victory only by means of huge destructive battles into which she
has ruthlessly thrown her millions of men. The British have never
tried to force large, destructive battles. They have tried to avoid

them and have only engaged in them if unable to reach their goal
by other, less expensive means.

The industrial centers of the Anglo-American powers have been
able to work on undisturbed, and their technical superiority has
made possible the rapid creation of aerial weapons. In this field
they gained superiority astonishingly quickly and have since further increased their lead.

Even if Italy has not dropped out as a belligerent partner with
the collapse of Fascism, the war strength and potential of the Axis
has been weakened considerably. The situation has grown very
much worse, so that it is now hardly possible to reckon upon an
Axis victory; indeed, their defeat is not out of the question. While
the German armies are fighting in the East and South against
overwhelming enemy forces, Germany herself is the object of
heavy destructive raids, which are causing civilian casualties having a detrimental effect on the morale of the army. These raids
have also caused perceptible confusion in the industrial program
and have affected the armaments position. A particularly grave
factor is that it has still been impossible to retaliate effectively
against enemy air raids or materially to reduce their efficacy by
inflicting heavy losses. There is for the moment no prospect of
Germany's gaining a decisive victory in this sphere. Nevertheless,
the German high command is determined to continue the war
and will continue it even if Italy, for whatever reason, retires from
the war as a belligerent. The German forces have a gigantic task
to face. The vast areas over which they are spread and the strength
of the enemy make it impossible for them to strike decisive blows
at any single one of the enemies. As far as can be seen, the aim
of further operations can only be to delay the hostile forces and
gain time.

. . . The war will be dragged out until an acceptable peace can
be negotiated.

In the Eastern theater of war Germany is retreating and on
the defensive. She may perhaps make a stand on the banks of the
Dnieper, and may even counterattack if she still has reserves when

the Russian attack is spent. At present, however, she has no large reserves in the East, since she has been compelled to send all she had to spare and more to Italy and the Balkans. The enemy's superiority in manpower has brought Germany into a very difficult plight. In this difficult situation, the Hungarian high command wishes to help Germany by sending troops to occupy the Balkans; this support would induce Hitler to "discharge" the Hungarian divisions occupying Russian territory. These might then be used in the defense of Hungary.

The withdrawal of the Second Army from the front after the heavy fighting has relieved our situation, but it must not lull us into feeling that the war has lost its real significance for us and that we have nothing to do now but to watch events and speculate upon them. These speculations invariably bring us to that point where we need not make sacrifices—in other words, the essence of speculation is that it is a loophole from our war responsibilities and that it may take us down the primrose path. If we are not careful the Hungarians may gradually slip into a subordinate role in facing the enemy and war responsibilities. We shall be afraid of everything. The nation must, therefore, be informed that the withdrawal of the Second Army from battle is merely a temporary relief and that newer and more difficult tasks must be faced, in the achieving of which we shall have to stand our ground.

The Germans today are undoubtedly in a difficult situation, but we should misjudge it if we were to think that we could simply renounce our alliance and leave them in the lurch. The might of the German forces is unbroken, their discipline unshaken; if they fight under difficulties, they can still fight and may act ruthlessly against those who revolt against them.

Precisely for this reason it is extremely dangerous to imagine that we could throw over the Germans, even at the risk of their occupying Hungary. Many people would like to see such an occupation, since it would earn us a good mark from the Allies and in any case not last long. The partisans of this idea have not

thought it out or they would soon shrink back from its consequences. Firstly, it would not be the Germans who occupied
Hungary, but the Rumanians, the Slovaks, and even the Croats
weak as they are, who would quickly take back the territories
which Trianon gave them. Moreover they would plunder those
areas bare. It will be sufficient for me to recall the few months
occupation of 1919 [2] to realize what can be done in this field. But
above all, they would do everything in their power to destroy the
only prop of our self-defense and our sovereignty—our army
They would disarm it, take away its arms, and intern the officer
and NCO's just as they did in 1919, but this time they would use
the Katyn method of settling affairs. Germany would perhaps hold
only Budapest and would bomb any centers of resistance. The
British, Americans, and Russians would then, of course, bomb
also. In a few months they could destroy us completely. Hungary
would lose her sovereignty and would never again retrieve the
lands her neighbors had taken away from her.

Today Germany is the only dam against Bolshevism. It would
be long before the British and Americans could build up a defensive bulwark against the flood of Bolshevism, and, in my view
they would not want to do so. We saw that too in 1918. Our interests still lie today by the side of Germany. Today we can still
defend them at her side and can prepare for the future in her
shadow, creating a place there for ourselves. Honor, too, binds u
to Germany, but this does not, of course, mean that we serve her
blindly. Let us not rush into escapades; but, on the other hand
if it is our duty, let us not draw back from a Balkan expedition.

It may be that the Germans will lose this world war also, bu
that does not mean that we shall also have lost as we did in 1918
when we collapsed helplessly because a peace-loving spirit whose
main aim was to avoid battle and bloodshed undermined the fighting force of the nation.

That was what Chief of Staff Szombathelyi said on September 4. On the fifteenth, when he set out for the German genera

[2] A reference to the occupation by the Rumanian army in 1919.

headquarters, he received a letter from me containing the following guiding principles:

I have studied with attention the text of your speech, and make the following observations: I share in every respect your arguments and ideas on military affairs, and also on the military and national spirit and morality.

I do not, however, see any connection whatever between these and what we are asked to do in the Balkans. And I regard such an undertaking as destructive and as an irredeemable mistake from the point of view of our national existence. In no circumstances can I give my consent to it.

I went on to say that Szombathelyi should try to bring the German high command to this point of view, and I produced an argument which could be used with them: that the Hungarian forces should be concentrated at a spot on the eastern slopes of the Carpathians where they could avoid contact with the Russian forces and in case of necessity be used for the defense of the Hungarian frontier. He must make the Germans understand that this did not mean that Hungary refused to defend herself against the Soviet attack, but common sense demanded that the Hungarian troops should be placed in a strategic position where they could actually realize that they were defending their own country.

I then asked Chief of Staff Szombathelyi to inform the Germans that we could offer them the use of only those railway lines which avoided Budapest and the industrial centers. In conclusion, I wrote:

These are the guiding principles which I ask you to keep in view; the Hungarian government cannot admit any deviation from them. I recommend the greatest caution during the discussions. Where a successful result does not appear attainable, I think it better in present circumstances not to secure any change. In any case try to obtain every possible relief in the interests of our troops.

Szombathelyi had discussions with Hitler, Keitel, and Kurt Zeitzler, then chief of the general staff of the German army. They made no further demands for our forces to be sent to the

Balkans. But we were not satisfied with the situation of our occupation troops, and Szombathelyi visited Hitler's headquarters again in November, 1943, and on January 24, 1944. On the latter occasion he argued that, since the German high command had transferred the greater part of the Germany army to the Western front in view of the expected landings there, the Russian advance would definitely accelerate and could not be held up. We had therefore to consider the defense of our frontiers, for which we urgently needed the use of our two army corps still in the field. Szombathelyi told Keitel that he had received definite instructions from the Regent to tell Hitler that he demanded the unconditional return of our troops. At the same time, the Regent, on the recommendation of the premier, had commissioned him to state that he wanted to entrust the defense of the Carpathians to Hungarian troops alone, to the complete exclusion of any German forces.

That last idea was based on my own plan. I reasoned that if the advancing Russian troops found a Hungarian army of half-a-million men defending their own country in the East Carpathians with no German units among them or on Hungarian soil in the hinterland, as I had expressly stipulated, the Russians would think twice before forcing this line. In the primeval forests and mountain ranges of the Carpathians—a belt averaging 100 kilometers in width—there were only a few passes which could be used by tanks and vehicles. It would be easy to block those passes and they had, in fact, already been closed. It would be impossible to find a way for large operations elsewhere, especially drives involving mechanized forces and heavy artillery. Troops hidden in the depths of the forests could not be seen and thus could not be attacked from the air. Naturally I did not suppose that the Russians would have been unable to break through those obstacles if determined to do so at all cost. Thinking in terms of politics, however, I asked: Why should they make the attempt? Why should they incur the sacrifices? What mattered to them was the defeat of the German, not the Hungarian, army. Why should the Russians waste their time—and it was quite likely that the operation in the Carpathians would be so protracted as to hold up the whole advance—on a minor battlefield, whereas their aim in the south was the invasion of the Balkans and in the north of Germany herself? By advancing north and south they could surround Hungary and cut her off from further participation in the war.

If this theory of mine worked out and if Hungary were not occupied by the Germans, we should not become a theater of war. The Russians would not come among us as combatants, and the Germans could not make a stand in my country or a retreat through it. That was my last hope. Even today I believe that that aim might have been achieved if there had been no German occupation; but it is also possible that my plan when advanced by Szombathelyi contributed to Germany's decision to occupy the country.

That my plan correctly estimated the Russian tactics is proved by the fact that they did not even try to cut through the Eastern Carpathians, although there were there only a handful of Hungarian troops. I think that this was chiefly because, even if they did not anticipate real resistance in that area, still they could not have brought up reinforcements. Later they came to Hungary by following on the heels of the retreating German army from Transylvania and the Balkans; thus they avoided fighting anywhere in the Carpathians.

My British and American advisers in Berne were against both the defense along the Carpathians and the occupation of Croatia.[3] On no account did I want Hungarian soldiers to set foot on Yugoslav territory. Nevertheless, I raised the question with Mr. Allen W. Dulles and Mr. Royal Tyler through George Bessenyey, our minister in Berne. If we transferred our troops then in Russia to Croatia, it would facilitate an Allied landing on the Croatian coast. I guaranteed that our troops would offer no resistance and

[3] See Chapter Sixteen, "My Foreign Policy," for the details about our relations with the Western Allies alluded to in this chapter.

would lay down their arms. I even left it up to them to make use of the Hungarian troops if they wished. The answer was definitely in the negative. Thus I, too, could do nothing else, since I had no desire at all for such an undertaking even though we should have secured the withdrawal of our troops from Russia. I had to submit to America's warning that she would take this action ill.

My suggestion that Hungarian troops be sent to Croatia and my plans for the independent defense along the Carpathians were, I believed, measures that would have defended more than the integrity of my country. By the first plan, I was speeding up contact between our forces and British and American armies. The second suggestion would gain time, I felt, not only for our own purposes but also for the Allies to reach Hungary, before the Russians perhaps or at least no later. Even if the Russian troops entered Hungary first, then maybe the Allied Military Missions would appear with the Russian soldiers. At that time I did not understand the heated rejection of these plans. Now, however, I can see more clearly why they had such a poor reception, for it seems that it had already been decided that Hungary was to be occupied by the Russians and to come into their sphere of influence.

I made systematic attempts to get the Regent to remove untrustworthy (in other words, entirely Germanophile) senior officers from the leading military positions, especially those who had decisive influence. Some were to be pensioned, others transferred to less important posts. The Regent readily agreed, but it was harder to carry out the changes.

We have already seen the mental attitude of Csatay, the minister of defense, and Szombathelyi, the chief of staff; those two were among the coolest and most loyal of our generals. Their colleagues were far more intransigent militarists, and they trusted blindly in a German victory. The Regent called a meeting of seventeen leading generals and lectured them. Horthy spoke strongly to them, reminding them of their oath and appealing to their loyalty, but his exhortations had little effect.

The forces we had on a war footing were on the eastern and northeastern frontier, and their commanders, Generals Stephen Naday and Louis Veress, were completely trustworthy, faithful to the Regent, and absolutely loyal towards me. The commanders of the other two armies were of a different mind, but the units under them were not fit for action. General Stephen Ujszászy and Colonel Julius Kádár, the commanders of the counterespionage system of the staff, were completely trustworthy and, in fact, anti-German. (Both of those officers and many other military and political officers who played an active anti-German role or leaned towards the British and Americans were dragged off by the Russians after they had been freed from the fearful tortures they had suffered in German captivity.)

Although there were many efficient officers on our staff, a great number of them lived under a spell that began with an admiration of the German army and slowly changed into fear of it. And behind all this was a deadly fear of the Russians. If the British and American armies had appeared in our proximity and the fear of the Soviet Union was thus ended, our officers would have joyfully gone over to the Western Allies. In the absence of such a turn of events, the Hungarian officers judged the situation non-politically and without regard for the long-range interests of the country. As professional soldiers do, the Hungarian officers gazed down at their maps and made their estimates of the situation on the basis of the dangers they saw surrounding Hungary—on the one side the Germans, on the other the Russians. It was natural for such mentalities to turn towards the Germans. These officers hoped to win the military struggle with Germany's help. In the eyes of these Hungarian officers, defeat fighting on the side of the Germans was better and more honorable than victory with the Russians.

But that was not the point—I repeat this to prevent misunderstanding. If British and American troops had appeared on our frontiers, the Hungarian army would have obeyed as one man the Regent and government, and they would have surrendered without firing a shot or gone over to the Western Allies if ordered to do so. The charge made against our army that it remained the longest on the German side *is only true in the sense that it fought the longest against Bolshevism*. This is the correct phrasing of the situation, and this must be the guiding point of view in any judgment.

We know now after the events that the part played by the Hungarian army in the final phase of the war meant nothing at all. Even before the end the Hungarian military effort was negligible; it did not prolong the war fought by the Western Allies as much as a day nor did it obstruct their victory. The Hungarian effort did perhaps have a slight effect on the rate of the Russian advance westward, but that deterring effect did no harm, regarded from a modern and historical point of view, for the Russian advance westward was in any case faster than was desirable.

It is undeniable, however, that I had considerable trouble because of the blindness of the Hungarian officer corps. When the minister of defense and the staff presented their estimates for 1944, with a six-year armament program requiring a credit of several billion pengö, I gave the whole scheme back and said that I would agree to any expenses incurred up to the autumn of 1944 but to no investment extending beyond that time. Their proposals included such projects as the establishment of a synthetic petrol refinery and another for making synthetic rubber, together with the research and experiment resources necessary for discovering how to make synthetic petrol and rubber (for the Germans characteristically had not given us information or knowledge about either product). The air force commanders wished to establish twenty-four air squadrons and twelve airfields in six years. I asked how many squadrons and airfields would be ready by autumn, and General Alexander Marossy said none—the air plan was conceived as an integrated long-range project and could not be split up. He in any case would not do so, and instead he resigned. All that characterized the political short-sightedness of our officers; they were like the inhabitants of an occupied country.

My view that everything would come to a head in the fall of 1944 and that we should prepare for that time of decision caused panic among the high officers. Chief of Staff Szombathelyi asked me to speak at a conference of officers at which every staff officer from the rank of colonel upwards would be present, and I accepted his invitation.

I began by saying that my predecessors had adhered to the Axis because they expected its members to defend Hungary from Bolshevism and insure the integrity of her territory. After Munich it seemed as though Hitler was the master of the fate of Eastern Europe. The Western powers did not subsequently aid their allies Czechoslovakia and Rumania against the Germans. The Hungarian thesis was, not service for the Germans, but the insurance of our own rights and interests. That was the underlying policy of Hungary at that time, and it would continue to be the nation's policy in the future. Thus if we saw that the Germans could not defend and preserve Hungarian interests, we should not sacrifice our interests and heritage but we should instead find a way of defending and rescuing them in spite of the deterioration of Germany's military situation. At the moment our task was to prepare for the independent defense of our interest in the future. That was the duty and task of our soldiers. Everything else was for the political leaders to decide and do.

Naturally I said all that at much greater length than in this summary of my talk. Chief of Staff Szombathelyi told me afterwards that I had opened the eyes of our officers in a very dramatic fashion. "From today," he said, "they're your men and will do whatever you want."

Among the senior pensioned officers there were one or two of considerable personality who had become followers of Imrédy. They tried to draw staff officers, especially the younger ones, into their circle. Contact with these older officers was therefore for-

bidden by order, as were meetings with the Arrow Cross and
Imrédy's parties.

The equipping of the army went on but very slowly. We had
to obtain many essential supplies and replacements from the Germans. They, however, reduced their deliveries to a minimum,
partly because we were not fulfilling our export program and partly
because they themselves were running short. Our soldiers looked
sadly at the trains from Germany which crossed Hungary full of
excellent war material for the Rumanians, whom the Germans
regarded as combatant allies and supplied without stint. Our
soldiers naturally concluded that the Rumanian policy was the
right one because the Germans gave them so much. It did not
occur to them that those who are paid do not always come off
best.

Nevertheless, as things were going we should have been able
by the fall of 1944 to put a fully equipped army of 300,000 into
the field, with about three times as many trained soldiers in reserve—a considerable force for the defense of Hungary and of
the Carpathians. Thus we tried to prepare ourselves at home,
abroad, and in the field to face what must come. I know that we
should have gone further in every sphere, but we could only go
as far as our strength allowed. Efforts to the full extent of our
ability are all that we can be held responsible for, and we did go
as far as we could go.

FIFTEEN

THE TREATMENT OF REFUGEES
AND PRISONERS OF WAR

❲WE ARE ACCUSED of many sins by the misinformed world, and, although no other people admit faults and failures as freely as Hungarians do, we reject categorically many of the accusations made against us. Now when the war is in the past we can face humanity with pride because of our one great accomplishment during those tragic years: the treatment of our refugees and prisoners of war. In this area Hungary, by exerting her strength to the utmost and by continually resisting German demands, fulfilled the obligations of humanity and civilization. Hungary did far more, I assert, than any other belligerent European nation did for the victims of prejudice and war. In this respect Hungary often acted far more bravely and humanely than the neutral countries. M. Jean de Bavier who was the representative of the International Red Cross told me his feelings in this matter when I myself was a refugee in the Turkish legation:

I could not report with exact truth the marvelous circumstances under which refugees are living because my report, such as it was, has anyway been considered biased and of a propaganda nature. Furthermore, the British and Americans requested that their exceptional position should not be made public for fear of a German reaction.

I wish to mention that the same spirit of charity and respect for fellow men prevailed in Hungary during the First World War. I was lord lieutenant of a county and living in a small town then. A group of women presented a request to me that the days on which movies were shown be changed from Saturday and Sunday—movies were shown only on week ends then—to weekdays because the Russian POW's who were working on farms around the town were occupying the movie houses to such a degree that the residents of the area could not get in. It never occurred to the people of this delegation to request that the Russian POW's be barred from attending the movie on one of the days. That was a wonderful and characteristic example of the feeling nature of the Hungarians. Magnanimity towards the vanquished is not only a superior human quality but it is also a realistic policy.

After the *Anschluss* of 1938, refugees began moving into Hungary. The number then was small because the way from Austria to Switzerland and other Western nations was still open. For the most part those who entered Hungary had relatives or social and business connections in Hungary. The first refugees were easily taken care of by the welfare agencies or church groups, and they presented no social or administrative problem to the government. They were all admitted and subsequently treated the same as other foreigners of legal residence.

When Slovakia acquired her independence with the collapse of Czechoslovakia in 1939, the number of refugees increased as people fled from the new Slovakian state. Most of these people were Hungarian nationals who had clung to their Hungarian citizenship and their relations with other Hungarians after the Treaty of Trianon had placed them outside of Hungary. The refugees were for the most part Hungarians and Jews. Few Slovaks fled to Hungary because most of the Slovaks were happy to be free of Czech oppression and they lived with the illusion that the new Slovakia of Tiso would under German protection safeguard them from every danger. Although nobody was threatening the Slovaks, Tiso's state did protect the Slovaks from everything except the one and only danger—Nazi terror. However, the fact should be stated that the Germans treated Slovakia the easiest of all the German-occupied countries, and life was endurable there in every way. The Germans supported the Slovak government in its anti-Hungarian tendencies, however, and consequently there was a constant migration of Hungarians from Slovakia.

The situation changed radically after the Slovak government committed itself to the elimination of the Jews. The Jews in Slovakia began leaving for Hungary, and all of them were admitted by our border patrol. Their number was estimated to be as much as 24,000. Because of German pressure the Slovak government protested our giving the Jews asylum.

We paid little attention to the Slovakian protests against our course, but the threats and interventions of Jagow, the German minister in Budapest, became more and more severe. The point of view of the Germans was that even though Hungary was not willing to follow all the other members of the Axis in taking drastic action against the Jews—a default which the Germans considered the shortsighted policy of a Hungarian leadership that had fallen under the degenerate influence of Judaism—the Hungarian government did not under any circumstances have the right to weaken the uniform procedure of the entire Axis bloc and to frustrate the total solution of the Jewish problem. Hungary's interference was considered an opposition to the Axis powers and a violation of the alliance that would not be tolerated.

It would have been absolutely useless to start an argument with the Nazis. One cannot argue with lunatics. Keresztes-Fischer, the minister of the interior, was forced to instruct the border control stations to take a more severe attitude and grant entry only to those refugees who produced a border-crossing permit. At the same time those authorized to issue the border-crossing permits were instructed to observe scrupulously the rules and regulations. Thus the entrances along the border were restricted by a tightening of the legal regulations; nevertheless, all the refugees who crossed the border illegally were permitted by the guards to enter and then were sent to the nearest police station, where they were assigned to refugee camps. It is true, however, that after the regulations were tightened many refugees were more easily apprehended by Slovak border guards. Despite the tighter controls along the border the influx continued because of our sufferance of illegal entries. According to the records of the ministry of the interior, more than 40,000 Slovak Jews crossed the Hungarian border. Only 4,000 of the refugees who entered illegally were kept in concentration camps; the rest, even most of those not registered, were cared for by relatives, friends, and fellow members of the Jewish faith.

The Slovak government made repeated demands for the extradition of the Jews who were in camps, and we repeatedly rejected those demands. One day the Slovak government handed the Hungarian government a list of one hundred names. The men whose names appeared on the list were accused of various crimes—mostly faked or irrelevant crimes—and their extradition was demanded on the grounds of international law. In order to prevent endless arguments and further deterioration of relations with the Germans, Minister of the Interior Keresztes-Fischer ordered the listed refugees to be put on the train in the presence of the Slovak minister and to be taken to the frontier. Not far away from Budapest, however, members of the committee of the Jewish congregation were waiting for this train, and they received the deportees, who were let out of the train, and resettled them. When the empty train reached the frontier, the Slovaks were told that the deportees had escaped. That ended that matter.

Refugees came to Hungary from Rumania and Yugoslavia, too.

The numbers from those countries were considerably smaller, and those people were treated in the same manner as refugees from the other countries.

Until the time of Hungary's occupation by the Germans, no Jewish individual, citizen or refugee was expelled or deported from Hungary. Minister of the Interior Keresztes-Fischer did, however, attempt to resettle Jewish refugees in Galicia after the German army had penetrated so far into Russian territory that Galicia was not considered an area for military supplies any longer. The refugees considered for resettlement were asked first if they had any objection to repatriation. This resettlement was undertaken as a means of easing the tense situation between Hungary and Germany that stemmed from our humanitarian attitude towards the Jews. Shortly after the first transports left Hungary, we learned that the Germans did not comply with the agreements that they made with us. The chairman of the Jewish congregation in Budapest reported that the transports did not reach their destination because SS units held them up over the border, killed some of the Jewish refugees, and sent others to Auschwitz for extermination in the concentration camp. Samuel Stern, chairman of the Jewish community, produced evidence to back up his reports, and consequently Minister of the Interior Keresztes-Fischer immediately stopped further shipments of refugees to Galicia, denying repatriation even to those who requested it.

Because there is general confusion on this issue, it seems necessary to state the fact that the arrest and the deportation of Jews in Hungary began after the German occupation on March 19, 1944. After the Germans invaded Hungary not only Jews were deported but also many non-Jewish citizens, such as Minister of the Interior Keresztes-Fischer, many high-ranking officers in the police corps and the ministry of the interior, and other Hungarian officials who handled the Jewish problem in a humanitarian way.

To summarize: the principal facts in the matter are that Hungary never discriminated among people seeking asylum, and Jews and non-Jews alike were admitted if they requested admission into

Hungary. Here I recall an incident bearing on this claim. During those years a steamer carrying some 300 Jewish refugees sank under mysterious circumstances in the Aegean Sea after it had visited a half dozen ports where the passengers had tried in vain to disembark. That experience was evidence of the correctness of the assertion of the principal rabbi in New York City that Hungary was the asylum of the Jews in Europe until the occupation of Hungary by the Germans.[1]

The problem of refugees became of the greatest importance in our internal and foreign affairs after the collapse of Poland. When Poland was partitioned by Germany and the Soviet Union, many large and small units of the Polish army and great numbers of persecuted civilians sought refuge in Hungary.

Directly after the Polish army was beaten in the field, a Polish colonel crossed the Hungarian frontier and asked Karoly Jákó, chief officer of the border control station in Ökörmezö, if Hungary was willing to grant asylum to units or individuals of the Polish army. Jákó immediately communicated the question to the ministry of the interior, and he was instructed to admit every Polish civilian or member of the armed forces desiring to enter.

Thus the gates of the Hungarian-Polish frontier were thrown open, and more than 150,000 refugees streamed into Hungary. On some days thousands entered. At first most of the refugees were members of the Polish army, but later civilians came, including many Jews. All of these refugees met with a cordial and helpful attitude on the part of the authorities and population.

The central office for the control of aliens was in charge of all foreigners in the country, and it was an independent department under the control of the minister of the interior. How very gen-

---

[1] "Among the reasons which induced Hitler to thus shear Hungary of most of its powers as a sovereign nation was the fact that its policies toward the Jews were unsatisfactory. It had become the great refuge of European Jews, who fled from territories which were occupied by the Germans and its satellite countries, and while, as we have heretofore stated, there was a strong current of anti-Semitism there, and numerous restrictive laws have been enacted, nevertheless, in comparison with what they have suffered elsewhere, the Jews' fate in Hungary was at least bearable." *Trials of War Criminals before the Nuremberg Military Tribunals.* Vol. XIV, Nuremberg, October 1946–April 1949.

erously the Polish refugees were treated from a police point of view is illustrated by the fact that all matters of registration and the subsequent processing of the refugees were assigned to Joseph Jakubovietz, a high-ranking Polish police officer from Warsaw.[2] Anybody who has but a vague notion of police duties, especially the police control of aliens, can see from that fact alone how we treated our refugees. Further evidences of our openhanded attitude towards them were our permitting members of the Polish army to keep their weapons until after they were registered, which often was at places some distance inside the border, and our allowing all the refugees to keep their personal possessions, including foreign currency on which the treasury regulations were very strict at the time.

A special office to deal with matters of social welfare, sanitary service, housing, and jobs for the Polish refugees was established under the direction of a high official from Warsaw; members of the ministry of the interior were assigned to this office as observers and helpers only. (Members of the Polish army were chiefly farm laborers, and the allocations of their jobs, salaries, rations, and working hours were strictly set and controlled by the ministry of the interior. I wish to emphasize in this respect that no complaints were heard; all the laborers expressed their complete satisfaction.)

An allowance was set for the refugees by the government, according to their social standards.

Schools for the lower grades were organized for the education of Polish refugee children, and it is a remarkable fact that the only Polish high school operating at that time was in Hungary. Special undergraduate and postgraduate courses were established for the refugees in the universities.

Those refugees who were unwilling or unable to work were settled by the government in health resorts, in boardinghouses, in country residences, or in villages with families. Camps were succeedingly dissolved after the government became aware that

[2] This Polish police officer received an apartment in the residential quarters of the police, and he resided there until the German occupation. The Germans wanted to arrest him, but the Hungarian police prepared his escape before he could be arrested.

living in groups was to the social and moral disadvantage of the
refugees, and from then on the refugees were assigned to families.
The refugees were free to move within the limits of the county
lines, and they were free to choose their hosts. Thus in time the
refugees were considered as guests by their hosts, who frequently
did not accept any contribution towards expenses from the refugees.

Among the politically prominent Poles to whom Hungary
granted asylum were Messrs. Slavic, Filipowicz, and Ipses,[3] members of the Polish parliament. These gentlemen were members of
the American Polish committee, which was an officially accepted
branch of the Polish government in London. They lived in Budapest and engaged in extensive political activity with the benevolent tolerance of the Hungarian police. Many other Polish politicians stayed in our country. The Germans demanded the extradition of those Polish officials, but we rejected the German
demands in every instance.

Marshal Edward Rydz-Smigly fled to Hungary in 1941 after
his security in Rumania was endangered, and he was placed
and harbored in the Pajor sanatorium, which is located in mid-
town Budapest. The Germans searched for him but never located
him. Rydz-Smigly returned to Poland in 1942, where he took part
in the resistance movement until he was finally reported missing.
Socha Lipinski Wadslow, the famous historian and director of
the Pilsudski Institute in Warsaw, hid in the very same sanatorium before he escaped to England. Stephen Hubichki, formerly
minister of social welfare in Poland, was one of many others who
stayed in the same institution in Budapest.

The Hungarian authorities not only tolerated but often supported the political activities of the Polish refugees, especially their
relations with the underground in Poland. A member of the Polish
government in London stopped in Hungary on his way to Poland,
and he visited Minister of the Interior Keresztes-Fischer and other
leading personalities in Hungarian public life. We not only tol-

[3] These names are quoted from memory, and so the spellings are uncertain.

erated but also supported the dispatch of military and political information to the West. To give one example, we organized a camp at the request of the Polish refugees in Dunamocs so that they could observe German shipments on the Danube. We harbored and covered their secret radio broadcasts from Balaton Boglár, which furnished the Allies and governments in exile with military and political information. Western information about movements in our area of Europe was at that time based chiefly on what was supplied by the Polish refugees in Hungary.

The encouragement and support given by the Hungarian authorities to the members of the Polish army and other Polish youths who wanted to fight with the Western Allies was most important and daring. Hungarian officials helped about 100,000 Poles cross the border into Yugoslavia, from where they found their way to the army under General Wladyslaw Anders, which was fighting with the British in Italy. We never gave up helping Polish soldiers to escape to the West even though the Germans backed up their protests of our support of the escape of Polish soldiers with photostatic copies of Hungarian documents and other evidence that was unearthed by their intelligence agents. In order to conceal the government's participation in these activities and to calm repeated German indignation, Minister of the Interior Keresztes-Fischer took some retaliatory action against, not the refugees, but certain Hungarian officials, who were previously informed of what was coming and who had previously consented to disciplinary action.

Thus Hungary delivered close to 100,000 soldiers to the Allied forces. *This was an actual military contribution to the West.* It is true that these soldiers were not Hungarians, but many Hungarian young men did join the escaping Poles. And German vengeance took many victims from our ranks.

The thirty to forty thousand Polish soldiers who remained in Hungary were placed in camps but were given the best possible treatment. (If the Allies had ever arrived in our area, these men could have been organized into several regiments under their own

REFUGEES AND PRISONERS OF WAR

officers and used by the Western forces.) The soldiers in our
camps were paid and the restrictions on their movements were
governed for the most part by the Polish officers themselves,
many of whom disliked having their men drift about uncontrolled.
Most of them were, therefore, restricted to a certain limited area
unless they were given special permits issued by the commandant
of the camp at the request of the Polish commanders.

In substantiation of the above summary, I should like to quote
here from the report of M. Jean de Bavier, of the International
Red Cross, on the camps for refugees that he inspected in late
1943.[4]

Many camps, all established under good conditions, were visited
between December 2 to 17, 1943. I shall briefly describe here what
was characteristic.

Camp Pesthidegkut: The new factory for synthetic silk—Magyar Viscosa near Esztergom—employs thirty Polish and three
French internees. They are living under excellent conditions in
the perfectly new boardinghouses of the plant, and all are completely satisfied. The Poles occupy the dormitory, while the French
have a nice room. Their salaries are equal to the salaries of the
Hungarian workers.

Camp Ipolyhidvég: Situated in an old barrack of the frontier
guards, eighty officers, about twenty soldiers, and one woman are
sheltered here under conditions similar to those in other Polish
camps. A very well-educated doctor is attached to the camp; the
morale of the internees is excellent. They had only one complaint
—the restricted amount of oil, which allowed only three hours of
light at night. The delegate was able to obtain an improvement in
this matter, although the Hungarian peasants were subject to the
very same restriction. The commandant of the camp is very
friendly and understanding.

Camp Süttö: This is in a large village, where close to sixty
Polish internees are working in the fields. They mostly live with

[4] This report was published in the Revue de la croix rouge of March, 1944.

farmers and are well roomed. Others are grouped in a little house under conditions characteristic of all Hungarian camps. There are no complaints except with respect to the price of food. Some of the internees prefer to feed themselves, and their provisions are supplied by their employers at the official prices. The population is most sympathetically disposed towards all these internees.

Camp Mosonmagyaróvár: This is a very large factory which processes bauxite and where fifty Polish internees are working and living under very satisfactory conditions. The kitchens are very well kept, and when one considers that the Hungarian worker has to pay for his board, light, and fuel, one concludes that the Polish worker is favored. On the other hand, the work is disagreeable because of the nature of the material processed. The sanitary conditions are good, however.

Camp Gencsapáti: This is a very nice mansion that was purchased by the government before the war as a convalescent home for servicemen. This building is actually completely at the disposition of Polish officers, and at the time of the visit by the delegate of the International Red Cross there were a hundred officers, eleven women, and three children present. All the large rooms were turned into well-furnished dormitories. The camp has good kitchens, baths, and an infirmary attached. There were no complaints in spite of the inconveniences of the communal living.

Camp Várpalota: The camp was made to hold several hundred Polish soldiers, under the supervision of five officers, who worked in a bauxite mine. A spacious kitchen and large assembly and recreation hall are at the disposal of the Poles, who live on a perfectly equal level with the Hungarian workers.

Camp Dömsöd: This camp, of less importance than others mentioned, is for Polish officers. It is located about 12 kilometers from the one previously mentioned, and the officers are billeted in various houses in the village. As in other camps, the internees are permitted free movement within a radius of 3 kilometers and further, including to Budapest, with special permission. The morale of the prisoners is good, thanks to the Polish commandant who has fine qualities. It should be mentioned that the officers have organized classes for their children.

In conclusion the delegate of the International Red Cross wishes to state that the camps made an excellent impression on him, and the prisoners were living under most satisfactory conditions.

The International Red Cross, the Catholic Action, and various Polish relief and aid groups abroad contributed towards the caring for the refugees. The envoy of the Holy See and other diplomatic representatives visited the refugees often. The Hungarian Red Cross received tremendous support from the Pope and from people in the United States and in England. For our own efforts in behalf of the Polish refugees the Hungarian government received thousands of letters of thanks, first and foremost from the Polish government in exile.

I wish here to remember those Hungarians who played the greatest part in this wonderful work. Stephen Horthy, the Regent's son, until his untimely death played an active role in the entire refugee program. Francis Keresztes-Fischer, the minister of the interior, who had my fullest backing, never hesitated, nevertheless, to take the initiative and full responsibility without consulting the premier if he thought that direct action was right and necessary. Special appreciation is owed to Joseph Antal and Aurel Kern of the ministry of the interior for their efforts on behalf of the refugees. I wish to express my thanks to them for furnishing the necessary material for this summary. Count Anthony Szapary was a leading spirit in all the Hungarian-Polish welfare agencies. For his activities he was deported during the German occupation to the concentration camp in Mauthausen. Count Julius Károlyi, the Regent's son-in-law, was Count Szapary's immediate assistant.

Great and noble work was done by Béla Varga, the parish priest of Balaton Boglár, who was a member of parliament and deputy chairman of the Smallholders party. In his hands were gathered the strings of all official and unofficial activities in behalf of the refugees. He acted independently of the government but with its full approval. His name became legendary among the refugees, and his deeds certainly deserve the gratitude of the entire nation. Mention must be made also of Béla Fábián who was also a deputy in parliament and Monsignor Varga's helper. Fábián was chiefly active in helping Jewish refugees—that is, in the most difficult area of the refugee work.

I should mention many hundreds, even thousands, of names. I hope that the time will come when the people who labored so valiantly and selflessly in that task will be remembered and honored for their achievements.

Mention should be made here, too, of the British, Americans, French, and members of other nations who were stranded in Hungary by the war. In their internment they enjoyed the same freedom as in prewar Hungary. They had to register with the police, but they suffered no other inconvenience. They could remain at their old job or seek new work. (An evidence of their freedom of movement is that on March 19, 1944, when the Germans occupied Budapest, they collected most of the British internees at the horse races in Alag.)

As the war continued and France and other nations were placing large numbers of laborers at the disposal of the Germans, word got around the labor and POW camps that everybody who asked Hungary for asylum was admitted. Streams of refugees headed for Hungary, therefore, but many were apprehended by the Germans along the way. The number of French, Belgian, American, and British laborers and POW's who did succeed in crossing our frontier was estimated to be about 2,000. In time we received Russian refugees, too, those who were being returned to their homes by the Germans for forced labor. If they escaped, they made for Hungary. All the refugees, whether from friendly, neutral, or enemy nations, were accorded the humanitarian treatment that I have described in discussing the Polish refugees.

We did not hand over to the Nazis a single refugee or POW. Later, however, we did allow the Germans, always in the presence of a Hungarian officer, to interrogate the American pilots who had made a forced landing in Hungary. But we—and perhaps we alone—adhered most scrupulously to the Hague and Geneva conventions. Our only violation of those international agreements was our refusal to discriminate between military and civilian refugees with respect to the treatment given them. The regulations for civilian internees were applied in every case because they were more humane than the regulations pertaining to military prisoners. All the refugees were treated by us not as prisoners but as guests. They received enough money for their necessities, and they could freely choose an occupation. Many of them did find work, and some of them made a better living than most of the Polish refugees because the refugees from the Western nations were qualified to do intellectual work.

In 1945 a pamphlet entitled *Asylum in Hungary from 1941 to 1945* was published in France as a gesture of appreciation for the treatment that Hungary accorded French refugees and POW's and as campaign literature for relief of Hungarian refugees and POW's in French custody. Paul Giraud, the French representative in Hungary during the war, and Paul Lamair stated the fact in their introductions to this pamphlet that up to 1943 French soldiers and deportees continually entered Hungary from German POW and labor camps. Men were helped by the Hungarian government to reach General Charles de Gaulle's forces in Africa. About 800 French refugees remained in Hungary because they could not escape. Paul Giraud wrote:

My young countrymen were accepted in a friendly manner and helped by everybody they met in Hungary. Our soldiers were transferred from camps to hotels around the Balaton, where they were under French supervision and the regulations were easy. The refugees were free to live in Budapest, if they chose, or in the country, where they could work in factories or on farms according to their abilities. Very many made use of these privileges. Members of the French armed forces were cordially accepted in the homes of families of all social classes.

After the two introductions, some of the French refugees told their stories about their experiences in Hungary and the spirit they found everywhere in it.

Marcel Fertier reported in his story that many French deportees or POW's tried to escape from German camps and get to Hungary. His group was among the first of those to cross the Hungarian border. At the time they did not yet know that Hungary rejected every demand of extradition. The news did, however, reach the German camps in some mysterious way. Fertier concluded his story with: "Hungarians, if you only knew how you are loved by those who were generously accepted in your country."

R. Klein's story told of how he arrived at Budapest in 1942 with a fellow prisoner from a camp in Rava-Russka. Their only concern, after escaping from the camp, was to reach Hungary. They had no decent clothing; his friend had received a good pair of pants, and Klein made himself a shirt out of a blanket and tied a shawl around his head. That is how they were dressed on the journey of 500 kilometers—a little more than 300 miles—on foot. After they finally got over the Carpathian Mountains, they came suddenly upon two armed Hungarian policemen. Klein reported:

The gendarmes looked us over with distrust, which considering our attire we could not take amiss, and they asked for our identification cards.

My companion, whose imagination was even greater than his courage, started to protest in a German language that he invented, declaring that we were Spanish technicians voluntarily working for the Germans and that we had lost our way in the mountains, where we wanted to spend a vacation. This story did not satisfy the gendarmes, however, and we were taken to the nearest police station. Here we were investigated thoroughly, and after we saw that further denial was pointless we admitted that we were French refugees from a German camp. A broad smile came upon the policemen's faces at this, and a young officer hastened to assure us *that we would not be handed over to the Germans. Our armed guards escorted us in a very friendly manner to Budapest. We became the very center of interest on the train, and our fellow passengers offered us food and apricot brandy, so that in the end our guards and we arrived at the lovely capital in very high spirits. Three weeks later we were walking around Budapest with full freedom and in brand new civilian clothes. Budapest is certainly a place where hospitality is more than a word.*

Jean Boussaquet also had a pleasant story to tell about his experiences in Hungary. He, too, was met by our well-known border guards, with their bowler hats decorated with dark green feathers. He was unable to make them understand his language. Finally one of the guards started to talk in a very primitive Latin. To this the Frenchman answered: "Ego sum gallieris captivus." The guard understood this and immediately treated Boussaquet to milk and bread and butter. The "prisoner" was then assigned to a de luxe hotel in Balaton Boglár. This refugee got work soon afterwards with the periodical *Revue franco-hongroise*, and in addition he gave French lessons. He also entered Budapest social life and made the acquaintance of Kalman Kánya, former minister of foreign affairs, of Count Ivan Csekonics, a former minister, and of other prominent persons.

G. Butte told the story about Balaton Boglár where actually the internees were those who did not wish to settle elsewhere in Hungary. He recalled a celebration on a French national holiday when the officers and the guards saluted the French flag that daily flew on the balcony of the hotel. Butte reported: "The German legation knew about us and repeatedly demanded our extradition, but the Hungarian government energetically rejected their demand every time." Later, after the German occupation, the situation, according to Butte, was: "Franco-Hungarian friendship really came to a test as the Hungarian civilians gave shelter to the refugees and did not register them with the police."

And so went story after story in this delightful pamphlet.

I personally had a serious and disagreeable matter to handle with respect to our relations with the French when Count Dampierre, the French minister in Budapest, broke off relations with the Vichy government and resigned. We, according to the rules and regulations, issued him a diplomatic passport and were prepared to put a special train at his disposal. He wanted to go to Turkey via Rumania. The Rumanians, however, denied the transit visa because of German pressure, and Count Dampierre remained in Hungary. We hid him in the country, and this caused difficulties after the German occupation. Jagow, the German minister, personally came to my office on the matter, and my answer to him was that they had no right whatsoever to interfere.

I should like here to express my thanks to those French refugees and POW's who after their return to France immediately tried to aid those Hungarians who, although they had lived for many years in France, had been imprisoned under very unpleasant conditions.

We also sheltered Belgian POW's. Here is a copy of the letter we received from some of them:

Gentlemen:

We, the undersigned Belgian former prisoners of war who succeeded in reaching Hungary after our escape from German camps, consider it our duty to petition the Allied military commands in favor of the Hungarian prisoners of war. We request that Hungarian prisoners of war be treated as we were treated in Hungary. We are glad to make the statement that Allied prisoners of war—Belgians, French, Polish, British, and Americans—were most cordially received in Hungary and enjoyed full freedom. The prisoners of war were not forced to live in camps but were permitted to live in hotels and other places. We received identification papers from the Hungarian authorities. Thanks to these documents we were able to escape from German persecution. We are writing this letter in the name of and for all fellow prisoners of war.

Signed: Armand Lobet, s/officier au 38 cme. de ligne, 65 rue

Crocq, Brussels; Charles Nicolas, brigadier, 15 reg. d'artill., 215 rue Morchamps, Seraing; Mean Joseph, 2 Reg. Dtca, Place Kuborn 12, Seraing; Delaisse Stephan, 116 rue St. Roch, Auvelais.

Although a few American and British POW's escaped from Germany, most of them parachuted into Hungary or made forced landings in damaged planes. I had not been able to gain the friendship of the American and British nations for my country, but American and British POW's were, nevertheless, treated as friends.

A general of our antiaircraft division made the following statement:

I was in direct command of all antiaircraft service up to October 16, 1944.[5] All reports on enemy air activity over the entire country came to me. I declare that it is absolutely true that every time reports of damaged or shot down planes or of parachuted pilots were made, strict orders were given to the respective authorities to take immediate measures for the rescue and safeguarding of the pilots. Up to March 19, 1944, strict orders were issued by the highest command that firing at Anglo-American airplanes was to be restricted to planes engaged in offensive actions against us.

Another high-ranking officer of the air force wrote:

In 1943 the crews of all airplanes flying across Hungary were making efforts to land on Hungarian territory if forced to land in the general area. The reason for this was that they knew that they would be treated exceptionally well in Hungary. As part of this special treatment, members of the Allied air forces were established in a residence of Count Apponyi near Szombathely, where they had good food and were even permitted to visit the city in civilian clothes. The crew members of the Allied aircraft that were shot down on April 3, 1944, during a raid on Hungarian targets, were, on the Regent's special orders, established on the island of St. Margaret and in special parts of the military hospital, regardless of the German occupation forces that were present on our soil. I wish to make a matter of record that those members of

[5] At a time when Hungary was being methodically bombed.

the American air force who were killed in the vicinity of the airfield of Kenyeri were buried with military honors at a ceremony attended by a unit from our air force academy. Members of the Hungarian air force and civilians covered the graves with flowers.

Now I should like to tell of two incidents only that characterized a humane spirit even in the life and death struggles of the war.

A member of the Hungarian air force who moved to the West after the war wrote:

I was a member of the training staff of the Hungarian air force academy in May, 1944. Once during that period I saw an American bomber hurtling to the ground, and as it thundered down towards the village, members of the crew parachuted out. The pilot remained in the plane, however. After passing over the village he dropped his last two bombs in the fields and crashed. The pilot was probably wounded and could not jump, but he still gathered all his energy to lift his plane over and past the village, thus saving it from disaster. He, however, was burned with the plane. We discovered the American hero's name; it was Joe Young, Lieutenant. He was buried two days later with military honors and with showers of flowers.

An air force captain wrote:

Master Sergeant B——'s experience is characteristic of the gallant spirit which prevailed between the fighting air forces. Sergeant B—— was flying back alone to his base after an air battle, when suddenly an American Mustang drew up alongside his plane. The American pilot made signs to Sergeant B—— to look back. On looking back Sergeant B—— saw that the tail of his plane was on fire. He turned the plane over on its back, opened the hood of his cabin, and jumped without hesitation. He landed without mishap, but meanwhile a tragedy happened up in the air: the sergeant's plane exploded after he jumped, and the plane's propellor was thrown right at the American pilot, who was killed. The Hungarian air force considered the dead hero their own and buried him with all military honors.

Sándor Szent-Iványi, the Unitarian bishop, who had an American wife, was the principal person in charge of American and British POW's. He organized the Emerson Guild for that purpose. I recall the following from his statements and from his book, *With God against Hitler*. Szent-Iványi listed the names of our American, British, and other POW's in his book.

The British POW's were first placed into the citadel of Komárom. After this proved inadequate they were transferred to Count Michael Andrassy's residence in Szigetvár. The prisoners were so well roomed and boarded there that possibly no POW's were ever so well taken care of anyplace else. They received a daily salary because they were officially supposed to work; however, they did not work, preferring to swim, hunt, go horseback riding, and even playing soccer with the local team. Szent-Iványi forwarded their mail through the ministry of defense.

The residence in Szigetvár could not take more than fifty POW's, and as the infiltration of them from German camps continued to grow, others were sent to the country residence of Countess Joseph Károlyi in Fehervár Csurgo. Others were assigned to the camp for Polish officers in Zugliget, where there were no guards and no fences either. Those who were sick were taken to the Pajor sanatorium in Budapest.

The first American POW's came to Hungary in 1943. A damaged American bomber made a forced landing not far from the frontier. The Germans demanded their extradition, arguing that the bomber was damaged over Austrian territory, so the crew members were their prisoners. The German arguments were brought to the judiciary department of the ministry for foreign affairs, and their demand was finally rejected. Later, after ceaseless German pressure, it was agreed that all crew members of Allied planes who were forced to land in Hungary after an assault in Austria were to be escorted to Germany territory for interrogation but that they were to be sent back before six hours had elapsed. The American POW's were sent to Count Anthony Sigray's country residence after February, 1944; his wife was American.

Szent-Iványi was informed in 1943 that the citadel of Komárom where Russian POW's were kept was not adequate for a prisoner's camp and that some of the localities there were unhealthy. This is what he wrote in the matter:

Upon my intervention the Regent and Premier Kállay ordered Colonel Utassy, who was chief of the department in care of prisoners of war, to investigate personally conditions in the citadel. This probably was the most unusual investigation ever. Colonel Utassy, at my request, took Colonel [Charles Telfer] Howie, who was a British prisoner of war, along with him on his tour of investigation. Thus the Hungarian army authorities consented to let a British prisoner of war investigate the establishment housing Russian prisoners of war. It does not seem probable that the Russians would have permitted a British colonel to investigate prisoner of war camps in Russia even during their warmest and closest relations.

Szent-Iványi sheltered among others in the Pajor sanatorium five Yugoslav army officers. Sixteen army officers from the Netherlands were also given sanctuary by us, and we rejected the German demand for their extradition. Their names were also listed in Szent-Iványi's book.

Colonel Howie, who was mentioned above, escaped from a camp in Silesia and came to Hungary with Tibor Weinstein, a British soldier from Palestine. After registering, Weinstein went to stay with relatives, while Colonel Howie spent some weeks as the guest of Szent-Iványi, an arrangement which had been approved by Colonels Utassy and Balogh, chiefs of the department for the care of POW's. Colonel Howie enjoyed perfect freedom of movement, so much so that he conferred with Count Stephen Bethlen and other politicians, with Francis Szombathelyi, chief of staff, and he even conferred with the Regent in an interview arranged by Nicholas Horthy, Jr. Colonel Howie worked out plans for Hungary's occupation by British air force troops, after which the Hungarian army would have attacked the Germans alongside the British.

We furnished Howie with a radio transmitter and a secret code by which he was able to report his plans to the navy command of the Mediterranean. The transmitter was first in Szent-Iványi's apartment, later in the apartment of Francis Durugy, counselor in the ministry of foreign affairs, and finally was set up in the royal palace.

Szent-Iványi recalls that the Regent issued a second order for the rescue and safeguarding of all POW's and crews of landed enemy planes and that the ministry of defense also instructed the military and police forces on the absurdity of Goebbels' propaganda about explosive fountain pens and dolls being dropped by Allied planes. And that was all under the German occupation.

And so I close my lineup of facts. All that I have said in this chapter amounts to a small part of a volume that it is possible to write about the humanitarian spirit and culture of the Hungarian nation as manifested in its treatment of other people in distress. All the conditions and events that I have described were possible only because the spirit of charity prevailed and ruled down the line from the Regent, the government in all its branches, to the entire population of the country.

It is painful to contemplate that my country's destiny was not decided with these facts and truths in mind, although I hoped for that eventuality, the more so when I read Minister Wodianer's last telegram from Lisbon before the German invasion. It read:

LISBON, MARCH 19, 1944. LETTERS FROM AMERICAN PRISONERS OF WAR OF THE AIR FORCE WERE READ AT THE UNITED STATES EMBASSY HERE IN THE PRESENCE OF HIGH-RANKING OFFICERS OF THE AMERICAN AIR FORCE, WHO HAPPENED TO BE PASSING THROUGH. THESE LETTERS MADE THE BEST IMPRESSION. THE AMBASSADOR CABLED THEIR NAMES TO WASHINGTON WITH THE COMMENT THAT A NATION WHICH TREATS PRISONERS OF WAR IN SUCH A MANNER DESERVES THE GREATEST CONSIDERATION.

SIXTEEN

MY FOREIGN POLICY

The leaders must all be killed. Peace must be concluded only after complete victory and total destruction.—JENGHIZ KHAN

⟨IN THIS CHAPTER I shall summarize my efforts during my premiership to prevent Hungary from falling under the German yoke, from sinking into the position then occupied by every state of Eastern Europe and the Balkans and even by Italy and the occupied countries in the West. To appreciate my position and my subsequent decisions and actions it is necessary first to consider the military situation in Europe at the time I took office.

A glance at the map on page 346 will show that the Continent of Europe from the Iberian Peninsula to the Caucasus lay during that phase of the war within the German sphere of power. Switzer-

THE EXTENT OF GERMAN POWER, MARCH 15, 1942

land was the only Continental state that had—with great difficulty—preserved its complete independence. Sweden had made a great many concessions and was wavering between neutrality and nonbelligerency; the same held true for Spain and Portugal. The only open resistance to Germany, therefore, was that offered by Russia on the Asiatic fringe of Europe and in the West by Great Britain on her unconquerable islands—the two nations that were fighting for their dear lives. The German and Italian troops were advancing victoriously in North Africa, and Allied naval casualties in the Mediterranean were severe.

As the map on page 347 shows, the situation for the Western powers in the Far East was also extremely forbidding at that time.

THE EXTENT OF JAPANESE POWER, MARCH 15, 1942

Considerable portions of the American and British fleets had been destroyed in the Pacific and the adjacent seas. American and British soldiers were surrendering one position after another. Nearly all the strong points of the Western nations, north and south and east and west of Singapore, had fallen into Japanese hands.

I mention this situation because I have many times heard or read the accusation that Hungary changed her policy by turning away from Germany and towards England and the United States when Hungary realized that Germany's cause was faring badly and her victory was unlikely—even that her defeat appeared to be inevitable. The two maps show beyond possibility of cavil that I started in the course, which I pursued for two years without halt or deviation, at the very moment when the Axis' territorial, military, and political triumphs were at their very peak. The charge of opportunistic behavior by Hungary is another one of those false accusations that have been uncritically accepted by a deliberately misled public opinion and have now become dogmas. In 1939 when Germany invaded Poland, the Poles showed a dash and courage unsurpassed by any other people. When Poland refused to bow to Hitler's will, however, Europe was still there—France, England, and Russia were intact, and the small powers, except for Austria and Czechoslovakia, were still in existence. Above all, Poland had allies—England and France—that had guaranteed her independence and territory. When, on the other hand, Hungary began to resist, to break away from Germany, to prepare perhaps to confront her, there was de facto only one power on the Continent: Germany. It is quite true that many people knew that Germany could not win. Early in 1942, however, the military situation determined whether resistance was possible, useful, or sensible. Poland had been able to hope for military aid, and it is infinitely tragic that she did not receive it. But Hungary could not hope for any kind of military assistance from any quarter whatsoever; the situation excluded the possibility.

As I indicated previously, until the Russo-German pact came into being there was one great danger threatening us—German imperialism. After the rapprochement, however, we had to be aware of Russian imperialism, too. Closely similar as the two dreadful systems were, there was still one great difference between them. One grew out of a European people, the other from Asian; the one from Roman culture, the other from Byzantine. And there was a certain hope that a system like Nazism could not hold its own for long in Europe: it was a fit of madness connected with the person of Hitler which had attacked the German people, and Germany would either cure herself of it or perish of it. Europe, European civilization and culture, and the orderly world that

ted on tradition would rid themselves of the infection of
zism.

Bolshevism, on the other hand, was no ephemeral system. It
not mean only Stalin, and it had long ceased to be an economic
l Marxist revolution. Bolshevism was a system of terror over
sses, masses as wretched and as patient as animals; it was an
iatic system that intended to preserve itself and that was op-
sed to and hated the West. The first and principal aim of
lshevism was to destroy the West; its commanders were despots
ose desires, disguised under ideological slogans, were to con-
er, rob, trample underfoot, and destroy as all Asiatic despots
ve done from Attila through Jenghiz Khan to the Osmanli.

Hungary, of course, wanted neither National Socialism nor
lshevism to triumph. When the two giants on either side of us
rned against each other the question did arise as to which would
victorious. I had no doubt at all, even before the Russian cam-
ign of the Germans, that the Nazis would lose the war. What
en could save Hungary? A Russian victory? We had seen what
e Russians or rather what the Soviets and Bolshevism were like,
d we knew consequently what a Russian victory would mean
us and to the whole world. It was bound to mean the end of
ungary, for it was quite natural that as a drop in the ocean of
olshevik and Slav peoples the Hungarian identity would dis-
pear by growing like the other nations surrounding it and then
king the last place among them. The Slav and Orthodox peoples
d identical roots, and it was possible for them to adjust them-
lves to the Russian national and ideological world. The Hun-
rians, with their utterly different intellectual ideas, views of life,
lture, and civilization could not do so even if they would. And
hy should Hungary survive? may have been the attitude of some.
Vhat difference would it make if a few million Hungarians lost
eir national existence, culture, and morale and sank into the
me morass of slavery as the Soviet millions?

To avoid absorption into the Soviet system and to find a way

out of the dilemma posed by our position between the Russi
and Germans was, however, the historic task that I had to und
take. Thus I came to the root of the questions that had so of
arisen in the history of Hungary: to adhere to the West or
East, to resist overwhelming force or to submit to it.

To resist or to submit is to solve a problem decisively, I
either of those extreme solutions to a complex problem rests
an oversimplified view of it. Either course demands a total re
lution. Resisting a powerful aggressor is a heroic policy, but
can also be irresponsible. It may mean keeping the good e
in mind but in practice sacrificing the nation's life and pos
sions in a heroic but vain opposition. Submission to force,
the other hand, sacrifices the honor of a people, and the elite
usually handed over to the conquerors. In our history we had of
chosen resistance but never once submission, for Hungary I
been a nation that struggled for freedom. The Czechs, for
stance, seldom in their history resisted the Austrians or the G
mans; they took things as they were and managed to live v
well. The southern Slavs and Rumanians learned how to com
during the five hundred years of their domination by the Tu
Those peoples could submit, but we could not. In the situati
that confronted us in 1942, however, did either resistance or su
mission offer a solution to our predicament?

I had watched the examples of resistance in Poland and Serk
but neither of them seemed to me worth emulating. The idea
submission I refused a priori to entertain. There was one shado
possibility: to turn to that quarter that we had always looked
for aid—even though we had not always been helped by them
to the West, to the civilized world and its representatives of I
manity and culture.

I felt that two principles had to inform our policy with resp
to other nations. First, we should refuse any demand that mea
adapting Hungary's culture to another nation's ideology. We h
especially to keep from being influenced by the spirits, metho
and terrors of Nazism and Bolshevism. We, together with Switz

d and Sweden the only islands of European culture in the
shevik and Nazi dominated sea of nations between Vladi-
tok and the Iberian Peninsula, must maintain our national
ependence so that we could resist both ideologies and remain
ropean and Hungarian. This defense of our national and cul-
al identity had to govern our attitude in a forthright manner
t would be visible to the nations of the free world. Secondly,
hould try to establish direct relations with the representatives
culture, civilization, and national and human liberty—with the
estern nations.

I wish, however, to emphasize that my decision to extricate my
untry from the German sphere and to take it into the Western
ance was not inspired by, born of, or matured by the fact that
id not believe in Germany's victory or that I foresaw her mili-
y defeat. I do not deny that in making my decision I took the
litary factor into consideration; to have done otherwise would
ve been unrealistic. But I am not a strategist capable unaided of
rectly estimating the military probabilities. Wherever I turned
ly in 1942, I could not get my belief in the ultimate defeat of
rmany confirmed by a military expert. Churchill wrote in his
moirs that, when he told the French that even if they sur-
dered the English would fight on alone, the French generals
orted to the French cabinet that "within three weeks England
l get her neck wrung, like a chicken's."

My decisions and policies were governed by different considera-
ns that were of a higher order than the military considerations,
en if predictions regarding the military struggle could have been
solutely accurate. I felt that *it was inadmissible that Hungary
ould become an inseparable partner of a country and share its
stinies if that country's philosophy and methods of ruling were
ntrary to Hungarian beliefs and practices.* That was the founda-
n of my decision to disengage completely from Germany and
row in our lot with the West. That decision of mine was made a
onth before Churchill uttered his great, tragic speech about
he darkest hour of England's history." The supreme objective

which I set myself was to preserve the honor and the human a
European character of my nation, which, I felt, should be p
served, irrespective of the hazards of war, of military victories
defeats. I made it my faith that what decides a nation's destiny
that nation's character, not the victory of this belligerent or th

Then, too, Hungary looked towards the West—Britain, t
United States, even conquered France and the downtrodden sm
nations—for the same reason that we had in the past: we prefers
their orientation. We had preferred Western culture in the pa
we were drawn towards it during the war when we were the g
graphic prisoner of Germany; and we hoped to be on a frien
basis with the West after the war was over. The attempts
rapprochement with the West did not stem from opportunis
After my release from imprisonment in Germany I was often c
gusted when reporters and even high officials of Western natic
would say to me: "You turned against the Germans, didn't yc
because you realized that we would win? Just the same, Hunga
is a war-guilty nation because she realized the turn of events la
than the other nations." That is a degrading and revolting es
mate of the situation. It is the caricature of our spirit that or
the grossest materialism could perpetrate. Do we not learn fro
history that the heroes and heroic nations are the men and cou
tries who oppose naked might for the sake of justice? That the
who strike a bargain with the strong merely because he is strong
are base? Britain, America, France, Germany, and the small x
tions with a long history do not in their backgrounds reveal con
tions that give rise to spirit and ideas underlying the questions a:
taunts addressed to me. Where did that spirit come from? Wh
business sense, what materialism, what defection from both r
tional and human ethics has brought it into being and flooded t
world with it?

An accusation leveled against my policy by the other—pr
German—side at home and abroad was that my policy of chai
ing sides was unrealistic because I got no assurance, no concre
promise, no tangible guarantee from the side towards which

s hoping to move. That charge was also untrue. When the
glo-American nations published the Atlantic Charter in 1941,
ey addressed an appeal and offered guarantees to Hungary as
ll as the rest of the world. Neither the Hungarians nor I ever
nted more than was promulgated in that document to which
e United States and England pledged themselves. It was as full
d definite a statement as any country or people of good will
uld have desired. My policy was not "up in the air." I had no
n—I asked for nothing—that was not in that document. I had
wish to bargain with other nations or to make bilateral agree-
ents since I was led to believe that that spontaneous declaration
ve me more than devious transactions could bring me. Every-
e knows the substance of the text, but I reproduce it here be-
use men and peoples forget all too quickly.

JOINT DECLARATION OF PRESIDENT FRANKLIN D. ROOSEVELT,
OF THE UNITED STATES, AND WINSTON CHURCHILL, PRIME
MINISTER OF GREAT BRITAIN, AT SEA, AUGUST 14, 1941

he President of the United States of America and the Prime
finister, Mr. Churchill, representing His Majesty's Government
the United Kingdom, being met together, deem it right to
ake known certain common principles in the national policies
their respective countries on which they base their hopes for
better future for the world.

First, their countries seek no aggrandizement, territorial or
her;

Second, they desire to see no territorial changes that do not
cord with the freely expressed wishes of the peoples concerned;

Third, they respect the right of all peoples to choose the form
government under which they will live; and they wish to see
vereign rights and self-government restored to those who have
een forcibly deprived of them;

Fourth, they will endeavor, with due respect to their existing
bligations, to further the enjoyment by all States, great or small,
ctor or vanquished, of access, on equal terms, to the trade and

to the raw materials of the world which are needed for their e
nomic prosperity;

Fifth, they desire to bring about the fullest collaboration
tween all nations in the economic field, with the object of sec
ing, for all, improved labor standards, economic advanceme
and social security;

Sixth, after the final destruction of the Nazi tyranny, they h
to see established a peace which will afford to all nations the mea
of dwelling in safety within their own boundaries, and which v
afford assurance that all men in all the lands may live out th
lives in freedom from fear and want;

Seventh, such a peace should enable all men to traverse t
high seas and oceans without hindrance;

Eighth, they believe that all of the nations of the world,
realistic as well as spiritual reasons, must come to the abando
ment of the use of force. Since no future peace can be maintain
if land, sea, or air armaments continue to be employed by natic
which threaten, or may threaten, aggression outside of their fro
tiers, they believe, pending the establishment of a wider and mo
permanent system of general security, that the disarmament
such nations is essential. They will likewise aid and encourage
other practicable measures which will lighten for peace-lovi
peoples the crushing burden of armaments.

FRANKLIN D. ROOSEVE
WINSTON S. CHURCHIL

I might almost say that my whole decision meant nothing mo
than the acceptance of the binding and unilateral offer made
the Atlantic Charter. In the document there is no discussion
"victor" and "vanquished" in terms of the side a nation took
was drawn into. In fact, the only mention of the two wor
"victor" and "vanquished" is in the fourth point, where it is de
initely stated that no differentiation will be made between the
in the economy of the postwar world. No finer set of principl
could have been offered smaller nations than those laid down
the Atlantic Charter. The statesman who did not try to grasp th

)ffered hand of the two great nations would have been guilty of
rime, a sin against his nation. And the tragedies of our recent
tory have come about because by the end of the war the ideals
the Atlantic Charter had been forgotten. There is not a word
the document about military service, resistance, underground
)vements, sabotage—anything which could be called military
:ion. We shall see presently why I emphasize this here.

I began by keeping the portfolio of foreign affairs in my own
nds in order to be able to take personal charge of my foreign
licy plans, control the execution of my instructions, and become
`ectly acquainted with the officials concerned. I was soon satis-
d that the foreign ministry was the most efficiently operated
inistry in the government. The mentality of the career diplo-
ats was all that could be desired; only a very few of the quite
nior men showed inclinations towards left and right extremism.
<ept the portfolio in my own hands, however, for more than a
ar—until July, 1943. The principal reason why I relinquished
then was to insert an intermediate person between myself and
e German minister, so that *I* would not have to receive *dé-
arches* from him personally. This was not because Jagow, the
erman minister, was personally offensive to me, but because I
shed to gain time to prepare my answers to German communi-
tions. Later the Wilhelmstrasse forbade the German minister
see me personally.

When I left the foreign ministry, Eugene Ghyczy, a career
plomat who was the permanent officer in charge, took my place.
entmiklóssy, chief of the political section, moved up into
hyczy's place, and Aladár Szegedy-Maszák into his. Thus no
al change occurred in the conduct of the business of the foreign
inistry.

The first time that I called together the leading officials of the
)litical section of the foreign ministry I told them that my
:finite and ultimate line of policy would be *to lead the country
to a position in which the points of the Atlantic Charter could*

be applied to us without reservation. This entailed following
appropriate internal policy, reversing our military policy, and
our foreign policy informing the Allies—that is, the British a
the Americans—of our intentions and activities. All this could
done by seeking direct relations, by informing the foreign pr
and public opinion in the required senses, and in general by
ethical attitude on our part. I regarded this as the essential p
gram to which everything else was subordinated.

I began by giving the appropriate instructions to the press. '
do this it was only necessary to bring the existing instructions
to date. I can best illustrate the way our press was told to wr
by reproducing the original text of the oldest set of instructio
in my possession.

INSTRUCTIONS TO THE PRESS

January, 19

Generally speaking, the press is following the instructions p
viously sent out from this office, so that serious objections fro
the point of view of foreign policy have been only occasional.
is not so much in order to correct its previous attitude as rather
insure that it preserves its present tone that the attention of
representatives is now again drawn to the chief ruling princip.
which should guide it. These are as follows:

The Hungarian press sees in the present European conflict
cause to conduct polemics against any side. The belligerent part
can appreciate this the more readily because if we have given
polemics in our own cause, no one can ask us to be the mout
piece of others. This point of view must, therefore, be strict
observed.

It follows that any offensive references to foreign states or lea
ing statesmen are forbidden. This applies also to caricatures.

It is most undesirable that the press should seek to lay dov
the government's foreign policy for it. Expressions of oppositic
to the government's foreign policy cannot be tolerated.

The utmost caution is recommended in reproducing foreig
political news items. In the case of any such item not received v

the Hungarian Telegraphic Agency [HTA] [1] editors are advised, if there is the slightest cause for doubt, to consult the press section of the foreign ministry.

As regards our connections with foreign states, the following rules remain unchanged:

a. Towards Germany, the tone of the press should be friendly. There should be no suggestion that Germany harbors any designs on this country. It is, however, unnecessary to reproduce Germany's own polemical matter.

b. Towards Italy the tone of the press should be most friendly. This does not mean that all the attacks against the Soviets in the Italian papers need be slavishly reproduced.

c. As regards the Allies (England and France) the press should bear in mind the foreign minister's statement in his recent speech that our relations with those powers are unaltered—that is, the present war is no war of ours. All expressions of sympathy towards Hungary emanating from those countries should be politely acknowledged but no attempt made to create immediate political capital out of them.

d. Towards Yugoslavia the press should be friendly. It should abstain from emphasizing in any way Yugoslavia's internal difficulties. It is, however, unnecessary for it to take over everything that the Yugoslavs write—probably on Rumania's suggestion—about plans for a Balkan bloc.

e. The press should take as little notice as possible of Rumania. Whatever has to be said will in any case come to it from the HTA; if any further communication needs to be made, the press section will speak to the papers individually.

f. The same applies to Slovakia.

g. As regards Soviet Russia, abstain from any attack, which does not mean showing sympathy for conditions in the USSR. The press will be issued with the requisite items from time to time by the HTA, possibly also by the press section.

[1] The Hungarian name for the agency was Magyar Tavirati Iroda, and so the initials on dispatches were MTI.

h. The Hungarian press has to date reported the Finnish nation's fight for its liberty with sympathy, without endangering our correct relations with the Soviet Union by pro-Finnish leading articles. This attitude is, broadly speaking, correct, and since we have received from Finland expressions of thanks for the attitude of our press, there is no need to go any further.

A. ULLEIN-REVICZKY

I will not deny that our press was occasionally guilty of lapses from these principles, but I know for a fact that there was not a single fundamental deviation during my administration. If we departed from the outlined program, it was under the compulsion of the momentary situation, never from conviction or because our principles had changed. Very often the only way of preventing a great evil or serious damage to our course was by making concessions of form that averted concessions of substance. Such compromises applied especially to the Jewish question, and it was a regular phenomenon that we wrote most violently against the Jews when most strongly resisting German demands for action against them. My own strongest anti-Semitic speeches were made after I had refused a German ultimatum, repeated three times in various forms, to enforce the wearing of the star of David, to segregate the Jews in ghettos, and to send 300,000 Jewish workers to Germany. It is true that this unavoidable double game had a bad side to it, since people at home and abroad heard, of course, only the words and were unaware of the actions that were behind the words.

From the inception of my administration onward the press in Hungary was guided by the following instructions issued to it.

1. The government press was to reduce to the minimum possible any expressions of sympathy for Germany. The National Socialist philosophy was not to be mentioned at all, and writers were to avoid affirming faith in the justice of the German cause and in a German victory. The writers were by no means to talk of a community of destiny between Germany and ourselves. German war communiques were to be published, but in the com-

mentary the reports of the Allies were to be included with the German ones under the guise of refuting the Western account with the German record.

2. The so-called left-wing press (which consisted of considerably more daily papers than the right-wing group possessed) was to be allowed more space for enlightening the public both on military and on foreign political events, and it was to be allowed a free hand in controversies with the Nazi papers and parties. Any kind of Bolshevik propaganda remained, however, strictly forbidden.

3. Strict censorship was to be applied to what the Imrédist and Arrow Cross papers wrote. Their publication was to be obstructed, and if a suitable pretext appeared, the administrative authorities were to use their powers to suspend them temporarily or permanently. (Soon after, in fact, the extreme rightists had only one daily left.)

4. The greatest attention was to be paid to the neutral press, which was to be supplied with or furnished the inspiration for articles indicating Hungary's intention of breaking away from the Axis.

5. The inevitable protests from Germany were to be parried by abstaining from attacking her openly and from time to time publishing articles flattering to the Germans [2] (but never touching on ideological questions) or offensive to the Anglo-American powers (but not excessively so).

6. On the Jewish question, the measures already taken were to be treated as *faits accomplis*, but no further demands were to be treated as admissible. Strict instructions were given that the Jewish question was a concern of the government that could not be influenced in wartime by party politics, popular feeling, or press campaigns.

7. Attempts were to be made to place in the British and Ameri-

---

[2] This came presently to take the form of eulogistic articles on the culture, learning, poetry, and music of the old Germany—which annoyed the Nazis exceedingly.

can press articles explaining Hungary's situation, point of view, and objectives.

As a consequence of the government's attitude, the newspapers went on for a long time publishing the official British and American war communiques. They wrote much about Germany, but the events in the Western nations were reported precisely and in most instances with favorable comment. Unfortunately we had to stop the public sale of newspapers of belligerent countries, but these could always be obtained in envelopes by subscribers. The sale of papers from neutral countries was quite unrestricted, so that the people of Hungary had access to information about the world outside. Our press was courteous to the Allies, and it never attacked Britain or America. Our newspapers did, however, defend Hungary against the regrettably frequent unjust attacks and libels upon us. Imrédy complained that the censorship was "in the service of the British." There was absolute freedom to listen to and own a radio, and foreign broadcasts could be heard freely in public places. (The Germans were extremely annoyed to hear the British and American national anthems through open windows.) Our radio did not attack the Western Allies, and very often it broadcast communiques and news which also gave the "enemy" point of view. The result was that in Germany and the occupied territories, Hungarian publications—books, magazines, and newspapers—were banned. This German ban included the official Hungarian press and even the extreme right-wing Hungarian publications.

In estimating what the government's liberal attitude towards the dissemination of news meant, it must be remembered that the Germans disapproved strenuously and that we struggled indefatigably to preserve our policy. The preservation of this policy was a principal reason for keeping the Germans out of Hungary, for if they entered, all this as well as other freedoms would end.

The Hungarian press observed the government's instructions in a way that was entirely satisfactory to me. A falling-away from these policies began early in 1944, when the news of the Czech-

Russian treaty and the Teheran Conference began to filter through and the military situation began to worsen seriously for the Germans while the Russians drew near to our frontiers. Tension and excitement gripped all groups from left to right, and it was no longer possible to keep the press in hand so surely as before. So much for the press.

Of the missions accredited in Budapest when I assumed the premiership only the German and the Italian were at all politically important. Of these two we had most to fear from the Germans.

The German officials established almost no relations outside the expressly Germanophile, right-wing circles. This reduced the social circles within which they moved to narrow limits. Hungarian high society at that time was composed of landowners, big industrialists and bankers, clergy, businessmen, and writers and artists. As I have explained before, hardly a man among them was pro-German or a right-wing extremist; it was only the minor figures in any of these classes who went that way. Thus, socially speaking, the German legation had no weight or influence.

In this area of our life, the position of the Italians was quite different. They were living proof that Fascism was not an article for export. The Italians themselves showed no signs of wanting to win friends for their country through propagation of Fascism. The members of the Italian legation maintained normal contact with the same circles of Budapest society as the other legations and as the Americans and British had before them. This shows, incidentally, what tendentious folly it is to use the name "Fascism" collectively, or rather how cunningly the definition of National Socialism has been blurred by first grouping conservatives, democrats, and Nazis together under the collective head of Fascist, until at last the conservatives became the Fascists in chief, followed by the democrats and socialists, while the Nazis slip out and take their proper places in the Communist Peoples Democracies.

These remarks are necessary, not only for the analysis of the social life of the two Axis partners, but also to show the influence that each exerted on Hungarian life. We had nothing to fear from the Italians, but much from the Germans, which made it necessary for us to obstruct their penetration into our various groups. We were reasonably successful, and as time went on the public appearances of the members of the German legation were restricted to ever narrower circles, and their social influence became nil. They did, however, seek intensive contact with the press, with certain political movements, and with individual writers and actors. Above all, they tried to win over members of our ministries.

Recognizing the danger in the attempted infiltration of our ministries by the Germans, I had a circular letter sent to all foreign missions in Budapest requesting them not to communicate—personally, in writing, by telephone—with any ministry or public office other than the foreign ministry, which would forward the message to the addressee office. The members of our ministries were also instructed to reject any direct approach made to them. Thus we not only made German interference with our missions impossible, but we were also able to check the subjects the Germans were interested in.

Another unpalatable but necessary step which I took was to have the German legation under constant observation and its telephone tapped.

One of my greatest problems was the men who were heads of our various missions abroad, especially those in neutral countries. I soon satisfied myself, however, that they were entirely reliable with two exceptions: Döme Sztójay in Berlin and John Vörnle in Ankara. Sztójay was heart and soul with the Germans; it used to be said that he, not the German minister, represented Germany's case in Hungary. Vörnle's sympathies were with Germany, and in Ankara he was strongly influenced by Franz von Papen, but I never had reason to doubt Vörnle's loyalty. Some of the other ministers had German sympathies, but no question of their reliability ever arose.

The ministers, except Sztójay, were instructed that I proposed to follow an independent foreign policy. That did not mean a reversal of our existing policy, nor anything impracticable, but I attached great importance to not allowing even a suggestion to remain that Hungarian diplomacy was in German leading strings. I was determined that ways be found to emphasize this both in the neutral countries and in those allied with Germany. There should be dissociation but no demonstrated unfriendliness. The ministers and their staffs should try to maintain the best relations, which might be as intimate as they cared, with the diplomats of neutral countries. Contact was not to be sought with the diplomats of countries at war with us. Indeed, no individual initiative with respect to unfriendly countries was permissible, but if meeting occurred on neutral ground, the greatest courtesy was to be shown representatives of those nations and any sign of tension carefully avoided. Szentmiklóssy drew up instructions laying down in detail what attitudes our representatives were to adopt on various instances which might arise, emphasizing always and everywhere that we regarded two considerations as directing and governing our conduct: (1) the general, human point of view, and (2) the specifically Hungarian. Those two were never to be allowed to conflict.

After that I called the ministers home one by one and informed each of them of the intimate objectives of my policy to the degree which I thought necessary and advisable. I was completely frank with Gabriel Apor, our minister to the Vatican; George Bessenyey, who was then in Vichy, and Andor Wodianer, in Lisbon. I thought of replacing some of the ministers but my colleagues dissuaded me. And they were right, for it made no difference, for example, who represented us in Berlin. The Germans went their own way without regard for others, and it was even better to have someone there whom they trusted. Sometimes Sztójay got useful information. If we had been represented by someone not friendly towards the Germans, they would have isolated our legation. It was better for the legation staff as things were, and

sometimes they reported to us independently. I did not like
Vörnle's ideas, but precisely his good relations with the Germans
made his reports valuable to us. We therefore retained him, too,
but we enlarged the consulate general in Istanbul to meet our
own special requirements and placed it under a trusted member
of the foreign ministry, Desiderius Ujváry. That arrangement subsequently fulfilled our hopes.

Anthony Ullein-Reviczky, the chief of the press section of the
foreign ministry, who had a team of excellent young men under
him, gradually expanded the service of press attachés, appointing
to these posts only reliable persons who made contact with neutral
and Allied journalists and did most useful work for our information services. Certain of them, by an altogether exceptional concession, were allowed to send in reports by the diplomatic bag, in
sealed envelopes, the contents not being shown to the ministers.

I should like to mention a confidential discussion in which,
besides Ghyczy and Szentmiklóssy, Keresztes-Fischer, Kánya, and
Bethlen took part. At this meeting I raised the questions of our
official attitude towards our participation in the war and the interpretation of our policy generally. Were we to say that we had
been dragged into the war by German pressure? That this had
forced us into our declarations of war and our similar actions?
Or that our decision had been our own? That our actions had
been and would be governed by the service of Hungarian interests?

There was much truth in the thesis that Hungary was pushed
into the war. I told the others that I did not think that internal
forces unassisted by German threats could have carried the nation
into the conflict. The course of events, our geopolitical situation, our friendlessness—all these were the circumstances that had
brought Hungary to the point where she stood at the time of
our conference. But to admit all that was equivalent to a public
declaration of Hungarian nonindependence. Such a declaration
might be regarded in the future as an extenuating circumstance,

but to admit our helplessness would mean losing our right of self-determination, which would have serious consequences. The greatest hindrance to the Germans in carrying through their plans was the forced respect which they had to pay to Hungarian independence. If we ourselves opened a breach in our national integrity, it would be easy for the Germans to widen it and march through it. To get us into a Quisling position was what both the Germans and their Hungarian partisans wanted, and an admission of weakness might facilitate this.

Then, too, a confession of impotence was no program for a government but a mere evasion of responsibility. The internal political effect would be catastrophic. It would entitle the opportunists and the self-styled realists to run some to Nazism, others to Bolshevism, in search of strength and a solution. It would give the nation one more cause—of which it already had enough —to be despondent; special emphasizing of our weakness would be suicidal. In any case it would be a deliberate weakening of our power of resistance, something that it was our duty to foster against the moment when the nation could act in her own interest.

Suppose then, I told the others, that we said that Hungary had made her policy on her own responsibility. One analysis of the facts might show that this was not true, for unquestionably Hungary had nothing to seek in the war. Yet it is a fact that a nation always bears the consequences of its actions and its fate. It must stand before her own sons and before the world with erect head, not disclaiming responsibility and in consciousness of right. What decides what is right is the possibility of action in given circumstances, whether there was another choice, whether the way chosen was in the interests of the people of the nation, whether everything that could be done in the common interest was done. All these considerations apply especially to members of a government whose plain duty is to assume all responsibility. This duty cannot be evaded with excuses, nor pushed on to fate or the enemy or anything else. To do this is to abandon the principle of national self-determination and therewith to abandon the right to require others to respect it. Some may call these arguments fictions. They are not. Even if they were, however, it would not alter the case. If nothing else remains, one may still clutch a fiction, and it may turn into a reality. If, on the other hand, we give up even the fiction, nothing remains at all. A fiction in difficult times is like a faith with great and fundamental tenets that must be held at all costs.

Those considerations seemed overruling to all of us in the meeting. We decided, therefore, that the fundamental thesis of our official attitude should be an independent Hungarian policy that was self-regarding; that accepted full responsibility for its actions; that adhered strictly to the Hungarian traditions of liberalism, humanism, and Christianity; and that would fight to the end for the last particle of our independence. What we had done in the past was accepted, therefore, as having been done in the interests of, not the Germans or any other people, but ourselves. And all our future actions would, of course, serve the cause of Hungary. Circumstances would undoubtedly play a part in shaping our methods and instruments, but it was our duty to make the means serve ultimately our purposes.

Someone asked whether this attitude would not appear too chauvinistic and thus make a bad impression in English and American minds. I answered that Western thinking might frown on our policy as being unduly self-conscious. The attitudes towards nationalism in the West had been embittered by the aggressive tendencies in Fascism and National Socialism. Yet we could not abandon the policy and direction we had decided upon, for I believed that the confusion in the thinking of the Westerners would pass away. True nationalism, I declared, can never be offensive in character, only defensive. True nationalism should not be confused with the imperialistic trends in Germany and Italy that stemmed mainly from the need for economic expansion. Italy's attacks on Ethiopia, Albania, and Greece, and Germany's on the non-German territories, had nothing in common with na-

tionalism. Nationalism may mean irredentism—the urge to liberate from foreign oppression people cut off from the mother stock
and gravitating towards it. The conquest of other peoples, however, can never be nationalism. It is simply imperialism, usually
of an economic nature. Hungarian imperialism ended with the
Turkish conquest. It was replaced in the Danube Basin by Habsburg imperialism, of which we were the principal victims. All our
wars of liberty were waged against Habsburg imperialism, and in
those wars the Habsburgs used the other Danubian peoples against
us. In our history, nationalism and imperialism took opposite
paths. In the soul of the Hungarian people nationalism lived as
a self-defense against foreign conquest. It was, therefore, very important to keep nationalism alive in Hungary.

It is also noteworthy, I said in conclusion, that only two forces
have been able to stand up against National Socialism and Bolshevism: religious feeling and national feeling. The Soviet leaders
know this well, and that is why the spearhead of their propaganda
is directed against these two forces. The third great thesis of Bolshevism, the proclamation of class war, is directed partly against
the cohesive forces of religion and nationalism. In addition, the
aim of class warfare is the destruction of other forms of community existence, chief among them the democratic, by the setting of one citizen against the other and so disintegrating the
institutions that make for their common existence amidst the
diversity of their experiences.

That then was the situation when I became premier and minister of foreign affairs. I knew that I was starting out on a difficult
path. All my informants told me that political thought in Britain
and the United States had been pushed into the background. The
leaders in those countries concentrated everything in winning the
war, and they viewed everything from that angle. The war became
the end. People forgot why it had begun, and what was to come
after it scarcely entered their thoughts. The Atlantic Charter be-

gan to take the place of Wilson's Fourteen Points, but both were ill-fated documents that eventually became the ideal, not of their authors and publishers, but of the enemy and the conquered.

When I took as my aim the policy that I have sketched, I naturally wanted to serve the interests of my country. I also continually saw to it, however, that the policy remained in harmony with European interests as a whole—with the struggle for freedom from dictatorship. The fundamental idea was to offer the maximum resistance without endangering the nation's interests: to give the least possible moral, material, and military aid to the Germans but to avoid by all means occupation by them. That was my hope and the faith that sustained my strength, naive as it may have been. I was not prepared to give Hungary up to the Germans or the Russians, and in those days not even to the Western Allies. Today I should be happy if I had been compelled to deliver my country over to the British and Americans on the basis of unconditional surrender. At that time, however, I thought that they should be liberators, for I was not seeking for a conqueror of my country.

The approach and understanding that I had hoped for never—as we all know now—materialized. The internal ideological, economic, and cultural resistance that we showed, even our humanitarian treatment of refugees and prisoners of war, did not earn us a just solution to our difficulties after the war. Other reasons apart, I believe it was because the military authorities in the Western nations were at that time not sufficiently interested in Central Europe. Perhaps they did not know what would happen in the Balkans—that, in fact, the decisive battle began there. In the political field, it was probably the mistrust created by the universal intrigues of Benes and his colleagues that was the primary obstacle.

Despite, however, the difficulties that I was aware of at the time, I did not lose heart and give up my plan to seek and establish a relationship with the British and the Americans, to arouse in them an interest in our little European island, which had preserved so much of its independence despite unremitting pressure by the Germans who surrounded us. I persisted in that course, not merely because all my hopes and feelings were set on it, but also because I could see no other way out. Between the two colossi whose armies raged around us, I spun a slender hope, an Ariadne's thread by which to lead my nation out of the unwanted war and destruction. On the basis of my thoughts and feelings about our predicament, I began the long work of establishing relations with the Allies. That work was begun through unofficial diplomatic channels, through articles in the press of neutral countries, and through speeches and announcements on our radio. I tried to voice my purpose in sentences and allusions in my speeches. I tried at the same time to lead the nation on the right road and form its ideas so that at the end of the war the "West" when it entered Hungary would find a nation, people, parliament, military forces, public order, and economic life so well organized that Hungary could without a jar join in a world reformed in the spirit of the Atlantic Charter.

Our first contacts with the British were made via the Poles. That was an indirect contact: we did not go so far as to negotiate, but we did try to send information to London through Polish channels. We forwarded the Polish correspondence from Lisbon in our diplomatic bag. We recognized Fietowic as representative of the Polish government in London, while Wodianer, our minister in Lisbon, represented us with the Polish government, receiving written credentials from our foreign minister. Later Fietowic traveled to London from Budapest, via Turkey and South Africa, on a Hungarian passport. It was through Lisbon also that we gave Eckhardt authorization to represent the Hungarian cause in America.

We succeeded in establishing actual, direct contacts with the British in the summer of 1942. Ullein-Reviczky reported that he wished to spend his summer holiday, as usual, in Constantinople with his parents-in-law (his wife's father was a retired

British consul general). Ullein-Reviczky was authorized to establish contacts with British official circles there. He was successful, and an agreement was reached that a Hungarian trusted agent, equipped with instructions from the government and powers from the military authorities, might be sent out. London and the GHQ in Cairo agreed to this. The choice fell on Andrew Frey, foreign political editor of the *Magyar Nemzet*, an independent conservative paper, not representing the government and enjoying great authority. The foreign ministry and Chief of Staff Szombathelyi jointly empowered Frey to make the following communication:

1. Hungary did not intend to oppose Anglo-American or Polish troops if they reached the Hungarian frontier and advanced into the country. Hungary wished nothing in return for this. It was, of course, understood that Hungary could undertake to adopt this attitude only towards the regular troops of the Allies, not towards partisan bands.

2. Hungary was in principle prepared to take positive action against the Germans if it proved possible to work out in advance a practical plan for co-operation between the armies concerned.

3. The purpose of this offer was not to save the existing Hungarian regime, but solely to serve the interests of the Hungarian people.

Unfortunately, the difficulties of getting Frey his visas caused protracted delays. He reached Istanbul only in January, 1943, when he immediately carried out his mission as instructed. The Americans replied that the British would represent them also in the discussions. A few weeks later we got the following answer from the British: "We propose that the Hungarian government send to Istanbul, as soon as possible, two senior Hungarian officers to discuss details of the proposal received."

That answer took us somewhat aback. It contained no suggestion of concluding, or even discussing, a political agreement with us. My own idea had been that some such agreement should be concluded first and that the military discussions begin only after that. The fact that the British answer to our message related to the making of military contacts suggested that the British wanted to take advantage of our approach in the military field but that they were not prepared to carry on negotiations that were in line with the point of view and interests of the Hungarian people. We were also influenced by an article in the *Times* that stated that certain states, including Hungary, should not fancy that they could save themselves by their belated efforts to escape from the sinking ship. What appalled us was not the stupidity of the article but the proof that some official indiscretion had taken place. The slipup not only made the success of the whole plan problematic, but it also seemed bound to provoke a reaction from the Germans, and it is not impossible that that was the purpose of the indiscretion. What made things particularly disagreeable for us was that the British had designated to conduct the negotiations with us an individual of Hungarian origin named George Pálóczy-Horváth, at that time employed by the organization which the British had established in Istanbul for counterespionage and sabotage in the Balkans. The British also named him as the man who would talk to the Hungarian officers when they arrived. We made many attempts to get Pálóczy-Horváth out of the negotiations, but the British refused all our requests. Everyone in Hungary knew that he was a spy of Gömbös in former days and that later he became a left-wing Socialist with strong sympathies for Moscow. In Serbian affairs, he was Tito's *homme de confiance*. The British only discovered in December, 1944, what we knew at that time, that Pálóczy-Horváth was regularly passing on information to the Russians.

In any case, the military situation did not seem to have reached a stage such as to make the immediate creation of military contacts an urgent matter. It was, however, I repeat, the designation of Pálóczy-Horváth by the English as their negotiator that disquieted me. Furthermore, I must say frankly that I should not have been able to find a single senior officer in the Hungarian army ready to negotiate with any civilian, least of all with a Muscovite agent. Frey raised the question with one of Pálóczy-Horváth's English superiors, who answered that Frey might be right from a political point of view but that he, the speaker, was not there to make politics but to create the maximum of confusion behind the enemy front. In that work, the Englishman said, a gentleman would be unwilling and even unable to help him; such people lacked either the training or the taste for underground work. Revolutionaries and adventurers, on the other hand, volunteered willingly for his service, and precisely the political passion which inspired them made them particularly suitable for it.

We therefore put off sending the soldiers. Part of the reason for our delay was that I was afraid that if they arrived prematurely some indiscretion would occur which would, not only hinder the military co-operation, but make it impossible to plan it for a future date. Then, too, my military advisers refused flatly to negotiate with such a partner. Indeed, they could not imagine what an officer of the general staff could discuss with an obscure renegade. Strategy? Tactics? Co-operation? What? When, however, a possibility seemed to arise that, if I sent down a professional diplomat, the contacts first established by Frey could be extended and made more intimate, I grasped at the chance. Given the peculiar situation in Turkey—that I could not trust Vörnle, our minister there, but could not replace him for fear of upsetting the Germans—it was inadvisable to send down a senior diplomat. His presence would have attracted the Germans' attention and Vörnle, too, would have demanded explanations. My choice therefore fell on a young man named Ladislas Veres, who at that time worked in the press section of the foreign ministry and who possessed English connections, whom we were about anyway to send down to the Smyrna Fair as our representative. Veres carried out the duties entrusted to him quickly and courageously. In the following pages I tell the story of his activities, as gathered from his reports and supplemented by notes from

Szegedy-Maszák, the chief of the political department of the foreign ministry.

Our official representative in Istanbul was our consul general, Desiderius Ujváry. Veres was specially attached to Ujváry for the purpose of his mission. On August 17, 1943, these two informed Mr. Sterndale Bennett, the British minister, representing the Allies, of Hungary's readiness to surrender to the Allies on the basis of the formula already communicated in the previous March (amounting, roughly, to unconditional surrender), which surrender could, however, only come into effect if Anglo-American troops reached the frontiers of Hungary. Ujváry and Veres further asked Mr. Sterndale Bennett to pass on their message to the British and American governments, with the request: (1) that they should accept this in principle as notification of Hungary's capitulation and (2) that they should communicate the preliminary conditions.

The British government submitted our message to the Quebec Conference, which was meeting at that moment. President Roosevelt and Mr. Churchill received the message as constituting Hungary's advance notice of capitulation. They passed it on to Moscow and informed the other governments of the United Nations. All this was done between August 17 and September 9, 1943.

On September 9 Sir Hugh Knatchbull-Hugesson, His Majesty's ambassador, met Veres on board a British vessel in the Sea of Marmora and informed him in the name of the United Nations that His Majesty's government, having taken note of Hungary's communication, thought it necessary to inform the Hungarian government that its preliminary conditions were as follows:

1. The Hungarian government confirm its communication of August 17 with respect to Hungary's capitulation and acceptance of the conditions set forth by the Allies.

2. Hungary's capitulation will be kept secret. It will be made public by the Allies and by the Hungarian government simultaneously, at a time agreed by both parties as suitable. At the ex-

press wish of the Hungarian contracting party, it is agreed that publication shall in no case occur before the Allies have reached the frontiers of Hungary.

3. Hungary shall progressively reduce her military co-operation with Germany and shall in particular withdraw her troops from Russia and shall assist Allied aircraft flying across Hungary to attack bases in Germany.

4. Hungary shall progressively diminish her economic co-operation with Germany and shall refuse to participate in Germany's war production.

5. Hungary undertakes to resist any attempt made by Germany to occupy her territory. To this end, the Hungarian high command is to be reorganized so as to make the army able to withdraw from the Germans and attack them.

6. At the given moment Hungary shall place her entire resources, her communications, and her air bases at the disposal of the Allies for the continuance of the fight against Germany.

7. An Allied air mission will be dropped in Hungary at the suitable moment to make the necessary advance preparations in connection with Hungary's surrender.

8. Regular radio contact will be established between the Allies and the organs of the Hungarian government. The Allies will be regularly informed of the German and Hungarian situation.

The first of these conditions was fulfilled by Wodianer's informing Sir Ronald Campbell, the British ambassador in Lisbon, that Ujváry had been granted plenipotentiary powers by the Hungarian government to conduct the negotiations and that Veres also had been regularly accredited.

A few days later Veres returned to Budapest bringing with him the code and transmitter, which worked thereafter satisfactorily up to the German occupation.

I have based these paragraphs on Veres' report. Our offer amounted in essence to unconditional surrender, and it was received as such by the British. Wodianer told Sir Ronald Campbell that Hungary was prepared to carry out any conditions lai

lown by the British and Americans. Only the formula of uncon-
litional surrender was unacceptable because it would mean the
bandonment and immediate cessation of the sovereignty of the
tate, whereas Hungary's aim was, on the contrary, to save and
o preserve its existence. Any condition would therefore be ac-
epted which in practice came to the same thing as unconditional
urrender, but in principle was poles apart from it. The English
iaturally had to stick by unconditional surrender, which had been
nade a principle of general validity. They explained that to us in
Constantinople. Our negotiators did not dissent; they only pointed
»ut that at the moment the question was of no practical signifi-
ance because, as the military situation then stood, a long time
vas likely to elapse before the British reached the frontiers of
Iungary. Frey, who attended the conferences as a nonofficial
»bserver, raised the question with the foreign ministry, and he
vas told in reply that at the moment the Hungarian government
vas not considering the question, it being not yet *actuel* in view
»f the military situation. It could say at once, however, as it had
n its first communication, that the Hungarian government was
»repared to carry out any condition which saved and assured its
ndependence.

One might go on arguing this question at length. It is a fact
hat we knew that the British government accepted our offer in
hat sense, but they also knew that at that moment it was only an
·mpty formula. The agreement had been concluded in the inter-
·st of collaboration and above all of preparation for collaboration,
nd there was no need to prepare unconditional surrender. But
»ne reason why the thing was differently understood may perhaps
ie in the fact that the enterprise did not work out thereafter as
had hoped. We had made a political gesture and expected it to
iave political consequences, by whatever conditions those were
ccompanied. The British, however, regarded the agreement as
inconditional surrender and sought only to derive military ad-
·antage from it.

But the essential fact is that *we were the first country within*

the German sphere—even Italy came after us—to notify the Wes
officially through diplomatic channels of our withdrawal fro
collaboration with Germany. Our action was taken before we ha
been subjected to any pressure from the other side, been invaded c
threatened with invasion, or otherwise been reduced to having n
other choice. It was a spontaneous gesture and made of ou
own free will. The British government took official note of ou
decision, and on that basis we continued to negotiate. We receive
their proposals, and I dare maintain that we fulfilled all of then
so far as lay in our power.

On the individual points of the agreement I note briefly:

1. The Hungarian government ratified the agreement in Li
bon.

2. The secrecy of the agreement was kept by both sides.

3. The Hungarian government did all it could to reduce mil
tary co-operation with Germany. Hungary was unable to brin
back all her troops, but she reduced their number and fightin
capacity and arranged that they should serve only behind the line
Thus the essential part of that objective was achieved. The Allie
including the Soviet aircraft flying for Tito, were able freely to us
the Hungarian air space. Germany, on the other hand, was allowe
no air bases in Hungary.

4. Economic resistance against the Germans was carried ou
on a large scale.

5. The attitude shown by the Hungarian government again:
the invading Germans on March 19, 1944, when the nation wa
left entirely to her own resources, is described below.

6. The placing of our resources at the disposal of the armies c
the West was the main point of the whole proposal, and it woul
certainly have been fulfilled at the appropriate moment.

7. The allied air mission did come to Hungary, belatedly.

8. Radio communication was maintained with the British.

By concluding that agreement I thought I had brought my na
tion into safe harbor. I hoped that the relationship would grov
more intimate as time went on. In our struggle to hold our ow

we had a safe backing, whatever happened. We enjoyed British protection in which we could trust. From that moment we were struck off the list of enemies and enrolled, if in disguised form, in the ranks of the resisting nations.

Such thinking was wrong. I am convinced, however, that the reason for the different outcome lay, not with the British, but with the development of the military situation. We and the other Danubian and Balkan states knew that, not only our own future, but that of all Europe, perhaps of the world, depended upon the military victory. That victory would have a purpose only if it were the victory of the West. More important than victory of arms was the victory of the Western spirit. If this did not come about, all the sacrifices of the Western powers would be rendered useless and far worse than useless. We thought in terms not of army corps but of eternal values of human and national problems. The democracies, on the other hand, the unmilitarist peoples on whom the war had been forced, thought only in military terms. They could not believe that Russia's victory meant, not only the defeat of the German imperialism and ideology, but also the victory of Russian imperialism and Russian ideology.

The people in the West did not realize that the left-wing forces with which they linked themselves, including those that were beginning to appear in Eastern Europe, were the advance guards of Bolshevism. The Western Allies were fighting National Socialism, that anachronistic product of medieval stupidity and untenable doctrine based on absurdities, but at the same time they were unknowingly helping into the saddle Bolshevism, the most pregnant form of international socialism, a modern, up-to-date, precisely and logically worked out system. The Western powers fought honorably to defeat Germany; they meant to make a just and democratic peace.

The Communists, on the other hand, never for one moment lost sight of the goal they had set for themselves. Their long-range plans were obvious. Communism's alliance with Germany, its complete support of Hitler's aggression and of his lunatic ide-

ology, made one thing clear beyond all question: the Communists
would ally themselves with the devil himself, and the Nazi devil
was more sympathetic to them than the democracies were. The
Communists knew that Hitler's madness was a passing phenome
non in Germany but one that was well calculated to disintegrate
those forces in the German nation that stood in the way of Bol
shevism: the great German conservative bourgeoisie, the real
strength of Germany; the Wehrmacht; and, above all, her reli
gious life. Nazism was the pathmaker for the Communists; it did
the pioneer work for them. The Communists could reckon that
the collapse of Nazism would leave the German people in con
fusion and ready to accept the Bolshevik propaganda for which
Nazism itself had prepared them. The Russians had wanted to
wait for that time while allied with Germany, and then, after
Germany had defeated the West, the Russians had intended to
realize their plans on Germany's weakened body.

It is undeniable that Hungary made her offer, not only with
the object of escaping from Hitler's grip and taking part in the
struggle against him, but also of securing her independence against
all aggressors and primarily against the Russians. Germany could
suddenly crush us at any moment, it was true. That was the nearest
danger in point of time and distance that threatened our inde
pendence, and somehow we hoped that the agreement would
help us here also. But the first task and object of the Hungarian
government was to protect the nation by linking up with the
Allies in order to avert the even greater devastation which threat
ened us from Russia. We should certainly have been able to free
ourselves by our own forces from the Germans, but not from the
Russians. The only Trojan horse that the Nazis could send into
our city was anti-Semitism, that is, agitation against one group
The weapon of the Russians, however, was the general war and
beyond that war against everyone, irrespective of class, who did
not bow the knee and the head not only to Bolshevism but also
to the biggest imperialism in the last five centuries. One of the

fundamental and catastrophic anomalies in the situation was that we were seeking the protection of the British and Americans, not only against our own "allies," but against their allies also.

We saw that quite clearly from the first moment. I do not know whether the British and American statesmen were not of the same opinion in their hearts, but they did not act as if they were in the policy they subsequently followed. Throughout her history England has always been the protector of the small nations, which was one of the characteristics that made her great. Now, it seemed, England had left that path.

The fact is that each partner to the agreement expected something different from it. England wanted to drive a destructive wedge into the body of the German rule. We were prepared to do that, but we were neither willing nor able to do it by the only means to which they attached importance—sabotage. We wanted to go over completely to the Anglo-American side, not to carry out trivial enterprises. Acts of sabotage by us at the most would have given some material to the Allied propagandists. They would, however, have resulted in the sacrifice of our national independence, our people, and the hundreds of thousands of refugees within our gates. I have already explained in detail throughout this account why we could not do that. Since we could not, there was no sense in sending the two senior military officers.

I wish, however, to say here a few words about the plan of dropping a mission by air. When I agreed to that, I imagined that the Allies were proposing to send to Hungary persons who would act as advisers and sources of information, as a small, secret diplomatic mission, collaborating with our government and keeping their own government constantly informed. I supposed that England would make up such a mission, established in the heart of Germany's power sphere, a watchtower for her policy and that the British government would send to the post a man who could speak for British policy. I thought, too, that the intentions of the Hungarian government were understood and appreciated and that the Allies would help us realize our aim of withdrawing from the war or, if it came to that, turning with all our armed forces against the Germans.

I soon discovered that the ideas of the English were quite different from what I had supposed; their emissaries were to be mere underground secret agents charged with the task of organizing conspiracies and sabotage and causing disturbances. Those British agents were not going to furnish support to my political program, which was backed up by the cream of Hungarian society and the overwhelming majority of the Hungarian people and which was—in a word—an Anglophile program. The British agents were to aid the small, subversive minority that Moscow stood behind. England began her conversations with us through secret service channels. We succeeded in having the negotiations raised to the official, diplomatic, intergovernmental level. Once the agreement was concluded, however, England insisted on putting the execution of it back on the secret service level.

England obviously wished to follow the example of her relations with Yugoslavia. She had dropped her support of King Peter and Mikhailovich, who represented the Yugoslav national ideal, in favor of Tito. England aided Tito, not only in his campaigns against the Germans, but in the atrocious civil war that Tito was primarily interested in winning. We did not wish to suffer a similar fate. Our object in offering our help against Germany had not been for the purpose of delivering ourselves over to another dictatorship. The principal reason for the breakdown in the negotiations between England and ourselves was this: The English would not recognize the fact that *resistance in Hungary was an official operation undertaken with the knowledge of the Regent and under the direction of the premier.* There was no other Hungarian resistance then or later.

The great majority of the nation was behind me when upon the assumption of the premiership I undertook the corollary task of leader of the Hungarian resistance to tyranny. In that dual role I did not represent only the progovernment circles. I forced into

my camp the military, ministers of opposing views, deputies in
parliament from the various parties, the entire apparatus of the
state—all those elements, different as their private views may have
been from mine. I was loyally supported in the resistance movement by the members of parliament, including the representatives
of the Citizens Liberty, Christian, Smallholders, and Social Democratic parties of the Opposition, and most keenly of all by our
million Jews, with their hopes and fears. With all those forces
behind me I counted on finding, as the crowning support, the
understanding and help of England. I assert that the destruction
of that great Hungarian camp, which comprised fully 90 per cent
of the nation, would have resulted in the end first of the resistance
and then of Hungary herself. A Nazi dictatorship would have been
established and hard upon it a Communist one—neither of them
Hungarian.

I admit that our position was peculiar and difficult to understand, especially for those predisposed against us. But even in London there were those who understood it. The French ambassador
there, André Charles Corbin, wrote that "la politique hongroise
est une acrobatie diplomatique, digne de toute éloge." One reason
for the misconceptions about our position was the maneuvering
of our neighbors who hated to see that Hungary still existed. Nor,
indeed, was there any position parallel to ours among the small
nations under the German yoke. Then, too, the peculiar independence we enjoyed in our external relations was enhanced by
our internal situation whereby those who thought differently from
the government, including the members of the Opposition parties,
refrained from any independent action and entrusted the struggle for the nation's independence and the defense against Germany, not to irregular, partisan forces, but to the government
itself. There were even suggestions from time to time that I should
reconstruct my government to advertise this fact.

I regard the failure of Anglo-Hungarian collaboration to become definitive and effective as one of the essential causes of the
tragedy of not only Hungary but of half of Europe, too. Had col-

382 MY FOREIGN POLICY

laboration between us developed, England could not have been voted down at the Teheran Conference, November 28–December 1, 1943, over the question of attacking in the Balkans. If Hungary could have been made into a base, British and American influence would be prevailing today in the Balkans and on the Danube. The strange thing, as it turned out, was that the two minorities in Hungary, the pro-German and the pro-Russian, could always be assured of the support of their patrons, while the pro-Anglo-Americans, who were the great majority of the population and were headed by their legal government, could not be assured of support.

We got one thing out of the agreement: the secret transmitter and code. These were brought back to Hungary and put into use at once. The texts of the messages were drawn up by the political section of the foreign ministry. We gave complete information on every question put to us. We for our part had few questions to put. If we asked anything of a political nature, we got snubs. On one occasion, for example, we sent documented proof of Tito's connections with Moscow and one-sided care for Russia's interests. We were rudely told to keep off such Goebbels propaganda, which was aimed at driving a wedge between the Allies. Many messages were exchanged about the English mission to be parachuted into Hungary. Interest in the project flagged, and it was only just before the German occupation that we reached an agreement on it, but by then, of course, it was too late.

After the occupation the Germans tracked down and found the transmitter, but they accepted the foreign ministry's explanation that it was used to keep in touch with our own men. Szegedy-Maszák burned all the papers.

The transmitter did the British good service. They received official information on the military situation, complete as regards ourselves and all that we knew about the plans and dispositions of the Germans. Thus the British did not have to rely on spies but got instead official information. Since Pálóczy-Horváth took the messages down, it is not impossible that he passed on totally false reports to his superiors. We discovered at the time that he was regularly supplying hostile and tendentious reports on leading Hungarians, describing such prominent anti-Germans as Bethlen, Baranyai, and Rassay—his own opposite number—as pro-Germans in disguise. Pálóczy-Horváth took pains to blacken everyone who was conservative—in fact, everyone not belonging to the extreme left. One reason for the failure of the Anglo-Hungarian agreement, which was concluded with such high hopes in Istanbul, may well have been the bad choice of an operator on the receiver.

It may be asked: If the Hungarians began along one line of foreign policy and made some contact in it, why didn't they stick to it exclusively? An important explanation is that we dealt with two partners, the British and the Americans. We made our first overtures to the British, as they stood nearer to us strategically and in their way of life. We had always felt that way about the British. After a while, however, we were forced to realize that the Americans handled matters with more courage behind their convictions and with less prejudice. The United States, not being a European or an Asiatic power, did not feel bound to pay so much regard to the 1918 Treaties, the League of Nations, or the Little Entente. Briefly put, the Americans were easier to deal with. We even got the impression that the British were not sorry to let the Americans take the front of the stage. But another reason for our trying many channels was that after my speech of May 29, 1943,[3] most of our ministers and also certain Hungarian individuals in neutral countries were approached, officially or privately, in one way or another.

First among these endeavors I wish to discuss those conducted through George Barcza, who was Hungarian minister to the Vatican for several years and then went to London shortly before the war. He did all he could to prevent the rupture of our relations with England. When they were severed in April of 1941, however, Barcza returned to Hungary. He was not given another active

[3] See pages 192–93.

post, but in his activities at home showed a strong antipathy to
the Germans that was notorious. Then, in the summer of 1942,
Bethlen sought me out and proposed that I send Barcza to Switzerland as representative of a group that had formed around Bethlen.
Bethlen, incidentally, had more than once refused my suggestions that he go abroad to represent Hungarian interests. The
members of the group that Bethlen wanted Barcza to represent
were from the upper house, the Revisionist League, various social
clubs, and the economic association and various banking and industrial circles. Bethlen recommended that Barcza be given a
memorandum on our situation generally and on our policy towards
England.

I thereupon asked Barcza to call on me, and I told him that
I agreed he should be sent abroad as an emissary of Bethlen's
group. He was to go to Switzerland where he was to represent that
group, not the government. He should, however, stress that, while
it was an independent group, it supported and thus was express-
ing the foreign policy of the premier of Hungary. Barcza was to
go via Rome and begin by getting his bearings in relation to the
policy of the Vatican. He was to maintain contact through the
foreign ministry and to have the use of our diplomatic bag. Szentmiklóssy, chief of the political section of the foreign ministry at
that time, was to act as liaison between Barcza and Bethlen. As
things subsequently worked out in practice, Szentmiklóssy first
reported Barcza's communications to Bethlen, and then he made
them a part of the official record of the foreign ministry, signed
by himself.

The preparations for Barcza's mission took a long time unfortunately, so that he left at the very end of 1942. The foreign
ministry gave him the necessary information. I authorized him,
as I had Frey, to say that neither Bethlen nor I had any idea of
trying to save the present regime. Barcza was, however, to oppose any suggestion either of bringing back Michael Károlyi and
his émigrés or of setting up any other regime of the extreme left,
not only because such radical groups did not have any real fol-

lowing in the country, but because a leftist government of those persuasions would lead Hungary into the arms of the Soviet Union as had happened in 1919. I asked Barcza to point out that to take up Károlyi would make Hungary a political satellite of Benes, and Benes had lost all his faith in the West after what had happened to his country and was turning towards Pan-Slavism and Russia. Barcza was to stress that the Regent's case was different. Horthy's Anglophilia was the very foundation of his being; if he ever acted against it, it was because he was misled or could not help himself. Once the period was over and the time came to seek a final solution Horthy would undoubtedly act solely according to the interests of his people. The popularity of a Hungarian premier or the success of a government were transitory things, but Horthy's twenty-five-year rule was a reality which nothing could efface from the people's soul. Horthy had become a legend. Where he led, the people followed. To take advantage of this fact was to insure the preservation of an order that would have beneficial effects reaching beyond Hungary's borders.

Barcza's first mission was, therefore, to enlighten the British about his group's and my attitudes. He was not authorized to enter into immediate, concrete discussions about Hungary's surrendering, jumping out, or turning against the Germans. Nevertheless, Barcza's mission was very important. His activities should have served the English as proof that the best men of Hungary were almost of one mind in their opposition to Germany and that nearly the whole of the Hungarian people agreed with their leaders. Barcza's discussions proved that the failure on the part of the English to realize our point of view had tragic consequences for us and led to the perishing of Central Eastern Europe.

Another intermediary in our negotiations with the West was George Bessenyey, our minister in Berne. His predecessor at that post was John Wettstein, who had carried out his duties admirably; Wettstein's sympathies, however, were with Germany or so at any rate the Western Allies thought, and he was hardly a suitable person, therefore, to negotiate with the Western representatives. At my request Wettstein sent in his resignation, and we decided to send Bessenyey, our minister in Vichy, to fill his place in Berne. Bessenyey was in every way suitable for the job: he was one of the old guard who had never succumbed for an instant to the German spell.

An important consideration was the presence in Berne of Mr. Royall Tyler, in an important position with the American legation. Mr. Tyler spent many years in Hungary as a commissioner of the League of Nations reconstruction loan, and he had learned to speak our language fluently. He had made numerous friends in Hungary, with many of whom, including Leopold Baranyai, president of the national bank, he had kept in touch. He knew our conditions thoroughly, and there was no doubt of his sympathies and his desire to help us. Mr. Tyler had received from Washington full powers to negotiate with us.

Bessenyey discussed our intention to appoint him minister in Berne with Mr. Tyler and only took up his post after the American agrément had been received. There can be no doubt that Wettstein's resignation and Bessenyey's appointment evoked much resentment in Germany, although we received no official or unofficial indication of the fact. The Germans never even dreamed of voicing so much as an opinion of their own in respect of an administrative measure taken by the Hungarian government (whereas we had asked the Americans before appointing one of our ministers).

Unfortunately, however, the United States was subsequently concerned with such great matters that our little individual concerns, which meant everything to us, were too small for America to heed or even to understand. Despite, therefore, all the good will and readiness to help us displayed by Mr. Tyler, and also by Mr. Allen W. Dulles, with whom Bessenyey was in constant contact, too, our discussions with them led almost nowhere. The only positive result was the sending of an American military mission, headed by an American colonel, that was parachuted into Hungary a few days before the occupation of the country by the Germans in March, 1944.[4]

Bessenyey made every endeavor to make the Westerners understand our point of view. But he, like all our diplomats, was inevitably ground between two millstones. Bessenyey saw from close up the power, superiority, justice, and certain victory of the Western Allies, and he got suggestions and warnings at first hand. They naturally impressed him, and he regarded it as his patriotic and official duty to pass them on to us. We at home, on the other hand, saw from nearer at hand our own position, which was perhaps less comprehensive but yet decisive for ourselves. We knew that the English and Americans would win the war, but meanwhile the German fist might descend on us at any moment, and the Russian clenched fist was already visible above our heads.

Both the Western Allies and Hungary were willing to negotiate, and for us it was a matter of life and death to achieve a result. We would undoubtedly have followed any practicable course, fulfilled any demand favorable, or at any rate not dangerous, to the interests of the Hungarian people. Unfortunately, however, no such situation arose: the suggestions of the Allies when Italy changed sides that Hungary should jump out (at a moment when the British and American troops were five hundred miles from our frontiers) or that we should "do something" were not requirements that we could fulfill. We could not undertake to commit a suicide that would have benefited no one. At any rate we are grateful for the good will that was shown us in the negotiations that were conducted through Bessenyey. I believe that if there had not been a German occupation these negotiations (which the Germans knew about through the decoding of American telegrams) might have eventually led to positive results.

[4] In the planning stages of this mission, an American diplomat was scheduled to accompany the military personnel. This officer was Mr. Howard K. Travers, who served as counselor in the American legation in Budapest from December, 1936 to December, 1941. He could not leave Washington at the appointed time, however, and the mission was dispatched without him.

Other overtures to the Allies were made through Andor Wodianer, our minister in Lisbon. The Lisbon post, lying outside the German iron ring, allowed Wodianer more scope than was enjoyed by any other of our diplomats in neutral countries. On the other hand, contact with Budapest was difficult, and Wodianer was thus out of touch with our prison atmosphere.

Wodianer had an important line to the Poles and through them to England. This provided us with excellent information and enabled us to communicate our point of view to London. The Polish line was kept open to the last, but we also soon began to get inquiries from America. This was principally because of the work of Archduke Otto, who succeeded in awakening the interest of President Roosevelt, with whom he had several conversations and who showed distinct good will towards the Hungarian question. The Archduke's and Eckhardt's reports raised great hopes in our breasts. Otto sent his younger brother, Archduke Louis Charles, to talk to us in Lisbon, and soon after Colonel Francis Deák, an American citizen of Hungarian origin, was sent to Lisbon and attached to the American legation with a special mission to talk to us officially.

If anything kindled our hopes after the Istanbul deadlock, it was the coming of Deák to Lisbon. We believed that through him we should be able to bring our discussions with America to a successful conclusion. Deák, too, arrived under that impression. But soon after his arrival he was forced to realize that there was still a large gap between what good will suggested and what was practically possible. He saw that we were looking behind the great problems to our own little problem of life and death, and he wanted America to see and understand this. There were delays and hesitations over this point, but since the good will and good intentions were certainly present on the American side, we should have reached agreement through this channel.

Unhappily, the whole atmosphere, especially with respect to our vital decisions at home, was ruined by the agreement between Benes and the Soviet Union, the abandonment of the Polish national government, Tito's advance to favor, and above all Teheran. Then, the German occupation of March 19, 1944, put a brutal end to everything. Wodianer's reports to us showed, however, that the accusation of instability and failure to stick to a single line was one which should not be leveled against us alone. Every initiative in Lisbon was taken by some official, semiofficial, or unofficial representative of the Western Allies. Wodianer never once began the proceedings, and throughout he maintained the most complete reserve.

Anthony Ullein-Reviczky, who went to Stockholm in September, 1943, also negotiated with representatives of the Western powers, and those discussions broke down as did those that I have just discussed. Ullein-Reviczky did what he could during his short term, but he could not have succeeded. He has written his own account in a book excellent alike in its subject matter and its title, *Guerre allemande, paix russe* (1947).

In all of those negotiations five points were uppermost: (1) jumping out, especially in connection with events in Italy; (2) bringing back our soldiers from the Russian front; (3) sending staff officers to an allied headquarters; (4) admission to Hungary of an Anglo-American mission; (5) bombing.

I have already dealt in detail with the first four matters.[5] I repeat once again that we never rejected any of them a *limine*. We weighed the sacrifices and risks objectively rather than considering only our point of view.

The bombing of Hungary, and particularly of Budapest, was a question that came up repeatedly. I can count only two positive successes for my whole policy: on the Jewish question and on the matter of bombing. There were certain tactical reasons also for abstention by the Allies: we were not in the first line in that respect. But while they bombed Rumania and Bulgaria, they did not

---

[5] On jumping out, see pages 203–12, 387; on withdrawal of troops, see pages 133–34, 183, 192, 305–9, 311; on sending staff officers, see pages 370–72; on Allied mission, see pages 376, 379–80.

bomb us. Formations from Italy flew over Hungary almost daily towards Vienna and its environs. They flew unmolested over our antiaircraft defenses and over the Lipse oil wells and munitions factories, and they assembled regularly in the air space over the Balaton. There was a sort of tacit mutual agreement by which we did not interfere with them or they with us. Once a subaltern (probably a German agent) let off one round. Our liaison officer in Constantinople immediately received a protest. We expressed our regret and sent word that the culprit had been punished and transferred to the infantry. That was, I think, a very unusual situation to prevail between belligerents. It amounted almost to an armistice. It went beyond nonbelligerency and became direct support of the Allies when we openly and definitely allowed them the strategic use of our air space. I may recall that the strictly neutral Switzerland opened fire on all aircraft flying over Switzerland and shot down several Allied planes, while Turkey, which was allied with England, shot down five British planes. We had proof that the Allied Air crews had been instructed to respect Hungarian territory. One American Negro who made a forced landing in Hungary after jettisoning his bombs showed us his orders which forbade, under pain of severe penalties, the dropping of bombs on Hungarian territory even in an emergency. If that was unavoidable, the bombs had to be dropped into water or forests. The penalty must have been severe, for he entreated us earnestly not to hand him over to his unit—a request which we were easily able to fulfill.

It is easy to imagine what resentment all that evoked among the Germans. They asked for permission to station antiaircraft units in western Hungary. We refused. They asked for the use of an airfield for their fighter defense of Vienna. We refused. Thus the Hungarian government, not only did not help prevent the attacks on German cities and factories, it assisted in them.

There are two considerations which I wish to emphasize about our actions in the air war. First, is it possible to imagine a stiffer resistance and a bolder attitude towards the Germans in this respect? Second, the Anglo-Americans were always asking us to do something positive to help them. Well, our policy in the air war was positive help.

I have already spoken of how we treated our prisoners of war.[6] Most of the English and Americans were airmen. Our treatment of them was another proof that we missed no opportunity to show that we did not regard ourselves as really at war with the West. None of our common practices were agreed to in writing. Our behavior was an expression of our feeling; the behavior of the Allies was an acknowledgment of our feelings towards them.

The maximum sacrifice was being asked of us, however, and we should have liked at least a minimum return. That was the sole reason why decisions were delayed. But the delays were so long that before the decisions could be made the Russian problem was on both of us.

Our Western partners in the discussions did not have complete freedom of action vis-à-vis the Russians. The possibility of a German-Russian agreement hung like a sword of Damocles over the Anglo-American negotiators. It was the fear of such an agreement (fostered by Goebbels' propaganda) that was largely responsible for their docile acceptance of Russia's wishes, the tragic consequences of which are so apparent today. The Russians knew this. They did not say so, but they felt it; and one could see it in their tactics, as when they would suddenly halt their advances and allow the Germans a breathing space. The threat was a mortal one to us, too. If Germany and Russia agreed, it would be at our expense. That was why we always insisted that we could do nothing until the relations of Russia to Central Europe were cleared up. On the other hand, it was natural that, as the situation then stood, the Anglo-American powers could not have fulfilled our wishes. I believe they would have liked to do so, and it would have been in their interest. We got no more than a promise from them, however, and that only semiofficial, that our merits would be con-

[6] See Chapter Fifteen, "The Treatment of Refugees and Prisoners of War."

sidered. Then, when Benes smuggled Soviet imperialism into Central Europe, Russia's westward penetration was an accomplished fact. The idea of a Danubian federation to replace the Monarchy or of a block of states was written off. There arose instead a system agreeable to Russia—that of spheres of interest.

It is all the more noteworthy that in that situation American officers, even Roosevelt himself, were entirely prepared to enter into conversations with us. That inclination was perhaps for our own sake, perhaps in the hope of saving for the West a position in the Danube Basin; for the West was certainly being progressively crowded out at every point. At first all the states crushed by Germany looked to the West. They had no thought other than to link up with the Anglo-American, Western world. And what happened? The national regime in Poland had to defer to Russia's wishes. Mikhailovich and King Peter were dropped for Tito. Benes turned to the Soviets. Those enormous successes of Soviet diplomacy are the harder to understand because all that happened at a moment when Russia was hard beset and only holding her own through British and American help. The secret, I think, is this: that the Soviets knew what they wanted and never diverged from their line by a hair's breadth, while the West, unfortunately, did not prepare in advance its postwar plans and its good faith blinded it with regard to the plans of the Russians. We saw all this, but we were never listened to. We floundered between wishes and reality, and wherever we turned we came to the same dead end.

I must clear up one more question, which arose several times in the minds of people in the West. What were the German pressures that we had to yield to sometimes and that prevented us from acting as we would?

The greatest and most paralyzing pressure was the sight of what was going on all around us: the fate and example of the Poles and the Czechs, of Slovakia, Rumania, and Yugoslavia. That nightmare weighed on us continuously, and the hope of escaping from a German coup and saving our people from the fate of the people in the occupied countries influenced all our actions.

Our second nightmare was that of being occupied by Russia and left in the Russian sphere of influence. We feared terribly a Russian victory or, what would have amounted to the same thing, a Soviet-German agreement. This was why I used to add fire to all our anti-Russian propaganda when there seemed any chance of such an agreement. I hoped that our intransigence might be an obstacle to the plans.

Thirdly, there was Germany's ever more intimate collaboration with Rumania and Hitler's great friendship for Marshal Antonescu, who was described as the "third personage in the Axis." Goebbels wrote that Antonescu was the only reliable one among the Eastern statesmen. (As I have said before, Goebbels characterized Horthy as a hireling of the Jews.) The Rumanians really took an important part in the campaign against Russia and fought well against her. They, too, kept aloof from fighting the other Allies. They were fully entitled to take part in the war against Russia—more so than we: the Russians had taken Bessarabia away from them, with, however, the consent of the Germans. But the Rumanians suffered from another running sore also: the loss of half of Transylvania, the prize they had held for twenty years. To that loss, too, the Germans had consented. The Rumanian army was greatly expanded in the course of the Russian campaign. It was more than twice as large as ours and incomparably better equipped because after we had withdrawn our combat troops from Russia we got no more arms from Germany. The Rumanian army also started from ahead of us because we had been disarmed under the Treaty of Trianon, while they, like the Czechs, got every support, especially from France. Naturally, when they entered the war they hoped to get back not only Bessarabia but also Transylvania, about which they cared even more. They stated that preference openly in their propaganda and in their proclamations.

It was thus quite obvious that Rumania's attitude towards us was a powerful weapon in Germany's hand. Germany did not keep her awareness of this to herself, and, in fact, the chief threat that Hitler used against the Regent at their meeting of March 18, 1944, was that Rumanian troops would participate in the occupation of Hungary. After our experiences of 1919, the Hungarian people feared this only slightly less than they feared an occupation by Russia.

Another difficulty and depressing factor for us was the tone adopted by the radio, the press, and the public spokesmen of the Western democracies. The propaganda line of the BBC and the Voice of America was the most unfortunate possible. It was quite indubitable that it was inspired by Benes' clients, the Michael Károlyi—Armin Vámbéry émigré group. Except to that group, the things that were said about Hungary served no purpose and were, in fact, senseless. The propaganda emanating from the West reinforced the propaganda of the rightist groups in Hungary and greatly impeded my efforts to seek rapprochement with the democratic and socialist parties. People in Hungary used to say: If the victory of the Anglo-American group is going to result in conditions that not one per cent of the people of Hungary want, why bother? Is that where Kállay wants to take us? There was a joke that circulated in Hungary too: Kállay's policy is like the traffic regulations in Budapest—it keeps to the left underground and to the right above ground.[7]

Finally, there were the threats in Hungary's domestic political situation. The Arrow Cross party and Imrédy's ambitious Rejuvenation party—the extreme right—were always ready to go the whole way, à la Quisling, and they enjoyed the unconcealed sympathy of the Germans. We always had to be on our guard against action by those groups and not to give the Germans a pretext for intervening, and so the freedom of action of the Government was sorely limited. What made the threats of the rightists and the Germans dangerous and important was the position of the Jews, the refugees and prisoners of war, and all the Hungarian people who were not pro-German.

[7] Until 1941 the rule on the roads in Hungary was as in England. In that year it was changed as a compliment to Germany, but the change could not be applied to Budapest's subway.

I only twice got direct and written ultimata from Germany. The Germans were very circumspect because they did not want written proof of their interference to be on record and they knew how sensitive we were in this respect (they still preserved a certain romantic recollection of "Hungarian pride"). The first ulti--matum came, when after several previous representations, I got a definite, ultimative demand to take action against the Jews. The second was the telegram commanding me to recognize Mussolini. I did not comply with either demand. I resisted absolutely *in merito*, but to avert a catastrophe I made certain saving surface gestures.

In these pages the expression of many German wishes are recorded. I fulfilled very, very few of them and then only in part. I have not even mentioned many of the demands the Germans made upon us. When Germany went to war with Chile and Brazil, for example, Germany asked us to declare war on those two countries also. I refused, in this, too, being one of the few "satellite" leaders to do so. Comically enough, both of those South American countries declared war on us a few months later, but that did not however, prevent the Regent's son, Nicholas, who was our minister in Rio, from being able to send to us messages over the radio. Then, too, such small questions as the German minority group in Hungary, German schools, the German press, the reichs-mark-pëngo exchange rate necessary to the financing of all German activities in Hungary, and the detailed requests for military and economic adherence to Germany—all these came up almost daily. We were always "at the ready." Once Clodius, the German minister plenipotentiary, said: "Look here, I never get anything I ask for. Let's try it the other way around. You offer something." Our answer to him was: "We shall be glad to provide you with a sleeper."

Finally a few words about myself. My book thus far reveals what my hopes and wishes for my country and people were. In the pages that follow I shall show how my two-year struggle ended. I was balancing on a razor's edge, but always with the best will and in the best faith. My policy was not a double-faced one. I had one motivating wish: the welfare of my people. I believed that the security of Hungary could be achieved only with the help of the Western democracies.

I had to think and act, however, with full awareness of our limitations and our appalling situation. Why was I hesitant? My awareness of our situation made me hesitant. Why did I let German troops cross our territory? Why did I allow Jewish labor battalions? Why did I not take more left-wing elements into the government? During the whole period of my premiership I heard those critical questions. My reason was: to gain the time necessary to establish relations with the West and to stave off a German occupation.

Even the dreaded occupation I could not avert in the end. I had tried to do that, and I had tried to find the path to salvation. The tragic event that abruptly ended my efforts proved that what I had tried to do was not possible. I was, however, not the only political official whose strength was insufficient to avert the great march of history.

But I had succeeded in giving two more precious years of Hungarian life to the people of my nation and two added years of life to a million human beings who found sanctuary in Hungary before the German occupation.

That is the balance sheet of my tenure as premier of Hungary.

As the last illustration of my foreign policy, I shall quote the instructions that I sent, just before the German occupation, to our ministers. I suppose that only the courier to Stockholm succeeded in getting through; that, at any rate, is the copy that came into my possession subsequently and that I reproduce below. I dictated the entire letter. The last few lines below the asterisk, which appears in the original also, are a postscript added later as a precautionary measure. When I gave the letter to Foreign Minister Ghyczy to read and send off to our ministers abroad, he expressed the fear that it might fall into the hands of the Germans. He suggested that I add some words that would soften the anti-German tone of the whole, and he would inform the ministers of that act through another channel. I accordingly dictated the last two sentences, but even in them I took care to dissociate myself from Germany's internal system as well as from the Bolshevik social system. I may remark that my views and judgments were already at that time as I have described them in these pages.

Here is the letter:

Budapest, March 1, 1944

Dear ——

I think it necessary to give you a written résumé of my views in relation to the present situation. Kindly regard these lines as a personal communication to yourself, and when using them in no case name the source. My first purpose is to acquaint the leading exponents of our foreign policy with my views on the present situation and Hungary's special problem and to insure that they know exactly the objectives that I hope to achieve by my policy.

The principal objective of the policy followed by the Hungarian government during the past eighteen months has been to recover, as fast as circumstances permitted, our full freedom of action and simultaneously to place both public opinion in the country and the army wholeheartedly at the service of this exclusively Hungarian policy. We started from the assumption that, although the Anglo-American powers were far away from Central Europe, yet their policy reached to us. Thus it was to be assumed that Anglo-American troops would reach this area before the Russian soldiers and that Anglo-American policy (the Atlantic Charter) would decide the future of Central and Eastern Europe.

These assumptions do not hold good at the present time. Today the Russian army is near our frontiers and Russian policy is penetrating Central and Eastern Europe. Owing to the inactivity of the Anglo-American armies and the political withdrawal that has accompanied it, our ideas have not hitherto been realized: the partners on whom we had reckoned have not materialized. Today the Russian question threatens our very existence, and independently thereof the other side continues to insist on its unaltered demand for unconditional surrender. The example of Italy, Poland, the Baltic states, etc., makes it impossible for any Central European state, least of all Hungary, to take such a step. This, today, would mean Russian invasion or Bolshevik penetration. It was exclusively the idea of defense against Russia which took us, like most of the Central European states, into the war. This may have been a mistake, but that does not alter the fact that there is no government or people that would hand itself over to the Soviets—unless it had itself gone Bolshevik first. This cannot be our object or the true object of our Western opponents.

In any case, in a constitutional country a government could only sign an unconditional surrender if authorized to do so by parliament, and even that authorization would be valueless unless it accorded with the will of the entire nation. But there is no nation which would accept such an unprecedented renunciation except under compulsive duress or, alternatively, without incurring certain destruction.

Hungarian public opinion is itself beginning to feel the shift of the balance away from the Anglo-Saxons and towards Russia. I had, with the object of creating an atmosphere which would facilitate our orientation towards the Anglo-Saxons, allowed great freedom of movement to all the political and social factors hostile to National Socialists, from the legitimists to the Social Democrats. Unfortunately the development of events has been such that the pro-Soviet agitation was able to take fuller advantage of these possibilities than the Anglophile circles. This has produced a reaction from the right, so that it is today far harder than it was at first to pursue our policy of increasing independence. Every word of the British radio propaganda is different from what our leading classes—90 per cent Anglophile since Széchényi's day— would have expected. The strongest Anglophiles, therefore, insist that the Hungarian service of the BBC does not reflect the opinion of British official circles and, accordingly, do not listen to it.

In this situation, then, we must draw up the balance sheet of what Hungary has done and what she can do in the future.

Hungary is the only state in Central and Eastern Europe to have resisted the National Socialist world philosophy. She has kept her constitution, her independence, and her way of living. Hungary has often given open expression of her friendship and sympathy with the West—when she was the only state in the area that was not allied with a Western power and that was forced by her losses at Trianon to seek revision, which, however, we always said that we wanted to achieve by peaceful means and did in fact achieve peacefully, before coming into conflict of war with any power, through the two Vienna awards, to which the states interested consented, while Rumania actually asked for the arbitration.

The only exception is the case of the Bachka, but in that case our troops did not move until after the Yugoslav state had disintegrated; of all Serbs anywhere, it is those in the Bachka which have been best able to preserve their national substance and their economic position, the bloody events of Ujvidek notwithstanding. I do not wish to minimize the serious character of that case; but it was Hungary's only mass atrocity, and the only one in all Europe where the offenders were brought, even if belatedly, before the courts to be punished.

Austria, Bohemia, Rumania, Bulgaria, Slovakia have all submitted unreservedly to the Nazi rule, without displaying any serious resistance to its system. In Hungary, too, movements in this direction have often begun to take shape, and we have had one government which inclined towards it and the military often flirted seriously with it; but the country always managed to prevent Nazification. Since I became premier the very possibility of it has been excluded. The Rumanians, Czechs, etc., say that they are under dictatorships and that the countries are therefore not responsible, only the dictators are. This is completely untrue; for, firstly, the country could have prevented the dictatorship; and, secondly, in Rumania the old parties have been able to work freely

enough, and it has been precisely their free activity that has sup
plied the government with that political backing without which i
could not have remained in office.

Austria received the Anschluss with enthusiasm and ratified i
by plebiscite. Czechoslovakia never showed any serious resistanc
and placed her highly developed industry, her manpower (wome
included), and her entire economic capacity at the service of th
German war production. There has been hardly any sabotage
Heydrich's and Frank's bloody enactments were rather preven
tive than retributive. The present Czech government is the d
jure successor of that of Benes, who himself sent a letter of wel
come to Hacha, who might be called Europe's first Quisling.

Of Benes it may be remarked that he was the prime instigato
of the disruption of the Dual Monarchy, which has since bee
recognized by all sensible people as, to say the least of it, a grav
mistake; his agitation and his false data were responsible for th
impossible treaties of 1919–20; his slogan of "better Anschlus
than Habsburg restoration" made it impossible to correct th
worst faults of those treaties. The Anglo-Americans themselve
are probably not overdelighted with his last effort: his demonstra
tive and exaggerated Russophilia has been and is a big factor i
making a settlement of Russo-Polish relations more difficult. Th
one constant element in Benes' policy is perhaps his Pan-Slavism
between the two wars Czechoslovakia made herself out to b
representative number one of the Western political idea, while to
day she preens herself in the role of the westernmost outpost o
Pan-Slavonic Russian policy.

The Slovak Protectorate and Croatia are so essentially colonie
that I need not waste many words on them; but from our point o
view they have one quality in common: they can always be used a
any moment against Hungary if Germany's momentary politica
interest so dictates. The same may be said of Rumania, with thi
addition, that of all our neighbors she is the best equipped. Firs
the Allies armed her; then Germany carried on the process and i
still doing so. Hungary never got as many arms from Germany a

Rumania did, but, of course, we never gave Germany so much military and economic support. This relatively well-armed Rumania today constitutes one of the chief reasons why we cannot take any premature step of serious character, for Rumania would gladly be the instrument of Germany's reprisals.

There is really no serious Hungarian emigration. It would certainly have been much easier for Horthy and Paul Teleki simply to take a plane out of the country, to preserve the fiction of resistance by the legal government, and to leave the country to the Quislings and the Germans. Such a Hungary would certainly have at least supplied several million workers for the German war economy—to mention nothing else. But Teleki killed himself, while the Regent lost his son and designated successor in the endeavor to save the independence and self-determination of the country and its control over its own army.

Much has been said about our occupation troops in Russia, but the circumstances that led to their being sent there have been forgotten. The only condition on which we were able to bring our army back after the defeat on the Don was that we should leave at the disposal of the Germans nine divisions, only lightly armed and understrength at that—amounting, with the labor battalions, to about 90,000 men—to occupy the hinterland and guard the railways. These troops were dispersed about the hinterland and in quite small units, and it was only the unexpectedly rapid advance of the Russian armies that brought some of them into contact with Russian forces. We have no aircraft at the front, only a few pilots doing reconnaissance work for the occupation troops, in German formations and using German machines. In any case, they are only a handful.

The government has repeatedly and urgently demanded the return of our troops of occupation. The Germans have refused to grant our requests, alleging technical reasons. I am convinced that they have two considerations at the back of their minds. The one is that they do not want to let them come into the ethnically Polish government, that is, the immediate vicinity of the Hungaro-

Galician frontier, which was one thing we suggested. But the more important point is that they fear—and probably with reason —that the Rumanians would naturally come forward with the same demand which, considering that the Rumanian forces in the line are very considerable, would be a serious matter for the Germans. A further consideration may be that the moment the withdrawal began, the Rumanian army, the superiority of which over our own is at least two to one in terms of manpower, and more in terms of equipment, might easily turn against Hungary. For the Rumanians represent the withdrawal of the Hungarian troops as a step aimed against themselves, which they must answer by similar countermeasures. Furthermore, the Germans are well aware that our troops of occupation constitute our only direct participation in the war today. If they were not in Poland, we should be de facto nonbelligerents. They wish to prevent this at all costs. The nine divisions are thus hostages and pledges in Germany's hands.

Nevertheless, all this does not alter the resolve of the Hungarian government, which has gone so far as, on one occasion, to order the troops to retire; whereupon the Germans answered with a counterorder that they were to be prevented from withdrawing by any available means.

Our occupation troops are not in Russian ethnic territory; the population with which they come into contact is exclusively Ukrainian or Polish, and the partisans whom they encounter are not Russians but Ukrainians who are not Communists but Ukrainian nationalists fighting against the Russians, the Germans, and the Poles. The Hungarian troops are on the best of terms not only with the local population but also with the partisans. Prisoners are exchanged, etc. One difficult decision which we have had to take has been whether to let into Hungary the masses of Ukrainian and Polish refugees. It is a requirement of humanity, but a certain provocation towards the Russians, and it also raises a problem with the Germans.

The refugees are not, however, the only problem raised by the

Russian advance. More serious are the questions of the defense of our frontiers and the attitude that we should take up towards the Russians. I see only one possible solution: to occupy the Carpathian line and to undertake the defense of it exclusively with our own troops, no foreign elements at all to be included, and under our own command, so that we remain masters of our own decisions. For this purpose we recently undertook a partial mobilization.

The country now stands between the dangers of a German and a Russian occupation. Our object is to avoid both. If we do not resist the Russians with our own forces, the Germans will certainly occupy us. This, however, would have tragic consequences for the Jews, Socialists, Anglophiles, etc.; and above all, and chiefly, it would mean the loss of our military and political independence. There is still the possibility that a Quisling government might be formed under Germany's shadows, which would either place the army at Germany's complete service or disarm it and place the manpower thus set free and the entire productive resources of the country, with its communications, unreservedly at the disposal of the German war effort. This would certainly be followed by bombing, naturally on a severe scale, and if Germany were defeated, we should get a Russian occupation after that. The influential Czech propaganda would certainly get the Quisling government's every act scored up against the entire Hungarian people, so that on top of our other heavy losses the atmosphere towards us in the West would be even worse than it is today. There would be no single item to be put to our credit; for we could never play Benes' game. We have no bad consciences about Munich working in our favor, nor have we Russian patronage on which to count.

There is, therefore, no other way, no other possibility, than to take the most difficult decision—not to take a jump in the dark, in either direction. An individual may often think with longing of suicide as a relief because it is an immediate, grand simplification, but a nation cannot take that hazard. Moreover, in the present international atmosphere, with Russia's power and influence at their peak, it would be fatal to force any solution, for this could only work out to the advantage of Czech-Russian policy.

And we may hope that time is working for us: that with time common sense, humanity, and impartiality will prevail. We must always, in every way, work for this, both at home and abroad. This is the angle from which we must observe and examine every move made towards us from the other side. Their interest is—how soon can things be ended; ours—what the end is to be like.

We must therefore make it absolutely plain that, as regards Russia, we cannot retreat from the defensive attitude described above. This in no way means that we are dedicating ourselves in advance and forever to some anti-Russian or anti-Comintern policy. Provided she does not interfere in our internal affairs, we are prepared to live with Russia as good neighbors; but we do not, of course, want to live in the Russian sphere of influence.

We do not, of course, think in terms of dogmas, and we do not want to make our present attitude overrigid. But it must never be forgotten that, given the situation sketched at the beginning of this letter, a decision favorable to ourselves cannot come at the present moment. I am, however, convinced—although I do not overestimate the present tension between the Anglo-Saxons and Russia, nor expect a split between the Allies—that the Anglo-Saxon powers recognize that Russia constitutes a danger to them, both ideologically and as a power, and that if Russia won, her victory would be followed by collaboration between Russia and a new Germany. It would be practically unavoidable that a beaten, proletarized, and occupied Germany—that certainly—would go Bolshevik, and failing other resource, would look to the Soviets for salvation. Germany's present strategy of defense—the Eastern front is neglected for the benefit of the Western—is significant in this respect. If this were recognized, the East European question might perhaps be judged in a saner and more favorable light.

Hungary must, therefore, gain time, for with time things will improve for us. Naturally, in the interval we must see to it that the atmosphere towards us on the other side improves. On the whole, we have a good press in the neutral countries, but this has not sufficient effect of the press of the other side. Our chief aim should be to make the favorable opinion of us held in neutral countries penetrate into the Anglo-Saxon press and public opinion, at least to some degree. Another very important aim of ours must be to disprove the three chief charges leveled against Hungary: that her political and social system is feudal, antidemocratic, and antisocial; that she oppressed the non-Magyars; that she mutilated her neighbors' territory (as though the world had begun at Trianon). It is these three charges which stand like a wall between Hungary and western public opinion, and make it impossible for the West to judge us objectively. We must at least get the rigid and absolute character taken out of the accusations. There is plenty of material for this; it has only to be used with due circumspection.

I am convinced that we can defend the Carpathians, always supposing, of course, that the Russians do not want to force the Eastern Carpathians at all costs and that we do not get a simultaneous Russian and Rumanian attack. Yet we mean to defend our frontiers alone, and the only difficulty which it seems might arise would be if the Mannstein army wanted to retreat along this route. But this seems unlikely because it would mean giving up the Rumanian oil fields, which would be the end of all things.

It would also be a difficult moment if the troops retreating out of the Balkans tried to pass through Hungary or to halt on our frontier. This situation, if and when it arises, may call for new decisions. It is the task of our foreign policy to make such decisions easier. It must improve the atmosphere, for an Anglo-Saxon war of nerves (the effect of bombing us would be similar, but worse) only strengthens the right-wing extremists and in no way advances the desired result of helping the left up. I can say this quite safely, the more so since the government's policy meets with full understanding in our so-called left-wing circles. They know very well that as things stand at present, the first result of any disintegration of the Hungarian state apparatus or weakening of the government's position would be to increase the prospects and possibilities of German influence and intervention. As it is, the rigidity of Anglo-Saxon policy has given great pleasure to our right and our pro-Germans; they point out triumphantly that they always said it was hopeless expecting anything from the other side. It calls for all the government's authority to restrain this reaction and prevent outbreaks against the Socialists, the Jews, and the National Casino.[8] But as things stand, the government gets no support in this from abroad; things are simply made more difficult for it on every side. In spite of this, I am confident that we shall be able to hold the inner political front also.

*

Everything I have written here has been based on the assumption of an Anglo-Saxon-Russian victory or, in part, of a compromise peace. This does not, of course, alter the Hungarian government's point of view that Hungary can expect a good and just peace, and one congruent with her national aspirations, only if Germany remains powerful; and from the same quarter she can still expect, if no further degeneration occurs there, security for her old, balanced internal order and social institutions.

Once again, I ask for your complete discretion in connection with this entirely sincere picture of the situation.

N. KÁLLAY

[8] See note 15, page 37.

SEVENTEEN

THE BEGINNING OF THE END

[DURING THE FIRST DAYS of March, 1944, reports reached us that the Germans were concentrating troops on a major scale between Wiener Neustadt and the Hungarian frontier. That in itself was suspicious, but certain bits of evidence confirmed our fears that the action was directed against Hungary. There was, for example, this concrete case: When a German telegraph patrol wished to string wires on a pole that was inside our border, the Hungarian frontier guards stopped them, and the officer in charge of the German patrol burst out, "You are still talking big now, but in a few days you won't be here any longer." I instructed Foreign Minister Ghyczy to ask the German minister, Jagow, what the troop concentrations meant. I also instructed Chief of Staff Szombathelyi to ask the same question of the German military attaché,

General Greiffenberg. The same reply came from both quarters:
they knew nothing about it, but they would inquire of the appropriate authorities.

Two or three days later Jagow offered the explanation that
the troop concentration was an exclusively German military matter and that he did not know why it was of any interest to the Hungarians, unless, he added arrogantly, it was because the Hungarians had a bad conscience. General Greiffenberg told General
Szombathelyi that the Germans had concentrated troops near
Vienna because that city was, as we knew, a primary railway and
traffic center from which reserves could be dispatched, especially
into the Balkans. Wiener Neustadt, moreover, being a great center
of war industry, was a target of air attacks, all of which broke
into Austria from the direction of Hungary. We had refused to
allow the Germans to place antiaircraft artillery inside Hungary,
and the Allied planes were flying over Hungary unchallenged.
Germany was forced in self-defense, therefore, to place antiaircraft artillery near the Hungarian frontier. Thus both German
representatives misled us as to the nature of the mobilization near
our territory.

I discussed the matter with several politicians, but mainly with
Minister of the Interior Keresztes-Fischer and Chief of Staff Szombathelyi. Keresztes-Fischer was convinced that something was
being prepared against Hungary. He did not expect an occupation
of Hungary by the Germans, but he felt that some heavy German
pressure against us was in preparation and that it would begin
with a demand for my removal and his. Szombathelyi viewed the
matter from a purely military angle and argued that a military
occupation of Hungary would not serve any German tactical
interest whatsoever. That move would only split up their forces
even more. The only expedient moment for Germany's occupation of Hungary would be when the fighting reached the Hungarian frontier. If the Germans entered Hungary before then, it
would only give the impression that they had lost their heads and

would convince the Allied general staff that the Germans could not count on Hungary at all.

I myself thought that it was entirely possible that the troop concentrations were merely for the purpose of threatening us, and I shared Szombathelyi's view that Germany's invasion of Hungary would be politically a strategic error and militarily a tactical one. I did not believe that the Germans, who attached so much importance to prestige policy-considerations, would make an error so contrary to their thinking. The military occupation of Hungary would announce a huge moral defeat because it would become evident that the only country which until then had adhered to the German sphere of interest in appearance at least— I repeat, in appearance because they could say that of us at least —could not be kept on their side except by open force. The use of force would make a bad impression upon the rest of the small countries, even if they felt some satisfaction at seeing us reduced to their own position, because it would be a revealing sign of weakness in the German power sphere. In a prize fight when one of the contestants feels that he is nearing the end of his strength and he begins wildly swinging for a knockout blow, even one below the belt, it is obvious to his opponent and the spectators that he has lost the match. I believed, too, that the Germans would refrain from invading us from a consideration of the situation within Hungary itself. I felt that the Germans would be deterred from entering Hungary, not by fear of all the elements opposed to them, but by fear of dividing their supporters and by the fear of creating a situation that would have to be controlled by force. For all those reasons, therefore, I was fairly certain that a German occupation would not take place.

I prepared myself, however, for increased pressure from the Germans. I talked over the possibilities with the Regent, beginning by asking him what he would do if the first German action should be a demand for the removal of me and Keresztes-Fischer. I reiterated to Horthy that I would not alter my policy and attitude—on the contrary, should there be a German tendency to involve Hungary more deeply in the war, I would stiffen my attitude and actions, to the point of open resistance if necessary. The Regent fully shared my point of view, and he assured me that he would reject a *limine* any attack on my person as an interference with our most intimate domestic concerns.

I conferred again with Chief of Staff Szombathelyi on the possibility of resistance. He replied that no resistance whatsoever could be built up with the troops in Budapest and western Hungary. Because the military evacuation of Budapest was in progress, the troops were widely dispersed in various villages and towns, and they did not have their equipment and war material with them. He could not raise one regiment in the immediate area. We had two army corps fit for action—one in the Northern Carpathians, the other in Transylvania—but it would take weeks to bring them over to the west. Those forces would be able to resist the German troops concentrated near Vienna if there were no other forces to reckon with, but it was certain that in an actual attack the Germans would also mobilize against us the Rumanian forces in Transylvania, which also were stronger than our two army corps. For all these reasons, Szombathelyi said, there was no possibility of successful resistance.

At about that time General Greiffenberg, the German military attaché, informed Chief of Staff Szombathelyi that the Germans wished to eliminate a Russian pocket of resistance to our east and they wished, therefore, to send to the front about 100,000 soldiers and some 3,000 vehicles via Budapest, which lay on the direct route to that sector—a detour would necessitate a delay of several days. I told Szombathelyi that, as before, we would not permit German troop transports to go through Budapest. In accordance with my instructions the chief of staff informed the Germans that, since Budapest was being relieved of military personnel and stripped of its fortifications in order that it could be declared an open city, Hungary could not grant the German request for troop passage. General Greiffenberg replied that the

Hungarians were again practicing sabotage, and the Germans did not return to the subject. At the time I believed that the passage was intended as a demonstration—to flash the German bayonets in front of the people of Budapest. Now, however, I believe that those troops would have upon reaching Budapest with our consent stopped there just at the time that an ultimatum from Germany arrived. It had perhaps occurred to the leaders of the Nazi movement, which was always solely built on and worked through brute force, that Hungary had actually not even seen German strength, German troops. In the whole of Hungary there were precisely 1,719 German soldiers—RTO's and medical personnel. You could walk the streets of Budapest for days without coming across a German uniform. According to Minister of the Interior Keresztes-Fischer, there were in Hungary a few hundred agents, agitators, and secret police disguised as journalists, merchants, and others who, when caught, were put across the border and who represented nothing of serious significance.

Days passed in this nervous waiting. I informed our ministers abroad, who passed the information on to the English and Americans, but no encouragement, no hope of help whatsoever, reached me from that quarter, although at that critical moment I was sure that they would urge me to offer military resistance and would offer air support to that end. I received one certain reaction: that if German troops entered Budapest the city would be bombed. The upsetting picture in my mind thus was: German occupation and Anglo-American bombardment. So the days wore on. Chief of Staff Szombathelyi ordered secret military preparedness, which meant that the army held itself in readiness—the first stage towards the state of war. He tried to create some sort of order among the troops in and around Budapest and to furnish arms and ammunition to the scattered units.

Many people came to see me. Bethlen, Rassay, Kánya, Maurice Eszterházy, Peyer, Chorin, Bajcsy-Zsilinszky, Samuel Stern, the leader of the Jewish community, and many others. Each gave advice according to his temperament. Bajcsy-Zsilinszky, who brought along with him a retired general, John Kiss, recommended the most resolute counteraction and the arming of the workers. Bethlen reiterated that now the Anglo-Saxons must decide whether they would help us or not. If they would, the time for armed resistance had come. If not, we were helpless by ourselves. Rassay asked whether I had received any ultimatum from the Germans and asked what their concrete objectives were; not until these were ascertained could we know how to answer. At any rate, if it came to any sort of negotiations with the Germans, we must defend, first of all, our Hungarian civil liberties and, above all, the Jews, for whom a German occupation and rule would mean annihilation. Stern of the Jews declared openly that he had one duty: to draw my attention to the fact that the country, our constitutional existence, our economic and social structure might bear the strain and survive a German domination, but the Jews would be annihilated to the last man. If I could not prevent that the great historic responsibility would be mine. If up to then it had been possible to save their lives, to which end the Hungarian Jews had brought unparalleled sacrifices and had borne suffering, to let them down at the last minute would mean the mockery and failure of my entire policy. Any concession could be made to the Germans and they would not reckon that against Hungary or me because I would be acting under duress. But to abandon the Jews would be an irreparable crime that history would never pardon. After saying that, Stern left the room sobbing.

I will not describe in further detail the uncertainty of those days. I confess frankly that I was at a loss for counsel.

So March 15, the national holiday commemorating the uprising in 1848, arrived. As was usual there was a gala performance at the opera house that was attended by the Regent, government officers, diplomats, and other dignitaries. No official invitations were issued, but the members of all legations except the German and Rumanian attended the affair. The festival was arranged not by an official organization but by students from the university. During an intermission one of the counselors of the German lega-

tion presented himself to the Regent's aide-de-campe, saying that
Minister Jagow requested an audience with Horthy after the affair on an extremely urgent matter: he wished to deliver a letter
signed by Hitler himself. The Regent agreed to see Jagow afterwards. Then Horthy immediately summoned me to his box and
informed me of what had happened. We decided that if the German minister asked any questions Horthy should not reply. I also
strongly recommended that if the letter contained an invitation
for him to visit Hitler the invitation should be refused.

After Horthy had received Jagow, the Regent telephoned me
that Hitler had asked him in the letter to go and see him. The
German minister had not asked Horthy a single question. Horthy
asked me to come see him the next morning, and he told me that
considering the nature of the foreign and military policies that
needed to be discussed he was going to invite to the meeting also
Foreign Minister Ghyczy, Defense Minister Csatay, and Chief of
Staff Szombathelyi, so that we could continue consulting with
each other after the meeting.

Prior to the meeting I learned that Hitler in his letter asked
the Regent to visit him because he was ready finally to discuss
with Horthy the question of returning to Hungary our soldiers
then in the Russian hinterland. As this conference would deal
with problems of a military nature, Horthy was asked to bring
with him the minister of defense and the chief of staff. The tenor
of the letter, incidentally, was very polite.

I at once warned the Regent that it would be extremely dangerous if he left Hungary before it had been made clear what the
Germans meant to do with the troops they had lined up on our
frontiers. If he went to Germany, no important decisions could
be made in his absence. The country, and even more the army,
would remain without supreme leadership and be at the mercy
of the arbitrary will of the Germans. And what would happen if
the Germans simply kept him there, having by this achieved all
their objects. It would be impossible for any order to be formed
from one day to the next that would stabilize the position of the

country both externally and internally. In conclusion, I pointed out that the subsequent disorder would be the result of our not having a deputy regent.

The Regent agreed entirely with my view of the situation, and we agreed that he should send the chief of staff instead of himself.

After that conversation we consulted with Foreign Minister Chyczy, Defense Minister Csatay, and Chief of Staff Szombathelyi. The Regent told them of Hitler's invitation and then informed them that he felt that he should not go to Austria but that the chief of staff should go in his stead. I followed the Regent in the discussion, and I seconded, of course, everything that he had said and presented the decision, in fact, as final. The Regent then asked Ghyczy's opinion. Ghyczy was rather undecided. He pointed out that if the Regent refused the invitation at that critical moment the bad feeling between the two countries would be aggravated. Csatay, who spoke next, identified himself fully with the Regent's position and emphasized that the Regent could not leave the country until the question at issue —that is, what the Germans wanted on our frontiers—was cleared up. Szombathelyi, however, then expressed in the most vigorous terms exactly the opposite view. He said that the fate of our troops on the Russian front would be cleared up at that meeting. For a year we had been continually harping on this question, demanding their return home, and so we could not back out at the moment when Hitler was willing to negotiate. He would, of course, undertake the mission alone if the Regent so wished, but he did not believe that, lacking the Regent's presence and authority, the whole excursion could have any purpose or result whatsoever. Only one man could impress Hitler and achieve results, and that man was the Regent. If we did not secure an agreement about our soldiers at this opportune time, then we would have to give up the idea of bringing home our troops. The same thing applied to the plan of making a Hungarian defense line in the Carpathians, as it was a plan that could not be defended solely on military grounds. Then, too, in a personal meeting with Hitler, the Regent possibly could clear up the disquieting problem of German troops on our frontiers. Szombathelyi concluded by saying that for twenty-five years the Regent had shouldered every burden for the nation's sake; he could not now, in its most difficult moment, refuse to undertake what was perhaps the hardest task fate had assigned to him. He himself knew, Szombathelyi declared, that the Regent was ready at anytime to venture his life for the nation, and the chief of staff begged Horthy, therefore, to undertake the journey. Szombathelyi assured us all that Horthy would not be harmed. Horthy would come back, as, the chief of staff hoped aloud, the savior of the nation.

Anyone who knows Horthy knows that the instant anybody appealed to his sense of duty, and especially to his courage, he accepted the challenge, and there was no arguing with him anymore. The Regent immediately agreed with Szombathelyi's view of the matter and said that he would go. He would not allow any more discussion of the matter. I tried, however, to effect a compromise, proposing that Horthy should write a letter to Hitler, to be delivered by Szombathelyi, stating that because of reasons of internal politics the Regent could not go to Germany until about a fortnight later but that meanwhile he requested that Hitler converse with the chief of staff. As Hitler in his letter had asked Horthy to come at once because he himself would have to leave on March 20 for general headquarters, Horthy should write that he would be willing to visit Hitler at headquarters. Szombathelyi, however, again rose and objected to my plan as being one of procrastination and indecision, and the Regent repeated his resolve to start the next day. This decision, therefore, was unalterable. I had previously offered to go with the chief of staff, but the Regent said my presence would only pour oil on the fire and that, rather than getting any concessions out of Hitler, I should probably never get a chance to see Hungary again. I then asked only that Horthy should take Foreign Minister Ghyczy with him, and he agreed to do so. He also decided that Chief of Staff Szombathelyi and Defense Minister Csatay would accompany him as requested by Hitler.

Before the Regent left for Hitler's headquarters, I talked over the problem with him in every detail. I told Horthy that if Hitler again asked for my removal the Regent should consent to his request, but only on the strict conditions that my dismissal should involve no change of any kind either in our foreign or in our internal policy and only if the concession helped to get our troops back and to prevent the German threats on our borders from becoming overt actions against us. The Regent absolutely refused to agree to my political sacrifice, saying that he would in no circumstances tolerate any interference with his rights and those of parliament and that he would not negotiate on that point. I thanked him for his firm and manly attitude.

I then told Horthy, however, that I felt it was my duty to tell him that I had certain knowledge that Hitler had been informed by members of the German legation, by other German agents in Hungary, and by the Hungarian right-wing groups that it was my person alone that stood in the way of better German-Hungarian relations, of greater understanding between the two nations, and of a common front. But I also pointed out to the Regent that we could save Hungary's independence only by standing absolutely firm in the course my government had pursued. The least retreat would lead to another and another, day after day, and as our moral position weakened refusal would be more difficult each time. In any case, if the Germans had now really decided on a showdown, they would not content themselves with trifles—some economic concessions, a few more schools for the German minorities, perhaps a few more regiments for the front. The Nazis would want to get everything that I and the nation's resistance had kept them from securing for themselves during the past few years. The present German demands could result in these various courses. The independence of our country might be saved by the Regent's voluntarily dropping me. Yielding to German demands that gave them more control than they now enjoyed would mean that I could not remain in office even a second after the surrender. Hungary might completely lose her independence, in which case, of course, I would not be able to remain at my post. In other words, however the problem was regarded, my own personal position seemed untenable.

The Regent replied that he did not believe that the nation's situation was as grave as I thought, and so far he had always been able to placate Hitler. Horthy said again that he would not drop me because he felt sure that nobody could carry on my policy. It would be easier for him to resist a German demand for my dismissal than to yield on that point and then be faced with the problem of finding a successor to me and the much harder task of resisting further demands. Anyway, we could not decide on anything in advance before we knew what Hitler wanted. The Regent told me that he would keep in constant touch with me by means of the radio on his train and that I must keep that line of communication open at my end.

On the next day, March 17, I saw the Regent to his train. There were tears in my eyes when we said good-by, and I even wondered whether I should ever see him again. The departure took place in absolute secrecy: public opinion was already so nervous that we dared not administer this further shock to it. On this point the Germans, who had promised most faithfully to keep silent about the matter, and we were in agreement.

A most harassing period followed. I got no news from any quarter, not even from the Regent's train. I did not even know whether he arrived at his destination safely or not. The German forces on our frontiers were quiet. Even the minor border incidents of earlier weeks—mostly cases of German soldiers trying to step across the border to buy chickens and our men stopping them— ceased. A bad sign in the ominous quiet was the fact that our couriers did not arrive when they were due. I could not even get a telephone connection with Vienna. There was a total lack of information, total uncertainty. I kept in constant touch with Minister of the Interior Keresztes-Fischer. He reported to me that both the Imrédists and the Arrow Cross group were in an extraordinarily excited state and were conferring continually. Nothing definite leaked out of those quarters, but we did learn that the leaders were saying that everything would be all right for their cause because Kállay was going. Keresztes-Fischer ordered full police preparedness, and we decided to put down any outbreak with all vigor. There were, however, no signs that a demonstration by the rightists was imminent.

During that period we continued to listen in on the telephone of the German legation, the only nation that we did that to. On the morning of March 18 our operatives reported to Keresztes-Fischer that Kornhuber, the German press chief in Budapest and a high-ranking SS functionary, had made a revealing call to Francis Rajniss, one of Imrédy's lieutenants. Kornhuber reported that Horthy was meeting with Hitler, that the old boy would be made to toe the line, and that if he did not sack Kállay he himself would go too. Kornhuber's expressions were not even so restrained as that, and he added further that the Imrédists should get ready because in a few days it would be their turn: they would be taking over the power.

I was infuriated by that report, not only because of the substance of the call, but also because of the breach of the pledged secrecy by a person in an official position. I called and told Keresztes-Fischer of the incident, and he immediately issued an expulsion order. The next morning Kornhuber was escorted to the frontier and put across it. (He probably returned the next night with the occupying forces.) In itself this small incident was of no importance, but it was altogether characteristic of the dishonesty of the Nazis, and it afforded one more proof of what we already knew: that the Hungarian Nazis were in touch with the German legation. But I also mention the whole incident to show how little subservient the Hungarian government was to the Germans, how independent it was in its decisions, and how little it hesitated, even at such a critical moment, to take the most energetic action. During the war and after we were branded as "satellites," but I think that this one case, small and unimportant as it was, is sufficient to refute that stupid generalization and to show what the situation really was.

Thus March 18 passed, without any news or major events. Worn out by the constant nervous strain, I went to bed at midnight and, contrary to my habit, took a strong dose of sleeping medicine to send me to sleep at once, as I wanted to wake up early in the morning. But I was hardly in my bed when my direct phone with the ministry of the interior rang. Keresztes-Fischer, who was on the other end of the wire, told me only to get dressed and that he would be with me very quickly because serious events were under way.

A few minutes later he arrived and he told me that the frontier guards had reported that the Germans had crossed the border in trains, tanks, and armored cars, the various units apparently heading towards Budapest. Then the reports from the army began to come in. These gave the following picture: the Germans sealed off the area around the Bicske railway station. Heavy armored cars and caterpillars started on the road to Budapest. A fresh troop transport, with many cars and tanks, reached the station. At a smaller station south of Cegled heavy armored cars were being detrained and already were moving in the direction of Budapest. Fresh transports were arriving and detraining. Ten or twelve German trains were on the line between Vienna and Bicske, the same number between Pozsony and Budapest, four to six between Szabadka and Budapest, eight to ten between Arad and Cegled.

At that moment Hungary had really become encircled in the ring of the Little Entente, as had been planned at Trianon, with the difference that the Little Entente forces would have moved on Germany's word had the Germans found themselves unable to carry out unaided the hangman's work.

According to the general staff, the following forces had been concentrated against us: on the western frontier, five German divisions; in the north and around Kassa, one German and one

Slovak division; along the southeastern frontier, ten Rumanian
divisions; in the Belgrade area, four to five German divisions;
westward of this, important Croatian forces had been disposed
against us. The only forces that we had ready for action were those
in the Carpathians. Our entire military resources, including those
in the hinterland that were not ready for action, included eight
infantry, one cavalry, and two armored divisions and two mountain brigades.[1]

After a short conference with Minister of the Interior Keresztes-
Fischer I asked to see the seconds in command of the ministry
of defense, the general staff, the foreign ministry, and other governmental officials. I did not arouse the members of the cabinet
until later. Keresztes-Fischer, calm as ever, gave the appropriate
instructions to the police and the gendarmerie, while I dealt with
the military. The deputy chief of staff, Colonel-General Joseph
Bajnóczy, could not be dug out. I sent cars after him, and he
was found in his flat; he arrived at the meeting two hours late
and even then proved perfectly useless. He was either incapable
of rising to the situation or unwilling to do so. I called the three
army commanders in Budapest, Stephen Náday, Charles Beregffy,
and John Vörös; Béla Miklós, chief of the Regent's military chancery attended the meeting and so did, of course, General Szilard
Bakay, the officer commanding the troops in Budapest.

At that moment two telegrams were handed to me. One had
been addressed by Foreign Minister Ghyczy to Szentmiklóssy. It
ran: PLEASE LET MY WIFE KNOW THAT I AM WELL. Before starting
out on his journey, Ghyczy had arranged with Szentmiklóssy a
few code sentences. The meaning of this telegram was: MILITARY
OCCUPATION TO BE EXPECTED. The telegram had been purposely
delayed in transmission. In the second telegram Chief of Staff
Szombathelyi had wired to Bajnóczy saying that nothing should
be done until the Regent got back and that the German troops
were to be received as friends.

[1] Some of this military data was drawn from Eugene Czebe and Tibor Pethö,
Hungary in World War II, a Military History of the Years of War (1946).

Soon after, a German general appeared and showed me a long telegram from Keitel, which said that German troops were going to occupy Budapest in accordance with an agreement reached between the *Führer* and the Regent. The Regent and the new German minister plenipotentiary would arrive the next morning. The German troops would behave "energetically but not inimically," but they would relentlessly crush any resistance. The general was to draw the Hungarian government's attention to the fact that the armies of our southern, eastern, and northern neighbors, with German units in these countries, were standing in readiness, and if Hungary resisted those forces, too, would march on Budapest.

After giving me that message, the general asked me what my attitude would be in the light of those facts. I answered that until the Regent returned I alone was responsible for what was done. I then politely informed the general that I would not tell him what we were going to do, and I asked him to leave.

The picture then began to become clearer. Ghyczy's telegram showed that the occupation had been decided at Klessheim. As regards the telegram from Chief of Staff Szombathelyi, I do not know to this day whether it came from him or was a forgery. The German military attaché soon informed me that eleven German divisions were on the march and that they would be in Budapest at 6 A.M. if they were not held up; our airfields were to be occupied by German parachutists at 4 A.M.

Thus I was faced with the first dilemma: should I act independently or should I wait for the Regent. My course depended, however, on what action I could take under all the circumstances. Deputy Chief of Staff Bajnóczy being, to put it mildly, useless, I consulted the three army commanders—Náday, Beregffy, and Vörös—and asked them whether, in the absence of the Regent, the minister of defense, and the chief of staff, they were prepared to accept my instructions to order resistance. All three military officers immediately answered that resistance against the Germans was absolutely impossible, that we had no forces at our disposal between Budapest and the Austrian frontier, that we were heavily outnumbered in other areas, and so on. I insisted, strongly and repeatedly, that the question now at issue was, not one of weighing up relative strengths, but of resisting to the best of our ability and thus showing that Hungarians were prepared to defend their independence.

Beregffy and Vörös then declared that, in the absence of the Regent, whose intentions were not known except that the telegram from Chief of Staff Szombathelyi indicated that they were the reverse of my own, they were under no circumstances prepared to order resistance. Both of those army commanders went on to say that they would forbid their subordinates to carry out orders to resist because Beregffy and Vörös believed that their oath of loyalty required that of them. Náday, on the other hand, said that he was willing to do whatever I decided. He himself favored resistance, but, naturally, only if carried out by the whole army. It would be very dangerous, Náday argued, if our forces disintegrated and split into several different camps before the return of the Regent, who might really be meaning, when he returned, to issue orders to resist. If that was the Regent's intention, all preceding action would only be harmful. Náday also pointed out that a premature resistance was bound to be unsuccessful and it would render impossible a later resistance in which our troops in Transylvania and Carpatho-Ruthenia might join and which might thus have a better chance of succeeding.

I did succeed, however, in reaching the following agreement with the three army commanders: The army was not to attack the Germans, but if any Hungarian military unit, garrison, camp, or depot should be attacked, the German attacking forces were to be resisted. The army commanders were to issue orders that the officers and other ranks were to be concentrated in the barracks, camps, and other places of military nature and that the gates of these installations were to be bolted, the ammunition distributed, and the guns made ready for action. The army was then to await the Regent's orders. I did not feel that the Germans should be informed of these measures, but I was unfortunately convinced that they would get the information in any case. At the same time I personally arranged that all mobile aircraft be removed from the airfields and dispersed throughout the country in secret locations.

These, therefore, were the obstacles to my giving orders for resistance against the invading German troops:

1. Successful resistance was a priori impossible.

2. I had no constitutional authority to give orders to the army in the absence of the Regent.

3. Chief of Staff Szombathelyi, in whose province this entire matter lay, was not only absent but he had even telegraphed orders not to resist. Deputy Chief of Staff Bajnóczy was useless in the situation. Moreover, the army commanders either refused to resist or thought resistance impracticable.

I did weigh the possibilities of other courses. Granted that organized military resistance was impossible, should I not try to find out whether some soldiers, students, and workers would resist enough to demonstrate that Hungary was not kissing the rod? But I had only three hours in which to work, and it was not possible to establish contact with the civilian masses at night. It was quite certain that the abortive demonstration that might have been organized would most certainly not be successful, and it was even to be feared that the moral point I hoped to achieve might rather become ridiculous. Both Minister of the Interior Keresztes-Fischer and I were certain that the Budapest police force was completely loyal and reliable and would obey every order. But how would things have looked, not only to the Germans, but also to other countries, if they saw that the army was not stirring to defend the country and that only the police force was making a stand? It would have been different if the people could have been mobilized. In fact, a rebellion by the citizenry despite the inaction of the armed forces would have been all to the good: it would have differentiated the people from their rulers. But, as I have already said, action by the police alone would only have emphasized the inactivity of the professional army. Moreover, it would have meant the annihilation of the Budapest police and its elimination as a factor of order for future occasions, for which this body, with its excellent and reliable officers and loyal rank and file, was indispensable. Both Keresztes-Fischer and I, therefore, dismissed the idea of calling in the police.

Above all, too, we had to reckon with the consequences of any sort of resistance. Eleven armed divisions would have defeated it in a few hours, and then the consequences would have followed. The Germans would have thought that they had acquired legal title to commit any brutality, to regard as not binding any agreement rendered with the Regent, to trample ruthlessly underfoot everything that was objectionable to them, and to destroy everything that they hated—the freedom of the country, the parliament, the leading social strata, the Jews, and the Socialists.

Those few hours were very long. I thought and thought, and in the end I could come to no decision other than that the nation should await the future and await the Regent's return, with hand on sword hilt but the sword undrawn. And I could do nothing else. At that moment everything depended exclusively on what had passed in Klessheim between the Regent and Hitler, and on that I had no certain information. General Greiffenberg's communication and Szombathelyi's telegram were not trustworthy bases in this regard. The communication might have been untruthful, the telegram forged. The fact that the Regent had not communicated with me seemed rather to indicate that he was not a free agent. Was he a prisoner? Or had he after all reached some agreement with Hitler? I could not believe the latter possibility, for why then had Horthy sent me no news? Before he left I had arranged with him some code messages which I should understand if telegraphed to me. I had received nothing from him, either open or coded. Then a report came that the Regent's train had crossed the frontier. I told the heads of his two chanceries, General Béla Miklós and Julius Ambrózy, to get on a locomotive, to go and meet Horthy, and to inform him of the situation and of what measures I had taken. They were to say that military resistance or civil rebellion were possible only if he ordered them. Miklós refused to transmit the message; his attitude during the whole crisis appeared pro-Nazi and hostile to myself. Ambrózy agreed to do so, but he said—with obvious truth—that the Regent would be in no position to give any such orders. They started and actually reached the Regent's train, but no report came from them.

I ordered the burning of the secret archives of the ministries of foreign affairs, the interior, defense, and others, of the more important offices, and, of course, those of my own ministry. My son Christopher sat at the telephone all night, calling up various individuals and groups and warning them of the imminent danger, beginning with the members of the left-wing parties, prominent Anglophiles, and the representatives of the Jews.

I was especially anxious about the 200,000 Polish, French, Jewish, and Anglo-American refugees in the country. I warned the commanders of the camps what was happening and gave orders that internees who wished to do so could leave and fend for themselves. They were to be permitted to go anywhere they wished and were to be given a month's wages in advance. In particular I gave special orders that the American military mission landed by plane a few days before should be safely hidden. In that I was successful.

Morning came. German tanks arrived by road and rail. At first they did not penetrate into the center of the city, but sealed off its approaches and occupied the district round the barracks. They tried to enter one barracks, but they were received with shots, at which they withdrew. I heard later that at one place the railway workers, or a military railway company, took up the rails and one of their trains was derailed. A few other minor incidents took place, but, generally speaking, the catastrophe went off smoothly. The airfield, which had been evacuated by us, was soon occupied by them.

The hours went by. The Regent's train approached at a snail's pace; it was delayed at every station under the pretext that troop trains were on the line. The Germans wanted still to retard his arrival.

In the early morning hours the German occupying army marched in in full style, bands playing. Budapest had to be shown the German bayonets. But a great surprise was awaiting the Germans. They had been told that the whole country was eagerly awaiting them, that only a wretched minority was holding the country down, that the Hungarian people must be freed from this gang and then its real face would appear. And so it did. There was no jubilant crowd in the streets to greet the parading Germans: not one hat was tossed into the air; not one handkerchief was waved; not one cheer was sounded. A profound silence was the reception the German soldiers got. The silence was perhaps at first the quiet of astonishment and curiosity, but the Germans were soon to see that indignation and hatred lurked behind it. This reception was not like the ones that had been accorded German soldiers in some other capitals. In Budapest, even the hooligans who had in the past noisily paraded their German sympathies were dumb on that day of German occupation. The Germans did not receive a word of welcome even in the Swabian villages around Budapest.

Thus the long-dreaded action was consummated, however. At the end of the First World War the Rumanians invaded the capital of Hungary; towards the end of the Second World War the Germans entered Budapest. In the first instance, the Rumanians were sent by the victorious Allied powers to crush the dictatorship of the proletariat in Budapest; the Germans, on the other hand, occupied what was to them an unreliable point in their fight against the great Russian dictatorship of the proletariat. In the past Hungary had asked for the protection of the Western Allies against the Rumanians. On the day the Germans marched in, too, we were looking to the West for salvation. Why is it that we have never got help from those towards whom our hearts yearned? Is it our fault—the fault of our bad policy? Or is it so written in the book of destiny? A people of the East, wanderers to the far West—we lose in one area, without gaining in the other. We are doomed to be ground between two millstones. But it may be that our fate is not a doom but a destiny. If that is so, then we must bear it.

When morning came my ministry swarmed like an anthill. The ministers from foreign countries came in search of information, the leaders of parliament and of our public life came to consult with me about the situation. I informed the ministers from other countries of our plight, and I asked them to report to their governments the true picture of events and the helpless position that Hungary had been maneuvered into: the Regent and the military leaders lured out of the country and then detained until the occupation was completed. I was all the more anxious that the ministers from other countries should get and send full reports because our own communications facilities had been disrupted. Before the Germans arrived, I had tried by radio to inform the country and countries abroad of what was happening, but all our transmitters had been put out of action. I sent military engineers to find out what was happening, but I never got their report. I suspected sabotage. I mention with gratitude that the ministers of Turkey and Switzerland, MM. Sefket Faud Kececi and Maximilian Jaeger, called on my wife and offered to give me asylum in their legations.

One of the first to arrive at my office that morning was Stephen Bethlen, but hardly had he reached the ministry when a Gestapo patrol broke into my office (in front of which, as always, one policeman and one detective were standing guard). The Germans demanded that Bethlen go with them because Jagow, the German minister, wished to talk to him. Bethlen answered quite calmly that if the German minister wanted to speak to him, he should come and see him where Bethlen was then. I ordered the Gestapo men, whose leader was a man with a face as terrifying as any I had ever seen, to leave the room.

At last the Regent's train was reported near. I went to meet him at Kelenföld station, where I found a big German "guard of

honor" drawn up and German staff officers, led by General Maximilian Weichs, head of the Balkan Army Group, waiting on
the platform. Weichs came up to me and introduced himself.
After saying our respective names we exchanged no further word.
When the Regent got out of the train, I was standing at the door,
behind his adjutant. Horthy was deathly pale, and he looked worn
out but still master of himself. Behind him, in general's uniform,
came Edmund Weesenmayer, whom the Regent presented as the
new German minister to Budapest; after him, Döme Sztójay, our
minister in Berlin, with whom I avoided shaking hands. In the car
the Regent began to tell me what had happened. Then I followed
him into his office, where he continued the story.

What follows here is the Regent's own account, as he gave it to
me then. I have not added any of the further details, interesting
as these were, which other members of the party provided afterwards.

Horthy arrived at Klessheim on the morning of March 18.
Hitler was waiting for him at the station, which is in the immediate vicinity of the castle. In the car, Hitler asked Horthy whether
he wanted the foreign minister and the generals to take part in
the conversation. Horthy proposed that their meeting should be
tête-à-tête. To his surprise, however, Schmidt, who usually took
down the minutes at such discussions, accompanied them into
the study. Horthy asked Schmidt to leave.

Hitler began his discourse by saying that Germany had been
placed in a very difficult position by Italy's surrender; now Hungary, too, was planning defection. He was not prepared to expose
himself to another surprise, and he was therefore obliged to make
the necessary dispositions. Horthy countered by saying that he
had not counted on such an attack, made without preliminaries,
without discussion, and ending with the announcement of a *fait
accompli*.

When Hitler had finished, Horthy asked him what proofs he
had for his accusations. Hitler answered that he had written proofs.

Horthy replied that reports of paid agents were worthless. Hitler said that Kállay had sent Albert Szent-Györgyi, the Nobel Prize winner,[2] to Constantinople to negotiate defection with the British and American ambassadors there.

Horthy replied:

Kindly take note that in the thousand years of our history no case of treachery has occurred. Should the situation and circumstances compel us, in the interest of our own existence, to ask for an armistice, I shall first inform the German government, openly and honorably.

I do not know what you mean by the phrase "make dispositions." If those dispositions are military ones and mean the occupation of a sovereign state which has sacrificed blood and wealth for Germany, in defiance of its own interests, that would be an unparalleled atrocity. The present Germany and its aims have earned the hatred of the entire world. If now you trample our freedom under foot, just the same hatred will flame up in Hungary against your regime. It is possible that we might be unable to defend ourselves against a surprise occupation, but only because all our troops are on the frontiers. But I warn you against any such ill-considered and irreparable step.

Horthy then gave me this account of what happened later:

Hitler repeated his accusations again and again, but in increasing confusion and in a tone of self-defense. But I saw that it was impossible to talk sense with him, so I stood up suddenly, broke off the conversation, and without further greeting went to my quarters, where I called the gentlemen who had come with me and told them what had happened.

I wanted to leave at once, but it appeared that my train had been put in a siding at Salzburg. Hitler asked whether I would be

[2] See page 181 and note 1.

Albert Szent-Györgyi, 1893–, received in 1937 the Nobel Prize in physiology and medicine. His researches were in biological oxidation. He discovered ascorbic acid in adrenal glands and identified it as vitamin C. Subsequently his studies were on muscle chemistry. He migrated to the United States after the war.

his guest at lunch. On my staff's advice, I accepted. At lunch I took part only in the general conversation: I did not exchange one direct word with Hitler.

In the afternoon Ghyczy talked with Ribbentrop, Csatay with Keitel, and Szombathelyi with Hitler. Hitler's conscience seemed to have begun troubling him, for he called Keitel and asked whether it was possible to cancel the occupation of Hungary. Keitel said that it was impossible: the occupying troops were already on the move, and the armies of our neighbors were standing ready.

Horthy said that in those circumstances he, of course, abdicated. Hitler implored him not to do so and said that, if Horthy would appoint a government which enjoyed his, Hitler's, confidence, he would at once order the occupying troops to leave Hungary, and in that case, but only in that case, he would call off the Little Entente troops.

The Regent did not answer and said that he wished to leave at once. On being told that his train was still not ready, Horthy asked whether he was to consider himself a prisoner. Baron Dörnberg, the chief of protocol, then appeared and said that the air-raid danger, which had held up the train, was past. The train could therefore be ready at 8 P.M. That was probably a subterfuge.

Soon after, Ribbentrop went to Horthy and asked him to agree to the text of a communique which he showed him. The message stated, among other things, that the German troops were entering Hungary as the result of a decision come to by Horthy and Hitler. Horthy protested indignantly against that falsehood and said that it only remained for them to add that the entry of the Little Entente troops had been his special heart's desire. Ribbentrop said that the wording of the communique was a necessary lie to give the occupation a friendlier appearance. Horthy answered that the world should see the foul, dastardly business in its true colors and that he was not going to allow that lie to be put into his mouth. In spite of his refusal, however, the Germans were so unscrupulous as to issue the original text to the German press, and, since it appeared the following morning, it had probably been issued to the press before being shown to him at all.

The train started at about 8 P.M. There were long delays in Salzburg and Linz: obviously they wanted to put off its arrival in Hungary until the military occupation was completed. In the morning Jagow went to the Regent and told him that he was being replaced. The new minister, who would have the further title of Reich plenipotentiary, was Weesenmayer, whom Jagow asked to be allowed to present.

Horthy also told me that he had made several attempts to get in touch with me but he had always met with blunt refusals. He was told that he could neither telegraph nor telephone until the conversation with Hitler was over, as the possibility of any leakage had to be avoided. Horthy was thus really completely in the dark about what was happening in Hungary.

The Regent expressly assured me, however, that he had concluded no agreement, given no promise, and given no indications of his intentions. He had instead insisted that he could take no action before arriving home as a free man. Horthy told me that the hatred the Nazis felt for my person was intense.

I then told the Regent what had happened in Hungary and what steps I had taken. He received my report without special remark, told me nothing of his plans or intentions, and did not ask my opinion about the future.

The Regent ordered a crown council for that morning. This was attended by the ministers, the members of the supreme defense council, the heads of the Regent's two chanceries, and the chief of staff. Before it opened I held a ministerial council at which I told the story as I had heard it from the Regent. Ghyczy also reported.

Then I stood up and began to speak, or rather, I tried to speak and could not for my sobs. I could say only: "I could not have acted otherwise . . ."

Keresztes-Fischer put his hand on my shoulder. I gripped it, saying, "Thank you all for standing by me . . . May God help us . . ."

At the crown council the Regent repeated what I have written here and said that he would have to make new decisions. Pending these, he asked the cabinet to continue in office. Keresztes-Fischer and I then said that from the moment of the German occupation all actions, including either the resignation of the old cabinet or the appointment of a new one, were legally null and void as taken under foreign duress. We could not therefore continue to function, either actively or passively, and accordingly could not comply with the Regent's request to carry on our duties. I added that I did not think it possible for me even to sign the minutes of the present meeting, nor would I issue a communique. Thereupon the Regent retired, and the crown council disbanded without having taken any decision.

In the evening I again went to see the Regent, who had by then been able to snatch a little rest after days of exhaustion. He told me that since his conversation on the train no German had sought an opportunity of discussing things with him except Weesenmayer, who had asked to be received after dinner. Horthy and I then talked together at length for the last time. I asked him what he meant to do. I said that the events of the day had created the impression that the Germans meant to keep their promises. They had promised that if I resigned and a pro-German, non-hostile government came in my place, Hungary's independence and internal liberties should remain unimpaired. Since the occupation, however, Hungary had ceased to be a constitutional state. Any measure of his, sanctioned by a parliament meeting under the shadows of bayonets, would not be constitutional. The principle of popular sovereignty had ceased to operate. Henceforward all the Regent's actions would be taken on his own individual responsibility.

He answered that he knew all this. He knew that he was left alone. Every bastion surrounding his authority had crumbled

away. Only the inner fortress remained, but in that he would hold
out until his last breath. He had assumed the chief responsibility;
it was he who was truly responsible. The so-called responsible ministers were responsible only until replaced, but he could not take
that easy way out because there was no one to replace him. I
pointed out that if he took that view he was assuming responsibility, not only for his own actions, but for everything, including
things done without his knowledge or even against his will. I
begged him earnestly to abdicate as a demonstration, since that
was the only way we could refute the story which the Germans
were spreading that he had consented to the military occupation.
His staying in office would mean that he was dropping and re-
pudiating the policy which I had followed, which he had always
supported and defended, and to which he had never once objected. He answered that he could not go, that he could not abdicate.

I cannot, he said, striking the chair on which he was sitting,
leave this chair empty. I cannot let a usurper sit in this place. I
have sworn to the country not to forsake it. I am still an admiral.
The captain cannot leave his sinking ship; he must remain on the
bridge to the last. Whom will it serve if Imrédy sits here? Who
will defend the army? Who will save a million Magyar lads from
being dragged away to the Russian shambles? Who will defend
the honorable men and women in this country who have trusted
me blindly? Who will defend the Jews or our refugees if I leave
my post? I may not be able to defend everything, but I believe
that I can still be of great, very great, help to our people. I can
do more than anyone else could.

I was deeply perturbed. I tried to argue with him calmly. I said
that, however honorable and heroic his attitude, whatever profit
it might bring, despite all, both he and Hungary would be branded
as criminals. Then I toned down my proposals and suggested that,
if he preferred, he should not abdicate but should withdraw from
the conduct of state business. He should appoint no government,
sign no document, adopt a completely passive attitude, go away

to the country. That might be the best solution. No one could be put in his place, nothing could be lent the appearance of legality. Everything done would be by virtue of the German occupation and on their responsibility. An inactive policy would create the same sort of situation as had happened under King Christian X of Denmark.

But Horthy rejected those proposals too.[3] He kept on repeating—I think unconsciously—Francis Joseph's words: "I have weighed everything. I have considered everything. I cannot act otherwise." He could not withdraw, for things would not remain as they were; the Germans always kicked the defenseless. The day would come when the nation would be strong enough to shake them off. There would be resistance in Hungary, but that resistance could take shape only if he remained at his post, if he kept the threads in his hand. If he was not there, who would constitute the focus round which anything could gather? The army would obey no one but him. Then, what would the people say if a possibility, a suitable moment, came for action and he was not at his post?

Alas, his calculations and ideas proved faulty. It is true that he helped many people; he saved nearly half the Jews. But he could not save Hungary. Most of all he harmed himself, but I know, and can testify before the world, that that was what he minded least. He was right, too, in supposing that resistance could not take shape except round him, for had he not remained at his post, the Sztójay government could not have been replaced in August by that of Vitez Geza Lakatos, with its new course [4]—an enormous change that was a reversion to a position something like that of the Vichy government before Laval. Nor could the proclamation of October 15 [5] have come—another failure, as was inevitable; yet in it Horthy was able to voice the true soul and will of the Hungarian people.

Horthy was every inch a gentleman. His own intentions were

[3] I repeated this suggestion in writing a few days later from the Turkish legation, but again without success. See pages 444–45.

[4] See page 454.   [5] See pages 458–61.

unimpeachable, and he believed in the good intentions and the honor of others. His gifts were not of the kind of the statesmen of our new world—a Nikola Pashitch, an Eduard Benes, a Nicholas Titulescu. But he could not help that. It was he, not such as they, that the Hungarian people needed.

When I got back to my office, Keresztes-Fischer was waiting for me. I told him in a few words of my conversation with the Regent. He received it without comment. We sat there in silence for a long time, then he got up, saying: "Well, I'll be going. God bless you, Nicholas!"

He went out. I never saw him again.

I remained alone in the room where I had been so little alone during two years. I had felt absolutely at home there from the first day, but now, suddenly, everything seemed strange. I looked round, not as one saying farewell, but as one seeing many things for the first time. Facing me was the portrait of Hungary's first premier, in 1848, Count Louis Batthyányi; next to him, on the other wall, the youthful Francis Joseph, a portrait painted about the time when Batthyányi was executed. On the other side were the two great Hungarians and great antagonists, Louis Kossuth and Stephen Széchényi. There was Stephen Tisza, martyred by the Communists in 1918; Stephen Bethlen, now somewhere in hiding; and behind my desk, Horthy. It has often been said that Hungarian politics are full of contrasts and incomprehensibilities. Here, in this room, a bundle of contrasts was brought together. Yet they represented the soul of Hungary: from these contrasts our synthesis was composed; they were the symbols of our independence and our love of liberty. No, I do not want to take farewell of that past, nor to break with it, for it is Hungary's past. If there is a Hungarian world again, it will be Hungarian only if it builds on the foundations of that past.

I tried to write down what happened in the last days; first of all, to think out why Hitler had decided to take the ultimate step —the occupation—and the timing of it. I have often thought that over since, and now I list the immediate causes as follows:

1. The Regent's last letter had put in the form of an ultimatum what we had been asking for a year past: that our troops should be brought back, together with our new proposition, that we wanted to defend the Carpathians alone and would allow no German troops on our soil. The Germans knew that we had informed the English and Americans of our requests and that my administration could not go back on them.

2. The Germans had got increasingly full information on my connections with the English and Americans. They had traced the transmitters through which I kept up this contact. They knew that I had agreed that an American military mission should be flown to us and be officially received by our soldiers. All that made them fear that those connections would soon bring results of some sort.

3. As the Soviet troops drew nearer, the Germans could not afford to have an unreliable country behind the lines, still less a hostile one. They could not know whether my connections with the Anglo-Saxons did not extend to the Russians. Hungary's behavior, her reluctance to take part in the Russian campaign, might affect Rumania's attitude.

4. Another determinant factor might have been the increased prominence of left-wing elements, the increasingly anti-German mood of public opinion, and the increasingly vehement protests of their own partisans against this and other phenomena.

5. The Germans were discontented at the slow progress and meager results of our economic negotiations. Both what we promised and what we sent were steadily diminishing. The German needs were great and could not be satisfied by other means.

6. The question of the Jews and of the refugees was of dominating importance. The greatest enemies of the Nazis, the targets of their deepest hatred, were living unmolested in the very heart of the German sphere of power—a million strong. Was one little country, one man, to hinder the execution of their totalitarian plans? Were the refugees—Poles, French, English, Americans,

and now Italians—to be allowed to escape the German death grip to live as free men? That was really too much for the Nazis.

These, I think, were the immediate causes of the occupation. There was perhaps one more that only someone who knows their mentality can understand: everything was going badly with them; one defeat was following another. The German soldiers, accustomed to victory, had to be given something which could be represented as such, shown something that was a sign of strength, and had to annihilate an enemy with a lightning decision. What could serve those purposes better than the crushing of the last partially free country?

Why did the occupation have to take place precisely on March 19? Why could the Regent's Canossa not be postponed one single day? My answer—and precisely because it sounds so grotesque it is probable—is that on March 20 I was going to speak on the anniversary of Kossuth's death to a representative audience. The Germans believed that I-was going then to announce that we were breaking away from Germany and asking for an armistice: a sort of repetition of Kossuth's declaration of independence. I heard that rumor from several sides. On the very day of the occupation the story was being spread by Rajniss, who professed to have it from Weesenmayer himself. Later, when I was being examined in Sopronköhida prison, I was again cross-examined about it. Actually, all these motifs were there in my speech, which I had composed a fortnight previously. It was not, however, to be an offer to the Allies, but a declaration to the free peoples of the world.

I was unable to work for long. I was tired. I had reached the end of my Calvary. All was finished—the destiny of a country, the future of a people. What had broken down, I knew, could nevermore be repaired. Rightly had I said in one of my speeches that what the world conflagration was deciding for the small peoples was the question to be or not to be. We had tried to survive and found that we could not. Was it ever possible? Even if verily nothing could have saved us, that is no consolation. Hungary died under my hand. When my dearest, my all, dies, it is no consolation if at her deathbed the doctor says that nothing could have saved her. To me fate gave Hungary to guard, lead, and defend in her last years. I did all that I could; what strength, what faith was in me, I threw into the struggle, and I do not know where I went wrong. Were I boastful, I should say, nowhere, in nothing. But I am but a lonely, tormented, simple child of my nation, just such a suffering member of my people as the other millions. It is terrible to have to write this. Teleki escaped from it; for him at least the nation wept, him the nation buried. Fate has willed it that I should live on, see my country, which I loved like a mother, a wife, a child, die in my arms. I must be the mourner, I dig the grave.

Lord, Thou alone knowest what manner of people this is: good, noble, fine. Perchance dreamy, perchance not always practical, fonder of fairy tales than of reality—but is that a sin? Who shall protect the little children, the weak, if not Thou? And, Lord, to Thee we cried out, of Thee we ask but one thing: punish us if Thou wilt, but have mercy on us; call us not guilty, for that we are not.

EIGHTEEN

AT THE TURKISH LEGATION

⟨AFTER THE FIRST hectic events of the German occupation, I retired to my own apartment. There I experienced an entirely different situation. The world seemed completely shut out. A stillness seemed to have gripped the city: no one came to see me; no one called me on the telephone. I was all alone except for my immediate family—my wife, my three sons, and my small grandchild. My son Andrew, who was in the Regent's bodyguard, came from the royal palace to see us. He told us that the Regent had gone to bed. The Hungarian guard had been reinforced, and the German "guard of honor" that had been posted at the gates of the royal palace had, on the Regent's protest, been withdrawn. There were no Germans on Buda Hill, but they had placed guards on all the roads leading up it. Those guards demanded to see the papers of all passers, although they made no attempt to stop them.

Feeling mortally exhausted, I went to bed. I could not fall right to sleep, however. For a long time I strained my ears to catch every sound, but all was still.

At about 6:00 A.M. I was aroused and told that the ministry buildings were surrounded by SS soldiers, that an armored car was standing at our own gates, and that an SS officer was hammering at the gate demanding admittance. My son Christopher went down to see what the knocker wanted, and Christopher was told that the officer had orders to conduct me to the German legation, where Weesenmayer awaited me. I had started to dress meanwhile and had laid out my revolver in preparation for any eventuality, when my wife and son entered my room and begged me to flee.

I had for the decision only the few minutes that the SS officer had allowed me for dressing. I decided immediately that we should all escape, and a moment afterwards all of us, including my grandchild, abandoned the premier's residence and hurried through the some three dozen spacious apartments under Buda Hill that had been fully furnished and provided with electric power for use by the principal ministries. The lower exit of these shelters opened onto the tunnel under the hill; another exit led upward to the royal palace. We headed for the latter, and after climbing the three hundred odd steps we found ourselves in the Regent's residence. He and Her Serene Highness were immediately awakened, and, after hearing with deep indignation the story of the attempted outrage, the Regent at once offered his protection to me and my entire family.

Horthy then phoned Weesenmayer, who was awake and thus must have been expecting me, and protested vigorously. Weesenmayer replied that, though he had given instructions that he wished to speak to me in the early morning hours, he had not ordered my arrest. That was, of course, an untruth.

I had no intention of availing myself of the Regent's invitation, which in any case was out of his power to honor. The Germans would never have allowed me, his "evil genius," to stay at his side. I therefore phoned M. Kececi, the Turkish minister, and asked him if his offer, made to my wife the day before, to give me shelter still held good. His answer being in the affirmative, I asked him to send a car to the entrance of the palace gardens. The car arrived shortly afterwards, and after saying farewells to my family and to the Regent and Her Highness, I was driven to the Turkish legation on the Rózsadomb.[1] I was greeted at the entrance of the legation by M. Kececi and his wife, and the minister remarked that I was the third person—Rákoczy [2] and Kossuth were the other two—to find asylum on Turkish soil.

Thus it was that I ceased to be a free man and entered on the life of a political exile.[3]

The Turkish minister, of course, immediately reported to his government what he had done, and the Turkish government signified its approval. Numan Menemencioglu, the Turkish foreign minister, then discussed the matter with Franz von Papen, the German ambassador in Istanbul. A few days later M. Kececi was informed that von Papen had proposed three possible actions for me: I and my entire family could go to Istanbul as a guest of the Turkish government, in which case the Germans would provide a plane for my use. I might go to my own house in the country, where a German "guard of honor" would watch over my personal safety. Lastly, I might continue to enjoy the hospitality of the

[1] A hill in the western suburbs of Buda.

[2] Francis II Rákoczy, 1675–1735, was a member of a noble Hungarian family that greatly influenced the history of Hungary and Transylvania in the seventeenth and eighteenth centuries, and he is a major national hero of Hungary. He led a Hungarian resistance against the Habsburgs, and in the Diet of Onod (1707) the nobles declared the overthrow of the dynasty and the total independence of Hungary. The movement was defeated a few years later, however, and Rákoczy fled, eventually settling in Turkey, where he died. Hungary brought back his remains in 1906.

[3] It is with feelings of warmest gratitude and friendship that I recall the kindness with which I was received by my hosts. The somewhat cramped apartment held no spare room, and the minister placed his own bedroom at my disposal. On the day of my arrival a chasseur was sent to fetch some of my more indispensable belongings and a few books and papers. I was a guest in that house for eight months, and I never once experienced anything but kindness and courtesy. And yet my presence placed the entire legation in a difficult position.

Turkish legation in Budapest. All that sounded very fine, especially the possibility of going to Istanbul—supposing that the promised German plane would really set me down there. But before I had time to decide which suggestion I would accept, a second telegram informed me that Berlin had vetoed von Papen's first proposal. I thereupon unhesitatingly rejected the second and begged to be allowed to remain where I was for the time.

After that, the Germans blockaded the Turkish legation. Day and night an armored car stood at the corners of each of the four streets that led to the house and garden, and between these cars patrols paced back and forth. As soon as anybody approached the legation, the motor horns signaled to each other. At night the entire building was lighted with flood lamps. For a while the minister and his staff were not hampered in their movements. Anyone who entered or left the building, however, was called on to produce his papers—principally to make sure that no letters were received or sent out by me. As a result of all these German measures the Turkish minister was extremely concerned for my safety, and a long time went by before he would permit me to walk in the garden.

Thus the days were passed in conversation, in listening to the radio, in reading, and, on my part, in much anxious meditation. M. Kececi was a man of wide and polished culture, a perfect French scholar, and a trained jurist. His wife, who came from one of the first families in Turkey, was the good angel of the whole house.

After a few days of unbroken calm, a few people succeeded in getting through to see me. The first to call was Count Ferdinand Zichy. He came to tell me that a thoroughly trustworthy friend of his, a pilot officer, would undertake to get me out of the country provided that I could manage to leave the legation. This could only be achieved if the minister accompanied me in person, and even so it would be no easy matter. By day I should be seen by the Germans; a departure by the minister at night would seem peculiar, and the Germans would probably—as they usually did—

shine their lamps into the car. The minister was definite in advising against this plan, which he thought in any case superfluous, since his government was carrying on constant negotiations with von Papen on my case and a solution might be expected at any moment. There was also the possibility to be considered that the Germans would treat my wife and sons as hostages and perhaps even deport them.

My next caller was Andor Szentmiklóssy, the deputy foreign minister, who told me what was going on in current events, particularly in the field of foreign affairs. He reported that everything possible had been done to destroy all papers and documents not meant for German eyes. But, he reported, the last foreign office messengers who had passed through Germany in either direction had been arrested and relieved of their diplomatic bags, which had held certain compromising material. That was the last time I saw this excellent fellow worker of mine. A few days later he was arrested by the Germans, and he perished in Dachau.

I was kept informed of all that was going on outside by the legation staff, the radio, the newspapers, and, more particularly, through the reports of my visitors. The arrests had begun that first Sunday evening and night and the following Monday morning, and then had continued ever since. The first of my ministers to be arrested were Francis Keresztes-Fischer, the minister of the interior, and Baron Daniel Bánffy, the minister of agriculture. Stephen Bethlen had escaped from his searchers and was in hiding, no one knew where. Leopold Baranyai, Count Anthony Sigray, Count Iván Csekonics, Count George Apponyi, and in general most of the leading members of the aristocracy, as well as Charles Peyer, Charles Rassay, General Louis Keresztes-Fischer, and many prominent Jews had been arrested and even more were in hiding to escape arrest.

The Germans had assumed complete control. Weesenmayer was complete master and director of the situation. The Gestapo had taken over the functions of the police, and it was continually being reinforced, while the regular German troops were being sent East. The Regent appointed a government under Döme Sztójay, which, however, was completely unable to keep the situation in hand. Although it was zealous in serving the Nazis in all things, the Nazis showed no intention of keeping their promise not to interfere in Hungary's domestic affairs after a Quisling administration had been formed; on the contrary, the German arrangements in Hungary resembled in every particular the procedure that they had followed in the Polish and Czech protectorates.

It is not my task to describe in this book the history of those days. I followed every phase with the utmost attention, and subsequently many people came to me for advice. But I did not participate directly in the events of that period, and I must leave it to others to put them on record. I shall restrict myself to relating a few episodes of a purely personal nature that occurred during those eight months and to unburdening myself of some thoughts about the events.

My wife remained as a guest under the Regent's roof, where she was treated with a tender solicitude and kindness that did much to comfort her and to uphold her courage. My oldest son, Christopher, was interned, with his wife and small child, at my sister's country place near Budapest. My second son, Nicholas, was advised by his army commander to rejoin his regiment, as the least likely place where he would be sought. My youngest son, Andrew, was a lieutenant in the Regent's bodyguard, and no better place could have been found for him then. I did not communicate with any member of my family at first. Later on, a youthful member of the Turkish legation undertook to convey a few letters to my wife.

Shocked by what I heard about the consequences of the German occupation, I thought it incumbent upon me to write a letter to the Regent shortly after I entered the Turkish legation. In this letter I repeated my contention that it was no longer permissible for him to retain his office—the time had come for him to abdicate. In explanation of my attitude, I referred to the reactions that the occupation of Hungary had called forth abroad which I had heard on the radio, and to what was reported to me by friends of the outrages committed by the Germans in Hungary.

After the Turkish minister had handed Horthy my letter, the Regent had a long conversation with him, the burden of which, as Kececi told me afterwards, was that he, as the Regent, had but one duty; to remain at his post under all circumstances and do the utmost possible in the interests of his country. Passing on to my own situation and the fate of those departed and those under arrest, the Regent said that he had received a definite promise that those questions would be solved before long. Everyone would be brought home again, but the politicians would have to be brought before a parliamentary tribunal in accordance with our own constitutional practice. The Turkish minister told me afterwards that he had not tried to argue with Horthy, that not being his metier. I learned later that Horthy unfortunately took Kececi's silence to mean approval of the Regent's line of action.

I recall a rather interesting episode that happened in those days. My son Christopher had written me a letter of two lines to say that our cousin Stephen Kállay had come up from my country place and wanted to speak to me, in order to report to me on questions connected with the farm. A person bearing my son's letter succeeded in passing through the German guard on the strength of it, and the messenger even got past the Turkish minister, who exercised a rigorous control over the persons admitted to see me. A servant conducted the messenger to my room, asked him to take a seat, and then brought me the letter, I being on the terrace at the moment. On entering my room, I saw a perfect stranger before me, and I could not restrain a start of surprise, which must have been observed by the servant who had entered with me (and who, as it later turned out, was an informer in the pay of the Gestapo). After the servant left, my visitor, a tall, good-looking young man of about thirty or thirty-five, introduced himself and then went on to say that he and my son had worked out together this plan for gaining him admittance. He was of

English descent on his mother's side and an agent of the British secret service. He had received instructions to arrange my escape, and he proposed the following plan: during one of the next air raids on Budapest, of which he would give me warning in advance, the Turkish minister was to drive me, and if possible my family also, to Lake Balaton, where, at a meeting place to be determined in advance, a motor boat and two British hydroplanes would be awaiting us. He could not as yet tell me the day or the hour; we should in any case have to wait for a dark night. When the time was ripe, I should be apprised through the radio: on the night preceding that of the escape the Hungarian broadcast of the BBC would refer three consecutive times to the date March 19, also mentioning an hour, which would be that at which I was to start. He asked me whether I was certain I could trust every single member of the Turkish legation. If so, he would pass the information on through them. He himself could not call a second time, for that would be too risky. He may have noticed a certain hesitation in my manner, for he said quickly: "Allow me to anticipate your answer. I am not going to ask you what your decision will be. You must do as you think fit."

With that he left. I cannot deny that my first thought had been that he had been sent by the Germans with a view to getting me out of the legation and at the same time compromising Kececi, the Turkish minister. But the fact that he had come from my son Christopher, who was sensible and coolheaded and who would never have acceded to a plan which might involve me in the greatest danger, militated against its being a German plot; nor did the bearing and address of the young man seem like those of a German agent. I reported the matter to my host, who said that it must be thought over. There would be plenty of time for this before the next communication reached me, whether by radio or in some other manner.

After that I listened carefully to the radio for any message for me. But I could never tell for sure that there was any. For one thing, the broadcasts were nearly always interfered with. Even when this was not the case and March 19 was mentioned, I could not tell whether the mention was repeated. I never again received any message from the agent. Subsequently I learned, on questioning my son, that there was no doubt about the young man's partial English descent; he had returned from abroad during the war, had been my son's comrade in the mounted artillery, and was known to him as a decent, reliable fellow. He told my son the same tale that he had told me, and it had been arranged between them that he would go back to my son after seeing me, since my boy would have had to inform the family and make the final arrangements. But the young man never returned to my son, and repeated inquiries failed to trace him or to find out what had happened to him. To this day I do not know whether he had really been commissioned to attempt the enterprise or was an *agent provocateur.*

At about this same time an unknown man called on my son Christopher and without giving his name laid 6,000 dollars on the table, with the words: "This has been sent for your father, do not ask by whom." I have not discovered to this day to whom I owe this sum. No one whom I have been able to ask has acknowledged it.

In the course of the summer I received a letter from Otto Winkelmann, the SS officer next in rank to Weesenmayer, who was in charge of the whole police organization, under authority deriving straight from Himmler himself. The letter ran as follows:

Your Excellency: I am convinced that the insecurity in which you and your family find yourselves at the present moment must cause you all much concern. I am authorized to inform you, on the direct orders of His Excellency Himmler, that if you will leave the Turkish legation you will be His Excellency's personal guest. You and the members of your family will be offered domicile commensurate with your rank in a hunting box, where you will be permitted to move freely about the vicinity, and you will be able to take with you anything you wish, not excepting even your radio and your guns. I must emphasize, however, that this offer and its acceptance must be kept clear of all diplomatic channels; it must remain strictly an agreement between yourself and Himmler.

Apparently my presence, even within the four walls of the Turkish legation, still caused the Germans disquiet. My host said that I could, of course, do as I chose; if I wished to leave the legation, he could not prevent me. But he begged me to remember that while under his roof, however unpleasant my situation, I was still a diplomatic problem; the moment I ceased to be one, I should be at the mercy of the Germans, who could do with me what they chose. I may say that I never dreamed of accepting Himmler's offer. I would, of course, have preferred not to continue being a burden to the members of the Turkish legation. My presence there could not but be inconvenient, both from an official and a personal point of view—all this quite apart from the fact that the apathy with which I envisaged my future fate robbed it of every vestige of romance, although I could not put an end to it by accepting a way out such as the Germans proposed. I might eventually be, as I did in fact later become, a prisoner of the Germans; I could not, however, be their guest.

I politely refused the Germans' offer, therefore, by saying that, since a settlement concerning my person had been reached between the German and the Turkish governments, it would be disloyal on my part not to submit to it. I could not, therefore, I told Winkelmann, accept His Excellency's offer. The offer was repeated later, not by Winkelmann himself but by his subordinates.

In the long hours of the nights I used to stand and gaze down on the darkened city. Until March 19, 1944, Budapest, perhaps alone of all the cities of the Continent, had still possessed a night life and had shown lamplit windows. The nights of a big city are a measure of the freedom that its inhabitants enjoy. Most people have their days prescribed for them by circumstances, but at night they sleep or read or write or amuse themselves as their whim dictates. After March 19, however, Budapest was lighted up only when it was in flames, noisy only when the planes droned overhead and the bombs and antiaircraft guns thundered. And I could hear, even though no sound reached my ears, the lamentations of men and the wailing of mothers and children. I could hear and I could see all the changes that I had strained every nerve to prevent. And it was no comfort, no satisfaction, to tell myself that while I had been at the helm we had managed to hold these troubles off. My heart was torn by doubt and by the ever-recurrent question whether a way might not, after all, have been found to save our people from these present horrors. What that way might have been I do not know to this day.

We reached March 19 without suffering an air raid, but after the German occupation Hungary was subjected to raid upon raid. The first were aimed at a big textile works and at the gigantic munition plant on Csepel Island. The airplane factory was the first to be destroyed, and after that the entire concern was crippled. At a stroke some 60,000 workingmen were left without a means of earning their bread. Man is the ultimate reason for all factories —their soul and essential substance. That is why the raids were aimed first and foremost against the workers. For after the factories it was the workers' quarters and the slum dwellings of the poor, not the inner city or the residential districts, which were attacked. We all know that it was done deliberately and that policy was based on a miscalculation. Later—much too late, alas —people in the West realized that the homeless masses did not, as had been expected, rise against the ruling powers. Rendered destitute and completely helpless, the workingmen fell an easy prey to Hitler, to reactionary regimes, to any authority which would give them bread and a roof over their heads.

Even if the purpose behind the bombing had been attained, however, it was not a defensible proceeding. So far as internal resistance is concerned, bombing did not shorten the war in any country. True, it was Hitler who began it, but inhumanity is not an example to be followed.

It is safe to say that the bombing of Budapest strengthened rather than weakened the position of the Hungarian Nazis. Logically, the opposite might have been expected, but desperation knows no logic. The raids were largely responsible for the anti-Semitic excesses; the masses do not pick and choose when it comes to wreaking vengeance—they smite where they can.

After March 19 there was no longer any organized order in Hungary nor any recognized governing authority. Horthy's continuance in office prevented the Germans from subjugating the country as completely as they had in Bohemia and Poland, but the presence of the Germans upset the existing order and the prestige and power of the authorities. A general disintegration set in all along the line, and as always happens in such times, the honest and decent people bore the brunt of the disaster. The dregs of humanity rose to the top; the satellites, the collaborators, and the unscrupulous who jibbed at nothing had it all their own way. The Germans who occupied Budapest were a mixed lot; there were probably as many decent men as blackguards among them. But the Hungarians who collaborated with them were one and all vile. Everyone, without exception, must be held to be so, who subordinates his country's good to other aims, even should those aims be ideological. But in most cases the motive force is self-interest. A nation that is led by such people does not reveal its true nature, since a nation is naturally represented by its elite. It is the elite that an occupying power casts aside in order to replace it with base and depraved men, traitors to their kind.

The Nazis were, however, the instigators of every act against human decency, and it was they who were responsible for the disintegration of the moral order in Hungary. I could always tell myself that they were to blame for all that was happening after they took over. Nevertheless, it hurt me terribly to witness and hear about the instances of demoralization in my country. My only comfort was that few of the persons involved belonged to my own Magyar race.

We estimated that those who made themselves tools of the Germans in those days formed about five per cent of the population. The same number are now Communists. But these twice five do not make ten, for in most cases they are the same individuals. It must be emphasized that none of the three principal groups of the Hungarian nation—the ruling class (including the civil servants), the peasantry, and the working classes—were Nazi or Communist; their members never collaborated with either party. Racially, they were the purest Magyars; and it was they who never subscribed to the theory of race purity.

Budapest faced utter ruin, and so did the country at large. The Germans took with systematic thoroughness whatever they coveted. The destitute Hungarians, who had lost all their possessions, threw themselves greedily on what was left. In the countryside the departure from some farm or country house of German wagons laden with loot became the signal for the villagers to raid the premises, with the slogan: "Why should the Germans have it all?" Later, after the Russians replaced the Germans, it was the Communist depredations that had to be "forestalled."

Factories were moved; they were being transferred "temporarily," the Germans said, to some safe place. Valuable assets became so much scrap iron. And the situation was no better after the Russians arrived. What, one is tempted to ask, was all this destruction good for? What ultimate profit did anyone derive from it? There may be some logic in the vandalism of the defeated. The vandalism of the victor is wholly illogical.

Worse than the material damage caused by the German occupation, however, was the moral havoc that it wrought in the nation. In this, too, it was in no wise different from the Russian occupation, as we were to discover later on. Both occupations set Magyar against Magyar, one with the racial slogan, the other with the call to class war. Every base human instinct and every form of meanness was set loose and ran riot. I had, long before, felt that these would be consequences of the occupation, and that was a primary reason why I had rejected the advice not to postpone the inevitable German occupation. Every day gained might, I felt, mean life for thousands of people—first and foremost for those of Jewish extraction.

Those gamblers who had advised me to cast our lot with the Germans could now see with their own eyes the consequences that an irresponsible policy could entail. The destruction of houses, factories, and valuable assets may be accepted as a normal concomitant of modern warfare. The loss of our sons in battle could be considered merely a mournful continuation of century-old traditions. But the persecution and deliberate extermination of innocent men and women—that we had not had before. To have lived to see that inhuman spectacle, to have had to look on helplessly and realize that there were those among my own people who participated in this hangman's work—that was the most horrible part of my life during that time.

Reports came to us of what was going on in the country districts. The country Jews were, strangely enough, the first victims. I cannot tell why that was so; one would have expected otherwise, since they had fused better than their city brethren with the rest of the inhabitants and had gained the liking and respect of their neighbors. The reason, probably, was that being more dispersed and less exposed to view they could more easily be dealt with. It was also said in explanation that Horthy was not meant to see what was going on.

But was it possible not to hear the agonized cries that were coming from every quarter of the country? Yet there must have been some truth in the supposition, for it is a fact that Horthy was able—until he himself was deported—to prevent the massacre of the Budapest Jewry. But why had he not intervened before? If he did not, it was, I know, because he lacked the power. Had he not resisted even the first, lenient Jewish laws and softened them as far as he was able? Even now he intervened again and again in the case of individuals, instituted a system of exemptions and even at times gave sanctuary to the hunted, as every decent person was doing in those days. But the question was no longer a matter of individual cases—it concerned a million men and women, and, more even than this, a nation's honor.

From the very first days, the Turkish legation was inundated with people who possessed passports, or a hope of obtaining them, and wished to get Turkish visas. But soon even this expedient failed, for those who entered the doors of the legation found, on leaving, the Gestapo waiting for them. The minister would have liked to offer sanctuary to these unfortunates; but apart from the fact that his instructions forbade this he lacked the necessary space. Even so, the consulate was soon crammed with uninvited but tolerated refugees. Yet how insignificant was their number compared with the multitudes who perished!

In Budapest the wearing of the yellow star was made compulsory for all Jews. Then, too, they were herded into special houses, from which they could only issue at specified hours of the day, and their own homes were looted. In short, all the things were done that had become the rule, years before, in the countries where the Germans were in power.

The Jews in their aggregate may have their failings, and it may be true that in the countries where they form a considerable percentage of the population they are a certain handicap, but in view of what they have suffered, there is nothing in their past that cannot be forgiven them and no act of desperation or vengeance of theirs that we are not bound to understand. Even in Hungary their fate had found them out. Until March 19, 1944, I had stood between them and their doom, but after the German occupation I was myself a hunted fugitive, and my fate was no better than theirs. Accursed be the brain that conceived and the hand that carried out the devilish work against them! There is no excuse for what happened—only one extenuating circumstance: Of all the countries under German domination Hungary was the one in which the greatest number of Jews escaped; more survived in Hungary than in all the German-ruled countries put together. I would ask all those who escaped, and all my fellow men, to note and give us credit for this fact.

Those, then, were the things that I felt and that I saw from my balcony. Budapest was burning, and already new lightning flashes were appearing on the horizon—the salvos of the Russian big batteries.

Seeing as I did the trend of events, I sent the Regent a letter via a member of the Turkish legation, asking for the Regent's views on the situation. In reply Horthy sent me his most trusted adjutant, Julius Tost, to acquaint me with his plans. The Regent had decided to sue for an armistice at the first possible opportunity. He also intended to dismiss the Sztójay cabinet—ridding himself of all the Nazi elements—and to appoint, if no other alternative offered itself, a government of civil servants under a general. With such a government, the Regent would be able to enforce his decisions and gain time to fill the principal military posts with reliable men.

On August 29, 1944, the formation of a government under General Lakatos was announced. Such a return from a Quisling regime to an independent one was an unprecedented decision and achievement. The new government was composed almost entirely of men of the highest character and integrity. What this meant may be gauged if we remember that of all the countries under German rule not a single one except Hungary succeeded in arresting the downward slide and regaining even a vestige of her former independence. The new government promised to do that, not only by implication through the personality of its members, but also openly in the program in which it announced its policy.

Subsequently the activities of the Gestapo were arrested, and the persecution of the Jews ceased. To have achieved that when the military situation for Germany had not disintegrated is sufficient justification of Horthy's resolve to remain at his post. Complete success was in the nature of things impossible. But Horthy saved the lives of some hundreds of thousands of human beings and demonstrated the nation's determination and ability to stop itself on the edge of the abyss.

After the appointment of the Lakatos government my personal situation changed for the better, too. A detachment of the Hungarian police was, by the Regent's orders, stationed in an adjacent building, with orders to keep an eye on the German guard lest they should kidnap me. A rumor arose that that was their intention because I had rejected Himmler's offer.

Subsequently, too, countless plans were being hatched to effect my escape. The most fantastic ideas were produced by relatives and acquaintances alike. Opposite the Turkish legation, in what had once been a boarding school for girls, was the headquarters of an air force squadron. The commander of the squadron proposed that he should pass our garden fence with all his men; I was to stand near the fence, and then the men were to lift me over, pop me into a car, and whisk me to the airport, where a plane would be waiting to carry me straight to Istanbul. A left-wing workers organization also declared itself willing to liberate me. It guaranteed that if I could make my way to its headquarters in Eskütér, it would find me a hiding place where I should be in complete security. My son Andrew, in the Regent's bodyguard, also had a plan to kidnap me with the aid of his men. And so ad libitum.

All those plans were conceived after Lakatos had become premier, when the German influence and absolute control of affairs was somewhat relaxed and a certain indecision could be observed in the attitude of the occupying forces. But I could see no advantage in an escape from the legation, however successfully managed, if, once out, I was forced to remain in hiding, lurking in some cellar, mine or wood, less capable of effective action than when I was in the legation.

Communication with the outside world became slightly easier. Joseph, the valet, undertook to fetch and carry my letters on his days off, taking them all, as I heard afterwards, to the Gestapo first for perusal and reproduction. The letters I sent by him were addressed exclusively to members of my family and contained for the most part purely personal matters, so the Germans gained little by their prying.

My son Andrew came to see me fairly often. When it was rumored that the Gestapo intended breaking into the Turkish legation, he brought me a Russian automatic pistol and a revolver —a fact our honest valet again promptly reported to the Germans, as they told me later.

Meanwhile German power had been receiving blows in other areas. On August 23, 1944, Rumania turned against Germany. Rumania, "the most loyal of all," as Hitler was fond of saying, that Rumania which had been held up to us as an example for her self-sacrificing zeal, her military contribution to the war effort, and her unshakable fortitude, was the first to secede. It would have made me laugh had laughter been possible in those days. Hitler had guaranteed Rumania's frontiers against us; it was at Rumania's wish that the Vienna award had bisected Transylvania. The most potent threat used by Germany against us was that she would give Rumania leave to overrun us. Hungary could not be given back her armies lest that should offend the Rumanians. Hungary could not be granted the privilege of defending her frontiers by her own efforts because Rumania would regard that as a provocation.

To all appearances, Rumania had done extremely well for herself. Having begun by giving unreserved assistance to Germany, Rumania now as unreservedly deserted Germany. At the moment it seemed that Rumania had saved herself. Today I, who did not ever want Russia's friendship, have been justified by events.

On August 26 Bulgaria followed Rumania's example. That vitally affected my own fate, since the Turkish government handed over Bogdan Filov, who had sought refuge in the Turkish legation in Sofia, to the Russians. The Germans would, I felt, obviously say, "If the Turks extradited Filov to the Russians, why should they not give up Kállay to us?" My position was rendered still more precarious by the fact that on August 2 the Turks had broken off diplomatic relations with Germany, so that there was nothing to prevent the Germans from resorting to drastic measures, unless it were a reluctance to provoke Turkey into a declaration of war.

Rumania and Bulgaria could turn against Germany; there was

no practical impediment to their secession because the Russians were already on their soil. Hungary had still only German forces on her frontiers. There was no other power within reach to surrender to, go over to, sue for an armistice to, and most important of all, appeal to for protection. At this juncture, as in the past, the situation can only be judged correctly if Hungary's geographical position and the military situation are taken into account, for it was those two factors which determined the trend of events.

NINETEEN

THE DEPOSITION OF HORTHY

⟨ON October 15, 1944, the Budapest radio broadcast a message from Horthy to the nation announcing his decision to ask for an armistice and to break with the Germans on the ground that they had tricked and deceived him and failed to keep their promises. He enumerated the outrages committed by them, including their attempt to arrest me, and in no uncertain terms he threw all their villainies in their teeth. I do not know how many men would have been capable of acting as Horthy did if they were in his situation —armored cars beleaguering his gates and his only surviving son in German hands. (Horthy did not know that the Germans were holding his son when he drew up the proclamation but he did know that when he ordered it to be broadcast.)

The proclamation ran as follows:

Ever since the will of the nation put me at the helm of the country, the most important aim of Hungarian foreign policy has been, through peaceful revision, to repair, at least partly, the injustices of the Peace Treaty of Trianon. Our hopes in the League of Nations in this regard remained unfulfilled.

At the time of the beginning of a new world crisis, Hungary was not led by a desire to acquire new territories. We had no aggressive intention against the Republic of Czechoslovakia, and Hungary did not wish to regain territories taken from her by war. We entered the Bachka only after the collapse of Yugoslavia and at that time in order to defend our blood brethren. We accepted a peaceful decision of the Axis powers regarding the eastern territories taken from us in 1918 by Rumania.

Hungary was forced into war against the Allies by German pressure, which weighed upon us owing to our geographical situation. But even so we were not guided by any ambition to increase our own power and had no intention to snatch as much as a square meter of territory from anybody.

Today it is obvious to any sober-minded person that the German Reich has lost the war. All governments responsible for the destiny of their countries must draw pertinent conclusions from this fact, for, as a great German statesman, Bismarck, once said: "No nation ought to sacrifice itself on the altar of an alliance."

Conscious of my historic responsibility, I have the obligation to undertake every step directed to avoiding further unnecessary bloodshed. A nation that allowed the soil inherited from its forefathers to be turned into a theater of rear-guard actions in a war already lost, defending alien interests in a slavish spirit, would lose the esteem of public opinion throughout the world.

With grief I am forced to state that the German Reich on its part long ago broke the loyalty of an ally toward our country. For a considerable time it has launched ever-new formations of Hungarian armed forces into the fight outside the frontiers of the country against my wish and will.

In March of this year, however, the Führer of Germany invited me to negotiation in consequence of my urgent demand for the repatriation of Hungary's armed forces. There he informed me that Hungary would be occupied by German forces, and he ordered this to be carried out in spite of my protests, even while I was retained abroad. Simultaneously German political police invaded the country and arrested numerous citizens, among them several members of the legislative assembly as well as the minister of the interior [Keresztes-Fischer] of my government then in office.

The premier [Kállay] himself evaded detention only by taking refuge in a neutral legation. After having received a firm promise from the Führer of Germany that he would cancel acts that violated and restricted Hungary's sovereignty if I appointed a government enjoying the confidence of the Germans, I appointed the Sztójay government.

Yet the Germans did not keep their promise. In the shelter of German occupation the Gestapo tackled the Jewish question in a manner incompatible with the demands of humanity, applying methods it had already employed elsewhere. When war drew near the frontiers and even passed them, the Germans repeatedly promised assistance, yet again they failed to honor their promise.

During their retreat they turned the country's sovereign territory into a theater of looting and destruction. Those actions, contrary to an ally's loyalty, were crowned by an act of open provocation when in the course of measures for the maintenance of order in the interior of Budapest, Corps Commander Field Marshal Lieutenant Szilard Bakay was treacherously attacked and abducted by Gestapo agents, who exploited the bad visibility of a foggy October morning when he was getting out of his car in front of his house.

Subsequently German aircraft dropped leaflets against the government in office. I received reliable information that troops of pro-German tendency intended to raise their own men to power by using force to effect a political upheaval and the overthrowing of the legal Hungarian government which I had appointed in the meantime [Premier Lakatos] and that they intended to turn their country's territory into a theater of rear-guard actions for the German Reich.

I decided to safeguard Hungary's honor even in relation to her former ally, although that ally, instead of supplying the military help it had promised, meant to rob the Hungarian nation finally of its greatest treasure—its freedom and independence.

I have informed a representative of the German Reich that we were about to conclude a military armistice with our previous enemies and to cease all hostilities against them.

Trusting your loyalty, I hope to secure in accord with you the continuity of our nation's life in the future and the realization of our peaceful aims.

Commanders of the Hungarian army have received corresponding orders from me. Accordingly, the troops, loyal to their oath and following an Order of the Day issued simultaneously, must obey the commanders appointed by me. I appeal to every honest Hungarian to follow me on the path, beset by sacrifices though it be, that will lead to Hungary's salvation.

So many false reports have been circulated about the broadcasting of this proclamation, that I feel it incumbent on me to relate the true story of what occurred. I have collected my information from the persons concerned, including the Regent himself, so that I have every reason to believe the following account to be an authentic statement of the events.

On the morning of October 15 a crown council was held. All members of the government were present, as well as General John Vörös, who had succeeded Szombathelyi as chief of staff, General Anthony Vattay, adjutant-in-chief, and Béla Miklos and Julius Ambrózy, of the Regent's military and civil chanceries. The Regent opened the proceedings by giving a brief sketch of the country's grievous state and our own military situation, which he described as hopeless. Horthy declared that Germany's imminent collapse was no longer in question, and if, when this occurred, Hungary were found on her side, the Allies would inevitably class us together. We must be prepared, in that case, to find them disregarding our struggles for independence and treating us, on the strength of the *de facto* situation, with extreme severity. He had therefore resolved to sue for an armistice. He had received information that if this was done then, we should be offered acceptable terms, which otherwise we could not hope for. The Russian forces already held a considerable portion of the country. Budapest still stood, but it must not be allowed to become a second Stalingrad. Every single life sacrificed in this hopeless struggle would be wantonly wasted. We would be exposed to the brutalities of Germans and Russians alike, and all for no purpose. By continuing the fight, we should be jeopardizing not only our country but the entire future of our race. He was saying all this to make it clear that his decision was irrevocable.

After this he asked Chief of Staff Vörös to describe the military situation. Vörös reported that a few minutes earlier he had received from the German GHQ a peremptory telegram in which General Heinz Guderian demanded the immediate revocation of the order to retreat which had been issued to the Hungarian First and Second Armies in the Carpathians and Transylvania. Twelve hours were given for the withdrawal of this order; if the demand was not complied with, Hitler would proceed to the most rigorous measures against Hungary. The telegram was couched in extremely rude and insulting terms.

Those demands and threats made a deep impression on the crown council. It was known that the chief of staff issued his orders in the Regent's name; it was thus evident that even Horthy's person had now ceased to command respect.

On the Regent's proposal, the crown council decided that the order should not be revoked and that the retreat should take its course. Chief of Staff Vörös issued the necessary instructions. The Regent then once again stated his resolve to ask for an armistice, adding that, since he had promised Hitler not to do so without apprising him, he had already invited Weesenmayer, the German minister, to call on him.

One or two timid ministers raised the question whether the

Regent was entitled to take such a step without first consulting parliament. A somewhat prolonged debate on this issue was finally brought to a close by the Regent's declaration that a decision on this question was a prerogative of the head of the state and outside the competence of parliament, an appeal to which was, moreover, impracticable under the given circumstances. Later, when it was once more in a position to take free decisions, it might reopen the question.

The council unanimously accepted that view; and therewith its proceedings closed. The time was then 11:30 A.M.

Meanwhile rumors had been filtering through that the Regent's son, Nicholas Horthy, Jr., had been lured into a trap by the Gestapo. According to the reports, SS men had arrested him at the offices of the manager of the free port. Young Horthy had defended himself and shot down one of his captors but had himself been wounded in the scrimmage. (This, as I subsequently heard from his own mouth, was erroneous; he was not wounded but was beaten on the head with a truncheon until he lost consciousness, after which a sack was pulled over his head and he was carried away.) For the moment it was impossible to ascertain his fate. The Regent was informed of the event only at the close of the crown council.

At noon the Regent received Weesenmayer. The audience, which lasted about half an hour, was dramatic in the extreme. The Regent began by taxing the SS troops and the Gestapo with the innumerable crimes and atrocities that they had committed throughout the land; according to authentic reports, they were treating Hungary like enemy territory, robbing and looting everywhere. Hitler had definitely promised him to support the Hungarian army in defending the country's frontiers, but, Horthy said, that promise had not been kept. Consequently the Hungarian army had suffered heavy losses everywhere, at Voronezh as well as later in Transylvania, at Arad and Debrecen, and a great part of Hungarian territory was then in Russian hands. At the same time the Germans had encouraged with money and promises the denationalized Hungarian Nazi parties, although knowing full well that he, Horthy, would never permit them to get the upper hand. Only a few days previously General Szilard Bakay, the commander of the Budapest army corps, had been kidnapped from his own car.

For all those reasons, the Regent said, he had decided not to continue the fight but to sue for an armistice, but unlike the Germans, he kept his promises and was accordingly informing them of the fact.

After his announcement the Regent indignantly accused his visitor of having trapped his son in dastardly fashion. He threw onto the table the clip of empty cartridges which had been fired at Nicky. "There is the proof," he shouted, "that your people have killed my fourth and last child!"

Weesenmayer feigned surprise. He declared that he had nothing to do with the attempt against young Nicholas Horthy; it was Winkelmann, the SS general, who was responsible. Having thus turned the matter into a simple question of competence, he proceeded to try to dissuade the Regent from carrying out his decision. All Weesenmayer's efforts in this direction proved unavailing, but he did get Horthy to consent to receive the German ambassador Rudolf Rahn who had arrived as Hitler's special envoy, bringing a message for Horthy, and who was to present himself within a few minutes. Soon afterwards Rahn arrived. His mission proved to be to try to improve relations between the Regent and Hitler.

Horthy replied that this was quite impossible and that he had nothing to discuss with Hitler. As soon as Rahn had left the room, Horthy personally telephoned instructions to the waiting staff of the wireless station to broadcast his proclamation.

During that time—simultaneously, that is, with the Weesenmayer interview—the Hungarian foreign minister, Gustav Hennyey, in another part of the royal palace, was communicating Horthy's decision to the Swedish and Turkish ministers and asking them to forward the request for an armistice to the Allied powers.

He sent special envoys to the commander of the advancing Russian troops. At the same time he telegraphed to the Hungarian diplomatic representatives abroad.

Various mistaken rumors have been circulated concerning the genesis of the proclamation. The truth is that it was drawn up by Horthy himself in conjunction with Julius Ambrózy, the head of his civilian chancery. It had been ready for some days, but no one outside themselves, not even the premier, had known about it.

Unfortunately the countermeasures—or, possibly, defective organization—prevented the Regent's move from developing into a comprehensive national movement. No military preparations had been made for it. There is no better indication of the situation in which Horthy was placed at this juncture than the manner in which the enterprise was conducted. He had to take this momentous step without previously consulting or even informing his government and the military high command. The real Hungary had ceased to exist.

I shall say no more about those days, interesting though they were, because I had no personal part in them. I shall only mention that the royal palace was put in a state of defense on the assumption that two Hungarian divisions were on their way towards Budapest. The Germans, however, intercepted them so that they never arrived, and soon German armored cars and batteries were drawn up all around Buda Hill. Weesenmayer called on the Regent, explained the situation to him, and told him that unless he surrendered the royal palace would be shelled to pieces a few hours later and the bodyguard killed to the last man. Thereupon the Regent, in order to avoid unnecessary bloodshed, ordered all resistance to cease. Andrew, my son in the bodyguard, who was in an advanced machine gun post nevertheless continued, with a few of his men, to fire on the advancing Germans, and he was afterwards accused of having caused the death of three of them. Of the members of the bodyguard only two were arrested and deported —the commandant, General Charles Lazar, and my son. They were taken first to Vienna and later to Mauthausen.

On the next day, October 16, the Regent himself was carried off. He was unable to keep his vow to remain at his post to the end. Hungary was completely delivered over to her fate, at the mercy, successively, of Germans, Hungarian Nazis, Russians, and Communists. The German invasion of March 19 was the logical consummation of that destiny which the dictated Peace of Trianon, twenty-five years before, had allotted to Hungary. October 16 meant only the end of Horthy's personal regime. He had tried to hold out after his country's fall in the hope of salvaging what he could of the wreck. It would have been better had he and his country fallen together.

Horthy's regime! How it has been abused and attacked! What a campaign of slander is directed against it even now in the countries calling themselves Peoples Republics! He has been called a dictator, a bloodthirsty sadist, an antisocial autocrat and oppressor. None of these charges is true. Horthy was no dictator, only a restorer of order and authority. It was he who gave liberty back to our people after the Communist terror of 1918 and the ensuing Rumanian occupation. Neither before and certainly not since, under the present regime, have so many social and welfare institutions been created as were during that quarter of a century. After the defeat of Communist rule, there came, certainly a judgment of the people—the vengeance of the incensed masses is not always just or equitable—and the procedure taken against the criminals was very mild indeed. But what happened then was not a thousandth part of what is being done today: a few hundred victims, compared with hundreds of thousands.

There has hardly been a period in the thousand years of our history in which our country developed so vigorously, and labored and created with such rich results, as in the course of the twenty-five years under Horthy. I am far from asserting that all of this should be set down to Horthy's credit. It is owing rather to the immense recuperative powers of the Magyar people. But it was under his rule that the nation found the means, the possibilities, the tranquillity, the self-confidence, and the faith necessary for such a regeneration. Of his fellow workers it is in the first place to Count Stephen Bethlen that credit is due.

Trianon deliberately and intentionally deprived Hungary of the conditions of existence. And what happened? Hungarian agriculture and industries flourished as never before. Hungarian currency was one of the most stable. And what of our achievements in the fields of art, music, and the sciences? We had during this period musicians such as Béla Bartók, Zoltán Kodály, Ernst Dohnányi, Franz Lehár; [1] we had Nobel Prize winners; our medical faculty and hospitals could vie with the best in Europe. I might mention also our book shops, with their array of foreign works, and our plays, which were welcomed on so many foreign stages. Then, too, at the Berlin Olympics Hungary, with her ten million population, took her place after America and Germany, with their hundred millions. Nor need we feel ashamed of our welfare and humanitarian institutions: the Beveridge Plan was largely realized in Hungary before the Second World War.

Of all the successor states of the Austro-Hungarian Monarchy, Hungary alone was sentenced to death. We were forced to undergo

[1] Béla Bartók, 1881–1945, first gained prominence with his nationalistic Kossuth symphony (1903). In 1905 he and Zoltán Kodály began collecting Magyar, Slovakian, Rumanian, and Transylvanian folk tunes. Subsequently Bartók wrote theatrical as well as musical pieces, and his compositions, which were written in a bold, contrapuntal style, included many works for the piano, which he played on concert tours. Bartók moved to the United States in 1940, and from then until his death he transcribed Yugoslav folk tunes under a commission from Columbia University.

Zoltán Kodály, 1882–, was a professor of composition at the Budapest Royal Academy after 1907. His musical compositions include operas, choruses, and various orchestral pieces. One of his best-known works is the "Psalmus Hungaricus" for chorus and orchestra.

Ernst Dohnányi, 1877–, is a composer, pianist, and conductor. He was director of the Budapest Royal Academy, later a permanent conductor of the Budapest Philharmonic Orchestra, and then musical director of the Hungarian Broadcasting Corporation. He composed operas and piano and orchestral pieces, among which is the orchestral suite Ruralia Hungaria.

Franz Lehár, 1870–1948, began his musical career as a band conductor in the Austro-Hungarian army. After leaving military service he settled down in Vienna and wrote operettas, and he is remembered, of course, for The Merry Widow (1905).

the harshest conditions. We had no support from any quarter. Each of our neighbors was, alone, stronger than we, and they combined against us in the Little Entente. The great powers of the West lavished on them material, moral, and military assistance. My sole request would be that those who visited the Danubian states before the war should bear witness to what they saw in Hungary and in the neighboring countries, and say whether Budapest did not compare favorably, in the matter of progress and civilization with Bucharest or Belgrade, or even with such cities of ancient culture as Vienna and Prague.

Tragic as was the close of Nicholas Horthy's rule, in the eyes of the Hungarian people he will always remain one of the country's great sons. His personal qualities, his high character and chivalrous disposition, the purity of his motives, his unquestionable good will and complete devotion to Hungary and its people, will decide his place in our history. Very few Hungarian statesmen have had success as their portion. It is the fallen heroes, the Zrinyis,[2] Rákoczy, Széchényi, and Kossuth, Stephen Tisza, and the two Telekis, who remain forever enshrined in the imagination of the people. Nicholas Horthy deserves to be remembered as they are remembered, and so it will be if ever there is a Hungary again. I for my part will remain faithful to him, in love and loyalty, as long as I live.

That faults were committed no one wishes to deny. But to see and harp on these alone is neither right nor honest. Those who sit in judgment on a country, its leadership, and its life should not listen only to that country's enemies, to the hostile Coriola-

[2] The Zrinyis were a noble Hungarian family of Croatian origin. Nicholas Zrinyi, 1508–66, fought in the defense of Vienna (1529). In 1542 he was appointed viceroy of Croatia. When Suleiman the Magnificent resumed warfare against the Habsburgs in 1566, Nicholas Zrinyi commanded the Hungarian forces that held up the Turkish army at Szigetvar, both Suleiman and Nicholas dying during the action there. His great-grandson, Nicholas Zrinyi, 1616–64, also distinguished himself fighting against the Turks. He was recognized as the leader of the Hungarians, and he was among the first to write poems and prose literary works in the Hungarian Zrinyi was the maternal grandfather of Francis II Ráckoczy, Hungary's national Zrinyi was the maternal grandfather of Francis II Rackoczy, Hungary's national hero.

nuses, but to the people themselves. And the judgment of the Hungarian people was, to my certain knowledge, different and despite all is different to this day from that voiced by our old enemies and the new renegades who, whether they know it or not, helped by their judgment to drive our country into the arms of the Nazis as they became afterwards the pathfinders and camp followers of Bolshevism.

After my flight, my wife, daughter-in-law, and little grandchild were the guests of the Regent and Madame Horthy. I shall never be able to thank them enough for their tenderness and helpfulness. But the arrangement was anything but pleasing to the Germans, and Béla Miklos, head of the military chancery, and Gabriel Gerloczy, the first adjutant, made constant efforts to bring it to an end. A few weeks before October 15 the situation became so precarious, as to make it seem quite possible that fighting would take place near the royal palace. In any case it seemed doubtful whether the Regent would be able to protect my family much longer. We therefore decided that my wife should join me at the Turkish legation. Notwithstanding the increased burden which this imposed on my host and his wife, they willingly consented and Madame Kececi went to fetch my wife in person. She even let us bring to the legation all those personal effects which we had salvaged from the premier's residence, from our own home, and from the royal palace.

It was a great day when my wife arrived, and we celebrated a joyous reunion. She had had a wearing time, too, with consuming anxiety for me and our sons. There never was woman more constant in her duty, more lovingly devoted to her husband, her family, and her friends. Alas, our time together was destined to be short.

TWENTY

ARROW CROSS RULE IN HUNGARY

⟨[ON October 16, 1944, Francis Szálasi's Arrow Cross party took power in Hungary. Their rule was worse than the German domination in that it was baser and more immoral. Szálasi was a madman; his followers were the dregs of the people. The Germans knew this. They gained nothing by Szálasi's accession to power. Their adoption of him was simply an action of revenge against Hungary. By then, however, there was no longer a nation for his leading. No one at that stage could have disentangled the hopelessly raveled reins and least of all Szálasi. Szálasi believed that it was the Germans whom he had to reckon with, accommodate himself to, and share the power with. That belief was an illusion, however, for there soon came into being another power in the country

—that of the advancing Russian hosts, who had planted their feet in Hungarian soil in late September.

At last, however, Szálasi the man had attained his long-felt ambition. He was the dictator and the "national leader"—or hoped that he was. In actual fact he remained what he had always been, a crack-brained, miserable puppet. To be a dictator without force or power, without obedient or mesmerized masses to follow, without real aim or faith, is to go through the laughable antics of a circus clown. Szálasi thought that provided he subscribed to all of Germany's demands in the matter of military assistance, the surrender of the country's assets, the sacrifice of the Jews, and the complete adoption of the National Socialist ideology, he would be master in the rest of his house. That was another illusion, however, for by that time the Germans had only one policy towards Hungary: to strip her bare. That was a realistic policy for them, in the execution of which most of Szálasi's followers joined with relish.

It seems quite evident that Szálasi tried to make a stand against the Germans, not by resisting their comprehensive demands for the assets of the nation, but by attempting to impose his own will and system in a restricted field of domestic affairs. He was, of course, completely unsuccessful in his power struggle with the Germans, who did not take Szálasi seriously. Another factor in his inability to assume control was that his own retinue was composed of picked and consummate ruffians capable of anything—except maintaining order in a country. Hungary had seen revolutionary regimes before and will see them again; but what makes Szálasi's administration so unique is that his so-called ministers, not only lacked any moral standing whatever in their public and their private lives, but they were on so low an intellectual level that it would have been hard to find one among them fit in the old days to fill the post of village notary.

Those ministers issued orders fully aware that they would never be carried out or obeyed. They were forced to recognize that not one man in the whole country with any claim to honesty, decency, or national feeling stood behind them. They resorted, therefore, to the habitual expedient of all revolutions—they pressed into their service the rabble and the misguided youth of the country. Naturally only a small proportion of the young people swallowed the bait—the kind who were pleased to be allowed at fourteen to exchange their lesson books for submachine guns and hand grenades. The streets, I am told, were a disgusting sight, with those youngsters employing the terrorist methods which are the usual adjuncts of dictatorships: they stood at the street corners, demanded to see the papers of passers-by, and made arrests and domiciliary visits. In short those young "guardians of order" did everything possible to render the existing chaos more complete. Szálasi's appeal to the nation's youth to take up arms was a complete failure, however, and nine tenths of the conscripted deserted. A certain percentage of the regular army did rally to him, but not the picked, seasoned formations such as Stephen Náday's and Louis Veress' army corps.

The arrests of "reactionaries" went on apace. Practically no decent and respectable person left in the country was safe from persecution. The peasantry remained quite aloof from Szálasi's movement, however, in spite of promises of land distribution. The entire Roman Catholic clergy, the Roman Catholic Church organs, and the Roman Catholic youth ranged themselves against the regime. Szálasi was opposed also by the industrial workers, except for a few who wanted to better their positions at all costs. In fact, it was conclusively proved that Szálasi's adaptation of Nazism, the so-called Arrow Cross movement, had no roots whatever in Hungary. It consisted solely of a disreputable gang of leaders without faith or honor and of the rabble.

The Jews were, naturally, the first and most important target. In this respect the new regime took over the role of the Germans, except that, instead of systematic extermination, desultory and indiscriminate persecution took place. It was a period of private despicable enterprises, of atrocities inspired by individual revenge. Until then the Jews of Budapest had been almost immune. Now it was their turn to suffer. The only brake, the presence of the Regent, had been removed; there was no longer anyone who could offer institutional protection. It is good to know that there were many honest people who in individual cases assisted the hunted and gave them secret shelter at the risk of their own lives. Special mention should be made, in this connection, of the Red Cross Society and the Swedish legation. Tens of thousands may be said to owe their escape to members of those bodies.

The only saving circumstance in those days was that the general disorganization of the Arrow Cross regime made it incapable of carrying any undertaking to its logical conclusion. The Germans naturally aided in all that was being done, but by that time the Germans had more important problems to face. They were at their last gasp, and serious symptoms of disintegration were becoming apparent. It must, in justice, be said, however, that the decline was more in evidence among the German leaders than among the troops, who still preserved an appearance of discipline and fought creditably. The German soldier remained to the last worthy of his reputation and his traditions; it was the Nazi leadership which broke down.

My situation at the Turkish legation meanwhile became more difficult. The Turkish minister received repeated demands to give me up, and the summonses grew increasingly peremptory as the relations between Germany and Turkey became more strained. The Germans also repeated to me their suggestion that I should place myself under their protection, and again I refused.

Finally, however, on November 18, 1944, Gabriel Kemény, the Hungarian foreign minister invited the Turkish minister to call on him and presented him upon his arrival with an ultimatum: Unless I left the legation by 4 P.M. on November 19, the police would enter it and take me out of it. When he returned to the legation, M. Kececi told me about the ultimatum, and he said that he did not feel able to resist an attempted entry by the police. He had consulted his staff and felt that the responsibility of making such a crisis in Hungaro-Turkish relations and placing his

legation in so difficult a situation was greater than he could assume
without instructions. The shortage of time and technical difficulties made it impossible for him to consult his government. I
made up my mind, therefore, to leave the legation the next day.

After making my decision, I thanked my hosts for the gracious
hospitality that I had enjoyed for eight months, and I bade them
farewell and I said good-by, too, to the liberty that had been
granted me in the sanctuary of the legation. I should perhaps have
said good-by to life as well, but that thought did not occur to
me at the moment. I could not bear to think of any future when
I had to bid farewell to my family—to my poor, long-suffering
wife, to those few relatives who were able to enter the legation,
and in my mind to those who were unable to come and see me. Of
my three sons I knew nothing but that the youngest had been
carried off by the Germans to an unknown destination.

I then packed two trunks and arranged my papers, committing
the most important ones to the care of the Turkish minister. I
earnestly entreated M. Kececi to assist and protect my poor wife.

The next day, November 19, at four in the afternoon, a whole
train of automobiles filled with Hungarian and German detectives,
as well as two armored cars manned by soldiers, drew up outside
the gate. A last handshake with the assembled company, a last
embrace, and I was on my way to the car, escorted by an armed
guard. My wife ran after us, broke through the cordon, and tore
open the door of the car I was sitting in to give me a last look.

TWENTY-ONE

FROM PRISON TO FREEDOM

¶I WAS TAKEN first to the ministry of the interior. There I had to wait for several hours in the care of guards with fixed bayonets. No one spoke to me in all that time. Finally, a police officer came, introduced himself as Colonel Orendi, and told me that I was in his charge. He gave me the customary warnings—not to attempt to escape and not to contact anyone because I knew the consequences of such behavior. Then we left the ministry and got into an automobile with drawn blinds that drove us away.

Our car stopped after a while in front of a building that I later found out was the Margitkörut prison. I was taken from floor to floor, but finally I was put into a cell and the door was locked behind me, the first of the many prison doors that I was to pass through until I was finally released from imprisonment by the Americans six months later on the island of Capri.

The cell was roomy enough, containing a paillasse and a wash basin, and a lamp hung from the ceiling. I did what I think all men do in similar circumstances—I threw myself on the bed and waited for something to happen. Like other men, too, I did not brood on deep problems, nor even on immediate possibilities; my thoughts wandered, and I waited for events to happen.

It must have been nine or ten in the evening when the door opened. Armed gendarmes and prison guards entered and ordered me to follow them. I was led into a larger room where a lieutenant of police named Demetrovics was waiting for me; with him there were two more subalterns and an NCO. Demetrovics ordered me to be searched, and I had to undress. When I was in my drawers only, I was made to sit down, although it was the end of November, the room was unheated, and the temperature in Budapest was well below zero. Demetrovics told me that no written record would be made of my deposition and that I could take it for granted that I should not leave the building alive. He told me that the same fate awaited my family, all my relations, and the whole liberal, Jew-hireling, aristocratic bunch. During this tirade Demetrovics kept swishing a riding crop in front of my face, and several times I thought that he would hit me; but at the last moment he always stepped back and then, nervously, drank from a glass of wine. Then he began a long, confused criticism of my activities. He was most offended when I refused a glass of wine that he offered me, and he smashed the glass on the floor. Finally, he gave me permission to dress, but, of course, my tie, collar, shoelaces, and similar dangerous objects were taken away, together with the contents of my pockets.

When I returned to my cell, I threw myself on the bed. I wanted to sleep, but it was impossible, partly because of the glare of the lamp, which could be switched off only from outside (and this the guards refused to do), and partly because of the bedbugs. The next day my door never opened once. On the following morning a German major came into my cell. He did not speak to me, but he looked around, told the guards to give me food and water for drinking and washing, and left two SS guards in front of my cell. At least in front of my cell some sort of Hungarian-German collaboration was achieved: I was guarded by two Hungarian gendarmes and two SS guards. But the Hungarian prison guards immediately became my bodyguards to a certain extent, and they did everything in their power to ease things for me. One of them was a gigantic Transylvanian named Erdey. He happened to be on duty when the German major and the SS came to visit me. The prison guard was already opening the cell when Erdey stopped him and said that he had orders from Colonel Orendi that no one was to enter my cell without the colonel's direct permission. Without the permission of Colonel Orendi, Erdey said, he would not open the door for God Almighty himself, and the Germans did wait for the colonel's permission. Later Erdey told me that he had been bluffing about the necessity for permission because he wanted to gain time and let his superiors know the Germans were there. He was afraid the Germans had come to take me away and finish me off somewhere on their own.

I spent two weeks in the Margitkörut prison. Nobody visited me. Only once Lieutenant Demetrovics came to tell me that all my "accomplices," Andrew Bajcsy-Zsilinszky, Lieutenant General John Kiss, and the whole "gang of rebels," were in their hands. He himself had questioned them, Demetrovics told me, and he could assure me that they had confessed everything. From the big room on the other side of the corridor I often heard the sound of pistol shots. Captured deserters were being shot, without either legal trial or formal sentence.

One evening I was told that I was to be moved. After endless confusion and chaos I was pushed onto a crowded truck. I sat on the last bench between two SS and two police guards. In the early morning we arrived at the great modern state prison of Sopronköhida, which was already filled with political prisoners. Prominent personalities against whom no specific charges had yet been made were placed in the fairly modern and clean hospital wing, fifteen to twenty in one big ward. I was in there a few hours. I spoke with Kálmán Kánya, who was gravely ill, and it was a great satisfaction to me to listen to him. Kálmán Töreky, the president of the high court of justice, who was almost completely blind, was also there. Among others I saw Prince Ferdinand Montenuovo; Francis Szombathelyi, the former chief of staff; Michael Arnothy-Jungerth, who had been minister of foreign affairs in the Sztójay cabinet; Gustav Hennyey, who held the same position in the Lakatos cabinet (later Lakatos himself with his wife); William Nagy, once minister of defense, and his brother; Count Maurice Eszterházy; Stephen Antal; many high army officers and younger pilot officers; several priests and some members of the aristocracy; and the person I should have mentioned first, Joseph Mindszenty, afterwards primate of Hungary, the great martyr.

The SS, however, said that they could not guard me properly if I was left with the other prisoners, and they demanded that I be placed in a special cell. I was placed, therefore, in the so-called lunatics' cell. That cell had a double steel door, and everything in the room was made of iron; next to my bed a thick chain was fastened to the floor. Then my life settled into a routine. A special detachment of sixteen SS guards came from Sopron to guard me. The Hungarians were sent away, and I was left under exclusively German supervision. The first SS men were elderly conscripts and a decent enough set. They did not bother much about me except to make sure that I communicated with no one; they apparently had strict orders on this point. Later, however, a detachment of younger men took over under an indescribably beastly officer and NCO, and these guards tried to make my life unpleasant in every way. The commander of the prison was Provost-Marshal Colonel Dominics. He treated me decently and politely. He allowed my lawyer to visit me and occasionally authorized other visits. I was able to receive some parcels and, what made me most happy, the prison doctor—an excellent, humane, and decent person who was completely on our side—visited me daily. The SS then reduced the effect of these privileges by ordering an SS man who understood Hungarian to be in my room whenever the doctor came to see me and by stopping all other visits.

During all this time only one of my fellow prisoners came to visit me. On Christmas night Paul Javor, the actor from the national theater, persuaded the SS guard to let him hand in to me through the cell door a fir branch, a glass of wine, and a slice of ham that had been sent by Maurice Eszterházy. I did not need all this, but I will never forget his kindness.

Otherwise I had no reason to complain. I was simply a prisoner. Perhaps I was treated worse than the others, but as far as my physical needs were concerned I could manage.

The psychological aspect of the situation was different. In spite of all precautions by the prison authorities news trickled through via nonpolitical prisoners who came to clean up and brought fuel and food to us in our cells. One of those orderlies told me one day that other prisoners were lined up in front of my cell door awaiting a medical examination and one of them wished to speak to me. The orderly told me that there were so many men lined up outside that the guard had been taken away and if he left the door open when he left my cell I might get a glimpse, perhaps exchange a word with my friend. The orderly did just that, and I saw Andrew Bajcsy-Zsilinszky standing in the corridor. I stepped out, and he opened his arms in greeting. But at that moment the jailers appeared. Bajcsy-Zsilinszky and the others were marched away, and I was ordered back to my cell. The next day I happened to be in the garden when he was executed in the courtyard, on the other side of a wooden fence.

Sometimes I received letters from my wife. To this day I do not know whether she ever received my answers. She wanted to join me, but I begged her urgently not to do this since I thought she was better off in the Turkish legation.

I got news occasionally from the fronts. In the wards where the others were, there was even a radio, and sometimes a prisoner walking in the garden would throw a piece of paper with some news scribbled on it through my window. I knew that the end of the war was approaching, but I was not optimistic about its outcome: I had lost hope. People say that hope and faith sustain the soul under conditions such as those which were then my fate. This was not so with me. My soul had been broken on March 19; it could not comfort me. I kept my physique and my nerves firm by not thinking at all about my personal future. Perhaps I should be executed, perhaps released. I took things as a soldier at the front does: fatalistically. Call this apathy, call it tranquillity—in any case, I never felt heroic in prison, but neither did I ever feel fear. I was completely indifferent to my own future. I was concerned only with the fate of my country, my people, my family, and my relatives. These thoughts filled the gloomy minutes and hours of my long days and nights, and they gave substance to my existence because I knew and had faith that whatever happened to me I would not, could not, ever deviate from my ideals, my traditions, my true self.

I have some pleasant recollections, too, of Sopronkőhida: of the affection and respect with which—as I could feel from afar—the other prisoners and convicts regarded me. After a time I was allowed to go to church on Sundays. The spacious prison church had two big galleries on either side of the nave. The inmates of the cells, most of whom were also political prisoners, sat downstairs. In one of the galleries sat the prominent personalities kept in the hospital wards—those whom I have named and, of course, many more. After all the others were seated, I was led in and marched, quite alone, to the second gallery. Behind me stood two SS guards with automatic pistols. Then the greatest honor of my life was paid me: When I entered the gallery, the whole congregation stood up and bowed to me. Even the priest, who had just come in, gave me a little bow. I cannot imagine a more sincere, greater, and more dignified homage than this tribute from one prisoner to another. This scene was repeated every Sunday. Kőhida belonged to the diocese of Gyor and its Bishop, Baron William Apor, afterwards to die a martyr's death,[1] sent me two priests to bring me his blessing and friendship.

After Christmas I got no more news from Budapest. I did not know what had happened to my relatives, but I was happy in the belief that no harm could come to my wife, who was in the safest possible place.

On the morning of February 15 the whole hierarchy of the prison officials, led by Colonel Dominics and with a number of Germans among them, filed into my cell. One of them, a young man who called himself a high official of the foreign ministry, told me that Budapest had fallen and that orders had come from high quarters that I was to be moved to the interior of Germany. I was given two hours to pack and prepare. When I left, the whole of the prison hospital was crowded with my fellow inmates and friends. They waved good-bys and called their farewells; I saw tears in many eyes. I could only wave back in silence.

I was taken to the SS headquarters in Sopron, where I had to repack my belongings in two suitcases. I was not allowed to take the rest with me but was promised that it would be sent after me. Then, under the guard of a captain and two NCO's, I traveled by car to Vienna, where we spent the night in a garage. The next morning we continued by train to what I already knew was to be Mauthausen.

At Mauthausen station I was placed on the top of a coal truck. It was evening, and on the road we drove between endless columns of miserable wretches, dragging themselves back to the camp from the stone quarries. We passed several rows of barbed wire, belts of fortified walls, and then the entrance to the camp. I was put down at the waiting room of the central office. At the door stood the colonel commanding the camp with his whole staff. My guards walked up to him and reported. I saw with surprise a strange excitement take hold of the group; they started to whisper and I

[1] Bishop Apor was killed in 1946 by Russian soldiers when he tried to stop them from entering a convent.

heard quite plainly: "Unmöglich! Ganz Mackensen!" I was wearing a long braided leather coat and a high fur cap; we had once presented an outfit like this to Mackensen, and it had become his favorite wear.

Then the commander walked up and said to me: "From now on you are a prisoner (Häftling). Mauthausen is not made to accommodate privileged gentlemen; you had better get used to this." I was led away, dragging my two suitcases, between the long rows of barracks.

That was the first and last time that I saw the notorious giant camp of Mauthausen; for during my whole stay there I was kept in strict isolation, and when I left I was driven out in a closed car. But what I saw at that time of the life in a German concentration camp was enough for one lifetime.

The barrack in which I was kept stood on the highest point of the ground, surrounded by a twenty-foot stone wall, topped by barbed wire in which a live current was passing. At two corners of the compound there were towers with machine guns, searchlights, and guards. All night watchdogs howled in the yard.

The building was clean and orderly. Right and left of the entrance stretched long corridors, each containing sixteen cells. At both ends there was a bath with a shower and other facilities. The rooms of the guards were at the entrance. The basement was less agreeable: on one side was the gas chamber, on the other the crematorium.

I was put in cell number 7. There was a wooden bedstead, a plate, a glass and a spoon, but no table and only a wooden stool to sit on. I was, however, given preferential treatment because I was allowed to ring when I wanted to leave the room to relieve myself; the other prisoners did not enjoy that privilege.

The daily routine started at four o'clock in the morning—to this day I do not understand why that was necessary. Reveille: the lights went on and shortly afterwards the door opened and a prisoner on duty entered and put in the cell a bucket of water, a mop, and a broom and a brush for scrubbing the floor. The prisoner made his bed, scrubbed the floor, and then waited. After another hour or two the door opened again, and the prisoner orderly would take out the cleaning utensils under the eyes of the guard. The door closed; and there was waiting again. Then it opened for the third time; a guard entered and marched the prisoner off to the bath. He was put under a shower, which was usually warm, made his morning toilet, and then was taken back to the cell. At about eight a hand reached into the cell through the Judas hole in the door with a mug of black liquid, called coffee, a piece of quite black bread, which had to last for the whole day, and a tiny cube of tasteless but not rancid ersatz margarine made from coal. At noon, lunch arrived in the same way. It was usually a big plateful of brownish potato soup; very rarely there was bean or cabbage soup. At six in the evening there was a pale brew, called tea, a piece of cheese or marmalade, and once a week a tiny piece of sausage. I do not think the diet had a caloric value of 1,000 a day; but somehow it was enough for me, and although I lost much weight I did not feel hunger. The central heating in the cells worked quite regularly: it was fed by the crematoria. Sometimes in the evenings I was allowed to stretch my legs in the corridor, but in all I went into the courtyard only three times.

I enjoyed one other privilege: unlike any other prisoner I could keep the light on until nine o'clock. Consequently, two prison orderlies had to come into my room every evening to fix the cardboard blackout curtain. To do this they had to bring a ladder, since my window was high up in the wall. Through this operation I kept a sort of connection—my only one—with the outer world. I heard of the war developments and learned with horror what was happening in my country. But the orderlies would not tell me who else was in the building or if there were any Hungarians. Later those two prisoners were unexpectedly changed for others. I do not know what happened to them. Both said they were left-wing Viennese journalists who had been in the camp since the Anschluss.

One evening when I happened to be allowed to walk up and

down the corridor, a group of SS men gathered in the hall and became engaged in lively conversation. To divert attention from themselves they let down the curtain between the corridor and the hall. Suddenly, a voice from one of the cells cried: "Uncle Nicholas! It's I, Nicky Horthy!"

I flattened myself against his door and he told me in great haste that he had been brought there from Vienna. He was near starvation and was treated brutally. We had to be very careful, for if the guards had noticed us we would have been severely punished. But on various occasions I managed to exchange a few words with him in this way. For the rest, the guards were fairly polite and the commandant held an inspection every fortnight. He always asked if I had any wishes, and I always declined to ask any favors with thanks. I was even allowed to use the SS library instead of the prison one, and thus I had the privilege of getting a deeper insight into Nazi literature, which at that time was known to me only through Hitler's *Mein Kampf*. I did not use my prison hours, however, to explore the world of Rosenberg, Goebbels, and others. I preferred to play chess by myself, and I solved problems, studied openings, and constructed new problems on my small pocket chessboard.

One day the commandant proved really human. He discovered that my son Andrew was in the camp, and Andrew was allowed to visit me. I was called into the entrance hall, and there stood my tall, handsome boy, whom I had last seen in the ceremonial uniform of the Hungarian royal guards. Now he was in rags with crosses sewn on them and with his hair clipped high and an inch strip shaved off the middle of it—the symbol of degradation created by the Nazis and constituting their contribution to the world. When my poor son saw how his appearance shocked me, he said that for this occasion he had collected the best rags from his friends and had washed as well as he could in order not to make me sad. We had to talk in the presence of the guard, in snatched half-sentences. Andrew appeared to be fully informed about world events, but he had no news of what we most wanted to know—the fate of his mother or brothers. Later he got permission to visit me a second time.

What happened to Andrew before he came to Mauthausen I heard only later when, after the inmates had been liberated by the Americans, he found me, after a long odyssey, in Capri. Andrew told me then that he had gone on fighting and shooting after the order to cease fire had come. He was taken to the Royal Hotel with Charles Lazar, the commander of the bodyguard, thence he was flown to Vienna and thence to Mauthausen. Lazar was placed in the same building as myself, but my son was thrown in the camp, where there were about 2,000 Hungarians. With him were Rassay and Peyer, the Liberal and Socialist leaders; several other Socialist and Democratic deputies; Count Anthony Sigray, the leader of the Hungarian legitimists; Count Iván Csekonics, president of the Polish Committee; many other magnates; and all kinds of people ranging from high-ranking civil servants to suspected communist workers, Catholic priests, writers and artists. My son—as I heard later from others—helped and assisted these ill and elderly people. By his powerful physique he impressed the guards, and he was most popular among his fellow inmates.

After I was taken away from Mauthausen, an SS man went to Andrew and gave him a few pieces of my underwear that I had had to leave behind. The poor boy thought that I was dead, and he arranged with the prisoners working in the gas chambers to go and watch the corpses that were prepared for the crematorium, believing that he might see my body among them.

From my cell I could observe little. Sometimes at night I heard people talking as they came and went under my windows, and sometimes I caught a few Hungarian words. On occasions the smell of gas through the open window was particularly strong. At that time I did not believe that the horrible human sacrifices were actually being done. I could not conceive them to be possible. Such practices were so alien to my whole being and past that the evidences I saw and heard about could not register in my mind.

Only when on Capri my son told me what he had seen did I realize among what conditions I had been living.

Some time in the first days of April a group of about thirty officers, including several high-ranking SS men, gathered in front of my opened door. I knew from my son that Himmler had visited the camp and given instructions for preparations for it to be evacuated. The commandant spoke to me, and now I recall that he occasionally looked back over his shoulder, as if hesitating whether to continue to talk to me. It was then that my fate was decided, that I should be taken away from Mauthausen.

I was moved on April 15. The almighty master of the barracks, an SS sergeant, told me that I was to pack because I was to leave in an hour. He did not know where I was going. I had very few of my belongings in my cell, enough perhaps to fill an attaché case. My suitcase was in the storeroom, and they fetched it for me. I was given back my watch, a few personal trinkets, my penknife, and even the five napoleons that were sewn into my suit at the Turkish legation and were, of course, found immediately when I was searched. It was one of the great surprises of my life to be reunited with my personal possessions.

A truck covered with a tarpaulin was waiting in the courtyard. In front of it Nicky Horthy and Marshal Badoglio's son Mario were already waiting. Horthy and I, fearing trouble at the last moment if our previous meetings were discovered, feigned not knowing that we had been kept in the same building. We were crowded into the truck with half a dozen SS men and then driven away. At first, not knowing what our fates were to be, we did not dare to talk, but later I turned to the guard next to me and asked if I might talk to my friends. To my surprise, he answered, "Ja, aber leise und nicht viel!" At last after so long a time I was able to talk to my own kind rather than only to SS men or to unknown prisoners.

Horthy had been brought to Mauthausen straight after his capture. He was still wearing the tweed jacket, grey flannels, and suede shoes in which he had been captured and beaten into insensibility, and he looked as immaculate as if he had just left not a foul prison but a first-class tailor. Even his shirt was clean and new looking; when it was being washed, he had to go without one. He had no overcoat, so I gave him one. I had some vitamin tablets and chocolate, and I shared them with him. I even had cigars in prison, which was a great comfort to me. Sometimes I saved them, sometimes I just wasted them. My smoking habit in prison depended on my mood: if I felt that my captivity would last a long time, I hardly dared to smoke; when I felt that I might not live to see the next day, I just smoked away—I could not bear the thought of leaving the cigars to them!

The next morning we arrived at Dachau. We were put in pleasant cells with big windows, spring beds, an armchair, table, hot and cold water in the cell, and separate water closets. All the cells in the two giant barracks that I came to know were so furnished. The barrack was surrounded by gardens where we were taken in groups for exercise. In the corridors there was a continual coming and going: the doors were open. After our recent experiences it was like heaven. The food was good, and we had hardly arrived when the guard asked me if I wanted light or dark beer from the canteen. Since I had no reichsmarks I went into my neighbor's cell, or rather cells because he had a bedroom and living room. Its tenant was Molotov's cousin, Flight Lieutenant Kokorin, and he lent me some money. (If I can ever repay that loan, it will be a sign that the world is again in order.) At first it appeared that I was to be treated exceptionally, for of the many hundred cells only mine was locked. It appears that very strict instructions concerning my care had come with me. But the strict watch lasted for only a few days.

One afternoon a few days later an SS man brought me an invitation to tea that afternoon bearing the name of Frau Schuschnigg. She had enclosed a message that said Léon Blum and a few other people would be at the reception and that they wanted to meet me and she was expecting me to come. I had known Schuschnigg of old, and I accepted the invitation with pleasure. At the recep-

tion I was introduced to Blum and his charming wife, and he told
me about how he had met a group of eight Hungarians a few days
before. Hjalmar Schacht, the erstwhile financial dictator of Germany, and Franz Halder, the former chief of staff of the *Wehrmacht*, were among the guests that I met at the affair. We had tea
and even cognac. I brought some chocolate. This was, indeed, a
different kind of life from that which I had just experienced. I
never had realized that it could be so pleasant to be a prisoner of
the Germans. Léon Blum told me that never in his life had he
been saluted so often or seen so many heels clicked as now during
his prison days.

I met many interesting people in the camp at Dachau. I saw
Blum again, and I thought him a fine Frenchman with an Olym-
pian view of affairs. I did not always like his politics, but he was
a most distinguished and pleasant person. Dr. Martin Niemöller,
the famous anti-Nazi Protestant pastor, was one of the oldest inmates of the camp and in a way its spiritual leader. Fritz Thyssen,
the industrial baron, was there with his wife. He was a grumbling
old gentleman, equally rude to guards and fellow prisoners, who
always wanted to play chess but was a very poor player. His wife
was just the opposite—reserved and quiet, although always wearing fabulously valuable jewelry. Dr. Joseph Müller, a lawyer from
Munich and extremely charming, friendly, and lively man, knew
that his death sentence was kept in the prison office; he had been
a leading personality of the Bavarian Catholic party and an or-
ganizer of the earliest resistance movements in Germany. He reminded me that I had once sent a messenger to him. There were
two Churchills with us—Captain Peter Churchill, of the British
war office, and Lieutenant Colonel Flack Churchill, of the British
army—but they said that they were not relatives of the English
prime minister. The Germans kept them as hostages, however,
and not as ordinary prisoners of war. Fabian von Schlabrendorff,
who later wrote an excellent book, *Generäle gegen Hitler*, was
also an inmate. In addition to the Lieutenant Kokorin whom I
have already mentioned, there were several high Russian gen-

erals and officers, but we had little contact with them. I do not
know for what special reason they were kept with us instead
of the prisoner of war camps with other Russian soldiers. Von
Falkenhausen, once military commander of Belgium, was one of
the pleasantest persons there and an accomplished raconteur. A
very interesting fellow prisoner, whom I should have mentioned
first, was Colonel Sigismund Payne Best, of the British secret
service. Even then he was interested in everything, and he was
everywhere. As the day of liberation approached Best's role became more and more important. He became the head of our group.
There were many other interesting people there, with greater or
smaller pasts and past records. What the future was to bring them,
or us, was still wrapped in ominous darkness.

For days rumors were in the air, including one that said we were
to move again. The advance of the British and American troops
and the German withdrawals accounted, of course, for these
rumors. On April 24 orders came that we were to pack and be
ready for the busses that were to come in the evening to fetch us.
No one knew where we were going. It is an unpleasant feeling to
be taken to prison, but it is almost equally unpleasant to leave one.
As one is removed from prison routine there is the lurking feeling:
"Selten kommt was besseres nach!"

In the late evening we were crowded into two busses. Horthy
and Badoglio were in my group. Only men were taken with this
transport: families, women, and children were supposed to follow
next day. Among my fellow travelers were Halder, Schacht, Kokorin, Richard Schmitz, formerly burgomaster of Vienna and
vice chancellor of Austria, the vicar general of Munich, Alexander
von Falkenhausen, the Polish Count Alexander Zamoisky, and
others. With us also were some inmates of the camp whom we
had not seen before because they were not kept with the "elite."
The first to appear was a skeletonlike figure, clad in rags, completely worn out, with the "convict strip" shaved on his head
—Xavier-Bourbon, Prince of Parma and brother of our Queen
Zita. Then came Prince Leopold of Prussia, the cousin of the

Kaiser Wilhelm, and the Prince of Hesse, the husband of the King of Italy's unfortunate daughter. (He had been a good friend of Hitler's and was pleasantly dining with him before his arrest.) Last, the bishop of Piguet-Clermont, who had been dragged away from Mass. My parcels were again divided between myself, young Horthy, and young Badoglio, who carried them faithfully and even with some pride: they had not so much as a handkerchief of their own. In the cold nights I gave them something to wear. We soon reached Munich; in the pale moonlight it made a ghastly impression. Like all the other German towns, it had become a heap of ruins, a hive of misery. This was where the "movement" had set out from: they had certainly achieved the realization of its leitmotiv of Gleichschaltung.

We learned that we were to be taken to Innsbruck and thence to a resort in the Dolomites. In due course we arrived at Innsbruck, and in the early morning hours stopped beyond the town at a barracks labeled "Polizeistelle-Innsbruck." We were not allowed to get out of the busses; we were waiting for further orders. Sausages were handed out and then again we waited, waited. At last towards dusk we were told to get out of the busses, and we were led to a very primitive shed with double wooden bedsteads. Here I met eight countrymen of mine for whom this place was their fourteenth camp since their abduction on October 16, 1944. Among those I knew were General Géza Igmandi-Hegyesi, Baron Peter Schell, who before October 15 was minister of the interior for a few days, and Andrew Hlatky, who had taken the Regent's declaration to the radio station on October 15. We rejoiced greatly to see each other again, and we exchanged stories about our experiences. They were much better informed than I because, in spite of all their adventures, they had kept together all the time and could maintain contacts with other people.

The next day the other members of the party arrived. The Schuschniggs, the Blums, and with them a whole party of women, young girls, boys, and even some quite small children. This was the Stauffenberg clan—more than a hundred relatives of the Count Stauffenberg who had made the bomb attempt on the life of Hitler. All who could in any way be connected with the attempt had been executed; the rest were dragged about as hostages.

The next evening the busses and trucks lined up again. We were told only that we were going towards the Brenner. As we approached our destination, Hlatky, with affected seriousness, gave me the draft of a telegram, which, by custom, I was supposed to send to Hitler from the frontier. It started in this way: "Your Excellency, as I cross the frontier of Germany at the historic Brenner Pass, I recall my unforgettable experiences, etc. . . . It is my deepest conviction that the New Order, with which I had the honor of getting acquainted, proves the prophetic words of Your Excellency that it would bring about the end of the world conflagration, end in total victory, and lay the basis for a new Europe. . . . May I assure you on behalf of myself and my friends that we shall never forget our experiences. . . ." The telegram was so worded that it would not matter even if it fell into the hands of the SS men. The whole company roared with laughter and many made translations of it which they saved for themselves.

At the Brenner Pass there was great confusion. Everywhere there were signs of bombing. We stopped in a small village. We struck up a conversation with a Tyrolean border guard, and one of us told him that Schuschnigg was in the car in front of us. He could not believe it; they all thought that Schuschnigg had been long dead. When the guard heard he was still alive, he went livid with rage that his chancellor was being dragged as a prisoner through HIS Tyrol. He ran back to his house near-by and returned with a small parcel of bacon which he asked us to give to the Schuschniggs. Next morning, when we caught up with the advance party at Niederdorf, we duly delivered the parcel.

I think that it was there in Niederdorf (Villa Bassa) that our fate was to have been sealed. The situation was that the "enemy" was approaching from all sides. In the mountains strong Italian partisan units had started to show themselves. For some time a German military car, driven by a German officer, followed us everywhere. Later we learned that he had been sent by the partisans. He contacted the Italians in our group and tried to arrange our liberation. We were made to camp on the highway, some two miles from the village, and were not allowed to go into the village. It was here that we discovered among the German trucks a strangely shaped, sturdy vehicle, continually guarded by an SS man with an automatic pistol. The German officers among us told us that it was a mobile gas chamber. We heard rumors that we were being kept outside the village to be disposed of but that there were not enough soldiers to carry out the executions. Later, Colonel Best got hold of the written orders issued to our German commander, a man called Stiller, which were that, if there was any danger that we might fall into enemy hands, he was to see to it at all costs that we should not do so alive.

We thereupon simply decided to go down to the village and camp there. This plan was carried out without opposition, and we found accommodation in the town hall and in private houses. We were even given some food. One cannot describe the friendliness and helpfulness of the local population. We heard later that during the night the Italian partisans came down quite close to the village and guarded our dreams. We had among us General Pepino Garibaldi, and he maintained liaison with the partisans.

It was then that news arrived that Hitler had died "in the heroic defense of Berlin." It was interesting to watch the total indifference with which people took this news—because it came from the SS, so we could not be sure, but also because we were almost completely apathetic by then anyway. The SS men seemed the least shocked. I remember now that I wondered then whether that had any significant meaning. Yes, if Hitler's death had happened eighteen months or a year earlier, many things would have gone differently. The fate in store for the German people might have been lightened; we might have been saved. But at the time when it did happen, Hitler's death was an episode of no importance. It is almost ignominious that he, too, should be numbered among the war's ten million dead. His death solved nothing. He should not have been born.

On April 29, a Sunday, there were almost revolutionary symptoms in the village. A Tyrolean committee was elected, and even we, prisoners, began to organize. The Italians appeared, resplendent in their generals' and colonels' uniforms, with red handkerchiefs round their necks. The SS men let us do as we liked.

A day or two later the real change came, when the Wehrmacht took us over from the SS men. We were not free, but we felt safe. We were taken to a big Kurhaus in a place called Praggs, near the Woldsee, 1,500 meters above sea level. There we were given decent beds in decent rooms, but the hotel had not been heated for some years and the central heating did not even work, so that the temperature sank below zero in our rooms. The food, too, was of wartime quality, but all that did not matter. The commanding officer of the Wehrmacht troops, Major Alwenzleben, who was an officer of the old school, correct from head to heel, at once got in touch with the Allied commanders, told them of our presence, and informed us that we were entirely free. If we wished, we could go away, but he thought it better if we waited until the Allied troops took us over. In the evening we enjoyed ourselves; Captain Churchill played the piano and the young people danced.

May 1. Apparently the war was over. I experienced its end there, on a peak of the Dolomites, with my Hungarian companions and those many foreigners. One felt as though time had stopped and some great vacuum surrounded us—the end of war's feverish excitement. Life had a meaning when I stood on the bridge of my country's ship and fought against fate. Even that long year which I had spent in one kind of imprisonment or another was life of a sort. But what was going to come afterwards I did not know, I could not understand, I did not feel. The past was gone forever. Never was the future of man and of humanity covered by clouds so dense as those at the war's end. All one could do is live in the past, in memory, and in the future, in hope. He who lives only for the day is a beast, not a man. He has no past and does not trouble with the future.

The Tyroleans showered kindnesses on us. They brought us food, clothes, cooking utensils, everything they could think of. The district commander called on us and asked us to consider ourselves the guests of the Tyrol.

Every morning we went to Mass in the little chapel near-by. We Hungarians and Schuschnigg were the most regular attenders. The bishop of Clermont planned to celebrate Mass there in the near future, and Schuschnigg and I were going to serve. We left, however, before that arrangement could be concluded.

Two Italian partisans came to take young Kokorin away, saying that their movement, too, was Communist. Kokorin thanked them very kindly, but did not avail himself of their offer.

We learned of the conclusion of the armistice from leaflets dropped on the orders of Field Marshal Alexander. On May 4, American troops, accompanied by Italian partisans, came into the hotel courtyard. The American troops looked fine. The next day I watched a parade; the behavior of the rank and file—ordinarily so casual—was exceptional. The Americans were very obliging towards us. We were sorry for Major Alwenzleben, whom they took off as a prisoner of war.

With the Americans arrived the spring and also the newspapers. Later, on May 9, the Stars and Stripes had a paragraph about me and my companions. The radio, too, reported our rescue. Would my dear ones read or hear of my deliverance, and where would the news reach them? An American general appeared on May 7 and told us that we were to be taken next day by car to Verona and thence by air to Naples, where further arrangements for us would be made. The village filled with American journalists and photographers; we had become interesting for a moment. Lieutenant General L. T. Gerow then called us together and informed us that we were completely free, that we could go where we wanted to, but he advised us to accept the invitation of the American command, because otherwise he could not guarantee our safety etcetera. He was as nice as could be and spoke in the friendliest way, but suddenly we felt that we were exchanging one prison for another. Certainly we were not yet free men, but the enormous change was that our fate was no longer in the hands of wild beasts but of decent, humane human beings.

Some two hundred of us were taken in jeeps, in two convoys, to Verona, next day to Naples by air, and then in a small destroyer to Anacapri on the island of Capri, where we were quartered in the admirable Eden Paradise Hotel. We were not allowed to leave the hotel grounds, but we were well treated. We got slightly less than GI rations, but even that was too much for us after the fare that we had been having, except for Igmandi-Hegyesy and Nicky Horthy, who regularly asked for second helpings. The restrictions were progressively lifted: we were allowed to go to church and were taken down in jeeps to bathe.

I did not avail myself of those favors because I was shocked to the core by the reception accorded to us. No one ill-treated me, and all the Americans were impeccably polite to me. But they were also entirely indifferent, which hurt me more than rudeness, not because I claimed more as a man, but because I felt that that indifference was not towards me alone but also towards my country, which had fallen with me. My Western hosts did not know what Hungary had been like during the war, what its struggles and sufferings had been, what my aims and motives had been, why I had become a prey and prisoner of the Germans. My Western captors probably thought that I was some disgraced Quisling from a satellite country—if they thought about me and Hungary at all. When I tried to explain to anyone my country's fate and history, I began to see myself that it was difficult to understand. But I met there some Irishmen who understood our situation at once. The Irishmen had voluntarily enlisted in the British royal air force, but they cursed the English horribly and drank repeatedly to Irish freedom. Yes, they said, of course, their country was nonbelligerent; yes, they hated the English; but it was natural that they should enlist under the English flag to fight Nazism. How many poor Magyar lads had felt the same sort of problem and had responded to it in the same way. They hated the Germans, but they thought that it was still better, while the fight was going on against Russia, if they fought the Russians under the German flag. None of the Irishmen were politicians but they understood my policy at once and Hungary's position between the German and the Russian millstones. Many an English and American politician and journalist was never able to grasp these things as those Irish boys did.

With deep consternation I saw that as warfare was becoming mechanized, a parallel process had taken place in politics. Politics, too, had become rationalized and mechanized, and it had adopted the leitmotivs of war. In war the man who fights with me is my friend, he who fights against me is my enemy, and so is he even who remains neutral in my life and death struggle. That is all right: it is simple and intelligible. But in politics it is not so. In politics there are no comrades in arms; my political ally is he whose aims are the same as mine. If the postwar aims of my fellow fighter are different from my own, he is not an ally or a friend anymore, but an enemy more dangerous than the beaten foe because he hides within himself the seeds of inevitable new conflict. I saw and felt all this, and I inferred the dangerous prospects inherent in the actual situation from the reception given me in Capri and from the little news that I gathered from papers or the radio.

I had never been so embittered, depressed, and hopeless in my prisons as I was then. For the first time I felt and I realized that my country had really lost the war, that it was all over with us. And I sadly saw that the Second World War had had one great martyr—Poland; one great hero—England; one great victor—America. But all that was to be of no avail. The profits were being cashed all the same by Russia, and that meant suffering, torment, destruction for hundreds and hundreds of millions.

The Allied Headquarters was at Caserta, and an English captain, the head of the Hungarian section there, came over to examine me. He knew the Hungarian situation fairly well, but he understood it not at all. It was an interesting experience for me to see how completely the anti-German propaganda had permeated this young and not unintelligent man, who had so absorbed it that he was now beginning to discover, in his own English people, all the faults of which Nazism was accused—imperialism, nationalism, racial discrimination, capitalistic feudalism, and so on. But he did not take the simple old English line that *si duo faciunt idem non est idem*, which nonetheless is a great and profound truth; he began to blame the British Empire for these sins and to fight against them. This surprised me; I thought that it indicated troubled times to come. I was also questioned by a Chicago lawyer with the rank of general. He began by saying that both London and Washington clearly understood what my role had been, but his orders were to keep me under American supervision. The same applied to Schuschnigg, whose position was like mine. That American officer told me that he had not been told why we were treated as we were, but he supposed it was because both our countries were under Russian occupation. He very obligingly promised to make inquiries about my son Andrew, whom I had left in Mauthausen, and to try and get some news of my wife from the Allied mission in Budapest.

Soon after this the Allies began to pick out the Germans from among us. Presently they put the whole Stauffenberg clan into airplanes and sent them home. Those women and children were simple, likable, very sad, and very hopeless Germans.

Soon only a few of us were left; it was not worth keeping the big hotel open for us. They moved us Hungarians, with a few Danes and Norwegians, into a smaller hotel, the Bella Vista. From its terrace we could watch every evening the setting sun going down behind Ischia, leaving behind it a glory of purple, silver, and azure. We stood there, the vanishing sons of a vanishing world. Within us there still shone some reflected radiance from that world, but dark night was coming into which all would be swallowed up. True, dawn would come, too, but a cold and hard one. It called man to work; but it also parched and burned, it sucked up the dew, it would not brook tears.

But my tears, when I learned that my poor, beloved wife had perished, struck by a German shell, nothing, nothing in life will ever dry. Only with sundown of my life will they pass away. It happened February 7. Two small dugouts had been constructed in the courtyard of the Turkish legation. They had been made for eight or ten persons; perhaps fifty were crowded into them. My wife went out to get a breath of air. The Turkish minister was standing beside her. Suddenly she said to him, "Je suis touchée." She walked towards the dugout door, collapsed on the stairs, and died, without pain.

M. Kececi wrote me the details. She had been the life and soul of the besieged party, strengthening them all by her fanatical courage and sustaining their spirits by her faith. When a burning airplane crashed on the legation, with frightful explosions and flames, she was the first to penetrate to the cellar to help those who had taken refuge there. At the time that she was herself hit, Russian troops guarded the legation. They fetched a Russian doctor, who could only confirm that she was dead. A priest rendered the last offices, and then they buried her there in the legation courtyard, in an improvised plank coffin, with a simple cross of rough wood at her head.

Such was her fate—the most loyal, the kindest, the noblest wife and mother.

She was still on her bier, poor creature, when the Russian colonel who commanded the guard appeared and demanded to be given all effects belonging to the dead woman and to myself which were in the Turkish legation. He had orders to take them over. The minister complied but made the Russians sign a statement that they were taking over our effects "sous titre de protection." The paper also stated the circumstances of my wife's death. The original and a copy of it still exists.

I rambled about Anacapri. I roamed, with my naked soul, on those naked rocks from dawn to dusk. Everything had become aimless, purposeless, and I knew that all my life would be so, unless the one miracle happened.

People are so good and kind, however. Those on the island overwhelmed us with affection and friendliness—the few families we knew there, but also the Americans, and most of all our fellow Hungarians.

The authorities took away from the Bella Vista our Danish and Norwegian companions. By that time we Hungarians, Schuschnigg and his family, and old Schmitz, the former burgomaster of Vienna, were the only internees left on the island of Capri. Schuschnigg and his family were left in a little villa in Anacapri, but the rest of us were housed in a larger villa in Capri. We cooked for ourselves from the ample American rations. Our other small needs were also taken care of—for example, we got a little money from the Allied headquarters in Rome, enough to buy an occasional glass of wine for our friends.

One August evening the lieutenant colonel who was commander of the section in charge of us came from Caserta to Capri and, accompanied by Lieutenant Gimser, the officer immediately charged with our affairs, he told us that our period of internment had been terminated. The villa was to be evacuated the next day. We were free to go anywhere that we liked.

This unexpected pleasure came a little suddenly. None of us had any money, few of us decent clothes even. Not one of us had made plans for the future. Our protests gained us a day's grace for the improvisation of personal programs.

The Austrians and all the Hungarians but I went to Rome, where the Americans found them quarters and the Hungarian monks helped them to make some sort of start. Four of the Hungarians reported at once to the displaced persons camp and asked to be sent home.

I remained on Capri. I had nowhere to go. A friend of mine in Rome sent me a pittance on which to live. There, where I had experienced the greatest sorrows of my life, came to me also the two greatest joys. At Christmas, 1945, my son Andrew arrived from Mauthausen after an adventurous journey, and in the spring of 1946 my son Christopher and his wife and child arrived from Hungary. From him I learned that my second son, Nicholas, was a prisoner in Russian hands.

That is the story.
Could it have been different? That is the first question.
My own view is that the war would have had a different ending

if different decisions had been made at Teheran, if the decisive blow against Hitler's rule had come from the south, and if Central Europe had not been handed over to the Soviets. My country would be living today. Europe could have been saved. The world would not have had to tremble before the prospects of Bolshevism, Russian ambitions towards world power, a third world war.

The second question is: Who is responsible?

In Nuremberg judgment was passed on individuals. There is no doubt that they were guilty. The chief criminals, led by Hitler, executed sentence on themselves. But is it wise or just to condemn a few wretched or insignificant individuals and to forget the frightful crime itself? Surely not. How was it possible for a handful of such little men to set a world aflame so that ten million human beings, priceless material wealth, and irreparable moral values of civilization perished?

The responsibility of Hitler and his movement is beyond doubt. There is no excuse for them, only at most a reason, now generally recognized—the Peace treaties of 1919–20. Those were unjust, dictatorial *octrois*, and neither the physical nor moral power necessary for their enforcement could be mustered. It is mere stupidity to imprison a man—particularly if one is not sure that the verdict is just—and then leave the prison door unguarded. It would be better to deliver a knockout blow followed by a handshake, a policy followed in the great wars of history, most strikingly after the Napoleonic wars. There was no moral possibility of that after the First World War, however.

The immediate author of the recent war is indubitable: it was Hitler. But his aggressions could not have been launched nor could they have succeeded without the conditions stemming from the embittered German peoples and the collapse of the healthy instincts of the people of Europe. The necessary preventive against those destructive forces was an alliance between the egotism of individualism and the cohesive forces of national feeling. Hitler's aggression was dangerous to only one people—the Czechs (the Austrians wanted to belong to the Reich). Hitler would not have dared to go further, and he could not have succeeded, had he not found an ally—the Soviets. The immediate purpose of that alliance, from the German point of view, was to secure Hitler's previous conquests; thereafter it was to be used to extend German control into Poland, Finland, the Baltic states, Rumania, and the Balkans. But that was to be only the first and modest stage: the great vision behind the alliance was the acquisition of European hegemony and world domination. There have been precedents for such combinations in history, but none for what was signified by the German-Russian alliance. The alliance and co-operation of two dogmatic ideologies such as German National Socialism and Russian Bolshevism was catastrophic for Europe, especially in the absence of firm alliance among freedom-loving peoples. Had the alliance between those two totalitarian nations endured, the inevitable consequences would have been—and there were many symptoms of this from the first—that they would have taken from each other their most horrible slogans and practices: racial warfare and class warfare. Hitler was resolved to eliminate the old leading classes and capitalist forces: he only awaited his moment. Hatred and persecution of the Jews lie much deeper in the souls of the Russians than in the souls of the Germans (practically all Western Jewry passed to success through Germany and the Monarchy, refreshed by German culture, as their names prove incontestably). Moreover, not only has Russia an old tradition of anti-Semitism, but the news coming today from Russia and from behind the Iron Curtain shows that racial discrimination has now reached a very advanced stage there: it is now not possible de facto to speak of Jewry there. I am convinced that the two beastly cruelties would not have hesitated to adopt each others' systems.

So much for the war criminals. But war is only a means or an unavoidable compulsion; for a sane man it cannot be an end. The true end of war in the minds and hearts of responsible individuals is what comes after the war—peace, reconstruction, the return of human liberty. If there are war crimes, there are also the crimes related to the peace that follows. He errs who starts amiss on the road of peace; he who prevents a just peace is a greater sinner than a war criminal.

My little country did not start the war. Hungary took no serious part in the war. During the war Hungary was an island of individual liberty and humanity in the Nazi sea. After the war Hungary had no voice in the peace. Nevertheless, Hungary was condemned to death, and the sentence is being executed.

In her thousand-year history as an independent nation, Hungary has often been in desperate situations, but never so desperate a situation as she is in today. This is the first time that she has had no voice in a peace treaty that decided her fate and no voice afterwards in the conduct of her destiny. In the past, too, the fortune of war was often unfavorable to Hungary: eastern hordes swept over her; the Turks ruled her for 150 years; she struggled against the Germans from the first years of her settlement; [2] in more recent centuries the Habsburgs threatened to absorb her. Always, however, Hungary rose again. Somehow one corner of the country's territory always remained free, and some of her leaders were able to carry on the fight; her refugees found some shelter, sympathy, even help for their country. Today there is no shelter, sympathy, or help available. There are today no free Hungarians, even though the chief characteristic of the Magyar historically has been that he fought for liberty. Hungarians played a part in America's War of Independence. They fought against the Russian conquerors not only at home but also in Poland and in Turkey. They helped Italians to win their liberty. The Hungarians have always been fighters for freedom; they have never been on the side of tyrants. The Hungarians would fight for their freedom today if they could, if a fight for liberty were going on in Europe.

If freedom had conquered in Europe, Hungary would have joined that movement and sought her historic destiny in it. But freedom was a catchword of the victorious side, and today there is no freedom for Hungary. Both world wars seemed to start for

[2] In 896.

the cause of freedom; their ends should have been to assure freedom for those who want freedom. Alas, after the First World War, not peace, but tyranny came to the beaten or weakened countries. Communism, Fascism, National Socialism—all are the fruits of bad peaces. Nor did the Second World War end with peace. The totalitarian slogan of unconditional surrender made this impossible and made freedom unattainable.

Today there is no peace, only victors and vanquished. Moreover, not only the vanquished have lost their liberty; the victors themselves are not masters of their own fates. They drag with them, like a convict gang, the peoples who have lost their freedom. In this mutual relationship, however, they are bound hand and foot, and their freedom is endangered.

Caught between the Nazi and Soviet tyrannies, Hungary strove as much as possible to link her destiny with the West and thus attain freedom. Perhaps that goal was impossible of attainment; it certainly was not our fault that we failed.

Today, too, we are fighting a war of liberty, with such arms as our position allows us. Now, too, it is from the West that we, our nation and every man in it, awaits its liberation. We know that we cannot achieve this for ourselves: our liberty is every man's liberty. It will come if the whole world is free. Freedom and tyranny, we Hungarians know, cannot live side by side. My nation and so many others are enslaved today. Vae victis! And let the victors, too, beware! The better part of the world went to war for freedom, for human welfare and happiness, and for beauty of life. Those nations certainly did not fight in order to lose millions of their men, their homes, their warships, their faith, and their life's purpose. Were we to break off the fight for liberty only the destroyers would remain, and that would be the greatest treason in history.

I believe in freedom, honor, and loyalty. I believe, therefore, in my nation and in the resurrection of my people.

INDEX

xiv; emigré activities of, 210, 240, 384-85, 394

Kassa, 63

Kececi, Sefket Faud, Turkish minister in Budapest, 427, 441-42, 446, 473-74, 498-99

Kececi, Mme Sefket Faud, 441, 469

Keitel, Wilhelm: and Hungarian military action, 64, 130; in German headquarters, 90, 93; and Hungarian occupation of Balkans, 309, 315; and German occupation of Hungary, 421, 430

Kelemen, Chrisostom, 186

Kemény, Gabriel, 473

Keresztes-Fischer, Francis: confidant and supporter of Kállay, 5, 17, 20, 70, 77, 122, 190, 204, 206; regulation of activities of parties by, 36, 224, 225, 256-57, 418; work in refugee program, 326-27, 331, 334; on German intentions, 408; activity during German occupation, 419, 420, 423, 424, 432, 434; arrest, 443

Keresztes-Fischer, Louis, 443

Kern, Aurel, 334

Kertesz, Stephen, 303

Kingdom of the Serbs, Croats and Slovenes, see Yugoslavia

Kiss, John, 412, 477

Knatchbull-Hugesson, Hugh, 373

Kodály, Zoltán, 467

Kokorin, Flight Lieutenant, 487, 488, 489, 494

Kölcsey, Stephen, 67

Komárom, 342

Kossovo, 46

Kossuth, Louis: biographical material, 22n; as historic symbol, 32, 435, 468; admiration of left for, 239, 241; fugitive in Turkey, 441

Kossuth, Paul, 5

Kovacs, Béla, 232n

Kristoffy, Joseph, 58n

Kun, Béla, ix, xiv, xv, 29n

Lakatos, Vitez Geza, government of, 3n, 434, 454, 460, 478

Lamair, Paul, quoted, 336-37

Land legislation, ix, x, 69-71, 194-97

Landowners: in politics, 31; position of, 36, 252, 253-54; and the Revisionist League, 47

Lazar, Charles, 465, 485

League of Nations: admission of Hungary into xix, 48; Hungarian attitudes towards, xxiii, xxiv; and Croat terrorism, 31; loan to Hungary, 48; and German aggression, 51

Left: defined, xi, 23; parties of, 35-36; supporters of, 42; support of Kállay's program by, 191; attitude towards foreign policy, 212, 240-41, 254; attitude towards military situation, 238, 241-243; attitude towards civil liberties, 239

Legislation, codification of, 194

Legitimism, xi, xiii, 35, 248

Legitimists, 138

Legrády, Otto, 48

Lehár, Franz, 467

Leopold, Prince of Prussia, 489

Lévai, Eugene, 114, 120n

Lisbon, negotiations in, 344, 369, 387-89

Little Entente; and Hungarian treaty revision activities, xx-xxi, 49; and West, xxvi, 44, 53; formation of, 47; and Bled agreement, 53; and Germany, 53-54

Lord lieutenants, 40

Louis Charles, Archduke, 388

Lower house, see Parliament

Lukács, Béla, 5, 66, 67

Luther, deputy secretary of state of Germany, 115, 116, 117

Macartney, C. A.: Foreword of, v-xxix; quoted, 239n

Mackensen, Hans Georg, 176

Maglioni, Cardinal, quoted, 173

Magyar Nemzet, 181, 370

Magyarország, 235

Magyars, 38, 39, 47; as minorities in successor states, 48-49; conquest of Hungary by, 57; in Transylvania, 57-58, 60; in Voivodina, 63; in relation to other nationalities, 81

March 15, national anniversary of 1848 uprising, 79-80

Margitkörut prison, Kállay in, 475-77

Marossy, Alexander, 320

Marxism, 24, 42, 163

Matthias Corvinus, 26

Máriássy, Zoltán, 144, 160, 219

Mauthausen, 334, 465; Kállay imprisoned in, 481-87

Menemencioglu, Numan, 276, 441

Rumania (Continued)
sylvania, 56-58; Axis-dominated, 72,
216; relations with Hungary, 84-88,
91-93, 156-57; treatment of Jews in,
118, 120n, 151; military manpower,
135; declaration of war against Germany, 456
Rumanians, in Hungarian population,
40-41
Rural population, described, 37-38, 39,
252-53
Russia, see Union of Soviet Socialist Republics
Ruthenia, see Carpatho-Ruthenia
Rydz-Smigly, Edward, 330

Sabotage, 286-87, 294; criticism of
West's request for, 304, 379; West's
attitude towards, 379-80
Saint Stephen, 167
Saint Stephen's Day (August 20), 102,
197
"Saint Stephen idea," 112
Sanctions, of League of Nations, 51
Saracoglu, Sükrü, 276, 277
Schacht, Hjalmar, 488, 489
Schell, Peter, 490
Schlabrendorff, Fabian von, 488
Schmitz, Richard, 489
Schuschnigg, Frau Kurt von, 487, 490
Schuschnigg, Kurt von, 52; imprison-
ment, 487, 490, 494, 497, 499
Sebestyén, Paul, 303
Serbia, 118, 120n, 149, 150-51
Serédy, Justinian Cardinal, 19, 168
Seyss-Inquart, Arthur, 89
Sigray, Anthony, 186, 267, 342, 443,
485
Simonyi-Semadam, Alexander, 3n
Slavs, xix, 56-57, 91
Slovakia: and Hungarian revisionism,
xxi, xxiii, 4n; and Treaty of Trianon,
44n; and Vienna award, 56; attack on
Poland, 62; German-dominated, 72,
216, 325; treatment of Jews in, 118,
120n, 151; refugees and, 324-25
Slovaks, in Hungarian population, 40-41
Small farmers: parties of, 35; position
of, 38-39, 252-53
Smallholders party: described, 34-35;
attitude towards foreign policy, 213;
attitude of rightists towards, 233;
memorandum of, 237-44; indulgence
of, by government, 256

Small nations: Horthy on, 15; Kállay
on, 143, 193, 269, 271-72, 274, 278;
Ghyczy on, 264
Smith, Jeremiah, Jr., 48n
Social classes, during interwar period, ix,
xi-xiv; described, 36-42, 252-56
Social Democratic party: attitude of
Conservative-Liberals towards, xiii;
described, 35-36, 255; attitude to-
wards foreign policy, 213, 246; atti-
tude of rightists towards, 231-33;
schools of, 232; indulgence of, by gov-
ernment, 256
Soldiers, see Army, Hungarian
Sopron, 46n
Sopronköhida prison, Kállay in, 437,
477-81
Sources, of this account, xxxii, 72; see
also Kállay, Nicholas: Speeches
Soviet Union, see Union of Soviet So-
cialist Republics
Spain, 149, 170
Stalin, 58-59
Stauffenberg family, 490-91, 497
Stern, Samuel, 327, 411, 412
Stresa Conference, 51
Struggle behind the Iron Curtain, The
(Nagy), 232n
Successor states, see Czechoslovakia,
Rumania, Yugoslavia
Sweden, 36, 149
Switzerland, 36; Hungarian diplomatic
negotiations in, 384, 385-87
Szálasi, Francis, xv, 33-34; followers, 39,
254-55; agitation by, 223; govern-
ment of, 470-72
Szapary, Anthony, 334
Szász, Louis, 21, 293-94
Széchényi, Stephen, as historic symbol,
22-23, 32, 435, 468
Szeged Idea, 231, 236
Szegedy-Maszák, Aladár, 355, 373, 382
Szekely, 57, 58
Szent-Györgyi, Albert, 181, 429
Szent-Iványi, Sándor, work in refugee
program, 341-44
Szentmiklóssy, Andor, 93, 160, 205,
355; instructions to ministers, 363;
and Hungary's negotiations with
West, 384; arrest, 443
Szigetvár, 342
Szöllösi, Eugene, 34
Szombathelyi, Francis, chief of staff,
103, 407; and Ujvidek case, 108, 109;